# The Complete Guide to Nonprofit Management

Second Edition

## WILEY NONPROFIT LAW, FINANCE, AND MANAGEMENT SERIES

# The Complete Guide to Nonprofit Management

## Second Edition

**Smith, Bucklin & Associates, Inc.**

**Edited by Robert H. Wilbur**

**John Wiley & Sons, Inc.**

New York • Chichester • Weinheim • Brisbane • Singapore • Toronto

*Library of Congress Cataloging-in-Publication Data:*
The complete guide to nonprofit management.—2nd ed./Smith, Bucklin &
Associates, Inc.; edited by Robert H. Wilbur.
    p. cm. — (Wiley nonprofit law, finance, and management series)
   Includes bibliographical references and index.
   ISBN 0-471-38062-8 (cloth : alk. paper)
   1. Nonprofit organizations—Management. I. Wilbur, Robert H. (Robert
Hunter) II. Smith, Bucklin & Associates, Inc. III. Series.

HD62.6 .C66 2000
658'.048—dc21                                       00-025513

Printed in the United States of America.

10  9  8  7  6  5  4  3  2

# Foreword

*What is most important is to have a family of strategies, such that one can vary the response to one's changing circumstances according to success.*
—*Murray Gell-Mann*

The world of nonprofit management is changing. Gone are the days when volunteers had generous amounts of time to give to support their causes, and gone are the days of accelerated growth in many nonprofit sectors. In fact, recent reports from Gales Research have indicated that for the last five years, the number of newly created national associations is being fairly evenly offset by the number of discontinued national associations—a testament to the fact that the industry is indeed undergoing a transformation.

These dynamics mean that volunteer leaders of nonprofit organizations are faced with increased challenges. They must provide effective leadership and governance to ensure that an organization's mission is fulfilled. To accomplish this, leaders must work to embrace new management practices that reshape organizations to remain competitive. In addition, they must build value within their organizations to satisfy the increasing needs of members, often with resources that are truly limited.

Nonprofit organizations can overcome these challenges by following three simple principles: (1) Organizing leadership such that it accepts its mission to strategically focus on building the services that satisfy member needs, (2) creating a culture that motivates and rewards volunteers, and (3) understanding and utilizing proven, dynamic association management practices to achieve success.

Smith, Bucklin & Associates has been managing nonprofit organizations—trade and professional associations, technology user groups, and medical societies—for more than 50 years. We have long maintained that with the exception of the volunteer aspect of associations and societies, the management practices of well-run nonprofit organizations are no different from the management practices of successful for-profit organizations. We have developed best practices in the areas of strategic planning, financial management, membership management, marketing and communications, trade show management, meeting planning, convention management, Internet services, and government relations—core areas critical to the stability and viability of an organization.

From these proven business practices, Smith, Bucklin has helped clients to achieve excellence in organization management by demonstrating:

- How to build an organization to be financially strong, efficient, and resourceful
- The management practices that contribute to organizational success
- How an organization can best use strategic planning to achieve its long-term goals
- The services, education, and information that should be provided to members
- The role of technology in servicing members with information, communication, e-commerce, and the like
- The proven methods of attracting, satisfying, and retaining members
- How the organization can use meetings, conventions, and trade shows to sustain the financial needs of the organization and define its presence in the marketplace
- The best sources of revenues to sustain long-term growth
- The best methods for providing rewarding experiences for volunteers, while also ensuring their loyalty to the organization

The internal sharing of best practices has allowed us to take the best ideas from the processes of nonprofit management and bridge the thinking across organizations and industries. This book contains some of the best examples of issues and management practices that Smith, Bucklin has gathered through serving thousands of clients over the years nationwide, as well as through participating as board members or volunteers with local and charitable organizations.

This book was prepared to provide readers with the insight required to lead a successful organization.

Stephen Fitzer
Chief Executive Officer
Smith, Bucklin & Associates, Inc.

# Preface

In the last 25 years, the nonprofit sector of the U.S. economy has grown rapidly in size and significance. More than 1,500,000 nonprofit organizations were registered with the Internal Revenue Service in 1996. Author and management consultant Peter Drucker, counting both paid employees and volunteers, has characterized nonprofits as "America's largest employer." Nonprofit organizations, including religious organizations but even without the contribution of (c)(6) trade and professional associations, had total revenues of $621 billion in 1996, equivalent to approximately 6.8 percent of the nation's total economy.

What accounts for this rapid growth? One reason is the evolution of our economy from agriculture to manufacturing to services and information technology. Another is the precedent set by increased government funding for health, education, and social welfare programs during the 1960s and 1970s, which stimulated the formation and growth of many nonprofit organizations, especially in service areas. When federal cutbacks occurred in the 1980s, local communities, corporations, and individual citizens, rather than seeing these service organizations disband, often stepped in to fill the void.

America's tradition of solving problems with the help of volunteers is not new. As early as 1835, French writer Alexis De Tocqueville noted the American tendency to band together in voluntary association to take on community problems:

> *Americans of all ages, all conditions, and all dispositions constantly form associations. They have not only commercial and manufacturing companies, in which all take part, but associations of a thousand other kinds, religious, moral, serious, futile, general or restricted, enormous or diminutive. The Americans make associations to give entertainment, to found seminaries, to build inns, to construct churches, to diffuse books, to send missionaries to the antipodes; in this manner they found hospitals, prisons, and schools. If it is proposed to inculcate some truth or to foster some feeling by the encouragement of a great example, they form*

*a society. Wherever at the head of some new undertaking you see the government in France, or a man of rank in England, in the United States you will be sure to find an association.*

&mdash;*Alexis De Tocqueville,* Democracy in America

More than 200 years later, volunteerism continues to spread, with nonprofit organizations providing the structure that makes volunteerism effective.

The word *nonprofit* is often misunderstood. Technically, it describes an organization that does not distribute profit (either dividends or capital gains) to its owners; it has no owners in the sense of the for-profit sector, and any income that exceeds expenses stays with the organization rather than flowing through to an owner or owners. But within this general category, the nonprofit world is immensely varied. It includes such large organizations as the Massachusetts General Hospital, Stanford University, and the American Red Cross, as well as trade and professional associations and local community organizations ranging from churches and temples to soup kitchens and shelters. Sources of revenues vary as well. A recent study published by the Foundation Center estimated that 51 percent of the income of all nonprofit service organizations comes from fees and other charges for services, 31 percent from government, and only 18 percent from charitable giving (the latter largely by individuals but also by corporations and foundations). Although those charitable groups that cannot charge fees inevitably depend more heavily on charitable giving, the point remains: "not-for-profit" cannot be "for-loss."

Despite the great variety of organizations, of purposes, and of sources of funding, a common element prevails: These organizations have become critical to the quality of life in America. They serve us and they deserve our support.

Despite the growing importance of nonprofit organizations in our society, relatively little has been written about the management issues facing their staff and leaders. Until recently, many believed that nonprofit organizations could not be "managed" in the same way as for-profit organizations. There was a bias against using the "bottom line" orientation of the corporate business world to manage nonprofit organizations. But nonprofit organizations today must operate as effectively and efficiently as for-profit organizations or they go out of business. With escalating costs and diminishing resources, nonprofit executives are now under the same pressures as for-profit organizations to justify every dollar spent. The days are past when a casual style of management, based on idealism rather than professionalism, might be excused because the work of the nonprofit was from the heart or because its staff were less well paid than those of comparable for-profit organizations.

For the most part, nonprofit organizations still do not face the same financial exigencies as the typical corporation: Extinction is not as likely if they fail to turn a profit (or, in nonprofit terms, provide a surplus of income over expenses.) But nonprofits are not excused from balancing their budgets. Under the pressures of "right-sizing," this exemption from the laws of economics is being repealed. Even the most loyal donors and contributors to nonprofits are now far less willing to support fund-raising campaigns whose goals increase in direct proportion to the shortfalls from operations, or that lack a compelling explanation of how the funds will be spent. When revenues shrink in the face of rising needs or desires, the bottom line exerts its discipline. Members of our boards of directors expect us, quite rightly, to operate at the same level of professionalism and proficiency that they demand from the staffs of their own organizations. Peter Drucker has noted the change, stating that nonprofits have entered the world of "accountability."

*The Complete Guide to Nonprofit Management, Second Edition,* is intended to help nonprofit executives and their volunteer leaders manage their organizations in this new and increasingly complex world of accountability. The contributors to this book work for a for-profit organization that manages more than 180 nonprofit organizations. Most have business backgrounds, often with additional experience in education or government. As our nonprofit clients always have the option of taking their business somewhere else, we live under a market discipline in many ways similar to that of the for-profit world. We believe our success, and much of what we have to share in this book, lies in our ability to adapt for-profit management strategies and techniques to the unique demands of the nonprofit world. Most of us also serve as volunteers, either on boards of directors or as participants in the work of charitable organizations. We've tried to bring both perspectives—paid manager and volunteer leader—to this book.

There are elements of art as well as science in managing nonprofit organizations. Relations between paid staff and boards of directors differ between nonprofits and typical for-profit organizations, and differ as well from one nonprofit to another. Management styles are perhaps more likely to be "interactive" in nonprofit organizations, based on teamwork and communication, but individual management styles and varying sizes of organizations make generalizations difficult. Nonetheless, the limits imposed by budgets mean that most nonprofit managers and staff wear several hats; CEOs must also perform much of the day-to-day work, not just facilitate.

We are pleased that the first edition of *The Complete Guide to Nonprofit Management* has helped many nonprofit managers address many of their common management concerns: clarifying their organization's mission, marketing their services, raising funds, managing staff and finances, deciding how to communicate with constituents, the public, and government. This second edition provides several new chapters, numerous new examples of successful programs, and a completely new discussion of how best to utilize the new information technology in both management and communication.

To help both the nonprofit executive and the board member who wants to know more about the tasks facing these organizations, we have structured this book in three sections:

    I. Building the Foundation
   II. Pursuing the Mission
  III. Managing the Organization

The first three chapters (Part I) deal with basic management issues confronting almost all nonprofits: establishing (and reevaluating) the organization's direction (or "mission"); maximizing board/staff effectiveness; and creating the "marketing orientation" necessary for growth. These elements of nonprofit management should, we believe, be reevaluated constantly. Without a practical sense of mission, organizations often flounder, unable to develop effective action plans. Without an understanding of board-staff relationships and of the way these may change in the evolution of an organization, much of the available talent and energy will be wasted. Without a realistic appraisal of its potential supporters and what it has to offer them—whether donors, members, or the segment of the public it wishes to serve—and a plan to make itself known, the best of dreams remain unrealized.

Part II, "Pursuing the Mission," turns to the design and execution of strategic and operational programs. As we have noted, nonprofits get more than half of their revenues from services. Establishing a marketing orientation does not mean giving up the goals on which most nonprofits are founded; it does mean developing the awareness that even a charity requires an assessment of the revenues the organization can expect from its services.

Chapter 4, a new chapter in this second edition of *The Complete Guide to Nonprofit Management,* provides real-life examples of nonprofit professional and trade associations that have successfully expanded their services and developed new sources of revenue to support these services. Chapter 5, on fund-raising, has been revised to cover the essential concept of developing a coherent case for support as the basis of all charitable appeals and the use of the Internet as a source of information and as a direct fund-raising tool. Subsequent chapters, dealing with specific programs—educational activities, meetings and conventions, public relations, and advocacy—have been revised with new case studies and examples. Chapter 10, another new chapter, provides case studies of nonprofits, both professional and charitable organizations, that have looked beyond our own borders to work with men and women with similar goals throughout the world. Examples from our own and others' experience illustrate how these activities can be effectively planned and executed.

Part III, "Managing the Organization," focuses on issues of day-to-day management, emphasizing the tools essential to running a nonprofit organization: choosing and managing the right information system in an age of technology, understanding basic nonprofit accounting principles, managing staff and resources, meeting legal requirements, selecting and using consultants. Most notably, the chapter on information systems (Chapter 11) has been totally rewritten, reflecting the dramatic change in nonprofit management that has occurred with the explosion of the Internet.

In addressing these management topics, we have outlined strategies that have been used successfully by professionals with responsibilities ranging from overall executive management to such critical details as staff management, finances, meetings, public relations, and member communication. We have reviewed such ever-present issues as the relationships between staffs and their boards of directors and the constantly changing role of information technology. We hope these discussions will be of value to the most seasoned nonprofit executive, as well as to those coming into new responsibilities. We also hope that our discussions will give nonprofit boards of directors a better understanding of the efforts and responsibilities of management in this vital part of our economy, as well as an appreciation of their own leadership role in working with both staff and volunteers.

Finally, we recognize that our observations and recommendations will not fit every organization's need. But we hope to provide a starting point for those looking for practical tools and techniques, drawn from experience and proven in practice, for meeting many of the day-to-day challenges of "accountability" in this growing world of nonprofits.

Robert H. Wilbur

Smith, Bucklin & Associates, Inc.
*January 25, 2000*

# Acknowledgments

We wish to take this opportunity to thank the dedicated officers, board members, committee chairs, and volunteers of the nonprofit organizations we serve. These men and women have been active participants in the programs and projects we describe; they have brought to these organizations their own knowledge and experience, providing us with ideas and inspiration; they have pressed us to think beyond what we have done in the past, searching always for new and more effective ways to work toward their organizations' goals.

To them this book is dedicated.

A large number of the experienced association executives of Smith, Bucklin & Associates have contributed to this book. Individual executives have authored some chapters, others are the product of teams. We wish particularly to recognize Ute Duncan, Susan Finn, Carolyn Freeland, William Greer, Carter Keithly, Jennifer Lewis, William Peyser, Dennis Smeage, Jill Rathbun, and Judith Thomas for their contributions. John Fisher provided content and counsel for the new chapter on the selection and use of information systems; Michael Payne, Deirdre Flynn, and Andrea Leiter reviewed and helped us improve a number of chapters. Michael Brodie provided new material and concepts for the important chapter on Fund Raising. Nora Greer worked successfully to convert our raw material and ideas for several chapters to the finished material you see here.

Stephen Fitzer, our chief executive officer, supported the project enthusiastically; his commitment was essential.

We also thank Marla Bobowick, our first editor, and Martha Cooley of John Wiley & Sons, for encouraging us to take on the labor that led to the first edition and then to the rewrites and additions that, we hope, will make this book more useful still. They have brought tact, prodding, and a sharp editorial eye to the difficult job of working with a consortium of writers more concerned with their responsibilities to client associations than to the deadlines of editorial production.

Finally, we express again our admiration and appreciation to William E. Smith, founder of Smith, Bucklin & Associates, who has been a friend, mentor, and supporter to us throughout our careers. While building a company with more than 600 employees, he has never lost sight of the fact that every one of us has an obligation not only to the nonprofit organizations we serve, but also to the communities in which we live and to our society as a whole.

# Contents

# PART 1

# Building the Foundation

# CHAPTER ONE

# Establishing the Organization's Direction

**"If you don't know where you're going, any road will do."
Identifying your mission will enable you to develop a blueprint for action, which can guide your organization down the road to successfully achieving its goals. This chapter outlines the steps toward defining that mission and strategic plan.**

Success does not come easily in our competitive society. For nonprofit organizations, the realization of goals is complicated by their structure of volunteer leadership. Here, more than elsewhere, a strong conceptual framework—a blueprint for action—is necessary. Yet this framework cannot be static, but must be reshaped as the needs and the governance of the organization and the environment around it change. Strategic planning is a management tool that can help focus—and periodically refocus—an organization's vision and priorities. This planning process establishes choices about how best to accomplish the organization's mission.

## STRATEGIC PLANNING AND MANAGEMENT

*Strategic planning* is a systematic process that brings consensus regarding priorities among the organization's leaders. As such, the planning process begins with *constituent building*. Before your organization can even consider its mission, it must obtain the commitment of its leadership to pursue such a course, choose participants to undertake the task, and conduct *preparatory research*—including a history and profile of the organization and an environmental assessment.

The selected planning group must then gather for a two- to three-day *retreat* to generate a strategic plan. First the *mission statement* will be developed or revised. The statement should concisely articulate why the organization exists and what it hopes to achieve—its purpose and values. Next comes an extensive *assessment* of how the external and internal environments are affecting and will affect this mission. From this analysis, priorities and goals are developed—that is, the *strategic plan,* which guides program activities, allocates resources, and assesses the organization's achievements. An *implementation plan* ultimately guides a more detailed *operational plan. Monitoring* and evaluating guidelines are set.

## Strategic Planning in a Capsule

The strategic planning process begins with a thorough examination of your organization's mission as it relates to its internal and external environments and moves on to ask:

- What is the essence of the organization? What makes it unique?
- What are the core values and beliefs of its constituents?
- What is its mission? Who is served? Should the mission be amended?
- What does the organization do best, and how does that relate to what is needed?
- What are its strengths? Its weaknesses?
- What are the keys to the success of the organization?
- Of those factors making a difference, what is changing in the environment and what is the competition doing?
- How can the organization really make a difference in the lives of its constituents and in society?
- What activities are worth undertaking and committing to over the next three years? Five years?
- What must be done to implement the strategy?

These questions and others can help the leaders of the organization to focus the strategic planning process. Strategic planning is not a wish list; rather, it is realistic, based on what is going on in the real world, taking into account the forces and trends that will occur both inside and outside the organization within the time frame of the plan.

A strategic plan broadly maps the activities the organization should pursue to reach its desired goals; it is not a detailed chronology of action. It is a tool to guide decision making by the organization's leaders on issues that are fundamental to the organization, containing a mission statement, principles, goals, and strategic objectives. In the end, the strategic plan should

- Establish the organization's priorities;
- Allocate human and financial resources to accomplish those activities;
- Assess whether objectives are being met; and
- Establish means to evaluate programs, staff, and resources.

Working from the strategic plan, nonprofit organizations then develop coherent, focused, realistic *operational plans,* describing the specific actions that must be taken to accomplish each objective identified in the strategic plan.

## KEY ELEMENTS TO SUCCESSFUL STRATEGIC PLANNING

Remember two maxims as you move through the strategic planning process:

1. A strategic plan is a statement of important, but flexible, guidelines, not rigid doctrine.
2. The process of strategic planning—the development, implementation, and assessment of a plan—is not a single, one-shot event; rather, it is an ongoing, continuous process, which must adapt to environmental changes, both external and internal.

Lessons learned over the years can help focus the strategic planning, making it more efficient and satisfying for all those involved, as discussed in the next several sections.

### Obtain Support and Commitment of the Organization's Leadership

It is critical to have the support of the nonprofit's elected leaders to pursue strategic planning. When there are board elections, be sure new board members also agree with the proposed activity. An executive who believes he or she "knows best" and therefore begins the process without the approval and commitment of newly elected policymakers will be jousting with windmills. In some cases, the nonprofit's leaders will need to be convinced that strategic planning is necessary. There may be those who have been through a poorly conducted process and may find little value in spending time and resources on such a "spurious" activity. Others may toss the responsibility back to staff, saying, "You know what we want. Handle it."

## Involve Leadership, Staff, and Other Major Constituents

Elected policymakers cannot just give lip service to the idea of strategic planning, but should be at the center of the planning process whenever possible. Other leaders or outside experts can likewise be involved in the process, including founders and other stakeholders or individuals considered to be "visionaries" or "futurists," as well as "distracters" or "outliers," of the organization. They will provide perspectives not readily apparent to those in the mainstream of the organization, challenging the status quo.

Without the support and commitment of the organization's elected leaders, your strategic plan will die a slow death. Their involvement, along with that of committee chairs, past and future leaders, key staff, visionaries, and even outliers, should facilitate the development of a good strategic plan. In addition, opportunities must be provided to allow other constituents to participate in the process, whether through a questionnaire in the organization's newsletter or through requests for review and comment on draft plans.

If recommendations for changes in the organization evolve from the strategic planning process, constituents must not only be aware of those changes but must also understand why the organization is changing.

## Identify a Consultant/Facilitator for Assistance

If resources are available, an outside facilitator can be immensely helpful. Specifically, a facilitator can:

- Assist in developing the overall strategic planning process that will be used by the organization;
- Assist in the development and analysis of questionnaires designed to assess emerging trends and critical issues;
- Assist in the development of meeting agendas;
- Assist in identifying individuals both within and outside the organization who should participate in the process;
- Facilitate the group process in a retreat atmosphere that will allow elected leaders and key staff to focus on the issues rather than on the process;

- Balance competing participant perspectives and facilitate consensus building;

- Prepare a summary report on the retreat, which should include the first draft of the organization's strategic plan;

- Provide ongoing counsel to the executive and elected leaders to ensure that the strategic plan is completed, an operational plan is developed, and monitoring and evaluation mechanisms are established; and

- Provide heightened credibility to the strategic planning process.

You will want a facilitator who has or will gain the respect of the participants. Costs, as for all consulting activities, will vary depending on location and the amount of time you will require of your facilitator.

If resources are not available to pay for an outside facilitator, nonprofits often solicit assistance from a governing board member whose for-profit organization may have used a facilitator or consultant for its own planning process. Sometimes, the consultant or facilitator may contribute his or her services in support of the nonprofit's mission.

## Conduct an Environmental Analysis

It is critical to understand the organization's position in society—how it is affected by trends, challengers, competitors, and other interested parties. One must also thoroughly understand all internal aspects of the organization—its constituents, structure, technical and economic capabilities, and culture.

Through an environmental analysis, the organization's leaders can identify these *external trends/issues* that may have an impact on the organization. Generally, it is helpful to begin with categories of trends to be analyzed, such as the following:

- Sociologic/demographic

- Economic/financial

- Technological/scientific

- Political/legislative/regulatory

- Professional/educational

Determine how each of these categories affects your organization. For example, current economic trends affect all organizations; however, the impact on each nonprofit may be different, depending on its mission and its usual source of funding. A social services nonprofit may depend heavily on state grants, which may be cut because of state financial difficulties; another nonprofit may look to philanthropic foundations and must therefore assess whether it can maintain or even increase their support. Trade and professional associations need to assess trends in their own sectors of the economy and the degree to which other organizations compete for their members' support.

An analysis of the *internal environment* means assessing the organization's strengths and weaknesses in all aspects of the organization:

- Communication and marketing capabilities
- Constituents' satisfaction with the organization
- Governance and staffing structures
- Culture of the organization—as perceived both internally and externally
- Financial and human resources
- Technological and scientific capabilities

Leadership and constituent questionnaires are often used to assess both the external and internal environments. These questionnaires may also be sent to outside publics to obtain their perspectives on the organization. Other sources of information also may be available through other data collected by the organization, as well as through meetings and current publications.

An environmental analysis is critical. Without a good, clear understanding of the trends both within and outside the organization, a "strategic" plan cannot be developed. The computer GIGO rule will prevail: garbage in, garbage out. An outline of the type of information needed for an organizational assessment is provided in Exhibit 1–1.

**Exhibit 1–1**   Sample Questionnaire

---

1. How would you define the mission of the _____ organization?
2. Currently, what are the main goals of the organization?
3. Using the attached form, (a) identify those environmental trends/changes that are occurring, or will occur within the next two to five years, that will have an impact on your organization. Next, (b) on the same form, identify the threats and/or opportunities

**Exhibit 1–1**   (*Continued*)

---

created by these same environmental trends for your organization. Consider Economic, Technological, Educational/Training, Sociologic, and Regulatory trends.

4. Using the same form, identify the organization's greatest assets or strengths in making an impact on those trends.

5. Again using the same form, identify the organization's greatest weaknesses in making an impact on those trends.

6. What do you perceive as the three (3) most critical issues for the organization at this time? Please prioritize. (1 = most critical).

   _____

7. Taking into account the organization's internal capabilities, which programs or activities do you consider most essential to the organization's ability to successfully implement its objectives?

   _____

8. What steps would you recommend to increase the organization's effectiveness? Please prioritize. (1 = most important)

   _____

9. What is your personal "vision" for the organization's future?

   _____

10. If one objective could be accomplished or one issue could be resolved for the organization, what would you want it to be?

    _____

11. In your opinion, what is the greatest obstacle to overcome to achieve this objective or resolve this issue? _____

---

A staff member facilitator can tabulate and summarize constituent responses. The summaries should be developed for use during the strategic planning process, along with any other documents or materials that provide information regarding the trends and environmental conditions of the organization.

## Plan and Conduct a Strategic Planning Session with Key Leaders and Staff

Generally, a meeting away from the office in a different environment eliminates distractions and gives elected leaders a clear perspective as they map out the future for their organization. Often this meeting takes the form of a 2- to 2 1/2-day leadership retreat, if an initial environmental analysis is completed beforehand. For very large organizations, several meetings over the period of a year may be required. Your facilitator, if involved, will work with you in developing the agenda for the retreat. This should allow for open discussion and active listening, testing of theories and practice, discussion by advocates and detractors, free time to allow issues to "gel," and sufficient opportunity to build consensus.

The amount of time provided for the retreat may have to be modified, based on the time elected leaders have free to spend away from home and their willingness to commit 100 percent of the time available to the task. Because strategic thinking and planning are arduous processes, requiring much concentration and creativity, the retreat should not be held following another meeting.

Two valuable guides to structuring and facilitating a strategic planning retreat *are Strategic Planning for Nonprofit Organizations,* by Michael Allison and Judy Kaye,[1] published by John Wiley & Sons, and *The Drucker Foundation Self-Assessment Tool Process Guide,* by Gary J. Stern,[2] available from the Drucker Foundation in New York or from Jossey-Bass Publishers.

*Test the Outcomes of Your Environmental Analysis.* During the retreat, the environmental trends and issues can be analyzed to determine whether they present *opportunities or threats* for the organization. Often, a trend or issue may present both opportunities for your organization and challenges to the status quo. The analysis, therefore, continues by assessing the *strengths and weaknesses* of the organization in dealing with these threats and opportunities. This process is often called a *S.W.O.T. analysis*—referring to Strengths, Weaknesses, Opportunities, and Threats. Again, information can be gathered via mailed questionnaires; however, the assessment is best conducted during a leadership retreat.

A S.W.O.T. analysis worksheet is provided to assist you in working through the process (see Exhibit 1–2). Identify one critical issue for your nonprofit; identify whether this issue provides opportunities, or threats, or both to your organization; and identify your organization's strengths and weaknesses in addressing the issue.

*Determine Whether Immediate Action Is Required.* It will be particularly important for the organization's leaders to identify spe-

---

[1]M. Allison and J. Kaye. *Strategic Planning for Nonprofit Organizations: A Practical Guide and Workbook* (New York: John Wiley & Sons, 1997.)

[2]G. Stern, *The Drucker Foundation Self-Assessment Tool Process Guide and Participant Workbook,* revised ed. (San Francisco: Jossey-Bass Publishers, 1999).

**Exhibit 1–2**   Strategic Planning: Environmental S.W.O.T.
Analysis Worksheet

| Environmental Trends | Threat | Opportunity |
|---|---|---|
| Trends: | | |
| | | |
| Strengths/Assets: | | |
| Weaknesses/Limitations: | | |

cific opportunities or threats that may require immediate action
or close observation in the immediate future. Using the chart in
Exhibit 1–3, identify those environmental issues and trends
(external and internal) that may have a high impact on your
organization and determine whether there is a low, medium, or
high probability of occurrence within the next five years. Those
that emerge as high priority—"high impact/high occurrence"—
become the critical "strategic" issues that will require the organization's immediate attention.

Nonprofit leaders who think and manage strategically can and
should develop mechanisms to continuously (not just during the
strategic planning process) monitor emerging trends, opportunities,
and threats to the organization. The earlier such elements are
detected, the more efficiently they can be addressed.

**Exhibit 1–3**   Environmental Issues Alert Matrix

## Impact on the Organization

| | **High** | **Medium** | **Low** |
|---|---|---|---|
| **High** | | | |
| **Medium** | | | |
| **Low** | | | |

*(Probability of Occurrence — vertical axis label)*

*Identify the Leadership's Collective Vision for the Organization.*
Once the environmental analysis is completed, retreat participants
are asked to step back and identify their *visions* for the future of
their organization. What consensus, if any, has emerged? What is
the "collective vision" for the organization? "Visioning" requires
letting go of preconceived notions about the organization and
allows for creative and strategic thinking about what the future
could be like. One facilitator used the tactic of asking the participants to describe the newspaper headlines about their nonprofit

that would appear five years into the future. Visioning helps to describe the organization as the collective group would like to see it at some point in the future.

*Develop Scenarios for the Organization's Future.* Some nonprofits find it helpful to develop both positive and negative *scenarios* about the organization's distant future (15 to 20 years into the future). In these situations, participants develop scenarios based on a future environment that has many positive opportunities for the organization and other scenarios that describe an organization confronting threats.

*One health care nonprofit, the American Association of Blood Banks (AABB), developed a series of scenarios that focused on various views of the world of medicine and the effects of potential future technological developments on the functioning of blood banking, transfusion medicine, tissue banking, and transplantation medicine. Although members who were involved in the development of the scenarios did not agree on all issues, the scenarios did present possible alternative futures that the organization could address proactively, rather than reactively.*

*Review the Organization's Mission Statement.* Strategic plans can never be well developed until the organization is clear on its fundamental mission. Most often, a number of board members cycle on and off the board each year, leaving staff to provide the continuing direction for the organization. Unless the board of directors, the chief executive, and staff are working with a *clear and concise mission statement* for the organization—one to which they are all committed—those working with different perceptions of the *actual* mission of the organization will try to lead the organization in a different direction.

All too frequently, however, it is not until the organization's leaders participate in the strategic planning process, identifying the trends and, consequently, the critical "strategic" issues that affect, or will affect, the organization, that they become aware of the group's lack of unity in direction. It is at this point in the process that the group should begin examining the organization's current mission, principles, goals, and strategic objectives.

Mission Statement: A succinct statement that sets forth the organization's purpose and philosophy. Although brief, the mission statement will specify the fundamental reason(s) for the organization's existence; establish the scope of the organization; and identify the organization's unique characteristics.

A good mission statement should be succinct, stating the non-profit's purpose and philosophy, identifying the uniqueness of the organization. It should provide the overall direction, guiding the development of the organization's principles, its goals, and its strategic objectives—those targets for the organization's primary activities. Goals, strategic objectives, or program activities not relevant to the nonprofit's mission should not be pursued; they would be a distraction for the organization.

In some cases, the *actual* mission is clouded by extraneous information included with the nonprofit's so-called mission statement. Because the nonprofit's mission cannot be culled easily from the mass of information, no one remembers exactly what the mission actually is. This allows individuals on the board, staff, and committees to selectively retain that piece of information that agrees with their singular perception of the organization, rather than acknowledging its actual mission. Keep the mission statement direct and focused.

*In 1960, the year Lamaze International (formerly the American Society for Psychoprophylaxis in Obstetrics, Inc./Lamaze (ASPO/Lamaze)) was founded, the mission of the association was "To promote the psychoprophylaxis (natural childbirth) method of childbirth education." In 1986, the mission statement was revised to read: "To promote an optimal childbirth and early parenting experience for families through education, advocacy and reform."*

*In 1999, the board of directors of Lamaze, now an international organization, conducted a thorough organizational assessment and again examined its mission statement in response to a changing environment. The mission of Lamaze International was revised to read: "To promote normal, natural, healthy and fulfilling childbearing experiences for women and their families through education, advocacy and reform.*

*"Education is defined as 'enhancing the knowledge and skills of women, families and professionals through education and certification.'*

*"Advocacy: 'Strengthening the voice of women and their families to speak on their own behalf.'*

*"Reform: 'Transforming the birth culture by fostering those attitudes in society that enable families to have a positive birth, breastfeeding and parenting experience.'"*

Some nonprofits, particularly one-purpose membership organizations, may perform well for years without ever having developed a mission statement. Usually, in these cases, the mission is implicit in the bylaws or the collective minds of the members or governing board members. Making the mission statement explicit, however, ensures the nonprofit's long-term success.

*Children's Hope Foundation is a mission-focused organization founded in 1986 by Steven Fisch, then a student at New York University Law School, to meet the needs of children with HIV and AIDs. Its mission is succinct: "To improve the quality of life for children and teens with HIV and AIDs by meeting their medical and social needs." Working in partnership with medical facilities and community-based organizations in the New York Metropolitan area, it responds with practical assistance to the unmet needs of children and teens in the communities hardest hit by AIDS. The tightly focused mission and programs developed accordingly have helped the Foundation obtain significant support from the New York business and banking community.*

Several other simple steps can help to make a mission statement more effective, as discussed in the following paragraphs. Take time to study these suggestions, as you compose or review your mission statement.

*Make Changes in the Mission Statement When Appropriate.* Test yourself, your organization's elected leaders, and your key staff with the same question: "How would you define the organization's mission? Do responses come easily? Are they consistent with one another?"

*Identify Your Organization's Principles.* Every organization carries with it its own life—its own values and beliefs—whether it exists for

---

Test your mission statement as it is identified in your organizational documents and publications.

Does your mission statement:

| | Yes | No | Unsure |
|---|---|---|---|
| • Specify the fundamental reason(s) for your organization's existence? | | | |
| • Establish the scope of your organization? | | | |
| • Identify your organization's unique characteristics? | | | |
| • Provide a consistent message to all constituents? | | | |
| • Provide overall policy direction for the organization? | | | |
| • Direct your short-term as well as your long-range and strategic planning initiatives? | | | |

issues that must be addressed, standards or professional education programs to be developed, or to support others who are less advantaged. These principles (values/beliefs) should both guide your organization's initiatives and help evaluate the success of those initiatives in fulfilling the nonprofit's mission.

*Principles:* Statements that identify the philosophical guidelines for all of the organization's activities.

Values and beliefs that recognize constituent needs and expectations can be captured as *principles* that define the philosophical guidelines for the organization's activities. For some organizations, principles may be embedded in a longer mission statement or not stated at all. It is important to list the organization's statements of organizational principles separately so that they are clearly understood by constituents, board, and staff.

*For Lamaze International, the following statement emerged to guide the work of the organization consistent with its mission and its values and principles:*

Integral to the work of Lamaze International is a fundamental philosophy of birth:*

- Birth is normal, natural, and healthy.
- The experience of birth profoundly affects women and their families.
- Women's inner wisdom guides them through birth.
- Women's confidence and ability to give birth is either enhanced or diminished by the care provider and place of birth.
- Women have a right to give birth free from routine medical interventions.
- Birth can safely take place in birth centers and homes.
- Childbirth education empowers women to make informed choices in health care, to assume responsibility for their health, and to trust their inner wisdom.

It is important for the organization's leadership to embrace and commit to the strategic plan as it is developed, to ensure it does not become a document that just sits on the shelf. With such a statement of principles included in the plan and in other organizational docu-

---

*Adopted at the ASPO/Lamaze Annual Conference in Pittsburgh, PA, October, 1993, and accepted with enthusiasm by members.

---

Test your own organization's documents and promotional materials. Do they include philosophical statements that:

|  | Yes | No | Unsure |
|---|---|---|---|
| • Identify the principles held by your constituents? |  |  |  |
| • Capture the essence of the organization's philosophy? |  |  |  |
| • Recognize and are sensitive to your constituents' needs and expectations? |  |  |  |

---

ments, it will be clear to all constituents, both inside and outside the organization, that the strategic plan will provide the direction for the organization's efforts and that the governing board has the responsibility to ensure its success.

*Specify Targeted Goals for the Organization.* Whereas the mission statement identifies general policy directions of an organization, *goals*—or purposes—specify how these general policy directions will be carried out. For our discussion, we will use the term "goals" rather than "purposes" to translate a mission statement into major policy directives.

Goals: A limited number of statements that translate the association's mission into *major policy directions.*

As noted previously, some organizations have included goals within their mission statement. Again, goals should be separated from the mission statement so that they can be used as tools to assess the success of the organization in fulfilling its mission. Goals will necessarily be broad statements, limited in number, and focused on the unique characteristics of the organization.

*The goal statements for the American Association of Blood Banks (AABB) clarified the Association's mission statement, but also, even more important, set out measurable tasks against which progress could be gauged:*
*Mission: "To establish and promote the highest standards of care for patients and donors through leadership in all aspects of blood banking, transfusion medicine and tissue transplantation."*
*Goals: The AABB provides leadership in blood banking, tissue banking, transfusion medicine, and tissue transplantation by:*

- *Educating members, other health care providers, donors, patients, policymakers, and the public;*

- *Providing a forum for professionals to exchange information and ideas;*

- *Improving the quality and efficacy of transfusion and transplantation practices by establishing and promulgating standards;*

- *Assisting our members in ensuring a safe and adequate supply of blood and transplantable tissue; and*

- *Assisting our members in effectively and efficiently implementing technological advances.*

*A regional nonprofit organization, the Fish Middleton Jazz Scholarship Fund, Inc. (FMJS), set its mission "to be a viable part of sustaining, nurturing and perpetuating American Jazz." This organization, which showcases jazz musicians through a number of music concerts, including an annual three-day music festival that provides the venue for awarding competitive scholarships, has identified two clear goals:*

- *To present quality music and educational events; and*

- *To promote and support emerging jazz artists to enter the international jazz arena.*

---

Test your organization's *goals* by asking yourself the following questions. Do the goals identified for your organization:

|  | *Yes* | *No* | *Unsure* |
|---|---|---|---|
| • Clarify your organization's mission statement? |  |  |  |
| • Specify the overriding purposes of the organization? |  |  |  |
| • Provide the foundation for developing targeted programmatic activities and operational plans? |  |  |  |
| • Provide the basis for assessing the major priorities of the organization? |  |  |  |

---

*Translate the Leadership's Visions into Strategic Objectives.* Evolving from an organization's mission, principles, and goals should be the major accomplishments (strategic objectives) the organization seeks to achieve over a specified period of time (e.g., five years). Organizations use a number of terms to identify these major accomplishments. Often, strategic objectives are confused with the more general policy directives (goals). The difference is the level of specificity: The term *"strategic objective"* is used to identify the major accomplishments the organization hopes to achieve in a defined time frame that address the critical, "strategic" issues identified during the environmental analysis. It is important to note that strategic objectives may relate to one or more of the organization's goals.

*Strategic Objectives:* The major *accomplishments* that the organization seeks to achieve over a specified period of time (e.g., five years).

More specifically, strategic objectives should:

- Support the mission and goals of the organization;
- Provide clarification of the goals;
- Translate the critical, "strategic" issues identified for the organization into *specific* policy directions;
- Provide the foundation for the development of detailed operational or business plans for the organization; and
- Provide the basis for assessing the organization's accomplishments.

Of major importance is that strategic objectives should not only respond to the needs of constituents, but also be realistic with respect to the organization's environment, both externally and internally, including the available human and financial resources required to accomplish them.

*The strategic objectives identified by the American Association of Blood Banks (AABB) related to those issues that are critical to the organization's future: quality management, education, legislative and regulatory issues, research, relationships with other organizations, and public image. Within AABB's strategic plan, the strategic objectives appear as follows:*

    *I. Develop and promote quality management and improvement programs for blood centers, transfusion services and tissue banks to ensure the safest blood and tissue supply possible.*

    *II. Increase professional educational opportunities for the membership and provide educational programs related to transfusion medicine and transplantation for the public and other related professionals (individuals and groups).*

    *III. Establish a legal, regulatory and public policy environment conducive to the effective and efficient operation of our members in providing the highest level of health-care services.*

IV. *Actively promote the application of basic scientific discoveries to the continuous improvement and enhancement of blood transfusion and tissue transplantation practices.*

V. *Form a mutually beneficial working relationship with other organizations, including state and regional blood banking associations, to address areas of common concern and promote the AABB as the leader in its chosen fields.*

VI. *Develop acceptance and understanding of the AABB members' activities and their roles in the health-care profession, with the public sector and other professionals.*

*The Fish Middleton Jazz Scholarship Fund identified four strategic objectives:*

I. *Sponsor annual jazz concert events.*

II. *Facilitate in-school programs.*

III. *Conduct jazz workshops and seminars to enhance students' skills and understanding of jazz.*

IV. *Grant scholarships to emerging jazz artists.*

A basic challenge to strategic thinking is the ability of the organization's leadership to create strategic unity among members of the leadership themselves, staff, and constituents. To build commitment to the strategic plan, everyone within the organization should be *aware* of what the organization is trying to accomplish, *accept* the organization's mission and goals and understand their implications, and *recognize* the actions that they and the leadership are taking toward the accomplishment of the stated mission, goals, and objectives.

*Develop a Three- to Five-Year Plan Based on the Strategic Objectives.* Typically, group consensus on all of the preceding retreat agenda items are captured on flip chart paper as they are developed, then taped to the walls of your meeting room so everyone can review them as the discussion continues. The individual who facilitates the strategic planning session is generally the person who develops summaries as the meeting progresses and prepares a first draft of your strategic plan (the draft strategic plan) for all retreat participants to review. Comments returned to the facilitator are incorporated into the organization's final draft, which can then be submitted to other constituents for their reactions.

To summarize, a strategic plan that focuses on the next three, four, or five years will not be a lengthy document; rather, your plan should consist of the following five items:

1. Introduction, which may include
   - The process the leadership pursued to develop the strategic plan;
   - A summary of the environmental issues, documenting those identified as "critical" issues; that is, having a high impact on the organization and a high probability of occurrence; and
   - Identification of the organization's strengths and weaknesses in addressing those critical issues.
2. The organization's mission statement
3. Statement of principles
4. Statement of goals
5. Strategic objectives

## EXAMINE THE IMPLICATIONS OF THE STRATEGIC PLAN FOR YOUR ORGANIZATION'S CURRENT PROGRAMS AND STRUCTURE

As the plan is developed, current programs and activities should be tested to determine their relevance to the *new* plan. Some programs or activities that have been part of the organization's past may not address the newly revised mission, goals, or strategic objectives and, therefore, do not fit within the *new* strategic plan.

Similarly, the plan should be reexamined in light of the organization's current governance structure to determine whether the current structure will facilitate the organization's new directions. In many cases, each board member agrees to accept oversight responsibility for one or more of the strategic objectives, to monitor both staff and committees' success in achieving the objective.

Depending on the needs of the new strategic plan, it may be wise to review both the number of board members and their terms, again to facilitate the organization's refocused agenda. The roles and responsibilities of committees will undoubtedly change. In some cases, new committees or task forces will have to be appointed, whereas in other cases, current committees should be dissolved. Just as changes may be necessary within the governance structure, so too the internal organizational structure will have to be assessed, including staffing patterns, activities, and the utilization of human and fiscal resources.

Once the organization's governing board adopts the new strategic plan, and as modifications within the organization are implemented, a carefully planned communications program should be executed so that all constituents and stakeholders, including staff and outside publics, understand the changes and how they came about.

## IMPLEMENTING THE STRATEGIC PLAN

An *operational plan* should accompany the strategic plan. Although there may not be enough time during the retreat to develop an operational plan, the process for developing such a plan should be discussed and assignments made. Generally, staff will prepare the bulk of the operational plan, with guidance and final approval from the governing board.

An operational plan describes the specific actions that must be taken to accomplish each objective identified in the strategic plan. It should include the responsible parties, time lines, resource allocations, and an evaluation plan that identifies specific, measurable outcomes to be achieved. The strategic plan, therefore, focuses on the *what,* whereas your operational plan will focus on the *how.* Without the accompanying operational plan, the strategic plan will languish on the shelf, perhaps serving as a reproach for what was not accomplished, but providing no real guide to action. Details within the operational plan should include:

- *Tactics:* Identify what should be done; that is, outline the specific tasks that must be accomplished to achieve the strategic objective.

- *Time lines:* Include exact dates (month and year) when each tactic should be completed.

- *Responsible parties:* Identify those individuals (staff members, board members, committee chairs, or others) who will be held responsible for accomplishing each task.

- *Resource requirements:* Identify all resources required to accomplish each task, including funding for supplies, equipment, staff time, board travel, and so forth.

- *Anticipated results:* Specify the desired or anticipated results and what will be accomplished according to the selected time line.

- *Evaluation measures:* Outline how you will determine that each task has been completed or that success has been achieved.

Exhibit 1–4 diagrams the strategic and operational planning processes, beginning with the environmental analysis and continuing to the determination of tactics and their implementation.

**Exhibit 1–4**  The Strategic and Operational Planning Processes

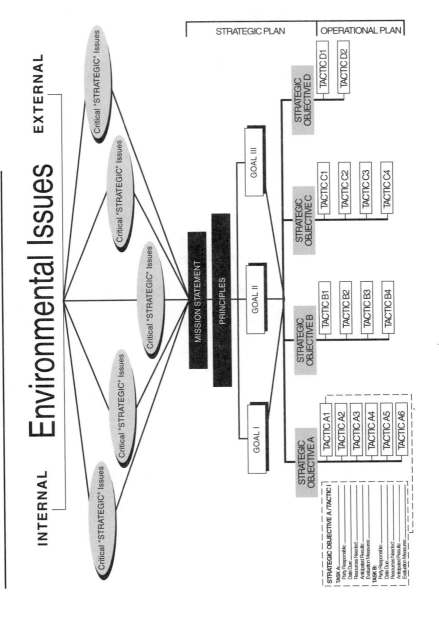

## DOCUMENT THE PROCESS, THE OUTCOMES, THE DRAFT STRATEGIC PLAN

The report of the process, the outcomes of discussion, and the draft strategic plan should be documented and shared with the nonprofit's constituents for review and feedback. This may take the form of a mailing to all board members or even to all constituents, based on the number of individuals involved and the resources available. In addition, committee chairs and members should have an opportunity to review the document to assist in identifying their roles (if any) in the new plan. It will be important, however, to involve the organization's constituents and other stakeholders, including outside publics, to ensure that leadership has correctly identified the critical issues for the organization as well as good strategies to affect them.

## MONITOR THE IMPLEMENTATION PLAN

Now that the organization has a strategic plan and an accompanying implementation plan, it is incumbent upon the executive director to monitor the plans and provide updates to the governing body on the organization's accomplishments in achieving the plan's strategic objectives. Mechanisms should be established, through a committee or staff assignment, to monitor and assess impending threats or opportunities and to recommend changes in the organization's course.

Again, there are two maxims to remember as you move through the strategic planning process:

1. A strategic *plan* is a statement of important, but flexible guidelines, not rigid doctrine.
2. The *process* of strategic planning—the development, implementation, and assessment of a plan—is not a single, one-shot event; it is an ongoing, continuous process that must adapt to environmental changes, both externally and internally.

The following chapters should help the nonprofit organization move from the essential first step, the strategic plan, to effective implementation—to turn from strategic planning to effective, strategic management.

### Why Strategic Plans Fail

There are a number of ways to approach strategic planning. A certain educational association began with a board-appointed standing committee on long-range planning. The committee took considerable time surveying the membership, conducting environmental analyses, and using a variety of processes to gain consensus. After two years, a document was prepared setting forth great expectations for the organization—expectations that had neither the intellectual commitment of the organization's leadership nor the financial resources needed to reach the hoped-for goals.

Does this sound familiar? Many nonprofits use this approach as their first step. But only when a governing board is convinced of its own responsibility and the need to match planning with reality will the process move forward.

Perhaps you already have a strategic plan that was developed a number of years ago but was not actually used by the organization or referred to since it came off the press. Have you analyzed why? There are a number of reasons that strategic plans fail. Among the pitfalls to avoid are the following:

- All of the ideas and all of the wish lists of the contributors are included in the document. So many ideas are presented that the real focus is unclear.
- The wish lists fail to take into account what is actually occurring in the real world or to realize that the environment and the organization have changed since the organization was chartered.
- The strategic plan is not tested against the current and anticipated resources (human and fiscal) of the organization.
- The executive directors, elected leaders, and/or staff lack commitment to the plan.
- No operational plan is developed for the strategic plan; thus, there is no carry-through on the plan.
- As leaders change, there are no mechanisms in place to gain commitment and continue the strategic plan; thus, again, there is no carry-through on the plan.

Don't let this happen to you.

## CHECKLIST FOR YOUR STRATEGIC PLANNING EFFORT

Has your organization:

- *Obtained support and commitment* from elected leaders *to pursue strategic planning* for the organization?
- *Involved leadership,* staff, and other major constituents in the process of strategic planning?

- *Obtained assistance from a person outside* the organization to assist in the development of your strategic planning process, as well as facilitate the group meetings of the leadership and staff?

- Encouraged all persons involved, throughout the process, to *think strategically?*

- *Conducted an environmental analysis,* carefully examining both the external and internal environments that affect the organization?

- *Planned and conducted a strategic planning session* with key leaders and staff?

  a. Developed a clear, succinct mission statement?

  b. Identified the organization's principles?

  c. Established goals that clarify your mission statement?

  d. Developed strategic objectives that respond to the organization's internal and external environments?

- *Established a process for implementing the strategic plan*—establishing priorities; identifying time lines, responsible parties, and resource allocations?

- *Documented the process,* the outcomes, and the strategic plan?

- *Continually monitored the implementation plan,* providing updates on the organization's accomplishments in achieving the plan's objectives?

## CHAPTER TWO

# Working Together: Maximizing Board and Staff Effectiveness

**The governing board and the executive staff share respon-
sibility for their nonprofit's success. The successful nonprofit manager must understand the relationship between
board and staff and be able to communicate effectively
with elected leaders. This chapter will help both you and
your elected leaders to understand the different—but
equally important—roles of each group.**

### GOVERNING BOARDS: CARETAKERS OF THE PUBLIC TRUST

A nonprofit organization is typically born out of a group's desire to
solve a problem, meet a need, help a profession to develop, or create
new opportunities. As the organization grows and gains strength
with time and experience, it often evolves from a group of volunteers
managing all aspects of its activities to one that depends on staff to
handle its day-to-day business.

Once the nonprofit moves into its formative years, most of its policies and procedures should be in place, with the governing board
working closely with staff to fulfill the defined mission. Nonetheless,
it is not unusual for difficulties to emerge as the nonprofit matures,
perhaps with new constituents interested in moving the organization
in a direction different from that of its founders. Often, it will not be
until the nonprofit fully matures that a settling in again occurs.

As nonprofit organizations change, so do their governing
boards. The relationships between committees, other volunteers,

and staff differ from one period to the next. This chapter will help organizations to identify troublesome areas before they become significant and to overcome these transitional obstacles more quickly.

## Types and Sizes of Boards

The size and nature of the board of directors is often determined by history, sometimes without adequate thought. Many nonprofits are established with a 15- to 20-person board of directors that includes officers and directors who chair each of the organization's committees. A smaller board (e.g., 10 to 12 persons) can, however, provide direction for the organization while other constituents chair committees and task forces.

Some nonprofits, because of their large size, their interest in involving as many constituents as possible, or simply tradition, have a small board (12 to 15 persons) but a larger "house of delegates" (individuals who represent regions or chapters and review policies recommended by the executive committee or board of directors). The size of a board will depend on many factors, including the laws of the state of incorporation (which generally dictate a minimum number of directors), the mission and philosophy of the organization, and its resources. However, any organization that has more than 20 board members should question its size. The decision as to the size of the board should be guided by several questions:

- What functions are required of the board?
- How many individuals, and in what roles, are needed to accomplish those functions?
- How many board committees are needed to accomplish the organization's goals?
- Are there sufficient individuals on the board to participate on board committees?

In most situations, the board will have an executive committee with the authority to act between meetings on behalf of the full board. Actions taken by an executive committee are reviewed, sometimes modified, and usually ratified by the entire board at its next meeting. With a large board, it is especially important to have strong, active committees to study issues in depth and make recommendations to the board. This streamlines the decision process by preventing the board from becoming enmeshed in details and unable to make decisions.

Most governing boards are elected—many by the constituents at large, some by the members of the governing board electing their own replacements. In some organizations, only the directors are elected by the constituents at large, and officers (president, vice president, treasurer, and secretary) are elected by the board. Decisions regarding policies and procedures for nominations and elections are organizationally unique. Although a certain approach may sacrifice democracy, it may also provide greater efficiencies for the organization. Decisions regarding such policies should be driven by your nonprofit's mission and the constituents it serves.

## ROLES AND RESPONSIBILITIES OF GOVERNING BOARD MEMBERS

Large nonprofits have sufficient staff to carry out all of the organization's activities, with the board setting policy and the executive committee responsible for oversight and any policy decisions that must be made between board meetings. In other cases, much of the organization's work is done by volunteers, through standing committees of the board or ad hoc committees and task forces. Regardless of the size or age of the organization or the number of staff available to carry through the policies of the board, an individual accepting a position on a governing board has fiduciary, moral, and ethical responsibilities.

As Richard Ingram has stressed in an excellent publication from the National Center for Nonprofit Boards, "the obligations of board members are considerable—they extend well beyond the basic expectations of attending meetings, participating in fund-raising initiatives, and making monetary contributions." Ingram recommends a "clear statement of individual board member responsibilities adapted to the organization's needs and circumstances." Such a statement, he writes, "can serve at least two purposes: it can help with the process of recruiting new board members by clarifying expectations before candidates accept nomination, and it can provide criteria by which the committee responsible for indentifying and recruiting prospective nominees can review the performance of incumbents who are eligible for reelection or reappointment." While Ingram's booklet is written principally for board members of charitable nonprofit organizations, much of his advice is applicable to trade and professional associations as well.[1]

---

[1]Richard T. Ingram, *Ten Basic Responsibilities of Nonprofit Boards,* Second Edition, (Washington, D.C., 1999), National Center for Nonprofit Boards.

## Ensure Mission Is Carried Out

Nonprofit organizations are established to achieve a specific mission. A misunderstanding or misperception of the organization's mission—its reason for being—can cause havoc among board members, between board and committees, and between board and staff. Board members must understand the organization's mission and work together, with committee chairs and staff, to ensure that the mission is fulfilled. Unless the organization's mission is clear, and all parties accept it and make a commitment to carrying it out, the organization will flounder: Disparate goals will be pursued, conflict will arise among and between board members and staff, and the organization will cease to be effective. (See Chapter 1, "Establishing the Organization's Direction.")

It is incumbent upon the governing board to establish policies and priorities, approve the procedures to accomplish them, and monitor and assess the organization's success in achieving its mission. Once tasks are identified and responsible parties and time lines are specified within an operational plan, nonprofit boards can better assess their organization's accomplishments between board meetings.

A board should periodically assess its own operations to ensure that both the board and the organization are working at optimum capacity and efficiency. Such an assessment can help ensure that the organization's mission remains in focus.

## Meet Fiduciary Responsibilities

In addition to ensuring that the nonprofit's mission drives all the organization's programs, governing board members have a responsibility to make certain that the organization remains financially sound. No board member wants to see the reserves of an organization depleted during his or her "watch." Although the chief executive officer (CEO), the treasurer, and the finance committee have the chief responsibility for developing and tracking the budget, it is every board member's responsibility to understand the budget, the budgeting and investment procedures, and the organization's financial history in terms of reserves and restricted funds (if any).

*The board members of an organization whose budget was well over $2 million were astonished to learn of imminent bankruptcy during a normal audit procedure. All had thought the organization was solvent, with plenty of reserves. When challenged, the executive director reported that he was planning to "get a bank loan to carry the organization through a rough spot." Unfortunately, the problem was much deeper. Had responsible board members closely monitored the organization's fiscal status, drastic reorganization and downsizing would not have been necessary.*

## Contribute to the Organization's Bottom Line

Members of nonprofit governing boards are well aware of the need to give willingly of their time for board meetings—time that translates into financial contributions for many volunteers. In addition, board members bring their expertise, providing free counsel on a variety of issues.

As discussed in Chapter 5, fund-raising is critical for most nonprofits. This is true for established organizations seeking to expand or maintain existing programs, as well as for small nonprofits whose success is measured by "getting to Friday." Board members will be expected not only to contribute their time and their expertise for program activities, but also to identify outside funding sources and, in some cases, to provide direct financial support. In addition to direct financial contributions, a board member's organization may provide in-kind contributions for such activities as printing or mailing a conference brochure, stuffing envelopes, or providing assistance at a function's registration desk.

Members of nonprofit boards should be willing to dip into their own pockets to support the mission and goals of the organization for which they advocate. The amount is less important than the principle. It is much easier to solicit other individual and corporate support for a nonprofit's agenda when all governing board members of the organization have contributed as well.

## Respect Other Board Members

Accepting of an appointment on a nonprofit's governing board requires a commitment of time, energy, and expertise. Depending on the maturity of the nonprofit, its size, and its resource base, the commitment may be significant. It is incumbent on all board members, however, to respect other members by both attending and being prepared for meetings. If an assignment is accepted, it should be completed by the agreed-upon deadline.

Although there may be unexpected circumstances that preclude attendance at a scheduled board meeting, any member of the governing board who fails to attend at least the majority of its meetings should assess his or her commitment to the organization and consider resigning from the board.

Respect for other board members also requires that members argue *positions,* not personalities. Decisions regarding the future of a nonprofit do not come easily, and there will often be differing points of view. At these times, stepping into the other person's shoes and carefully listening to his or her perspective will be particularly critical to quality decision making.

## Maintain Professional and Ethical Standards

Members of a governing board are entrusted with the care and nurturing of their nonprofit organization. Board members must maintain high professional and ethical standards for the conduct of all activities within and outside the organization. Two areas of particular concern include confidentiality and conflict of interest.

*Confidentiality.* The issue of confidentiality in regard to board meetings and board decisions is often not addressed until a problem occurs. Although there may be disagreements within the board room, once board members leave the room they have a responsibility to maintain the confidentiality of the discussion and support the outcome, whether or not they agreed with it. When board members leave the board room and comment to other constituents that they did not agree with the outcome and that "so-and-so said . . . ," constituents lose confidence in the board's ability to lead. Airing dissension also creates distrust and additional conflict among board members and strains possibly fragile interpersonal relationships.

*Conflict of Interest.* Depending on the organization's mission and goals and the program activities it pursues, board members may have opportunities to benefit from board actions. Providing services for a fee, although not illegal, gives the appearance of self-interest. Contracts with board members for direct mail campaigns or other fund-raising services have been a cause of destructive publicity for several national nonprofits in recent years. When confronted with a potential conflict, board members should identify the conflict and remove themselves from the discussion and any vote on the matter. Some organizations have conflict of interest policies to prevent even an appearance of wrongful activity.

## Respect and Support Staff

It is important for the board to support the executive staff leader. Whatever his or her title, the executive staff leader works at the pleasure of the governing board, implementing policies approved by board action. To ensure an effective, long-lasting relationship, the lines of communication between staff and board must be clearly identified and maintained.

*Lines of Communication.* Most nonprofits clearly delineate the roles and responsibilities and reporting channels of the executive director. Although the executive is accountable to the board as a whole, quite often the direct line of communication is with the elected president or chairperson of the governing board. In some cases, the executive works just as closely with both the executive committee and the president. All board members should feel free to contact the executive; however, the executive generally should confirm decisions with the president and/or executive committee, particularly if there are new policy or resource implications.

Staff, on the other hand, report to the executive, who has the authority to hire and terminate employees. In nonprofit organizations, whether small or large, board members should work with the executive in requesting staff time or support for activities.

The person hired to provide administrative leadership for a nonprofit organization (whether "president" or "executive director") is chosen to accomplish the tasks identified by the board at the time of hiring. Occasionally, a nonprofit outgrows its executive and chooses to hire someone who can meet the new demands of the organization. Ideally, with the support of the board, the executive grows along with the nonprofit. Boards need to recognize the talents of their executives and support them with opportunities for professional development. An executive director who has gained knowledge and responsibility through experience can be an organization's most valuable asset.

Generally, the chair of the board of directors (or "council") has the closest working relationship with the executive and should provide feedback on the executive's performance on a routine basis. A more formal review process, however, can also be developed so that all board members have an opportunity to provide their assessment of their organization's chief staff executive. The process developed should be agreeable to both parties.

*Separation of Roles.* An area of particular concern for many executives is the distinction between the board's role as policymaker and the chief executive's role as administrator and implementer. Often, the line is quite fine; the executive will be expected to provide policy guidance for the board, not just take orders, and board members, as volunteers, may be called upon to handle some specific administrative tasks. It is important, however, for board members to refrain from managing the office activities. That is the purview of the nonprofit's executive. The board's responsibility is to identify priorities and establish the policy directives so that staff can manage the day-to-day activities of the organization.

As an organization grows, it is often difficult for board volunteers to wean themselves from the day-to-day activities, particularly those at which they have been successful. In working with such board members, the executive will need to be particularly sensitive and identify ways to involve them in the organization's activities.

Relationships between board members and the executive staff will change as an organization grows and matures. Unless both the board and the executive are sensitive to changing needs, the process of maturation will be difficult.

*After taking several courses in teaching students with learning disabilities, Mary Johnson found that she was able to help her own dyslexic son overcome, at least partially, his reading difficulties. Once he was in high school and no longer needed special tutoring, she founded a small nonprofit organization to make tutoring available to other dyslexic students.*

*Mary initiated a fund-raising campaign and raised sufficient funds to hire a full-time professional head tutor. Gradually, the nonprofit acquired a staff of professionals, some working full-time and others part-time, and Mary was able to lease, at very low cost, an unused building that had formerly been an elementary school. Tuition income was now covering about half the organization's costs. A board of directors was formed, consisting largely of parents of former students who were willing to help the school in fund-raising and lobbying with the city government. Mary Johnson, still unpaid, became chairman of the board. The director of tutoring became the full-time paid executive director of the organization, with responsibilities for hiring and supervising tutors, keeping books, managing space contracts and other administrative activities. But when fund-raising fell off, Mary Johnson, frustrated, decided to resume more of a day-to-day management role. The professional educational staff, however, looked on Mary as an amateur, unable to guide them as educators. Conflicts grew, and the executive director, believing that she could no longer be effective as an administrator, resigned.*

*Mary Johnson had selected and recruited most members of the board of directors. Nonetheless, the board agreed that Mary, despite her role in creating the organization, was not the person to be the day-to-day administrator of the much larger, more professional organization it had become, 15 years after its creation in her living room. Reluctantly, the board pressured her to resign as chairperson. But, because the relationship between the just-resigned executive director and the past chairman was so strained, the board members concluded that they could not rehire the director. They recruited another trained educational professional.*

*Although no written job description existed at the time the new executive director was hired, she had an agreement from the executive committee that she would develop one, with their input, as one of her first assignments. She met daily, at first, with other members of the professional staff, both in groups and one-on-one, to solidify their support and get their ideas on the future of the organization, and involved both her faculty and the executive committee in decisions. She communicated frequently with the executive committee members, telling them of decisions she was making in a way that allowed them to demur if they wished, but without expecting them to make decisions for her. This style evolved into her job description, giving the executive director the authority and autonomy necessary without displacing board responsibilities.*

*The new executive was also very careful always to show respect for Mary Johnson, who still had close friends on the board and among the parents of alumni. Although Mary boycotted the annual fund-raising dinner the first year, by the second year she had been won over and attended the banquet, receiving a standing ovation and an award for her creativity in founding the organization and guiding it through its formative years.*

As in the preceding case, changes in staffing and board/staff relationships are often inevitable, particularly during the early years of an organization's growth and maturation. Board members should be alert to situations when the board chair and the chief executive, perhaps for historical reasons, cannot work together effectively. Recognizing and addressing issues early can help to ensure that personal conflicts do not interfere with the overall well-being of the organization.

## Enhance the Public Image of the Organization

Members of the governing board of a nonprofit organization must assume an advocacy role on behalf of their nonprofit. Often board members are called upon to speak on behalf of the organization. The request may come internally from the president, through a board assignment, from staff, from another organization, or from the press. Board members should accept such invitations to speak for their organization only with full knowledge of the requester's expectations so as to be sure they can respond "on behalf of the organization." Any board member accepting such an invitation should notify the organization's chief elected officer or executive director (sometimes both) so that all parties may discuss how best to present the organization's policies.

Because such requests may come at any time, it is important for board members to know the official position of the governing board on all issues facing the organization. Many nonprofits have fact sheets or position papers clearly identifying the organization's point of view and the rationale for the position. Again, board members should review these carefully and obtain clarification on any points they do not understand or do not agree with.

Whether in formal or informal situations, it is also important to acknowledge that even if a board member says, "This is off the record" or "I am not speaking on behalf of the organization," those listening will not hear these words. Instead, they will assume that the position the board member is advocating is the nonprofit's position. If a board member holds an opinion that is in conflict with the board's official position on an issue, the board member should either be willing to provide the "party line" or refrain from stating any position. If questions are expected, it is advisable to refer the invitation to another board member. If a board member continues to be in conflict with the board's official positions, he or she may wish to consider resigning from the board.

## Recruit Other Volunteer Leaders

Among the responsibilities delegated to members of a nonprofit's governing board, one that is most crucial to the future of the organization is identifying and developing future leaders. The future of the organization depends on the quality of new board members. Even though the recruitment and nomination process is absolutely essential, it is often overlooked or left to the last minute. Current board members are in the best position to know the kind of expertise needed on the board to replace those board members whose terms are ending. Is expertise needed in the financial area? Fund-raising? Strategic planning? Research? Education or certification? Are there other considerations for the selection of board members, such as regional or racial representation? Careful thought should go into the qualifications and expertise required. Current board members can help identify individuals who meet the criteria and who would be willing to be nominated for a position on the board.

Most often, new leaders will be identified from having worked on a committee or task force. Equally important, therefore, is helping to identify new individuals for the organization's working committees.

*A social service agency located in a major metropolitan area asked individual members of its board to personally recruit at least two new volunteers for the organization. One board member who had served on and off the board for the past 20 years and felt she had called on nearly all her friends and acquaintances to actively support the agency during her tenure with the organization, decided to carry out her new assignment in a unique way.*

*She arranged to host an informal "get to know us" reception in her home, to which she invited all other board members and their potential recruits. The reception provided a nonthreatening atmosphere in which the potential volunteers could chat with board members and other volunteers about the benefits of becoming involved in the agency's activities. Once everyone had gathered, the president gave a brief welcome and asked each board member to introduce and give a short biography of each of his or her potential vol-*

unteers. *The president continued with an overview (approximately 10 minutes) of the agency and its mission. This was followed by 2-minute reports by each of the agency's standing committee chairs, highlighting the major programs and activities of the committees.*

*At the close of the reception, each potential volunteer was given a summary sheet of the information presented. Board members were asked to follow up by personally contacting their potential volunteers to obtain a commitment from each to serve on at least one committee and to participate in one program or fund-raising activity.*

*Within two months of the reception, 18 of the 20 potential volunteers who had attended the reception became actively involved in the agency.*

Assess your governing board members' understanding of and commitment to their roles and responsibilities by identifying the extent to which each of the roles and responsibilities indicated in Exhibit 2-1 is carried out.

**Exhibit 2-1**   Roles and Responsibilities of a Governing Board: An Assessment

| | Always | Often | Sometimes | Never |
|---|---|---|---|---|
| All members of the governing board work to: | | | | |
| 1. Ensure the mission is carried out. | | | | |
| 2. Maintain fiduciary responsibility. | | | | |
| 3. Contribute to the organization's bottom line. | | | | |
| 4. Maintain ethical standards. | | | | |
|    a. Maintain board confidentiality. | | | | |
|    b. Recognize conflicts of interest. | | | | |
| 5. Respect and support staff. | | | | |
|    a. Maintain appropriate lines of communication. | | | | |
|    b. Understand and maintain separate roles. | | | | |
| 6. Respect other board members. | | | | |
| 7. Enhance the public image of the organization. | | | | |
| 8. Recruit other volunteers. | | | | |

## Position Descriptions for Governing Board Members

In addition to the general roles and responsibilities of governing board members, officers will usually have specific tasks that are carried out on behalf of the board and the nonprofit organization. Titles vary, depending on the nature and history of the organization. For many nonprofits, the chief elected officer carries the title of president, indicating that this person is the primary spokesperson for the organization. Sometimes, the title of president is conferred on the chief executive staff person, for the same reason. In this case, the chief elected leader is generally identified as the chairperson, or "chair," of the board.

Exhibit 2-2 provides sample position descriptions for these and other officers (vice president, secretary, and treasurer), along with a generic position description for a board director.

**Exhibit 2-2**     Sample Position Descriptions—Elected Officers

PRESIDENT (OR CHAIRPERSON): Chief elected officer of the organization

Primary Responsibilities:

Ensure that the organization abides by its bylaws and established policies.

Serve as chairperson of the board of directors and the executive committee.

Preside over all meetings of the board of directors and executive committee, and the annual business meeting of the organization.

Support the executive director.

Represent the organization to other organizations, the media, and the public at large.

Appoint committee chairpersons.

In collaboration with the executive director, develop agendas for all meetings of the board of directors.

Report to the membership.

Additional Responsibilities:

Communicate regularly with the executive director.

Report periodically to the board of directors.

Train and otherwise prepare the president-elect for the responsibilities of the presidency.

Charge committees.

Receive reports from all officers and committees.

Review communications, reports, and proposals of the staff.

**Exhibit 2-2** (*Continued*)

---

VICE PRESIDENT: Assume the role and duties of the presidency if the president is no longer able to continue. (The role of the vice president is sometimes performed by the president-elect.)

Primary Responsibilities:

Perform the responsibilities of the president during absence or disability of the president.

Accede to the presidency in the event that a permanent vacancy in the presidency arises.

Serve as a voting member of the board of directors and executive committee.

Familiarize him- or herself with the responsibilities of the president, the activities and positions of the organization, and the functioning of the executive office.

Additional Responsibilities:

Assist the president as appropriate.

Represent the organization at the request of the president.

Serve on appointive committees.

SECRETARY: Custodian of records for the organization.

Primary Responsibilities:

Generally oversee record keeping of meetings, policies, activities, membership, and any other records required by law.

Oversee minutes of all meetings and teleconferences of the board of directors and executive committee, as well as the annual organizational business meeting.

Within 30 days after a meeting, provide the board of directors with minutes, including a list of motions made and the voting results. (Preparation of minutes may be delegated to staff, with the secretary responsible for approval.)

Review the policies of the organization and present to the board any policies that may have to be amended, rescinded, or reaffirmed.

Serve as a voting member of the board of directors and executive committee.

Additional Responsibilities:

Assist the president as appropriate.

Represent the organization at the request of the president.

Serve on appointive committees.

**Exhibit 2-2**    (*Continued*)

TREASURER: Monitors financial condition of the organization.

Primary Responsibilities:

Oversee, with the executive director, the fiscal affairs of the organization.

Present to the board of directors an annual budget for the organization, developed in concert with the executive director.

Monitor budgetary performance of the organization, recommending modifications as needed.

Review for approval all actions and policies with major financial implications.

Serve as a voting member of the board of directors and the executive committee.

Additional Responsibilities:

Serve as chairperson of the finance committee.

Assist the president as appropriate.

Serve on appointive committees.

DIRECTOR: Assists officers in overseeing health and direction of the organization.

Responsibilities:

Attend board of directors meetings and participate in conference calls.

Attend any annual business meetings of the organization.

Participate actively in organizational strategic planning.

Vote on organizational policy and program issues.

Serve as a resource of knowledge and counsel to the executive office, committees, and other board members.

Assist in locating and developing funding sources for the organization.

Review and respond to all action and information requests from the executive office.

Serve as a liaison between the board of directors and committee chairs.

Represent the organization at the request of the president.

## COMMITTEES

Any experienced nonprofit leader will tell you that committees can be a boon to, or the bane of, a nonprofit organization. The function of a committee is to assist the board and staff with the work of the organization. When committees fulfill their charges, the organization's strategic plan can be realized, advancing the organization's mission. When committees fail, work is not accomplished and expectations are shattered, frustrating board members, staff, and committee members alike.

For the most part, the governing board determines the types and sizes of committees that will assist in the conduct of the organization's business. In most cases, the chairperson and members of a committee are appointed by the president, with nominations from and approval by the board. Terms of appointment vary, depending on the number of volunteers who are interested and willing to serve on the various committees. However, terms are usually designated as one or two years, with the opportunity for reappointment for a second and, sometimes, a third term.

Only standing committees—those that relate to the basic governance of the organization—should be included in a nonprofit's bylaws. In most organizations, these standing committees include the executive committee, the finance committee, and the nominations committee. Other committees, perhaps even more important, are appointed as needed.

Other committees, that do not relate to governance issues but are ongoing committees of the organization—such as the annual conference program committee, awards committee, research committee, education committee and legislative committee—should not be listed in the bylaws, but may be referred to as "special" committees or committees of the organization. Keeping lists of committees out of the bylaws allows the board more flexibility to conduct its business. In addition, many nonprofit boards also appoint ad hoc committees or task forces that are given a specific charge to be completed in a specified period of time. Ad hoc committees are often the most productive, specifically because the charge and time lines are clear.

## Governance Committees

As noted earlier, standing committees provide guidance on the organization's governance issues.

*Executive Committee.* The role of an executive committee is to provide guidance for the nonprofit organization between meetings of the governing board. The roles and responsibilities of the executive committee should be explicit; only in emergencies should the executive committee make policy decisions. The executive committee then reports its actions to the board at its next meeting, at which time the board ratifies, amends, or negates those actions taken. An executive committee can be a useful instrument of the board but should be careful not to usurp board responsibilities. Decisions reserved for the board should be included in the bylaws; for example, the board should be responsible for hiring the executive, encumbering funds, and approving the budget.

An executive committee is generally composed of the officers of the organization, with the executive director serving as an ex officio (nonvoting) member. Some nonprofits include one or two additional members from the board to expand board input into the organization's policy decisions.

*Finance Committee.* A nonprofit's finance committee should work closely with the executive in the critical role of financial oversight for the organization, advising the board on issues related to the budget and the financial affairs of the organization. The finance committee is usually chaired by the treasurer and includes other members of the executive committee, with the executive director serving ex officio.

*Nominations Committee.* The critical role of the nominations committee is to identify the future leaders of the organization. To eliminate conflict between potential nominees or factions in the organization, policies should be in place to govern the procedures the nominations committee follows to select a slate of officers and directors.

As noted previously, the nominations committee is often elected by the nonprofit's constituents. There are organizations, however, in which the president appoints the nominating committee members— in most cases, from members of the governing board. Because of its critical function, the procedures for electing or appointing members of the nominations committee are included in the bylaws.

Exhibits 2-3 through 2-5 provide sample charters for these governance committees.

## Other Committees

The number and assignments of other committees will vary, depending on the size of the organization, its resources, and the number of volunteers willing to serve. Often, organizations will have a program planning committee to design and promote the annual meeting of the organization. Other committees may include an audit committee, a fund development committee, an awards committee, a membership committee, a public relations or marketing committee, a government relations committee, an ethics committee, a research committee, and/or a certification committee. Again, depending on the needs of the nonprofit, these types of committees are generally ongoing, long-term committees, appointed on a yearly basis by the president in consultation with the board of directors.

**Exhibit 2-3**  Sample Charge for Executive Committee

Provide consultation and guidance to the executive director on matters related to the affairs of the organization between meetings of the board of directors.

Approve any extraordinary expenditure of funds, subject to board ratification.

Evaluate the performance of the executive director.

Perform other such duties as established by the board of directors.

**Exhibit 2-4**  Sample Charge for Finance Committee

Develop, with the guidance of the executive director, a budget for the organization based on forecasted income and expenses.

Recommend to the board of directors fiscal policies and procedures for the organization.

Review budget requests from all organization components.

Advise the board of directors regarding budget considerations and financial affairs of the organization.

Review all grants and contracts regarding their fiscal implications for the organization.

Review monthly financial statements of the organization.

Develop a long-range plan with strategies to ensure the fiscal viability and growth of the organization.

**Exhibit 2-5**  Sample Charge for Nominations Committee

Solicit nominations for elected positions from the membership at large.

Select, from the nominations submitted by the membership, a slate of nominees for each prospective vacancy in elected positions.

Verify and submit election results to the board of directors.

## Ad Hoc Committees and Task Forces

Short-term, project-specific committees are generally termed ad hoc committees or task forces. These committees have a time-related, specific charge, and when the task has been accomplished, the ad hoc committee or task force is thanked for its work and disbanded. The following are examples of such ad hoc committees and task forces: Ad Hoc Committee on Certification Test Development, Task Force on the First World Congress, Ad Hoc Committee on the 25th Anniversary Celebration.

## Successful Committees

There are certain ingredients necessary for successful committee outcomes. Examine each of your nonprofit's committees to determine whether it meets all of the criteria listed in Exhibit 2-6.

## ROLES AND RESPONSIBILITIES OF THE CHIEF EXECUTIVE STAFF PERSON

The titles—and, therefore, the responsibilities—of chief executive staff persons vary, depending on the size, maturity, and philosophy of the nonprofit organization. Most organizations identify their chief executive as executive director: the individual who provides leadership and guidance to the governing board, administers and manages all aspects of the organization, and speaks on behalf of the organization as delegated by the elected president and governing board.

As noted earlier, some nonprofits want their chief executive staff person to be the *primary* spokesperson for the organization, with the title of president. (See Exhibit 2-7 for a sample position description for an executive director.) As nonprofits grow and mature, their governing boards usually become more willing to delegate spokesperson responsibilities to the chief executive staff person. Whatever the title, there are common roles and responsibilities that the chief staff person must fulfill to ensure the success of the nonprofit.

## Understand the Organization—Inside and Out

A good chief executive will be familiar with all aspects of the nonprofit he or she is managing. A new executive staff person will want to review all organizational materials: bylaws, policies and procedures manuals, past board meeting minutes, publications, historical documents, and promotional materials. The bylaws of an organization, depending on their specificity, can be an excellent source for determining the roles and responsibilities of the executive and the purview of the board. This should be supplemented with conversations with past officials and minutes of previous board meetings, with the focus on specific motions addressing board/staff relations.

The day-to-day reality of working with any particular governing board may differ from what is written in the bylaws or position descriptions. The personal interests and the personalities of board members are important factors in how the executive relates to the board and carries out its directives. Often, the executive will have to rely on intuition, interpersonal relations, and management skills in deciding how to proceed in a particular circumstance. The bylaws may not, for example, contain information regarding conflicts of interest between board

**Exhibit 2-6**    Criteria for Successful Committees

- Clearly defined task(s) to be accomplished.
- Established time lines.
- A committed chair who has the time to pursue the task and prepare concise reports on the committee's accomplishments for board review.
- Committee members who, likewise, are committed to the task and are willing to expend the time to accomplish the task.
- Time for the committee to meet face to face as needed (other business can be conducted by mail, fax, e-mail, or conference call).
- Resources, based on a budget developed by the committee, adequate to accomplish the task(s).
- A board member, appointed as liaison to the committee, who will act as both advisor and advocate.

**Exhibit 2-7**    Sample Position Description of Executive Director

EXECUTIVE DIRECTOR: Chief executive staff person of the organization

Responsibilities:

Provide leadership and policy guidance for the organization.

Manage and direct all operations, programs, and activities of the organization.

Implement the policy decisions and directives of the board of directors.

Uphold and adhere to the policies and bylaws of the organization.

Report regularly to the board of directors and otherwise ensure that the board is fully informed of all organization activities.

Advise the board of directors in a timely fashion of any developments which may affect the organization's well-being.

Approve all financial disbursements and otherwise monitor all financial and accounting activities of the organization.

Prepare annual budgets with the assistance of the treasurer and finance committee.

Hire, supervise, and evaluate office staff.

Maintain organization records, files, documents, and archives.

Enter into contracts on behalf of the organization, with approval of the board of directors.

Regularly inform the membership at large of organization activities.

Represent the organization to other organizations, the media, and the public at large.

Prepare agenda books, bulletins, reports, testimony, daily correspondence, and other necessary materials and communications.

Maintain confidentiality of sensitive information.

Provide policy guidance and leadership for the board.

members on a specific matter pending before the board. Clearly, if such an instance surfaces, the executive will want to ensure that board members are not embarrassed or placed in difficult situations.

Clear and concise bylaws, board directives, job descriptions, and other written documents are critically important in establishing the executive's role and associated relationship with the board. Written directives, however, should be supplemented with a more personal and thorough understanding of the board and the way individuals on the board wish to operate. The executive director should spend time with the chief elected officer, as well as with other officers, board members, current staff, and former executives (if appropriate), to obtain a historical perspective on the organization and insights about the organization and its future. Particularly for a new executive, these discussions can be very helpful in understanding organizational issues, board politics, and individual sensitivities.

In most nonprofits, the role of the executive extends well beyond day-to-day activities. It is critical for the staff executive to monitor the organization's environment (both internally and externally) on an ongoing basis, identifying for the governing board those issues that will affect the organization. As noted in Chapter 1, the organization's strategic plan should be evaluated constantly in light of changes in either the internal or external environment. It is the responsibility of the executive to be able to discuss the implications of any significant change in the environment in which the organization exists and provide recommendations for board action.

By thinking and managing "strategically," providing insights for board members who may have limited time to consider all of the issues' implications, the executive has an opportunity to help shape the policy directions for the organization.

## Establish and Maintain Effective Communication Systems

A good working relationship between the nonprofit executive and the board of directors is critical to an organization's success. Nonprofit executives who do not communicate appropriately with their leadership or fail to read correctly the politics of their boards, create major, sometimes irreversible, problems.

Establishing good rapport and communication with the board is basic. This requires *respect* for members of the governing board: respect for their talents, their experience, and their perspectives. When respect between and among the executive and board members is mutual, honest and open communication will result. Without such respect, communication channels become strained, opening the door for mistrust and misperceptions.

Most often, nonprofit executives prefer flexibility and independence to manage activities without excessive oversight by their governing boards. However, caution is warranted. With each degree of independence granted, an equal degree of responsibility is assumed. If mistakes are made, the executive is held wholly responsible. Conversely, when success is achieved, the board will assume credit, and rightfully so. After all, the board established policy and granted the executive the authority to pursue board directives.

Through the executive's leadership, communication systems can be developed that are satisfying to all involved. In some nonprofits, and depending on the current issues for the organization, contact is made with the chief elected leader several times a week. In other nonprofits, a telephone or conference call may be scheduled with the elected leader once a week or every two weeks. In still other cases, no schedule is maintained for regular contact, and staff members use fax and mail to provide updates or obtain decisions when necessary.

Some nonprofit organizations find monthly updates of the organization's activities to be extremely helpful in keeping board members informed. These updates also can include action items that require board members' immediate response. One organization, which depends heavily on its volunteer board for accomplishing many of its activities, issues a monthly board bulletin with updates of both staff and board member activities and accomplishments. An "action list" is included that identifies the task(s) to be accomplished, party responsible, and date due, and confirms when the task is completed.

Similar communications must be considered for the rest of the nonprofit's constituents. In some organizations, a quarterly newsletter is sufficient to provide constituents with information relevant to the organization. Others may mail a "Friday Letter" at the end of each week to communicate with constituents. Most often, a monthly newsletter provides constituents with updates on activities of the board, committees, and other members, upcoming conferences or seminars, and/or information on legislative or regulatory issues. Unusual circumstances require more frequent communications.

It is also very important to remember that board/staff relations are not static. An executive cannot assume that the way things are done one year is the way it will always work. Presidents and officers change, and board members rotate off the board in some cyclical pattern, establishing a new set of dynamics at the board table. To succeed, the executive must be able to adapt to these changes. Note how one executive handled two different situations in the following case.

*A newly hired executive director was given no specific charge and very minimal direction from the board of directors. He met with some of the board members and solicited their areas of concern and interest to determine the organization's needs. At his first board meeting, he proposed a program focusing the resources of the organization on regulatory and legislative issues and provided specifics on how this would be achieved. The board endorsed the plan and strongly commended the executive director's proactive initiative.*

*About a year later, however, the same executive director was criticized for using his own judgment in another matter. The board learned that a program being managed by an outside consultant had developed in such a way that it now advocated a position not supported by the majority of the board of directors. Believing the position to be appropriate, the executive director had exercised his leadership to support the consultant. He was unaware that the board did not support this position until his management of the issue was criticized. The executive director successfully resolved the issue by calling a meeting of interested board members, modifying the position according to their input, and assuring the board that it would be party to any subsequent discussions on the issue.*

## Educate Board Regarding Board and Staff Roles and Responsibilities

As noted previously, newly elected board members may be long-standing and active constituents of the nonprofit organization. In their new positions as directors on a governing board, however, they will need more detailed information regarding the organization's policies and procedures. Indeed, to fulfill their roles as knowledgeable spokespersons for the organization, they will require additional education.

*Board Orientation.* Many nonprofits schedule an orientation session for new board members and, sometimes, as a refresher for existing board members. Such orientations may be scheduled for two to four hours prior to a board meeting or for as long as 1½ to 2 days in a retreat setting. Without a thorough orientation to the organization and the roles and responsibilities of the board, new members will be ineffective and possibly even counterproductive. They may well assume one set of expectations when the organization requires quite different activities. Unless they are properly oriented, they will proceed on the basis of their assumptions. Currently serving board members should be encouraged to attend the orientation sessions as well. They can add a valuable perspective, and the refresher is always beneficial to them.

**Exhibit 2-8**   Topics for a New Board Orientation Session

- Mission and goals of the organization.
- Overview of the organization's history.
- Strategic plan; strategic planning process.
- Roles and responsibilities of the governing board.
- Roles and responsibilities of the executive and staff.
- Organizational structure and policies; reporting lines of communication.
- Resources available, including the financial structure and financial policies.
- Review of major activities; e.g., fund-raising events, annual meeting, or government relations activity.
- Headquarters office operating procedures.

Generally, the executive conducts the orientation, along with the president and treasurer and perhaps other members of the executive committee. Note the list of topics typically included in a board orientation in Exhibit 2-8. The list is not all-inclusive. Executives should design an orientation approach that best suits the circumstances of their organizations and the various interests and sophistication levels of board members.

Some members of the board will have business experience and some will not. Some will have served on previous boards and some will be novices. The level of interest and expertise of board members, even if they are all from the same discipline, will not be uniform. Briefings and other communications (written and verbal) should reflect the diversity of board members.

In addition to the more formal presentation, it is helpful for the executive director to meet with new board members for an informal lunch or dinner. This not only creates a more intimate atmosphere but also enables board members to ask questions they may not be comfortable asking in a larger gathering. To establish a framework for working together throughout the year, it is particularly important for the executive director to have such an informal meeting with the incoming president or chairperson.

*Board and Staff Interactions.* Executives often find themselves in a quandary in determining how much direct contact should be allowed between the board and staff. Decisions should be based on the expertise or skill level of the staff and the size and complexity of the organization. If the staff is small, with two or three persons, the board members will generally deal directly with the executive. If it is a larger, more complex, and multidimensional organization, the executive will not have the in-depth knowledge of all topics needed to discuss them sufficiently with board members, and direct communication with the key staff person will be more appropriate.

Whatever the reason for contact between board staff members, however, the executive should ensure that there is a specified reporting mechanism to learn about that contact. Even if such communication is on a short-term, day-to-day operational matter, the executive should be informed. Staff want to please and will often accept an assignment from a board member without considering the consequences in terms of time, resources, and uncompleted priority projects. No matter how small or inconsequential the matter may seem, the executive director should never be left "out of the loop."

Further, board members should respect the executive director's role as staff supervisor. The executive reports to the board through the president or chairperson, and staff report to the executive. All board requests for organization resources or staff time should be channeled through the executive director. It is the executive's responsibility to coordinate the activities of the staff, and this becomes impossible if the executive is not aware of all activities.

The board orientation meeting provides a good opportunity for the executive to discuss board and staff interactions. If problems occur, the executive should address the issue directly with the responsible board member or solicit assistance from the chief elected leader.

## Maintain Fiscal Control

Monitoring the financial condition of the organization is a responsibility that neither can nor should be delegated. Not only must the executive fully understand the income and expense statements, but he or she must also have a thorough knowledge of the overall financial health of the organization. Financial statements provided during the year and year-end external audits should be presented clearly and concisely.

Just as staff should keep the executive informed so that there are no surprises, so it is with the board. Board members should be apprised of impending problems with income or expenses. Most organizations have both a treasurer and a finance committee who take responsibility to work with the executive in developing budgets and long-range financial forecasts. Often, the treasurer chairs the finance committee. Whatever the situation, the executive should prepare both the treasurer and the finance committee so that they can become the spokespersons for the financial reports during board meetings.

## Encourage and Support Involvement of Volunteer Board Members

With very few exceptions, individuals serving on a nonprofit's board do so in a volunteer capacity. It is critically important to remember that volunteers are motivated to serve by different reasons. Some are active in an organization because they are strong advocates of the particular cause or mission of the nonprofit group. Some become involved for the networking or business opportunities. Others serve on the board because of the recognition they receive from the nonprofit for their high visibility and/or their ability to raise funds. Still others agree to serve on nonprofit boards because of the recognition they receive from peers at home or in their own offices.

Understanding a board member's motivation for serving will provide the executive with tools to support that board member and, likewise, to obtain support from the board member. In some nonprofits, the amount of volunteer time required is extensive, yet expectations of how much time the volunteer will be able to contribute must be reasonable. Sensitivity to the board member's other demands, particularly if the member is an active public figure at the local or national level, will ensure that expectations will not be excessive.

Similarly, when working with volunteers, even those who appear to have unlimited time to serve, the executive must keep expectations in check, eliminating the possibility of volunteer burnout. As noted earlier in this chapter, clear and concise committee and task force charges that are realistic in terms of time lines and resources required will support and encourage volunteer involvement.

## Strategically Manage All Aspects of the Organization

A basic responsibility for an executive is to manage the nonprofit efficiently, effectively, and, for best results, strategically. Although each executive may have particular interests or strengths in some aspects of nonprofit management, it is necessary to become a jack-of-all-trades to manage a nonprofit organization well. Skills in all aspects of nonprofit organizational management will be required. Mastering the areas identified in this book is a good first step.

A major resource for any organization, in addition to its financial income and its volunteers, is its staff. Just as volunteer management and development are important responsibilities of an executive, so too are the management and development of staff members, whether there is one additional staff person in the office or more than 100 persons. (See also Chapter 13, "Your People and Their Environment.")

Nonprofit executives who excuse or cover up for poor staff work often find themselves looking for another position.

*A certain executive, because of his generosity and kindheartedness, allowed several staff members to work part-time because of family commitments. Rather than hiring additional staff to take up the slack, he took on their responsibilities to save the organization money. The work of the organization was not accomplished, and the person responsible, the executive, was replaced.*

*Another executive for a local charity, whose personal expertise was in research and grant writing, retained an office manager who could not track finances adequately or provide her with the answers to questions board members raised regarding the organization's financial status. This executive likewise was replaced when end-of-the-year audits indicated a more negative picture for the organization than had been presented in previous executive reports.*

Thus, it is critical for the executive to have good staff, but also to be knowledgeable about all aspects of the organization and to be prepared personally for any and all questions. Nonprofit cannot mean nonperforming.

## Maintain Flexibility

A critical lesson for nonprofit executives to bear in mind is that issues, responsibilities, and board relationships may not be the same next month as they were last month, and almost certainly will not be the same next year as last year.

Elected board officers come and go. Issues arise and are either solved or, at the least, outlived and put behind. New opportunities or new board members lead to changes in the nonprofit's strategic and operational plans, sometimes even to changes in mission. These changes, along with changes in personality or in operating styles of the elected leaders, require the chief staff executive to respond, creatively and constructively. The nonprofit executive who expects to do everything the same way every year is in the wrong profession.

Change can be difficult. It also brings opportunities, both for the individual and the organization. The chapters that follow outline specific management techniques that experienced nonprofit executives have used to enhance their effectiveness and that of their organizations.

Executives can assess their understanding of and commitment to their roles and responsibilities by identifying the extent to which each of the activities listed in Exhibit 2-9 is carried out.

**Exhibit 2-9**  Roles and Responsibilities of an Executive Staff Leader

|  | Always | Often | Sometimes | Never |
|---|---|---|---|---|
| The executive staff leader works to: | | | | |
| 1. Understand the organization— inside and out. | | | | |
| 2. Provide policy guidance and leadership for the board. | | | | |
| 3. Establish and maintain effective communication systems. | | | | |
| 4. Educate board regarding board and staff roles and responsibilities. | | | | |
| 5. Maintain fiscal control. | | | | |
| 6. Encourage and support involvement of volunteers. | | | | |
| 7. Strategically manage all aspects of the association. | | | | |

To maximize board and staff effectiveness, governing board members, committees, and staff must work together cooperatively, recognizing how the roles and responsibilities of each link with those of others, and all performing with one goal in mind: achieving the nonprofit organization's mission. Use the following checklist to assess how well your organization is maximizing the effectiveness of its governance structure.

## CHECKLIST FOR MAXIMIZING BOARD AND STAFF EFFECTIVENESS

Has your organization:

- Developed policies for board size, composition, nominations and elections processes based on its mission and the constituents it serves?
- Established a policies and procedures manual?
- Included the following in its policies and procedures manual?

  Roles and responsibilities of board members

  Position descriptions for officers

  Position description, roles and responsibilities for executive staff

- Developed a new board orientation program?
- Established effective lines of communication between and among the executive, the governing board, and committee chairs?
- Established effective communication systems for interactions between and among board, staff, committees, and constituents?
- Established a program for recruiting new volunteers?
- Established a review process for the executive's performance?

Does your organization:

- Hold board members accountable for timely completion of assignments?
- Hold committee members accountable for timely completion of assignments?
- Hold staff accountable for timely completion of assignments?
- Provide opportunities for informal interactions of board and staff?
- Conduct a periodic assessment of board operations?
- Provide support for the executive's professional development?

**CHAPTER THREE**

# Creating a Marketing Orientation in the Nonprofit Organization

**Do you know what they want and how to provide it? Have you identified *all* of your potential markets? This chapter includes strategies for identifying all of your constituencies, assessing their interests and needs, and planning and promoting programs that meet those needs.**

## THE ROLE OF MARKETING IN THE NONPROFIT ORGANIZATION

In the "old days," marketing had no role in a nonprofit organization. Nonprofits were content to set lofty goals, create a program of products or services that the board or staff liked, and wait for the consumer to participate. But times have changed, competition has grown fiercer, and like for-profit organizations, nonprofits have been forced to develop programs that are actually market- or consumer-driven.

In the for-profit sector, the change began to occur in the mid-1950s, when companies first began seriously studying consumer needs. Nonprofits generally lag behind for-profits in business trends, and marketing did not become an important issue for the nonprofits until the mid-1970s. Consumers of nonprofit services had begun to make their dissatisfactions known. Churches were losing members; colleges were having difficulties attracting quality students; cultural organizations were finding it difficult to interest donors and volunteers; and many professional societies and trade associations were experiencing declines in membership. These substantial problems, along with a tightening of economic conditions, forced nonprofit organizations to change the way they related to their markets.

The first steps were small ones, and it took about 10 years for marketing to assume its role as an orientation that pervades entire organizations and drives the daily work environment. Some organizations are still not there.

## WHAT IS MARKETING?

Marketing is often confused with selling. For years, nonprofits did not engage in *marketing,* because they equated the term with the "hard sell," something that was viewed as unprofessional and inappropriate.

Even trade associations with members accustomed to marketing their own company's products often thought their role was limited to collecting dues, publishing a newsletter, and putting on a good annual meeting. In reality, however, although the outcomes may appear the same, marketing and selling are quite different.

Selling is offering something in exchange for money: "*I* have *something* that I want you to buy." The emphasis is on the seller and the object being offered. An executive with a marketing orientation might say, "*You* have a *need* that I understand, and I am offering a product or service to meet that need." The central difference is one of perspective, and with a marketing orientation the emphasis is clearly on the consumer.

> Note: The terms *consumer, market,* and *audience* are used throughout this chapter. The "consumer" will vary, depending on the type of nonprofit organization; it may be a client, member, donor, visitor, patient, parishioner, or other such person. All are assumed in the general terms of consumer, market, and the like.

In *Strategic Marketing for Nonprofit Organizations,*[1] Philip Kotler defines marketing as "the analysis, planning, implementation, and control of carefully formulated programs designed to bring about voluntary exchanges of values with target markets for the purpose of achieving organizational objectives." Although that is a comprehensive definition, one that is probably more useful for nonacademics and nonprofit executives is that marketing is "a management process directed at satisfying customer needs and wants through an exchange process."

---

[1]P. Kotler, *Strategic Marketing for Nonprofit Organizations* (New York: Prentice Hall, 1995).

Consider the following example:

*A community hospital found that its surrounding neighborhood was changing, with young families replacing many elderly inhabitants. As a result, the hospital improved its maternity wing, began offering tours to expectant parents, and established training classes in delivery and parenting of infants and young children.*

*The hospital recognized that a secure and pleasant place to deliver a baby and information on how to deal with the stresses of pregnancy and caring for infants were important needs of its potential consumers (patients), and thus it developed both a tangible product and services to meet those needs.*

## THE BENEFITS OF A MARKETING ORIENTATION

A marketing orientation enables a nonprofit organization, whether a trade association or a charitable organization, to achieve its objectives more effectively and will produce four major benefits.

1. *Greater consumer satisfaction.* Effective marketing is "user-oriented," and it stresses the importance of measuring and satisfying audience needs. Thus, the products or services developed are far more likely to provide a high degree of satisfaction. Here's an example:

*A social service agency wanted to offer a program for recently widowed women. First, the agency surveyed the community and held a focus group. From these activities, the agency learned that although there was interest in the program, the widows in its community were less likely to need traditional information on managing finances, returning to the work force, and similar topics, because many were seasoned money managers who had worked out of the home for some time. What they did need was a place where they could express their grief and learn to cope with widowhood in a society where immediate families often live at great distances and fewer people are available to provide strong emotional support.*

*Armed with this information, the agency changed the focus of the planned program and the times at which the sessions would be held (from afternoons to evenings). The program was ultimately very well received by its clients.*

2. *Increased consumer participation.* It naturally follows that products developed to meet known consumer needs will be sought after, thus benefiting the organization as well as the audience— the classic win-win situation. If the agency in the previous example had not learned that most of its potential clients were

in the work force, it might have planned a very good program that was held in the afternoon, reducing client participation significantly. Instead, the marketing focus helped to ensure participation.

3. *Better attraction of market resources.* To serve their audiences and accomplish their objectives, nonprofits must not only *provide* resources, they must also *attract* resources such as volunteers, employees, donors, public support, sponsorship, and so forth. Marketing provides a framework for doing so.

An example from the for-profit world probably illustrates this best. If you wanted to start a business, and you had a product, you might need a bank loan to get started. If you approached the bank, but had no plan showing that there was a need for your new product or that you had an efficient strategy for producing, delivering, and promoting your product, you would certainly not get your money.

The situation is the same in the nonprofit world. Your resources may not be money from a bank—they may be donors or volunteers. But you will not attract these resources if you cannot show them that a need exists, and that you can meet that need through a well-designed and communicated program that will effectively serve your target audience.

4. *Greater efficiency.* To market means to exert total control and coordination of program development and delivery. Outside a marketing framework, decisions regarding programs are made arbitrarily, and the results may be ineffective, unnecessarily costly, or both. Nonprofits frequently operate on tight budgets, so it is imperative that they achieve maximum cost efficiencies. A well-integrated marketing plan is a giant step toward that goal.

## A Pervasive Orientation

It is important to keep in mind that marketing is a pervasive consumer orientation, one that holds that the very purpose of the organization is to determine the needs and wants of its markets and to satisfy them through the creation and delivery of appropriate and effective programs.

If you serve disabled or indigent persons in a nonprofit program, they should be treated like the wealthiest legal clients or the most socially prominent diners in a four-star restaurant. Clients do not exist to fit the needs or culture of an organization. A marketing perspective dictates exactly the opposite—that the organization exists to fit the needs of the client. Indeed, without the client need, there would be no organization.

A marketing orientation will transform a "top-down" or board-driven organization to one that is highly responsive and adaptive. Peter Drucker has said, "Marketing is so basic that it cannot be considered a separate management function.... It is the whole business seen from the point of view of its final result, that is, from the consumer's point of view."

## IDENTIFICATION OF THE MARKET AND ITS NEEDS

Market and needs identification can be one of the most time-consuming yet fascinating aspects of marketing. Exactly who are your consumers or potential consumers, and what do they need and want? This research is most important, because the more you know about your consumers, the better decisions you will make on how to serve them.

Useful information may already be in your files and is also available from public opinion polls, surveys, related organizations, government statistics, local or regional chambers of commerce, and other sources. The Census Bureau and the Bureau of Labor Statistics can often provide data, and colleges and universities, especially those that concentrate in your area of interest, are also good sources of information.

Trade and professional associations usually know their membership market—their industry or profession—but all too often fail to think through what they can provide to those members to make membership truly valuable.

### Targeting the Market

A common mistake made by inexperienced marketers is to assume that they have only one market. Someone who runs a small museum, for example, may think that current visitors are the only market. That is not likely to be true, but even if were, within the "current visitor market" lie several different markets, such as young people, older adults, members of minority groups, those who visit frequently rather than rarely, those visiting for education. All represent special interests, and their needs and wants are likely to be different.

Breaking down a large potential market into special interest groups is called *market segmentation*, or targeting the market, and that is how marketing is done today. Remember when radio stations just played some middle-of-the-road music and news on the hour? No more. That approach was designed to offer something to every potential listener with no thought to special interests. Today we have stations dedicated to rap, all news, all talk, religion, classic rock, and other formats. These programs are designed to appeal to a very particular group within a wide potential listening audience, and the kind of programming, the advertising, and the time slots are strongly related to the listening habits and demographics of that special group.

Consider other audiences in addition to those you currently serve. What about people who haven't yet joined, visited, participated, volunteered, or contributed? Those who previously participated in some way, but are no longer involved? Those who are involved in an associated way, perhaps as suppliers? All of these groups are potential markets.

In addition to the consumers of services, a nonprofit organization will have other very different audiences to be served. For example, you may have a board of directors or trustees that must be kept involved and committed to the organization's mission. Or you may rely on the goodwill of the greater community, or need to attract a significant amount of government support. Although quite different from one another, these markets must all be researched and well served by your program.

In addition, you probably have individual donors and volunteers, and to attract their continued support, you must identify and meet their needs. In fact, in today's climate, with diminished government resources and both men and women working long hours in the workplace, the attraction of individual donors and volunteers is one of the greatest challenges faced by nonprofits. To be successful, you must identify potential donors and volunteers, determine their needs, and position your program to meet those needs.

## You Know Who They Are—What Can You Do About It?

Once you have identified potential markets, two important questions emerge.

*Is the market accessible—that is, is there a way to identify the actual members of the market and reach them with information about products and services?*

You may be able to purchase a mailing list that includes the kind of people you need to contact. This is especially true if you are trying to attract donors or volunteers. Check your local library for the *Standard Rate and Data Service* (SRDS) book of mailing lists, which gives descriptions and prices of thousands of lists available for rent.

Moreover, other organizations may be willing to exchange or share lists of clients with you. If you cannot identify individual prospects by name, you may be able to predict the kind of publications they would read and reach the market through those outlets. For example, an agency planning to serve the Hispanic community might advertise in a newspaper oriented to this audience.

Sometimes, even creative approaches fail to identify a market. For example, one nonprofit health service agency would like to put together a national roster of people suffering from a rare bone disease. New treatment services are available for this small population, but until now there was no cost-effective way to identify them.

*Is the segment large enough to warrant the development of products/services to meet its needs?*

It may be that the market is too small to support such development; however, unlike for-profits that are usually driven only by bottom-line considerations, nonprofits may choose to go forward anyway, if they determine that the service is mandated by their mission.

A program that cannot support itself but makes a valuable contribution to a community or a profession can become an excellent example for the organization's fund-raising or membership promotion department to use for solicitations. A good fund-raiser can highlight the program and emphasize how the organization has stood by its mission—even at great cost—and that "only with the support of its givers is it able to survive." Frequently, more money can be raised in this manner than is lost in running the program!

A cautionary note must be heeded, however. "Nonprofit" is a legal identification, not a state of being. You must have a positive balance sheet to stay in business and continue to aid the people whom the organization was established to serve. A well-researched marketing plan enables managers to undertake an unprofitable but important program with a high degree of certainty that other activities will generate the funds to subsidize it.

## Assessing Consumer Needs

Once you have identified your consumers, learn everything you can about them. If you have an existing (fairly recent) survey of your donors or clients, get it out and study it. If it does not yield useful information, or if a recent survey does not exist, consider spending some funds for a well-designed and well-executed survey. Exhibit 3–1 illustrates the kind of information you will want to have on your markets. This is an investment in future success. In addition to surveys, focus groups made up of current or potential consumers and run by a skilled facilitator are an excellent means of gaining information. Evaluation forms are also a good source of feedback.

Do not be tempted to forgo market research on the assumption that you know what the market wants and needs, even if you consider yourself an expert or a member of the organization's market. Organization leaders and staff are sometimes out of touch and may be

**Exhibit 3–1** Checklist of Market Information

- Age
- Sex
- Race
- Habitat (e.g., urban, rural)
- Socioeconomic level
- Religion
- Occupation
- Family size
- Education
- Hobbies
- Publications read
- Level of knowledge about your organization
- Expectations regarding your organization
- Other organizations in which they participate
- Products/services used
- Level of satisfaction

quite different from other members of the market in terms of commitment, age, wealth, career progression, and so on. In addition, board or staff members often have strong proprietary interests in particular programs, and thus they cannot be objective. It is not uncommon for a board to fashion a program with great enthusiasm, only to have it met with total lack of interest by the potential consumers or donors.

Comprehensive research is the only solid basis for future marketing successes. The following example illustrates what can happen if market needs are ignored or misunderstood.

*A major national organization, concerned that too many people die while awaiting a liver, kidney, or other organ transplant, wanted to alleviate the critical shortage of donated organs. Some nonprofit organ procurement organizations had proposed that donors or their families be financially compensated (i.e., paid) for organ donations as a means of encouraging these donations. However, market research revealed that the three main reasons that people do not become organ donors were (1) religious beliefs, (2) lack of trust in doctors and hospitals, and (3) belief that organs would not be fairly allocated. Concerns about lack of compensation were not evident. Thus, if everything else remained unchanged, this market (potential organ donors) might not be moved to donate based on a new program of compensation. The market research may lead the procurement organizations to seek other programs to better serve both donor and recipient audiences.*

*In addition, society views organ donation as a singularly humanitarian and philanthropic act—perhaps second only to giving up one's life for another person. To offer payment for such an act may be interpreted as cheapening its value, and thus procurement agencies would run the risk of losing the community's goodwill and alienating another important market. Good market research would confirm or deny that speculation as well.*

Research does take time, but if you do not ascertain the needs of your market, you will proceed blindly with no assurance that the course you have chosen is the correct one.

Diligent research will uncover a variety of needs within your market segments. Some will be for specific products or services such as job training, shelter, medical treatment, educational or cultural programs. But other, less tangible, needs will also arise, such as the need for flexible access to services, group identity, information, recognition, fraternity, or prestige. You should consider both tangible and intangible needs when developing or evaluating products or services.

A final note on identifying market needs: Once is not enough! Our environment is fast-paced and ever-changing. That means your market and its needs are changing too, so needs assessments should be conducted on a regular basis.

Sometimes a board-driven organization has an "epiphany," whereby it comes to understand what it means to be market oriented.

*The board of a national health agency introduced a journal as part of the member benefits for its professional membership, even though no assessment had shown that those members actually wanted such a publication. The board thought that the journal "would be good for the organization." Dues were increased to include a required subscription to the new journal.*

*The reaction to this new "benefit" was lukewarm, and over the next few years many of the clinical members expressed dissatisfaction with the journal. At a long-range planning meeting, the issue of the journal was raised, and the board, somewhat wiser, decided to initiate another journal, this one positioned to meet the needs of the clinical members. Discussion ensued about whether members should be allowed to choose either journal as part of their membership or still be required to take the original journal and pay an additional fee for the new one. Finally, one board member said, "We can't allow members to choose, because it's possible that too few people will want our original journal, and we won't have the base to keep publishing."*

*After a moment, another person said, "But if very few of our members choose the original journal, why would we want to continue to offer it? Isn't satisfying the members what we're trying to do?"*

*The room was silent as several individuals grappled with and then acknowledged the truth of that simple statement.*

## EXAMINING THE ENVIRONMENT

Once target markets and their needs have been identified, you must look further to internal and external environments that may affect your ability to deliver a program that meets those needs. This is called an *environmental scan.* Such a scan will be extremely useful in considering your future service offerings.

### The External Environment

The assessment process may uncover a need for which you believe you can develop an excellent program, but a scan of the *external* environment reveals a barrier to market entry.

*A local birth control clinic was alarmed by the rapidly increasing rate of sexually transmitted diseases (STDs) among the community's adolescents and began working with the local high school to fashion a program of education to combat the problem. The program included the free distribution of condoms at the school. Clearly, there was a market need, and the two organizations had the necessary resources and the established delivery channels to put forth an excellent program. Before beginning, however, they found that the community was not willing to acknowledge the problem and was uncomfortable with the notion of teen sexuality. This was a barrier to market entry in the external environment. The program could not go forward unless community attitudes changed.*

Lack of consensus in the community is a common barrier to market entry from the external environment. There are many others, including government regulations, strong competing organizations, unusually high start-up costs, and unfavorable political forces.

External forces include anything outside your organization that can affect your market or your ability to enter the market or deliver a product or service. Such forces can generate good or bad outcomes, and sometimes a good outcome can be bad for an organization's market or mission, or vice versa.

*The National Foundation for Infantile Paralysis, better known as the March of Dimes, worked in the 1940s and 1950s to fund polio research and assist those stricken by this dread disease. A vaccine was discovered in 1955, and quite suddenly polio, and the March of Dimes' raison d'être, disappeared. This development in the external environment forced the organization to either rethink its mission or cease to exist. The board recognized that the organization's strength was the existing fund-raising structure, so its response was to redefine its mission to raising funds for birth defects, thus serving a new but related market.*

When looking at external environments, also focus on the ramifications of the current forces, which can affect every aspect of the marketing process.

For example, how might emerging communications technology affect the way in which your activities are conducted? Perhaps soon your organization will no longer communicate with members or donors through a newsletter, but rather through electronic mail, CD ROM, or Web site. The product (information) will remain the same, but the delivery of the product will be different.

A scan of the external environment will not only tell you about the factors affecting your market today, but also give you information about how you can plan for the needs of your market tomorrow.

## The Internal Environment

Like external environments, internal environments have a significant impact on your ability to develop programs to meet consumer needs; however, internal environments can sometimes be changed, whereas external forces cannot.

Internal environments include the size and wealth of the organization; the availability and expertise of staff to direct projects; the existing equipment; the commitment and orientation of the board of directors and donors; and the current program, mission, strategic objectives, bylaws, and policies that dictate how the organization is to be run.

For example, assume that market research identifies several needs for which the organization may create successful programs, but your internal scan reveals that the current staff is not large enough to develop and manage all those products. Your board must decide whether it should change the internal environment by expanding the existing staff, use outside consultants for project management, attract volunteers to provide the necessary labor, or set priorities regarding the market needs it will serve.

*A local clinic wanted to immunize a poor population not covered by Medicaid, and research clearly identified this as a serious need. However, the clinic did not have enough staff or volunteers to administer the vaccines, nor did it have the financial resources to purchase all the vaccine necessary to cover the population identified. These were limiting internal environments. However, with persistence they could be changed. The clinic director contacted the local medical society, which offered to provide the volunteers necessary to administer the vaccine, and, through a board contact, also reached an executive in the pharmaceutical company who agreed to provide the vaccine at cost. The small clinic then had the internal resources it needed, and it went ahead with the program.*

It is possible that an assessment will identify a need that the organization can serve, but a scan of the internal environment indicates that serving that need is not appropriate to the organization's mission as it is currently defined. The governing board may then decide to expand the organization's mission, that is, change the internal environment (remember the March of Dimes) or not to service the need.

## THE WRITTEN MARKETING PLAN

A marketing plan for a nonprofit organization is really just a blueprint for action that follows from your market research and needs assessments. Exhibit 3–2 lists the basic elements usually found in a marketing plan.

Information on market needs, along with the knowledge acquired from environmental scans, will be used to develop the beginning of the plan. Generally, you will review that data in an opening section that may be called a "Situation Analysis." Here you will describe

**Exhibit 3–2**   Marketing Plan Checklist

---

### The Marketing Plan

1. Identification of your target audience (markets) and a description of their need(s).
2. Discussion of problems and opportunities.
3. Listing of measurable objectives and strategies.
4. Budgets.
5. Methods of evaluations.

---

your various "publics" and discuss the results of your market research; your organization's strengths, weaknesses, and marketing objectives; and the overall plan of action. The presentation should make it easy for anyone to pick up the plan and understand your markets, your objectives, the needs you plan to serve, and the reasons the organization can and should meet those particular needs.

## Developing Objectives and Strategies

Objectives and strategies form the heart of a marketing plan and make use of all the items in the *marketing mix* (see Exhibit 3–3).

For nonprofits, we can convert the word *Product* to *Program.* Your product is actually the program of services (or in some cases tangible goods) that you offer to your clients. Programs (e.g., job training) or products (e.g., low-cost housing) are what you produce in response to a need. They are what you deliver and promote.

*Price* may not seem relevant if you provide services at no charge, but in every case, for proper financial management you must know the price to your organization for the services you provide. There is another "price" component for nonprofits to consider. What is the "price" that donors or volunteers pay to support your organization? It may be actual money expended on the organization or the loss of other opportunities because of time devoted to your organization.

*Place* and *Promotion* remain the same for nonprofits. Like a corporate manager, you also need to think about the geographical area that your services will cover, the methods through which you will deliver services, and the means by which you will let your various audiences know of the value and availability of your program.

Your marketing plan may actually include two different objectives. The first is a *marketing objective,* which addresses the way in which an organization intends to interact with its market. The appropriate marketing objective will be determined by the environmental scan.

**Exhibit 3–3**   The Marketing Mix: The Four P's

| | |
|---|---|
| PRODUCT | The good or service developed in response to perceived market need. |
| PRICE | Price at which good or service will be offered. |
| PLACE | Area to be covered by good/service, e.g., local, national, etc.; the method of delivery. |
| PROMOTION | Methods used to communicate to the market the availability and benefits of a product or service. |

**Exhibit 3–4**    Interaction Between Programs and Markets

|  | Present Programs | New Programs |
|---|---|---|
| Present Markets | Market Penetration | Program Development |
| New Markets | Market Development | Diversification |

For example, a group that finds itself with several successful programs would probably not choose to concentrate resources on new program development, but rather on promoting the current programs to its existing market to achieve *market penetration.* On the other hand, a group whose current markets are growing smaller would be interested in *diversification,*—that is, introducing new programs to new markets. Exhibit 3–4 illustrates the possible interactions between programs and markets.

*A small Midwestern museum had an excellent children's program offering "museum school," special tours, field trips, and other hands-on activities. However, the number of children in the locale surrounding the museum was decreasing as families grew older and were replaced by singles and childless couples. Because one of its markets (children) was declining, the museum was interested in diversifying or offering new programs to new markets. As part of this plan, it developed a "Singles Night" when the museum stayed open late, waived admissions, and offered wine and cheese to singles visiting the museum. This became one of the museum's most popular programs and was the start of other programs to be offered to this new market (singles).*

The preceding example illustrates a wise marketing decision. Because the children's market was declining, it did not make sense to move toward *program development* for children or to try to achieve greater *market penetration. Diversification* was the smart move, followed by *program development* (more programs for the current singles market). *Market development,* perhaps by offering the same kind of special museum night for seniors, might be the next step.

The overall marketing objectives should be explained in the situation analysis, before moving into the specifics of the marketing plan.

The second kind of objectives may be called the *plan objectives.* These refer to the objectives you hope to achieve as a result of the marketing effort. Such objectives should be clear and measurable, listed in order of priority, and followed by detailed strategies. Specific objectives will provide a method for assessing the success or fail-ure of the marketing plan once it is implemented.

Suppose you are creating a marketing plan for a church with a declining congregation. You might develop the following objective: "To meet middle-aged adults' (particular market segment) needs for fraternity and flexible access to organized religion by offering several church activities at a variety of times and places (your program of services), by the end of the calendar year attracting 15 percent more middle-aged adults than we are currently serving."

An organization usually identifies several objectives, and each is formulated the same way. For example, the church just mentioned may have another objective for attracting teenagers, still another to meet the needs of seniors, and so on.

Once the objectives are articulated, strategies must be formulated that detail the exact means to reach the objectives. Other compo-nents of the marketing mix such as *place* (the location and channels of program delivery) and *promotion* (the way in which you will com-municate with your market regarding your program) will be explained in your market strategies.

Returning to our church example, the strategies supporting the marketing objective for adults might be as follows:

- To offer a worship service with sermon and readings geared to working adults every Wednesday night, to be followed by coffee and dessert in the social hall. These will be highlighted in the church bulletin and listed in the "worship section" of the local paper. Eighty people should be attending by the end of the year.

- To introduce a regular column in the church bulletin geared to the problems of working adults.

- To develop a church bowling team for adult couples during the winter months and recruit through the church bulletin and com-munity newspapers. Twelve couples should participate the first year.

- To facilitate the organization of adult groups to work in other exist-ing social programs at given times. For example, Monday will become St. Stephan's night at the community clothes closet. By the end of the year more than 100 people should be participating in these groups. Announcement of this activity will be made regularly from the pulpit.

Promotion and price are integral parts of marketing strategies. Although many nonprofits offer services at no charge, not all do; managers may have to determine a price for various services, as well as their cost to the organization. The price will be determined by a combination of factors, including the cost of developing and delivering the program, the ability of the market to pay for the program, costs of similar programs, and the niche that the organization has created for its products in general.

*Market niche* is determined by the image of the organization and the kind of product it is known to offer, and it is an important factor in creating the marketing mix. For example, does the organization have an image as upscale, always delivering high-end products or programs that are expensive but well done, or is it known as an organization whose products are not fancy but reliable and inexpensive. Market niche affects the market's acceptance of a product and the price it is willing to pay, and it is difficult to market a product outside an established niche.

*A voluntary health organization in a large Eastern city was known as a very upscale organization, attracting big-ticket donors and many socially prominent volunteers. For years the organization held a glitzy grand ball with roving celebrities, breathtaking decorations, and irresistible displays of food. The ball was the highlight of the winter social season and raised thousands of dollars for the organization. However, as the economy weakened, and the well-to-do became concerned about perceptions of "conspicuous consumption," ball organizers decided that the event should be significantly toned down.*

*The result was a disaster. Attendance and donations were dismal. The market associated the organization with a very upscale, high-end product. It was not willing (or ready) to accept a "plain brown wrapper" social event, because that was not the niche that the organization belonged in.*

*In retrospect, the organizers realized that rather than attempting to move to another marketing niche by substituting a toned-down version of an existing product (the ball), they should have created an entirely different product or service.*

A change in image and marketing niche for nonprofits is possible, but it requires time and careful planning. The following example has a more positive outcome.

*A small Midwestern university attracted its student population in large part because of its popular and nationally recognized football team. The academic program was acceptable, but the school was known for football, not scholarship. A new president was installed, who was determined to turn the school into a strong academic center, thereby changing its image and its market niche. The president used the term "academic excellence" as a rallying cry*

*and the point of communications to all the school's various markets, includ-
ing students, faculty, administration, alumni, trustees, and donors, and slowly
went about making changes in the program. He upgraded the faculty, built a
new award-winning library, increased the academic offerings, tightened the
entrance requirements, and generally raised the academic standards. Over a
period of years, the school started attracting a more scholarly faculty and more
highly qualified students (two important markets for the university). Today
the university has successfully completed the change in market niche and is
regarded as an outstanding academic center (it still has a fine football team!).*

One of the reasons this transformation was successful was that it
took place over time. Many small steps were taken, and the school's
markets were able to slowly change the way they regarded the university. Had the president tried to present the school to its various
markets in this new niche within a year or two, and raised the tuition
accordingly—even if he had the program and faculty to back it up—
it is unlikely that he would have been successful.

Note: In the for-profit world, companies can sometimes get around this
problem by establishing a new brand with which they are not identified.
That is how Honda brought to market the Acura Legend—many people
don't realize that this expensive luxury sedan is made by Honda, the company best known for delivering a quality, low-maintenance, moderately
priced product. But this option is generally not available to nonprofits.

Let's explore the museum example again. Suppose one of the
museum's objectives is to attract young single people, and one strategy is to have a "Singles Night." The museum staff must make several pricing decisions: Should the admission fee be lowered, waived,
or left as is for that evening? Should wine and cheese be free or
offered for purchase? Should the event be at cost or at a profit?

First, the total cost of the service must be determined; that includes
all direct and indirect costs. Next, the staff must decide whether the
museum budget can support whole or partial costs or whether the
program must pay for itself. If it is decided that the event must raise
X number of dollars, the attendance must be estimated, which will
then determine the per-person price. Finally, the staff must look at
the potential consumers of the service. Are they upscale consumers
with high incomes who can afford the necessary price and more, or
working-class singles for whom anything but the smallest price
would be restrictive? If the staff determines that the audience cannot
afford the necessary price, and the museum cannot cover the event,
either an outside sponsor must be found or the event must be scaled
down, for example, offered less frequently or without refreshments.

However, market niche plays a role here too. If the museum has an upscale image (e.g., a museum of contemporary art), and the intended audience is consumers with high earnings, they are unlikely to participate in a pared-down event, such as a brief hour of viewing with pretzels and soft drinks.

If this market is important to the museum, a market that may eventually be not only consumers of services but also volunteers and donors, then it is even more important that staff devise a way to offer a program in keeping with the museum's image.

*Promotion—The Final "P."* None of the components of the marketing mix operates independently. They are related almost by definition. The type of program will affect the channels (place) through which it is delivered; the price will influence the quality and image of the program, and so on.

The final "P" to be considered is *Promotion,* and promotional strategies are influenced by all of the other P's as well as by the readiness stage of the consumer.

"Readiness stage" refers to the progression of consumer behavior that most experts believe occurs before purchase. The stages are awareness, comprehension, conviction, and purchase. The consumer first becomes aware of the organization or program (perhaps only by name recognition); next, he or she understands the offering; then the prospect becomes convinced of the value of the offering; and, finally, he or she becomes a consumer of the product or service. The marketer tries to ascertain the readiness stage of the target market and match it to an appropriate message and medium.

The four most common types of promotion are *advertising, direct mail, personal selling,* and *publicity.* They may be used alone or in concert, and an effective marketer will establish a blend that tells the consumer that the right program is available at the right price and at the right time.

For consumers in the early awareness stage, the message will have to be one of introduction, to acquaint them with the organization or the program. *Advertising,* which is paid promotion, may be a good way to do this, especially using a moderately priced vehicle that reaches a large percentage of the target market. If yours is a new organization, or you are offering a new service to a new market, advertising is an effective way to make potential consumers aware of your new program.

Recently, hospitals have begun to develop highly targeted programs for conditions like obesity, substance abuse, and eating disorders. Because it is difficult to identify exactly those who suffer from these problems, hospitals frequently use radio and television advertising to make the programs known to the general public, many of whom may be potential consumers (or know of those who are).

*Direct mail* can be targeted to a very specific group and provides an opportunity to explain at length the merits of an organization or product. It can be particularly effective at moving potential consumers from comprehension to conviction, or from conviction to purchase. Many highly specific mailing lists are available for rent, and users can purchase by area of the country, state, or even by zip code.

This is the time-honored method for reaching potential donors, because the cost per contact is low and a mailing can simulate a personal letter and even include photographs to provide a strong emotional appeal.

St. Jude's Children's Hospital in Memphis makes masterful use of direct mail. Each month those who have made a pledge receive a letter that usually includes a story about a young patient and his or her family. Sometimes the letters are signed by parents of a current or former patient; every letter includes at least one picture. Some letters tell of triumphs and some of losses, but each has a heartrending story that moves the donor to give over and over again.

*Personal or direct sales* is most often used during the advanced stages of consumer readiness and is frequently the method employed to "close the sale" (particularly if a substantial donation or complicated purchase is involved).

*Publicity,* that is, unpaid stimulation of demand, may be sought throughout the consumer readiness stages. If, for example, your organization has established a shelter for battered women, you may try to interest the local reporter who covers women's issues in the program. You may send a press release describing the program or invite reporters to visit the shelter. Any resulting coverage will be publicity—a highly sought-after commodity, partly because publicity is assumed to be more honest than advertising.

For example, a hospital or university seeking large contributions to a capital campaign, a charity hoping to obtain support from a local corporation, or a trade association seeking a new member at the top of its dues scale may build awareness of its activities and contributions through publicity. A colleague or board member, however, will almost always make the actual request during a personal visit.

Because members of a target market will not move through the readiness stages at the same time, an effective marketer uses a variety of promotions simultaneously.

A small crisis hotline in Kansas found that use of its services by people in severe psychological distress was declining, but at the same time the agency became aware of a growing need for "latchkey children" to have a similar service. Thus, the hotline was extended to these children to call whenever they felt frightened, unsure, confused, or just lonely.

This is a new service to a new market; let's explore what promotional strategies might be used.

*Advertising.* Because this is the introduction of a new service to a new audience, advertising is a very desirable means of promotion. The agency might place small space ads in community newspapers, PTA newsletters, and/or church bulletins. Flyers might be posted in places where children and their parents are likely to gather, such as an ice rink, swimming pool, or day-care center.

*Direct Mail.* Although a list of latchkey children will not be available, the agency can rent a list of parents of young children. A letter can be written that announces the phone number and describes the service. In addition, the letter can do "double duty" by asking for a donation to help maintain the service. Letters might also be written to principals, elementary school teachers, ministers, pediatricians, and any other reachable group that is known to work with children.

*Personal Selling.* Members from the agency might make themselves available to speak about the new hotline at PTA meetings, church meetings, scout gatherings, women's clubs, and other such events. Again, the staff can "sell" the service, not only to potential consumers, but to potential supporters as well.

*Publicity.* A press release describing the new service must certainly be written and sent to local news outlets and to any other locally read publication that includes a column on what's new in the community. In addition, staff might collaborate with related groups and approach television or newspaper reporters about doing a story on children at home alone in the community. A description of the hotline can be a part of that larger story.

Obviously, many of these strategies cost money, and the agency is unlikely to have the finances or the staff to handle all of them at once. A plan with a budget can be developed that sets priorities and develops a systematic program of promotion. As the various promotions are used, they will be evaluated for effectiveness, and as the hotline program matures, strategies will probably be adjusted.

Volumes have been written on promotional strategies, and more information on this topic can be found in the chapters covering fundraising (Chapter 5) and public relations (Chapter 8).

## CREATING THE MARKETING BUDGET

The marketing budget is not just a series of columns with numbers. It should be an integral part of the plan that flows from the organization's goals and objectives. The budget is actually a quantitative expression of the narrative statements in the plan.

In reality, marketing budgets take many different forms, ranging from budgets that merely attempt to capture the direct costs of promotional activities, to very sophisticated budgets based on sales response optimization—the theory that increased sales revenue is a function of increased marketing expenditure (often used in planning for major donor solicitations).

Ideally, the marketing budget will be comprehensive, technical, and based on known sales formulas.

But even someone not formally schooled in cost-benefit analysis or surplus maximization can develop a marketing budget that will work for the organization as long as the manager keeps in mind that the budget is essentially a projected profit and loss statement based on stated goals and objectives.

The budget should include a detailed list of the assumptions on which the numbers are based (e.g., how many members will attend the meeting, how many full-time employees are required, how many brochures will be mailed and at what rate) and cover both revenue and expenses. Expenses usually include the direct costs of production, distribution, promotion, and personnel.

More sophisticated budgets will also include indirect costs covering a portion of the organization's overhead. Not all organizations allocate indirect costs, but for realistic future analyses of what a program really costs the organization, indirect costs should be assigned. Your organization may already have a formula for doing this. If not, you might apportion indirect costs based on resource usage.

Some common mistakes made in the development of the marketing budget are (1) not allowing sufficient funds for market research, evaluations, or effective promotional strategies, (2) underestimating the costs involved in developing new programs, and (3) overestimating the level of contributions.

Revenue projections should be based on real numbers and past experience. It is unrealistic to project a 30 percent increase in donations if increases have never been more than 7 percent for the last three years (such hyper-optimistic projections can occur under outside pressure to balance the budget, save a pet project, etc.), unless a new variable is operating that will account for such a large increase. If that is the case, it should be documented in the budget narrative. (For example, a moving television story about people suffering from a particular disease may produce large increases in donations to organizations working to eradicate that disease or aid its victims.)

A well-planned marketing budget emphasizes organizational objectives and relates them to the inputs and expenditures necessary for their achievement. The result will be grouping by program area. This process facilitates making "tradeoffs" which may be necessary to reach objectives. If one program is performing much better than anticipated, while another is underperforming, it becomes easy to move additional promotional dollars to the latter program.

## EVALUATION

Evaluation is the final step in the marketing process, and no marketing plan is complete without this activity. It is interesting to note that the marketing process began with the consumers—who are they, and what do they need—and so it will end with the consumers—what is their level of satisfaction, and how well did we meet their needs?

Although evaluation is the final step, this does not mean that evaluation takes place only at the end of a program. On the contrary, to be effective, evaluation should be built into the beginning, the middle, and the end of a program. Evaluations actually serve two purposes: to ascertain whether the consumer is being well served, and to determine whether the organization is meeting its marketing objectives efficiently.

The first evaluation process may take place after a program is researched and designed, but before it is actually launched. Such an evaluation can take the form of a pilot project (launching the program on a small scale) or employ a focus group to respond to the new program (remember the agency that planned to offer a program for recent widows).

Sometime after implementation, another evaluation should be done. Surveys or user response forms will provide useful information on program use and consumer satisfaction, and may stimulate small adjustments or a refocusing of promotional strategies to make the program more effective.

*A library offering a bookmobile program learned through an intermediate evaluation that a small adjustment in schedule could greatly increase participation. It arranged to have the bookmobile in a church parking lot on Tuesday mornings instead of Wednesday, because that was the day a senior support group met at the church. That information had been overlooked when the program was being planned.*

A *sales analysis* is a method of evaluation that will help determine whether marketing objectives are being met, but it does not yield any information about how much better you might be doing. A *market share analysis* will give you a sense of the total possible universe and the portion that you "own." For example, a sales analysis may show that last week you served 200 meals to homeless people in your program, but how "good" is that? A market share analysis will tell you that there were 500 people that could have partaken of your free dinners, and you served 200. That makes it much easier to gauge your level of success.

A *marketing expense-to-sales analysis* will help you go beyond the limits of your existing budget and consider how much more you might sell if you increased marketing dollars. For example, how many additional donors would be generated by one extra mail promotion? Would the additional revenue cover the costs of the promotion and the "servicing" of the donor and still provide cash to the organization?

In addition to overall program evaluations, analyses of individual components can also be very important in determining the efficiency of a plan.

*A national association hired a director of marketing to increase membership. The association had always used direct mail as the main promotional strategy, but the new director wanted to introduce telemarketing. The board resisted, saying "Telemarketing is too expensive," but the director pervailed, and eventually the board agreed to a limited pilot project using telemarketing.*

*When the board members first saw the expenses from the telemarketing project, they were appalled, saying that it proved their assertion that telemarketing cost too much. But an analysis of the cost per actual new member showed that telemarketing was actually* less *expensive than the direct mail they had been using.*

*Telemarketing is now a part of the organization's promotion, but if the board had seen only comparisons of expense without the analysis, an effective strategy would have been lost.*

## WHO HOLDS THE MARKETING RESPONSIBILITIES IN THE ORGANIZATION?

This chapter would not be complete without a discussion of who should be responsible for the organization's marketing activities. The discussion is most meaningful here, now that you have an understanding of how marketing operates and what it means to an organization's structure.

Organizations vary greatly in the way in which marketing is handled. In many nonprofits, each individual function area is responsible for marketing its own programs. While that is probably better than no market orientation, it is not an effective way of using marketing resources or serving consumer needs. No overall marketing calendar is kept, and opportunities for joint promotions or cross selling are missed.

> *A large museum runs tours and day trips and has a meeting department to organize and market these events. The meeting department is very good at marketing the museum's tours, but the person who has just gone on a 10-day tour of the Roman ruins is probably not part of the market for the next trip to the Galapagos Islands. He or she is part of a market for a new publication on the Etruscan Civilization, but that book is developed and marketed by the publications department, which is independent of the meetings department.*
>
> *What both departments fail to realize and exploit is that in many instances they serve the same need, though the product or service meeting that need may be different. Without that understanding, joint planning and promotions don't occur and many marketing opportunities are lost.*

Some organizations go further and create a marketing department. Although this is a better plan, it, too, has limitations. Frequently, unrealistic expectations are placed on the department manager, and once such a department is created, no one else expects to do any marketing. In addition, because that department manager is generally viewed as a peer by other department heads, he or she has little authority to establish a marketing orientation throughout the organization.

Because an effective marketing program requires support and commitment from the highest levels, when the chief executive officer (CEO) takes on the responsibility the chances of establishing a market-driven organization are greatly increased. The CEO has the power to hire staff and insist on a marketing approach, and he or she can channel organization resources to this effort. In addition, being at the top of the organizational chart, the CEO has a broader vision of how the marketing program is working throughout the organization.

However, this model is not always an option. The CEO may lack a strong personal commitment to marketing or may not be trained in marketing functions. He or she may have been hired for other skills and experiences. Or the CEO may have the interest and the ability, but lack the time to properly manage marketing activities in addition to the other duties for which he or she is responsible.

Should that be the case, the CEO may choose to hire a senior staff person to be responsible for overall organizational marketing. This position would be above that of department heads and may carry a title such as Marketing Vice President, making it clear that the person will be a part of the senior executive team. With the appropriate authority and reporting lines, the person in this position can be as effective as the CEO in driving the establishment of a marketing orientation.

Regardless of who is ultimately assigned responsibility for the marketing function, the success of any marketing program will depend in large part on the enthusiastic support and understanding by the entire staff—from the receptionist and the mail room clerk to the CEO—of the premise that the reason the organization exists is to understand and serve the needs of its markets and its mission.

## FINAL MARKETING CHECKLIST

Want to Market? *Ask the right questions:*

- Whom do I want to serve?
- What are their needs?
- Can I provide a quality product/service to meet those needs cost-effectively?
- Are outside conditions right for my products/services?
- What is the most convenient way for my markets to use my products/services?
- What are the best ways to let my market know my product/service exists?
- Are my markets satisfied?
- How can I make things even better?

# PART 2

# Pursuing the Mission

# CHAPTER FOUR

# Sustainable Growth: Developing Profitable Activities for the Professional and Trade Association

**Overdependence on either member dues or charitable contributions will leave a nonprofit organization stagnant, at best. Growing organizations look for new ways to serve their members or their publics, and at the same time to diversify their income stream. Trade and professional associations have led the way in developing "non-dues" income to augment their resources and increase their services to members. This chapter examines ways in which trade and professional associations have developed new resources, new activities, and new visibility for their organizations and their members.**

No organization will survive without income. Not even a high-tech start-up can keep the doors open indefinitely without income in excess of expenses. A nonprofit that outspends its resources lacks even the option of trying to convince Wall Street that it is a "buy"; it either reduces expenses, goes out of business, or finds new revenue.

Chapter 3 stressed the importance of developing a marketing orientation in a nonprofit organization. This means thinking through the opportunities to provide new services and activities that will appeal to your "clients"—whether members, related publics, constituents, or other groups the organization reaches out to. Even organizations with the broadest social benefit need to build the base of income from services to members, or to the organization's intended beneficiaries, before they appeal to outside sources.

Human nature being what it is, most of us expect the world to see quickly the virtue of our enterprise and the value of our services and to support the organization to which we are committed. It's rarely that easy. Good planning and good marketing are required to nurture a nonprofit, whether it is a charitable organization, a giant university, or a membership organization. It is up to the nonprofit organization to define and develop its offerings within its basic mission or charter, just as the for-profit organization develops, defines, and markets its products or services.

Where do you start, in looking for sources of income beyond the traditional? This chapter focuses on the ways in which trade and professional associations can build additional activities into their basic revenue base, enhancing their services and activities beyond those that in the past have been thought of as "traditional."

## THE MEMBER-DRIVEN ASSOCIATION

A marketing orientation will help any organization to meet its goals. This is perhaps most obvious for a membership organization—the trade association, professional society, or technology user group—or other group created specifically to assist a profession or industry. Members of these organizations join, come to meetings, and use the services offered because these services provide a direct benefit to them as individuals. There may be an altruistic component—furthering medical research, for example, or establishing a foundation for the next generation of a profession—but the membership organization that counts on altruism alone will find its role and its activities quite limited. Service to members and to the broader range of society with which the organization's members interact requires offering services that directly benefit members or those in related fields and that members are willing to support financially. These programs and services are, in one sense or another, *for sale.*

For trade and professional associations, this concept is often called "non-dues income." The premise is that the revenue basis of a membership organization was traditionally membership dues. That is no longer necessarily true. Some membership organizations have now eliminated the requirement of members paying dues.

More commonly, however, the dues base remains intact or even expands. As a result, resources are augmented and the organization provides additional services to members, creating increased membership value. The payoff to the organization is twofold: First, the new activities and services bring in additional income; second, the additional activities add to the value and appeal of the organization. New members can be attracted, and the new resources can provide the springboard for other programs that increase the value of membership.

The organization with a membership orientation will constantly be alert for opportunities to provide new services and thereby to enhance its benefits to members.

## WHAT TYPES OF ACTIVITIES SHOULD AN ORGANIZATION CONSIDER?

The kinds of activities and services that a membership organization can sensibly undertake are varied. Nonprofit organizations have to be careful not to stray from their charter or mission. The core services for which members pay their dues cannot be compromised or ignored; activities cannot be unseemly or crass; the nonprofit status must be protected. There may be taxes on "unrelated business income"—income from activities that the Internal Revenue Service (IRS) may judge "unrelated" to the purpose for which nonprofit status was granted (see Chapter 14, "Knowing Important Legal Requirements.")

Some activities that generate income beyond dues are obvious. Almost every membership organization has a convention or annual meeting, which often generates income above expenses. Publications are also a common source of revenue, derived from subscriptions, book sales, or advertising. But other sources of income are not so obvious. Exhibit 4–1 provides a list of activities you might consider.

Two of the most traditional sources of income for trade and professional associations—educational programs and conventions (including trade shows)—are considered at length in Chapters 6 and 7. These activities can often provide the framework within which other activities can be developed.

As examples, consider three types of nonprofit organizations—a professional association, a trade association, and a computer technology user group—which have developed overall programs for sustainable growth, to the benefit of their members and their professions.

**Exhibit 4-1**   Checklist of Potential Revenue Sources

Trade Shows

Conferences

Continuing Education Programs

Journals, Trade Magazines
- Subscriptions
- Display advertising/classified ads

Special Publications
- Research
- Independent studies
- Books
- Educational materials
- Directories

Sponsorships
- Conference activities and amenities
- Publications
- Networking functions
- Working groups, chat rooms

Research/Statistics

Certification Programs

Grants
- Government
- Private
- Foundation

Cause-Related Marketing (but be careful of endorsements)

Event By-Products
- Tapes (audio, video)
- CD-ROMs
- Conference proceedings

Web Sites
- Chat rooms
- Banner advertising
- Job postings

Sale of Mail Lists

Warehousing Supplies

Franchised Chapters

Cost-Sharing Alliances

## THINKING BEYOND THE TRADITIONAL: SPONSORSHIP PROGRAMS AND THE PROFESSIONAL ASSOCIATION

The Society of Gastroenterology Nurses and Associates (SGNA) is a specialty nursing association. Like most specialty nonprofits, whether in medicine or in other areas of activity, SGNA needs to carve out its own niche—what it can do to serve its members and the broader public with whom its members interact—and then carry out those activities well.

In 1988, SGNA had 2,000 members and total revenues of $800,000. Only $18,500 of revenues came from sponsorships. By 1998, with a membership of 6,800, SGNA had revenues exceeding $2,000,000, of which $373,000 came from sponsorships.

To begin expanding its activities, the SGNA board of directors assessed, first, its members' needs (beyond those that were being met by other organizations) and second, its strengths. Through this assessment, it was realized that the professional activities of gastroenterology nurses created a need for a variety of programs within their organization, activities that could not be maintained by dues alone. The SGNA board had to reach out for other sources of support, but it knew that if it created strong, creditable programs, support would come.

Over the last 10 years, SGNA has developed:

- A monthly journal, *Gastroenterology Nursing*
- A monthly newsletter
- Seventeen special-interest groups (such as one for those in the field of hepatology), many of which have their own annual meetings
- Expanded educational events at meetings, including precourse sessions, vendor educational programs, and a video learning center
- Educational videos, through which gastroenterology nurses receive continuing education credits
- A Web site that also facilitates interactive "distance learning" programs over the Internet
- Manuals in the practice of gastroenterology nursing, so that nurses and other professionals have the most up-to-date practice information
- Guidelines and standards that address issues directly affecting the practice of gastroenterology nursing

Providing educational opportunities to its members is one of the primary ways in which SGNA carries out its mission. Approximately half of all gastrointestinal (GI) nurses are certified by the Certifying Board of Gastroenterology Nurses and Associates, a related association that certifies nurses in gastroenterology. To retain this prestigious credential, GI nurses must either retest every five years or obtain specialty-specific continuing education credit hours. To respond to this need, SGNA has developed a variety of educational activities:

- *Annual Course:* Each year, SGNA's annual course brings together almost one quarter of its membership for a concentrated array of plenary and concurrent sessions, special interest group activities, poster displays, workshops, and hands-on courses. Members pay a discounted fee to attend the annual course and may elect to participate in more focused precourse optional sessions at additional cost. SGNA now typically offers as many as 50 focused sessions at each annual course, at which attendees can earn an average of more than 35 contact hours toward the 100 they must earn over a five-year period for recertification. The annual course generates revenues not only from membership attendees, but also from vendors and exhibitors. Exhibitors and vendors purchase space in the exhibit hall and many also purchase space from SGNA to provide "vendor programs" at which they can teach GI nurses about their products and services.

- *Independent Study Activities:* As more GI nurses become certified, the demand for cost-effective, flexible educational options has increased. Many nurses report that their attendance at conferences must be rotated from year to year with other staff in their department, so they must seek other avenues for continued learning. SGNA has responded by developing materials to address these needs. These include video and audio modules, based on highly rated presentations from past annual courses, that members can use to gain more knowledge in their specialty. These modules are bundled with written study guides, references, and a posttest; learners can select topics of interest and complete the activity at their own pace. For a small processing fee, contact hours are awarded for successful completion of these modules.

How did the organization develop the resources to provide these services? SGNA was not shy about reaching out to corporations for support of its activities. Medical equipment companies, medical suppliers and distributors, and pharmaceutical companies support these activities through sponsorships, exhibits, and advertisements in the journal and newsletter. Credit is tastefully given for sponsorships of luncheons—for example, at the annual meeting—and other major activities. No product endorsements are provided or expected, nor is there any exclusive link to any one corporation. But these sponsors do, of course, receive exposure to and recognition from the members of SGNA, who are leaders in their field.

SGNA revenues have increased almost threefold over the past 10 years, mostly as a result of the attention focused on the activities made possible by this non-dues revenue stream. The actual dollars raised from sponsorships are important, but, as SGNA's experience shows, not as important as the contribution the new activities make to the Society's health, vigor, and service to its profession. Over the last 10 years, as sponsored activities grew, membership in the Society grew even faster—almost tripling. Dues income increased proportionately. Membership grew rapidly because of the additional educational programs and related services.

Management and oversight of these additional programs and the supporting resources do require further effort. The executive director and staff annually develop a detailed marketing plan. This nonprofit association has a part-time fund-raiser whose only function is to find sponsorship revenue. In addition, an active board of directors and membership participation has helped gain increased sponsorship dollars. The president of SGNA often writes letters and participates in conference calls and/or vendor meetings. Members of the SGNA board of directors each personally work with exhibitors and vendors at the SGNA annual course to thank them for their support at the course and throughout the year. Finally, the SGNA membership itself participates by showing vendors that their support is recognized. On average, SGNA members spend three to five hours with exhibitors at their booths during an annual course. The large amount of one-on-one time that exhibitors (many of them also SGNA sponsors) are able to spend with individual members is a significant benefit of meeting participation.

Overall, the key to an organization's successful sponsorship programs is the development of relationships with vendors. These relationships must be maintained by those at all levels within an organization—from the president of the board to individual association members. Follow-up by a fund-raiser or other staff member who is responsible to keep and grow those relationships is also essential. This person maintains continuity when there is a turnover of board members, handles any problems that arise, solicits exhibitor input, and continually updates vendors on how their companies are being recognized by their target audience.

What should SGNA undertake next? This nonprofit is now developing various Web site activities, also to be supported by funding. The Society's Web site, launched in 1997, now averages more than 300 hits by 50 visitors per day, and these numbers continue to grow. From this base, SGNA has now launched the first of a series of auditorium chat rooms consisting of a "speaker" and an "audience" on-line. The association presents an expert on a specific gastroenterology topic, communicating on-line to an audience of its members and others in the field. In this format, the leader opens with a short presentation, transmitted as she writes it—the Internet version of a live presentation before an audience. Questions then come from participants to a moderator, who selects and relays to the discussion leader the most relevant. The leader then responds to the full on-line audience via the Internet, stimulating follow-up questions. Audience members have an opportunity to interact with each other as well as with the speaker. The first chat room discussion in the fall of 1999 covered conscious sedation. SGNA plans to offer four chat rooms per year.

## TRADE ASSOCIATIONS—STRENGTHENING THE FRANCHISE

Trade associations, whose members are typically corporations rather than individuals, usually do not have the sponsorship opportunities available to professional associations. But other opportunities abound for the trade association looking for ways to best serve its members.

Industry-specific trade associations serve a specific purpose, relevant to their industry. These organizations focus on programs directly targeted to their industries that the larger "horizontal" business organizations—The U.S. Chamber of Commerce, the National Association of Manufacturers, the National Federation of Independent Business, the National Wholesale Distributors Association—cannot provide. This specificity of purpose gives them a niche, a franchise, which the creative nonprofit associations extend.

*For example, the North American Association of Food Equipment Manufacturers—at that time the National Association of Food Equipment Manufacturers (NAFEM)—decided in 1970 that it was no longer content being an organization of firms that exhibited their products at trade shows and conventions organized by others. Why pay for exhibit space and entrance fees at trade shows organized by other groups if you can do it yourself?*

*The first NAFEM trade show event, positioned as an "educational exhibition," was held in 1973. Emphasizing for buyers and sellers alike the important role of education in enabling informed purchases in commerce, the show was unlike any other trade show of the time. Foodservice equipment and supplies were exhibited exclusively, without the involvement of food purveyors, who had taken the spotlight at other industry events. The new venture was well received, as the foodservice industry welcomed an exclusive forum for display, demonstration, and education about foodservice equipment and supplies.*

*During the last 25 years, the NAFEM Educational Exhibition has grown to more than 10 times the size of its first event. In 1999 the show featured more than 650 equipment and supplies manufacturers, exhibiting in 320,000 net square feet of exhibit space, with over 20,000 foodservice professionals in attendance, including representation from 70 countries worldwide.*

*The NAFEM Educational Exhibition remains the number one benefit of membership within NAFEM. Exhibit privileges are limited to NAFEM members, resulting in increased membership for the association and a dependable pool of exhibiting companies who support the show. NAFEM takes an integrated approach to marketing its Educational Exhibition, combining direct mail, advertising, media relations, electronic promotion (via e-mail and the NAFEM Web site), and promotional partnerships (including co-promotion through affiliated industry organizations and the U.S. Department of Commerce).*

*Two thirds of the association's revenues now come from the biennial trade show and conference. These revenues have enabled the association to carry out other activities highly valued by the membership, such as energetic representation before Congress to defeat protectionist trade legislation and support of activities to help members market their products overseas, which would not have been possible had the association relied primarily on dues.*

Other income-generating activities of the association hew to its marketing orientation. The association holds an annual sales and marketing conference and an executive management conference on issues specific to the design and sales of commercial food preparation equipment. It oversees a certification program—providing the Certified Food Service Professional designation—that requires study of materials prepared by the association and passage of a stringent examination. This professional accreditation has created a new level of quality in the industry, leading most members to insist that their sales executives become certified.

All new activities should meet a cost-benefit test. This does not always mean that additional activities have to pay for themselves, or even that they produce income. Additional membership benefits justify the support members give their association through dues.

*For example, consider the American Bearing Manufacturers Association (ABMA), formed in 1917 as an informal committee to aid the U.S. production of bearings in World War I. Bearings are highly engineered, precision-made components that enable machinery to move at extremely high speeds and carry remarkable loads with ease and efficiency. Members' products are used in everything from automobiles and aerospace equipment to computers, ceiling fans, medical equipment, refrigerators, railroads, and hundreds of other everyday and complex products.*

*In recent years, ABMA has developed a number of new services for its members. One is a standards program. ABMA serves as the secretariat of one of the American National Standard Institute's (ANSI) industry committees and for several International Standards Organization (ISO) technical committees, and as administrator of the USA technical advisory group. Through these activities, the association has been able to define both national and international standards for its members' products—an activity essential not only to industry growth, but to the many sectors of the global economy—to which these little-noticed products are essential.*

*Second, there is the critical task of collecting and disseminating vital industry statistics. Through a separate market research and statistics department, ABMA collects information on industry production and on imports and exports, which is tabulated and distributed to member organizations. Individual member information is kept secure and confidential. The generic, tabulated information is shared only with the companies that participate in the survey, with one exception: The association has granted access of its information to the Federal Reserve Board, which has used the statistical information to help in its analysis of economic trends. More recently, as the markets have become internationalized, the association has also worked with counterparts in Europe and Japan to share information on trends in world markets.*

*ABMA staff have also worked with volunteer leaders to create a third significant association resource—engineering courses specifically designed for the bearing industry. An alliance was formed in 1995 with two prestigious schools, Pennsylvania State University and Georgia Institute of Technology, and since the inception of this program, more than 430 industry representatives have benefited from these specialized courses tailored to the industry.*

## USER GROUPS—ADAPTING TO CHANGING INDUSTRY TRENDS

A "user group" is a specialized type of nonprofit organization. Typically, its members are customers—users—of a technology product usually available from a specific vendor. There is a symbiotic relationship between the users and the vendor. The rapid development of sophisticated information technology (IT) has created the need for these independent specialized groups, which provide a vehicle for practical user-to-user continuing education regarding product applications and for dialogue between the customers and the vendor regarding product enhancements and upgrades.

SHARE Inc., one of the oldest technology user groups, was organized by users of IBM mainframe technology. Throughout the 1980s it saw rapid growth in conference attendance, reaching more than 11,000 attendees annually toward the end of the decade. IBM itself provided significant direct support to the association.

Conditions changed, however, in 1991, as the industry experienced a dramatic shift, including the downsizing of the IBM Corporation. Most IT user groups at this point went into a downward spiral, losing 20 percent or more of their conference attendance that year alone, and many subsequently went out of existence.

Despite the industry news that "the mainframe is dead," SHARE was not about to give up. As IBM began to "reinvent" itself and the industry underwent a period of renewal, SHARE's headquarters staff, working with the board of directors, similarly redesigned its own programs. The staff led a nine-month evaluation, collecting data on members' perception of SHARE, what its volunteers thought were SHARE's core competencies, and what IBM and other key vendors were seeing as the major trends in IT. On the basis of these results, educational programming was refocused and new marketing and promotion programs undertaken.

Following a staff recommendation, the board authorized creation of a trade show to supplement the annual conference. As part of marketing the new SHARE, its old logo, which was identified with the outdated mainframe on which the "old" user group had depended, was replaced with a new logo and tag line. This step permitted SHARE to redefine its marketing programs and get away from its previous "mainframe only" stereotype. A year-round advertising campaign was also initiated to promote the benefits of SHARE to a new target audience of younger technology professionals.

Although the first trade show, in 1993, produced revenues of only $122,550, this was deemed sufficient to continue. In 1996, as a result of conference growth and editorial marketing by staff, the combined conference and trade show was selected as one of its "hot picks" by *Computerworld*, a leading trade magazine. By 1998 the trade show was bringing in more than $700,000 annually in booth revenue and sponsorship sales, far exceeding the direct support SHARE had previously received from IBM.

## DRAWING THE COST-BENEFIT ANALYSIS

Careful planning of any new activity is essential. Market research may be needed to find out whether the market you anticipate really is there, or whether potential users of a service are willing to pay a reasonable fee.

Some associations have made the mistake of believing that all non-dues income is good income. Quite apart from the risk of diluting the purpose of the organization, there is always the potential that a program will cost more than it earns. Publications—particularly those that are self-serving, like a glossy magazine for members of a relatively small profession—can be money losers. Some association executives naively believe that the higher the percentage of non-dues income, the more successful they are as managers. That is not necessarily true. It is critical to understand the true costs of the programs that generate the non-dues income. Costs are not just the outside expenditures—the costs of meals provided at a convention, or of printing and mailing a publication—but the time and indirect (or "hidden") costs of all staff who work on a project and their true overhead, including office space and fringe benefits.

Consider the following example:

*The board of directors of a professional association headquartered in New York, with a budget of more than $4 million dollars a year, awakened to the fact that the organization was losing $300,000 a year. That was not an immediate crisis, because the association had $3 million in reserves, largely in the form of bequests from founding members, that could cover the deficit for some time. But the trend was sobering. How did this happen?*

*In the last several years, the board of directors had authorized a rapid expansion of activities recommended by its executive director: a glossy monthly magazine, headline entertainment at a black-tie banquet to cap off the annual meeting, an extensive series of videotaped educational programs. The staff was proud that non-dues income was 65 percent of total income, well above the average shown by the annual survey of the American Society of Association Executives.*

*By the association's accounting, each of the activities was profitable— income exceeded direct costs. The problem was that the headquarters payroll had expanded exponentially to support the staff needed to create, manage, and market the new materials, and all personnel costs were in an administrative budget.*

*On a project-by-project basis, after allocating all staff and indirect costs, only the association's annual trade show was profitable. The rest, although worthwhile programs in themselves, were draining rather than contributing to resources. Only when an outside consulting firm made this reality clear did the association's directors face the difficult choice that they had to cut back, jettisoning some programs and scaling down others.*

It is not necessarily wrong to support activities that don't pay for themselves. But the test needed to prove membership benefit is obviously a higher standard. If a program serves only a handful of members but pays for itself (or, even better, generates income above costs), it is a benefit not just to those members but to the entire association. If a program is losing money and must be subsidized, the executive director and the board of directors need to know the facts and recognize that no matter how much "income" the program is providing, it is being subsidized out of dues or by the income from other programs. If it is a clear membership benefit, that may be fine; but the executive and board of directors should make the decision to retain or eliminate programs only after they have a full understanding of costs as well as benefits.

## CHECKLIST FOR DEVELOPING YOUR INCOME RESOURCES

- What is your organization's mission?
- What is your organization's vision?
- What strategic objectives have been defined for your organization?
- Who are your members or other direct beneficiaries?
- Are they able to pay for your services? Willing to pay? If not, why not?
- What can you do to upgrade present services? What are the resources needed to do that?
- What new programs/services can you provide to enhance your organization's value to your members and build loyalty? (Think about related groups, not just present members or beneficiaries.)
- What additional educational, industry-related, or professional information can your organization provide to benefit members?
- Who depends on the services your members provide to them? Who are your members' suppliers/customers (in the broadest sense)?
- What can you do to draw your membership and related groups closer together?
- Is your board/membership willing to network with related groups? If not, how can you motivate them?
- Will your great new ideas be self-supporting? Profitable? If not, are they sufficiently valuable that they will justify increased dues or attract other outside support?

# CHAPTER FIVE

# Raising Money to Serve Your Cause

**Fund-raising is both an art and a science. The art is in developing and nurturing relationships with people; the science lies in using data, research, and tested fund-raising models to achieve your organization's revenue goals.**

**How do you ask for and get the funds needed to advance your organization's mission? What return can you expect on your fund-raising investment? Which fund-raising tools are best suited to your particular constituency? How can technology enhance your organization's fund-raising effectiveness?**

**This chapter provides answers to these and many other questions related to your fund-raising program.**

*Fund-raising. Financial development. Non-dues revenue.* Whatever words are used to describe it, all nonprofit organizations are in the fund-raising business. Whether you undertake a capital campaign to raise funds for a building or to create an endowment, organize a community barbecue to underwrite a specific project, or solicit corporations for contributions to an educational foundation, fund-raising is an essential element for your nonprofit organization's continued viability and success.

According to *Giving USA: The Annual Report on Philanthropy for the Year 1998,*[1] individuals, foundations, and corporations contributed more than $143 billion in that year to approximately

---

[1]A. Kaplan, ed., *Giving USA: The Annual Report on Philanthropy for the Year 1998* (New York: AAFRC Trust for Philanthropy, 1999).

620,000 nonprofit organizations in America. Your organization can capture its share of this largesse through thoughtful fund-raising plans and activities.

The key to success in this competitive environment is to demonstrate that there is a reason for people and institutions to give to your organization. Nonprofit organizations must clearly define their mission and their "niche" in the marketplace in order to keep pace.

With the aging of the "results-oriented" baby boomer generation, increased scrutiny by watchdog agencies, and the emergence of the Internet as a communications tool, nonprofit organizations will be increasingly judged by their *effectiveness* in meeting stated goals and their *efficiency* in the use of donor funds.

This chapter will help you to:

- Create a case for support for your organization
- Identify sources of support
- Choose from among the best fund-raising approaches
- Develop an action plan for positive results

## RELATIONSHIPS ARE KEY

It is important to remember that fund-raising, or "development" as it is most commonly called, is based on relationships, particularly relationships with individuals.

Although a professional-looking solicitation letter may get the attention of a new prospect, that perfect letter will never substitute for a personal relationship with a donor. Consider the chart of giving for 1997 (Exhibit 5–1). You will notice that 77 percent of all gifts given to nonprofit organizations, or $135 billion, was given by *individuals.* These figures include contributions to religious organizations and therefore are not representative of other social service or other nonprofit organizations. But, there is no denying that successful fund-raising, no matter what your type of organization, has to start with the individuals who share your organization's goals. *Cultivating relationships with individuals should always be your first fundraising concern.*

It is important to recognize that doing all the right things may increase your chances for success, but it does not guarantee it. In fact, only about 25 percent of your total fund-raising "asks" will be successful in any given year.

**Exhibit 5–1**   1998 Total Giving in the USA

| Source | Amount (in billions) | Percent |
|---|---|---|
| Individuals | 134.84 | 77.3 |
| Foundations | 17.09 | 9.8 |
| Bequests | 13.62 | 7.8 |
| Corporations | 8.97 | 5.1 |
| Total | 174.52 | 100.0 |

Source: Giving USA 1998: The Annual Report on Philanthropy for the Year 1998.

Your goal should be to focus first on those prospects with the greatest likelihood of making a gift in the current fund year. In fund-raising there is a tried and true saying, "Solicit inside-out and top–down," meaning that you should solicit those closest to your organization first (e.g., your board and previous donors), then donors with the highest giving potential, and on down to those with the lowest potential.

## CREATING THE CASE FOR SUPPORT

Funding-raising must have a purpose, an identifiable and quantifiable need. Ask yourself: Why are we raising money? Is it for a new project or a continuing program? Is it for an endowment? Are we raising money to offer something to the public, such as a new wing for a hospital or computers for schools?

The case for support is *your justification for philanthropic support.* The case will form the basis for proposals to corporations and foundations, appeals to donors, copy for promotional brochures and publications, and communications to all of your constituencies.

Principal elements of the case for support are shown in Exhibit 5–2.

A successful case statement must interest, inform, and involve prospective donors. It must persuade them to see your cause as significant and the need as urgent. It must convince them that your organization has the capability and commitment to reach its goals. It must excite them with a vision of what can be accomplished with their support. And it must motivate them to positive action.

A risk in any fund-raising activity is the temptation to accept money from a donor for programs or projects that do not fit the mission or goals outlined in your case for support. Never let money drive your mission. Stay focused on your priorities and stick with them.

**Exhibit 5–2**   Elements of the Case for Support

---

1. A description of your organization, to include:
   - Name
   - Purpose/function—Why do you exist? What is your purpose in the world?
   - Services—What activities help you perform this function?
   - Targeted population—Whom do you serve?
   - Geographic reach—Where do you operate? What communities do you serve?
   - Philosophy—What core principles, values, and ideas direct your approach?
2. What is the social problem or issue that you address?
3. What strengths qualify your organization to address this problem/need/challenge?
4. What new challenges now face your organization in carrying out its mission?
5. How do you plan to address these challenges?
6. What is estimated in terms of time and costs?
7. What opportunities and options do you offer other than to participate?
8. What will be the benefits for the prospect, community, or society as a whole?

---

## GOAL SETTING

Carefully assess how much money must be raised to achieve your organization's goals each year. How much of the organization's current operating budget must be supported through contributed income? How much of this is for general operations, how much is for program support, and how much is for other expense items?

Set what you believe to be achievable, realistic goals when starting out, and make sure you meet or exceed every one of them. It is essential to establish a strong track record of results and successes early on.

When setting your fund-raising goals, remember that it takes money to raise money. Estimate all costs involved in fund-raising, both variable and fixed. Variable costs include postage, printing, telephone, supplies, brochures, graphic design, and staff time. Fixed costs include accounting services, data processing/computers, and rent for office space. Other costs that should not be overlooked are those associated with research, training, marketing/promotion, travel, and consultants' fees. Be sure that your overall fund-raising costs do not exceed a reasonable percentage of the total amount raised. There is no hard-and-fast rule, although most watchdog agencies consider fund-raising costs over 25 percent of the amount raised to be excessive.

What is a good estimating ratio between money expended and money received? Jim Greenfield states in his book, *Fund-Raising Management: Evaluating and Managing the Fund Development Process,*[2] that the national average in fund-raising costs is $0.20 to raise $1.00. Percentages of expenses against income will vary depending on the event, but Greenfield suggests the following reasonable fund-raising administration cost guidelines:

| | |
|---|---|
| Direct mail acquisition | $1.00 to $1.25 per dollar raised |
| Direct mail renewal | $0.20 per dollar raised |
| Benefit events | 50 percent of gross proceeds |
| Corporation/foundations | $0.20 per dollar raised |
| Planned giving | $0.25 per dollar raised |
| Capital campaign | $0.05 to $0.10 per dollar |

## FUND-RAISING PROGRAM OPTIONS

As you define your mission and goals, it's time to consider the types of fund-raising approaches you will choose. Among the established fund-raising methods are the following.

*Membership solicitations*—Revenues derived from membership dues or annual assessments can help support general operating expenses, usually the most difficult costs to cover. Membership is most often solicited and renewed via direct mail. Most organizations now also have Web sites, where members and friends can join or give on-line via their credit cards.

*Contributions above dues*—An organization may solicit funds from its membership above and beyond membership dues, often to bridge the gap between operating expenses and dues income. If the organization does not have a formal membership program, an annual fund drive should be conducted each year, asking all con-stituencies on record to make a gift to the organization. Annual fund campaigns usually solicit gifts at calendar year end, when more than 90 percent of Americans make gifts to charity. Most organizations mail two or three gift solicitations each year to their target popula-tion, following up with a telemarketing appeal to their best donors and prospects.

*Special appeals*—At times, an organization may appeal to its mem-bership for special gifts, centered on an urgent project or particular

[2]J. Greenfield, *Fund-Raising: Evaluating and Managing the Fund Development Process* (New York: John Wiley & Sons, 1991).

program that needs funding. Many organizations mail two special appeals each year to supplement membership renewals and/or annual fund drives.

*Acquisition mailings*—Nonprofits use acquisition mailings to acquire new members or donors. An organization usually rents lists of donors from similar organizations, then mails a solicitation letter and return envelope along with a membership brochure or premium offer. Mailings of this type are usually handled by outside vendors and can be extremely effective in generating new members and friends of the organization. Remember, though, that the costs of acquisition mailings are high. The benefits of such a program come from renewing and upgrading donors for three years or more.

*Special Events*—Special events are the most labor-intensive activities in the fund-raisers arsenal. They are also the least cost-effective method of fund-raising, with costs sometimes exceeding 50 percent of total dollars raised.

Nonetheless, special events can be used to cultivate major donors, raise money, and bring name recognition and visibility to a nonprofit organization.

Special events are as varied as the organizations that plan them. A common event is an awards program at which individuals are honored for their outstanding contributions to the organization. Other widely used fund-raising events include balls, marathons, and auctions. On a smaller scale, churches and schools hold bazaars, "white elephant" sales, bake sales, car washes, and holiday gift-wrap programs. Look for something unusual or creative to distinguish your event.

*Building on an idea first tried in 1994 in Israel and by the Hospice of Metro Denver in 1998, the Visiting Nurse Association (VNA)/Hospice of Northern California sent 500 ceramic masks along, with acrylic paints and paint brushes, to prominent citizens in sports, politics, entertainment, and the business community (mostly local but some national figures), inviting them to decorate and sign the masks and return them to the VNA/Hospice. The masks were then auctioned at a gala dinner and, with assistance from eBay, over the Internet. Three hundred masks were returned, from individuals as diverse as actors Robin Williams and Kirk Douglas, Katie Couric of the Today Show, author Danielle Steele, San Francisco Forty-Niners coach Steve Mariucci, and local mayors and councilpersons. Auctioning the masks raised $80,000, supplementing the $230,000 in sponsorships and ticket sales from the gala. Perhaps even more important was the publicity: An enthusiastic story about the mask project in the* San Francisco Chronicle *and the display of selections of the masks in prime locations, including the world-*

*famous Gump's department store. (For more on this project, including pictures of some of the masks, see www.MaskProject.com.)*

For big events, well-known, high-profile personalities are often invited to help attract media attention to the cause. Sponsorships may be solicited and corporate tables sold to raise additional revenue. Markups on individual event tickets are often twice the actual cost of the meal.

Whatever the special event, it should appeal to a wide range of people and be well planned, publicized, executed, and evaluated. Planning a special event should start with answers to the following questions:

- Why have an event? Or can the goal be reached without the event?
- What kind of event will it be? A theme can help focus the event.
- Who will chair the event? Consider a prominent community personality.
- Who will be invited? Target your market.
- Where will the event be held?
- When will the event be held? Check community calendars, as well as your own schedule.
- Who will staff the event?

Establish a budget with costs versus projected income (see Exhibit 5–3 for an example of the expenses incurred by the Arthritis Foundation-Maryland Chapter for a Lifetime Achievement Awards Dinner, held in September 1999 as the kickoff for a three-year fund-raising campaign), as well as a time line of critical dates and a list of those responsible for mailing invitations, telephone follow-up, and event publicity.

*Capital Campaigns*—Usually undertaken by large institutions with a long track record of successful annual fund drives and a committed cadre of major donors. Campaigns support a wide variety of purposes, including building projects, renovations, new program development, endowments, and special projects. Capital campaign goals usually exceed annual giving targets by a factor of 10 or more. Campaigns are volunteer-intensive and focus on the acquisition of major, multiyear commitments to the organization. A feasibility study, usually conducted by outside experts, is recommended in order to determine realistic goals, availability of major gifts and volunteer leadership, the campaign budget, and a realistic campaign time line.

**Exhibit 5–3**   Sample Budget for Awards Dinner

Arthritis Foundation-Maryland Chapter
Lifetime Achievement Award Honoring Senator Barbara Mikulski
490 Guests
September 14, 1999

### EVENT INCOME AND EXPENSES

Donor Benefit with Honoree

*INCOME*

Corporate Sponsors

| | |
|---|---:|
| 4 @ $10,000 | $ 40,000 |
| 9 @ $5,000 | $ 45,000 |
| 8 @ $3,000 | $ 24,000 |
| 18 @ $2,000 | $ 36,000 |
| Ticket Sales | |
| 90 @ $200 | $ 18,000 |
| *Total Income* | *$163,000* |

*EXPENSE*

| | |
|---|---:|
| Crab Cards | $ 831 |
| Dinner/Reception | $ 33,321 |
| Flowers | $ 3,025 |
| Invitation—Design and Printing | $ 3,609 |
| Piano | $ 100 |
| Postage | $ 726 |
| Program Design and Printing | $ 3,446 |
| Save the Date Postcard—Printing | $ 693 |
| Save the Date Postcard—Design | $ 1,040 |
| Vellum Paper for Invitation and Program | $ 716 |
| Video Equipment | $ 1,628 |
| Video Production | $ 7,740 |
| Voice-over | $ 1,500 |
| *Total Expenses* | *$ 58,375* |
| *NET INCOME* | *$104,625* |

*Note:* This cost report covered direct expenses only, not including costs of staff or overhead. A complete accounting would include an allocation for staff time and other overhead. See additional discussion of event planning in Chapter 7, "Making Your Meetings Work—For You and Your Members."

*Planned Giving*—Allows donors to make gifts to nonprofit organizations, which will be realized in the future through the following vehicles:

- Wills and bequests—A gift is bequeathed in a donor's will, often as a percent of the estate.

- Pooled income funds—Cash or securities are transferred to a charitable organization in return for a stated percentage of the assets each year for the life of the donor.

- Life insurance/wealth replacement trusts—These vehicles allow an individual to make your nonprofit the beneficiary of his or her life insurance policy or, in the case of a wealth replacement trust, to use the annual income to purchase a life insurance policy in the beneficiary's name, thus transferring the value upon the donor's death.

Considering that $8 to 10 *trillion dollars* will be transferred by death over the next 30 years, nonprofit organizations would do well to have at least a simple bequest program. Also significant is the fact that 70 percent of Americans at the present time *do not have a will.*

(For a comprehensive overview on planned giving, consult Ronald Jordan and Katelyn Quynn's *Planned Giving: Management, Marketing, and Law, Second Edition,* Jim Greenfield's *Fund-Raising Management: Evaluating and Managing the Development Process, Second Edition,* and Bruce Hopkins's *The Law of Fund-Raising, Second Edition.*)

*Income from programs* or *services*—or from such sources as product sales, publications, affinity credit cards, cause-related marketing partnerships and/or licensing—can be an excellent source of revenue.

In addition, revenue generated from buying and selling goods and services on the Internet, called e-philanthropy, is now taking root. Many experts say that the Internet is the future of charitable giving because of its ability to reach millions of donors and prospects instantaneously at little cost. The following are among the Web sites offering guidance for those who want to contribute:

*www.helping.org*
Allows users to search for charities by location and topic, to find out about volunteering, and to donate on-line via credit card.

*www.guidestar.org*
Has a searchable database of more than 620,000 nonprofit organizations in the United States; includes postings of U.S. tax form 990, whereby charities report their finances and operations.

*www.greatergood.com*
Builds, markets, and manages "on-line shopping villages," for a
nonprofit partners' sites, where at least 5 percent of every
purchase benefits the nonprofit's cause.

*www.igive.com*
Enables users to choose charities, including local ones, that will
benefit from the users' on-line purchases at the igive mall.


## THE INTERNAL ACTION PLAN

Remember the words of wisdom from Sun Tzu's *Art of War:* "Every bat-
tle is won or lost before it is fought." In fund-raising, there is no substitute for proper planning. The three steps to creating a winning action
plan are to visualize a result, think backward, and implement forward.

If yours is a volunteer-driven organization, consider establishing
an advisory committee or subcommittee of the board to oversee
implementation of the action plan so that someone always has the
"big picture" in focus. In such a case, the executive director or CEO
will be the driving force and principal "asker" for funds.

If you have staff dedicated to fund-raising, carefully review, by
constituency, where your projected income will come from, based on
your prior year's giving history, remembering that your best prospect
is one who has made a gift in the past.

Establish a time line for the solicitation of your board, for renewal
requests, special appeals, corporate/foundation proposal submissions and event deadlines, with total ask amounts equal to four times
your anticipated annual goal. Then follow the results monthly and
alter the plan as necessary.


### Establish an Organizational Structure

Whether your organization is small or large, you need people
assigned to specific areas of responsibility, as explained here:

*Executive committee and board of directors/trustees*—Establish priorities and goals and approve the action plan. The board also provides
early money to any fund-raising project.

*Communications committee*—Coordinates efforts to promote the
project through publications and the media.

*Development committee*—Assists in the identification, cultivation,
and solicitation of donors and prospects.

*Information processing*—Staff assigned to keep the database and
other records accurate and up to date.

*Accounting*—Staff available to constantly maintain the latest, most
accurate account of monies collected. If you do not have an account-

**Exhibit 5–4**   Sample Donor Form

---

DONOR RECORD

Name:

Title:

Address:                                City/State/Zip:

Phone:                                  Fax:                    e-mail:

Employer's name:                        Employer's address:

Spouse's name:                          Spouse's occupation:

Children's names:                       Children's ages:

Children's schools:

Giving history:
   (Yr./Amt./Purpose)

Community affiliations:                  Religious affiliation:

Education:

General comments:

History of personal contact
   (from Call Reports):

Other significant information:

---

ant on staff, be sure to have one affiliated with your organization to serve as the accounting advisor.

*Gift processing*—Staff to process contributions, promptly acknowledge each donation, and maintain records. The items in Exhibit 5–4 represent necessary components for a donor's record. A database with this information should be set up accordingly.

## Understand Your Responsibilities

No one should raise funds for your organization without the knowledge and approval of the leadership, which may include, but not be limited to, your executive committee, board of directors, and chief executive. And, of course, all individuals who solicit gifts for your organization should be trained before they do so. There is one other hard-and-fast rule about volunteers soliciting for gifts: *They should always make their own gifts before soliciting others.*

Be sure to consider any disclosures that may be required by law when fund-raising. (See Bruce Hopkins' book *The Law of Fund-Raising,*[3] *Second Edition,* for an in-depth discussion of disclosures.)

---

[3]B. Hopkins, *The Law of Fund-Raising, Second Edition* (New York: John Wiley & Sons, 1995).

The importance of accurate accounting, record keeping, gift processing, and follow-up cannot be overstated. Regardless of the scope of your project, you must be certain you have sufficient staff to take and process gifts and/or follow through on other administrative activities.

Often, an organization agonizes over whether it should hire a development officer. If your nonprofit has a budget under $300,000, you most likely cannot afford to hire one. Use trained volunteers. If your budget is between $300,000 and $500,000, you can probably afford to designate a part-time fund-raising specialist on staff or on contract. Charitable organizations with budgets over $1 million usually have a staff person with designated responsibilities to coordinate fund development.

## PROSPECT IDENTIFICATION

Consider the "The Fund-Raising Universe" depicted in Exhibit 5–5 when creating your list of those to approach for contributions. Cast your net far and wide when identifying individuals or organizations that may be interested in contributing to your cause. Your list of potential donors should include the following:

- Individuals
- Corporations
- Vendors
- Board members/former board members
- Foundations
- Federal and state agencies
- Trade and professional organizations

When your prospect list is complete, create a computerized notebook of potential donors, through which you can track all donations. This database should be comprehensive and contain records of all past donations with pertinent comments. This database, then, will serve as an accurate resource for future projects.

### Individual Donors

Soliciting individuals may take a variety of forms, from the annual giving appeal to a personal request for a major gift. (See Exhibit 5–6, "Relationship Model".)

**Exhibit 5–5**   The Fund-Raising Universe

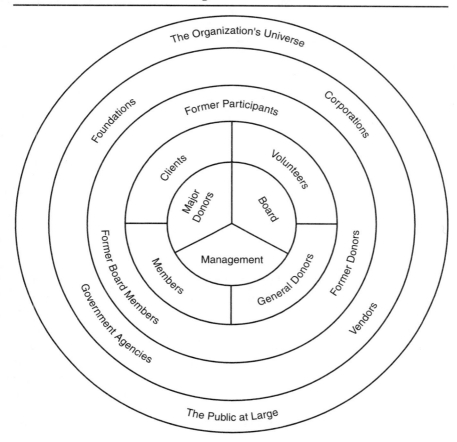

*Direct Mail.* Requests to a large group of potential donors are most likely to be made through *direct mail.* If they are targeted letters to people who know and support your organization, direct mail letters may be the most effective tool to generate money. The recipients are already designated as interested parties by their prior donations or by referrals from friends or colleagues. Start with the list of your former and current supporters and add referrals from friends, colleagues, or other organizations. Targeted mailings usually yield less than $500 per person; often the donation requested is in the range of $10 to $250.

Keep in mind direct mail postage costs. You will need to determine whether the mailings will be sent first class or via the less expensive bulk rate or third class mail available to nonprofits. Third class mail,

**Exhibit 5–6**   Relationship Model

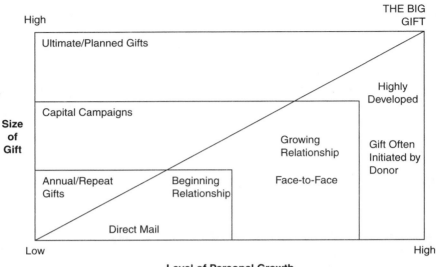

however, may take substantially longer to reach a prospective donor, so mailings that require a timely response should be sent first class. The use of bar codes and nine-digit zip codes can expedite your mailing. (Domestic mail manuals may be obtained by writing the Superintendent of Documents, Government Printing Office, Washington, D.C. 20402-9371.)

Your fund-raising letter must be designed to quickly capture the attention of the prospective donor, considering the deluge of unsolicited mail delivered these days. Spend time on designing an enticing envelope and letter. If possible, enlist help—perhaps a volunteer(s)—from a local public relations or design firm for an effective, eye-catching design. It may make the difference between success and failure. Bear in mind that direct mail to prospects on lists that are not well chosen or targeted can often cost more than they bring in contributions.

*Telemarketing.*  For many potential donors, the *telemarketing* call may be the only personal contact they have with your organization. This is an opportunity to answer any questions a prospective donor may have. When planning a telemarketing campaign, be sure to create an effective script for your callers that provides accurate information and anticipates questions as well as objections. Your telemarketers may be staff members or volunteers, or you may hire a telemarketing firm. A side benefit of a telemarketing campaign can be market research, because the telemarketers may learn the extent of support for your program.

According to the American Red Cross's *Manual for Financial Development,* a telemarketing campaign is best conducted as part of a larger fund-raising effort, rather than as a stand-alone device. Many groups use telemarketing for renewing donors or for lapsed donor appeals. The more personal approach of a phone call is also successful in trying to upgrade donors. Many colleges and universities have student volunteers for annual fund-raising drives who help to raise a substantial amount of money for their institution.

Through personal visits, volunteer intelligence, and prospect research you will begin to discover which donors have the capacity to make major gifts. These major donors will form the backbone of your individual, high-dollar giving program.

*Major donor solicitations* are most often coordinated by staff and are board driven, meaning that board members usually provide access to the prospect and at times go on the solicitation call with a staff member, usually the executive director or the president. Major gifts are larger than annual gifts, although the amount depends on the organization and the donor. Major gifts always involve personal contact as well as special acknowledgment and recognition once the gift has been made. Major gift development is the most cost-effective type of fund-raising.

When soliciting major gifts, remember these essentials: Know your prospect, make sure the right person is asking for the gift, and always ask for a specific amount. Jerold Panas, in his book *Finders Keepers,* reviews the solicitation process in great detail; this is a must read for volunteers and staff engaged in face-to-face soliciting.

## Corporations

Corporations often support nonprofit organizations through their charitable giving, marketing, or advertising budgets; however, finding the right corporation to fund your project is not always easy.

Personal access to key corporate decision makers is extremely beneficial, so it is best to start with your board. Check for board contacts with corporations in your local area first, then with national corporations with area plants or local offices.

Remember, too, that corporations frequently sponsor events, such as dinners or auctions, and that they can be a good source of in-kind contributions.

Be sensitive to the fiscal policies of corporations; most fund-raising is done in the fall of the year when corporate monies are allocated for the following year. Also consider the following general rules for approaching corporate giving sources:

- Never send a form letter to a corporation.

- Avoid sending letters to corporate CEOs if you do not have a direct access point through a board member or volunteer. Identify the individual who handles corporate contributions and communicate with him or her.

- As indicated earlier, charity usually begins at home with most corporations, so look first at those in your own backyard.

- If possible, have someone who knows the company make the first call.

- If you have an idea that appeals to a corporate giving officer, discuss how best to package it. Your chances of approval are almost ensured by doing this.

- Big companies like big projects, those with elements they can call their own.

- Do your research. Know each company's products, market, interests, issues, and concerns. Find common ground between your interests and those of the company's customers.

- Plan ahead and get your submissions in early.

- Remember that the company that says no this year may be a donor next year, if you come back with a better idea. And once you receive a company's support, inertia may keep you on its contributions list.

- Always say thank you. The best form of thanks is a report of what has been accomplished with the gift. Business people, now more than ever, expect something to happen when they invest in a nonprofit organization.

Corporations like to feel that they will be getting some visibility and recognition for their contributions. Be prepared with a "Corporate Recognition Plan" that outlines various benefits and levels of giving for corporate donors. Exhibit 5–7 is a sample corporate recognition plan for a national awards event held by a nonprofit organization.

## Foundations

There are more than 45,000 private foundations in the United States today, and the number grows weekly. There are four types of foundations:

**Exhibit 5–7**   Corporate Recognition Plan

---

CORPORATE SPONSOR - $15,000 to $25,000

- Press release announcing contribution and support
- Recognition plaque
- Head table representation at annual benefit
- Table for 10 at annual benefit dinner
- Listing in the printed program
- Special recognition at the annual benefit with plaque presentation
- Discount for all corporation's attendees to annual benefit
- Corporate name on scholarship program
- Article in national newsletter on contribution
- Complimentary ads in annual publications
- Full page ad in printed benefit dinner program

CORPORATE BENEFACTOR - $10,000

- Press release announcing contribution and support
- Recognition plaque
- Head table representation at annual benefit
- Table for 10 at annual benefit dinner
- Listing in the printed program
- Special recognition at the annual benefit with plaque presentation
- Discount for all corporation's attendees to annual benefit
- Full page ad in printed benefit dinner program

CORPORATE PATRON - $5,000

- Recognition plaque
- Prominent listing in annual meeting brochure
- Head table representation at annual benefit dinner
- Table for 10 at annual benefit dinner
- Half-page ad in printed benefit dinner program

CORPORATE DONOR - $2,500

- Framed certificate
- Prominent listing in annual meeting brochure

---

1. Independent foundations established by persons or families of wealth (which constitute the largest group)
2. Company-sponsored foundations
3. Operating foundations established to do research, promote social welfare, or engage in other charitable programs deemed worthwhile by the donor or governing body

4. Community foundations supported by and operated for the benefit of a specific community or region

Giving by both private and corporate foundations, bouyed by the rising stock market, increased almost 40 percent in the two years of 1998 and 1999.

Unlike government agencies and other funders, foundations rarely use standardized application forms. Some prefer a brief letter of inquiry about a possible match between your program and their interests *before* you submit a proposal. The objective of a letter of inquiry is to get the funder to invite you to submit a full proposal.

A few foundations supply detailed instructions on what a proposal to them should include, and they expect these instructions to be followed. Some groups of funders have adopted common grant application forms that grant seekers may use when submitting proposals to them. Find out what style of approach your prospective funder prefers.

Researching foundations requires the same care as researching corporations. Personal contacts of a board member or volunteer can be extremely valuable. Although many worthwhile projects inevitably go unfunded, foundation grants have been an important source of start-up funds for new organizations or for creative projects of established groups. Foundations are far less likely to finance operational budgets or to cover the deficits of existing programs.

To start the grant submission process:

- Commit your ideas to paper.

- Thoroughly describe your program.

- Construct a time line.

- Estimate costs for staff, materials, and equipment.

- Plan for the evaluation of the program.

- Create a prospect list, using print or electronic sources.

- Research potential foundation sources, using Foundation Annual Reports and Guidelines, IRS Form 990 (which identifies foundation board members, areas of interest, and grants approved), and information available through the Foundation Center (*www.fdncenter. org*).

- If at all possible, meet with foundation program officers in person to discuss your program.

Foundation grant writing is probably one of the most competitive areas of fund-raising today. It can be a very demanding process, requiring detailed answers to a series of questions. Submitting an incomplete application may immediately disqualify you from consideration. To be successful, a proposal must be well written, clear in its purpose, and include specific information about every aspect of the project.

It is best to submit your proposal six to nine months before your program is to be implemented, allowing time for you to apply elsewhere if need be.

*City Lights, a nonprofit organization created to provide alternative schooling and intensive counseling for alienated teenagers in Washington, D.C., many of whom would otherwise be in juvenile detention, initially had difficulty in obtaining funding from city government sources, who thought the concept unlikely to succeed. The organization was able, through persistence, to obtain a 3-1 challenge grant from the Agnes Meyer Foundation. Other foundations followed the foundation's lead, and the program was launched. Subsequently, after City Lights demonstrated its ability to help teenagers who had repeatedly been expelled from other schools and seemed headed for a lifetime of failure, the city school system provided the funds to continue its programs.*

## Government Agencies

Government grants are tax-based dollars and may be in great demand and, therefore, difficult to obtain. In addition, the preparation of grant applications may be extensive and require careful attention to details. Grant record keeping and staff administration may be extremely time-consuming; therefore, before you submit a grant you should research all of the direct and indirect costs of receiving a grant. Lead time could be a year or more for federal grants. If neither you nor anyone else on your staff has expertise in this area, a consultant skilled in this field can save you a great deal of time and money.

Funding and a variety of in-kind professional services for international programs and projects are also available through the federal government. U.S. nonprofits can benefit directly from the assistance provided by federal agencies to organizations interested in expanding their work into other countries. The majority of these programs are underutilized, because American nonprofits do not know what programs exist or how to find them.

*Sister Cities International is an organization whose purpose is to "twin" cities in the United States with cities abroad for cultural, municipal, and educational exchange. In addition to receiving donations and funding from their membership, Sister Cities has also received government grants from the United States Aid for International Development (USAID) and the United States Information Agency (USIA).*

## Trade and Professional Associations

Charitable nonprofits and business associations can often work together for the benefit of both. Typically, trade and professional associations support projects that relate to their business or that of the members they represent. Careful research is needed to develop projects that clearly benefit both organizations.

*Delta Society, headquartered in Renton, Washington (www.deltasociety. org), promotes mutually beneficial relationships between animals and people to help people improve their health, independence, and quality of life. The goals of the Delta Society are to expand awareness of the positive effect of animals on human health and development, to remove barriers that prevent the involvement of animals in everyday life, and to expand the therapeutic and service role of animals in human health, service, and education. Delta realized that better appreciation of the human-companion animal bond could result in increased respect for and care of animals, and that scientific studies were essential to increase the appreciation of the bond.*

*Initially, funding for the Delta Society was very small. To stimulate research into the human–companion animal bond, Delta approached the Pet Food Institute, a trade association of dog and cat food manufacturers, with a creative proposal: Delta would issue a request for proposals (RFP) to its network of academic researchers interested in the relationship between people and companion animals; a panel of academic researchers would review the proposals for quality; Delta would send those proposals approved by its peer review panel to the Pet Food Institute, which would have the option of funding one or more. Over a period of seven years, the Pet Food Institute funded 12 of the proposals recommended to it by the Delta Society, as well as reimbursing the Society for its management costs to solicit, review, and monitor the proposals.*

*The results were valuable to both organizations. One research project, for example, showed that men and women over the age of 65 who owned a pet made fewer visits to physicians for minor illnesses than those who did not have pet companionship. Another showed that heart attack victims who were pet owners were more likely to recover than those who were not. The research was widely reported in the press and provided invaluable impetus for academic research in this new field, as well as elevating the stature of the Delta Society.*

*From this research and its other activities to promote understanding of the human-companion animal bond, Delta has grown from a struggling organization to one recognized throughout the world.*

## The Importance of Research

As you develop your fund-raising strategy, draw upon useful information and data from various sources such as government reports, newsletters, computer databases, and industry associations. Use these resources to learn about your prospective donors, about their issues and concerns. With this knowledge, you can tailor your solicitation to the donor's perspective.

Research will certainly yield benefits, inasmuch as targeted lists promise a greater return than nontargeted ones. Always investigate the interests of potential donors, as well as funding histories and appropriate contact persons. A donor with a track record of giving to similar projects is more likely to contribute to yours. The more closely a donor relates to your organization's image, resources, and objectives, the more likely a donation will be made. Many companies, nonprofit organizations, and associations produce annual reports and/or promotional materials along with newsletters, magazines, and journals, which may provide background information.

Experts say that over 40 percent of the information you will need on prospective donors and prospects can be found on the Internet. The following is a sampling of some of the Internet sites that fundraisers say they use most frequently:

Development Research Links (*www.princeton.edu/one/research/netlinks.html*) is a compilation of nearly 300 sites with links to salary information, on-line newspapers, stock and other business information, and genealogy sites, among others.

Internet Prospector (*www.w3.uwyo.edu/~prospect*) has many useful links provided by fund-raising researchers and grouped in categories, such as corporations, people, and on-line news.

Price's List of Lists (*www.gwis2.circ.gwu.edu/~gprice/listof.htm*), compiled by a librarian at George Washington University, includes links to such lists as the Fortune 500, *National Law Journal's* Top 50 Woman Lawyers, and *Red Herring's* Top 10 Entrepreneurs.

The objective is to know what the existing resources are, decide which ones are useful, and then take stock to see what information you still need and where to find it.

## SOLICITATION TOOLS

Information given to prospective donors about your fund-raising campaign must be well thought out and attractive and should reflect the image of your nonprofit as a professional organization. Be creative with solicitation tools, but be sure that you develop a clear and concise message for prospective donors.

*Solicitation letters*—A direct appeal letter should be produced on your organization's stationery and contain a personalized salutation, persuasive wording, a brief description of need, and a request for the gift amount. When writing a solicitation letter, consider the following:

- Keep the letter to one page.
- Ask for a specific amount.
- Use clear and concise language.
- Use letterhead with the organization's main phone number.
- Address letters to the appropriate person. Never write to "Dear Sir or Madam." Refer to any prior visits and/or telephone conversations.
- Capture the reader's attention in the first sentence. State project objectives in the first paragraph.
- Outline only the highlights of your request. Details may be covered in the proposal itself or discussed at a future meeting.
- Show how your program/project addresses the prospective donor's expressed interests.

*Donor gift card or pledge form*—A gift card or reply form may be appropriate, especially when soliciting small amounts from individuals. This may produce higher results because of the convenience to the donor. (See Exhibit 5–8.)

Most gift cards allow prospective donors the opportunity to choose from several gift levels, or "clubs," commonly ranging from $10,000 for a benefactor down to $25 for a general member or friend.

If yours is an annual campaign, donors should also have the option of renewing their gifts. You might also give donors the option of making a substantially larger pledge over a longer period of time.

*Proposal*—A comprehensive proposal should contain the following:

- Title page
- Table of contents
- Project description
- Statement of need

**Exhibit 5–8**  Sample Gift Card

---

(ORGANIZATION LETTERHEAD)

*PLEASE COMPLETE THIS FORM AND MAIL WITH YOUR CONTRIBUTION IN ENCLOSED ENVELOPE.*

Name _____

Title _____

Affiliation _____

Address _____

Home Phone/Fax _____

E-mail address _____

Amount Enclosed/Charged: $_____

DONORS WHO MAKE CONTRIBUTIONS IN THE FOLLOWING AMOUNTS ARE RECOGNIZED BY INCLUSION IN THE SPECIAL GIVING GROUPS BELOW:

|  |  |
|---|---|
| President's Club | $1,000.00 and over |
| Benefactor | $500.00–999.99 |
| Patron | $100.00–499.99 |
| Contributor | $50.00–99.99 |
| Friend | $25.00–49.99 |

Please charge my contribution to my credit card (circle one):

VISA  MasterCard  American Express

Name on card: _____ Exp. Date: _____

Credit Card Number _____

_____ Please send me more information about including XYZ charity in my estate plan.

The Foundation of (organization) is a nonprofit 501(c) (3) foundation. Contributions are tax-deductible to the fullest extent allowed by law.

---

- Organization capability, philosophy, and history
- Budget; that is, income/expenses
- IRS letter of tax-exempt status
- Other relevant documents

*Support materials*—Annual reports, brochures, press clippings, and any other materials that help sell the project and demonstrate its legitimacy.

## DONOR BENEFITS

Prospective donors want to make a contribution to the betterment of their community in exchange for appropriate recognition by their peers and the public.

Donors often appreciate invitations to exclusive previews, private luncheons, and opportunities to rub elbows with other donors. At gala events they may be seated next to celebrities or people they might admire and would not otherwise get to know. That is enough of a "thank you" for some donors. Corporations that sponsor special events usually stipulate that their names appear on all press releases and printed materials.

Not everyone wants public recognition when he or she makes a donation; respect for a donor's wishes of anonymity must also be honored. It will, obviously, depend on the donor, but a fund-raiser must be sensitive to special requests and be as accommodating as possible. Most of all, let donors know that they are appreciated. This helps pave the way for long-term relationships.

### The Importance of Follow-Up

Always follow up on proposals or significant gift requests to confirm that prospective donors have received your information and to answer any questions they may have. And when gifts come in, promptly follow up with thank-you notes from your organization's leader, preferably within 48 hours. For substantial contributions, a personal call should be made immediately upon receipt of a check or letter of commitment from a donor. Plan a personal visit to the donor if the donation is over a certain established amount; many organizations call donors of $100 or more just to say "Thanks."

## FUND-RAISING CHECKLIST

The following checklist can help you to become a more successful fund-raiser.

- *Clearly identify your organization's mission and financial goals through a well-written Case for Support.* Develop criteria and specific reasons that people or organizations should give to you.

- *Develop a realistic list of prospects* and an action plan to approach these sources each year.

- *Research potential funding sources* and search for contacts to these funders.

- *Remember that individuals* give most of the money in America. Focus your attention on developing relationships with people.

- *Identify and recruit good board members,* those with the capacity to provide wealth, wisdom, and work. They will be the foundation for all your fund-raising efforts.

- *Send personal letters of thanks* immediately after all visits.

- *When a gift arrives, send a thank you promptly.*

- *Be prepared on visits.* When meeting with prospects and donors, know your case, know the prospect, listen for common interests, anticipate objections, and *always* ask for a specific gift amount.

- *Believe in yourself and in the value of your organization.*

- *Remember that your best prospect is the one who contributed to you last.*

## Fund-Raising Resources

- American Association Fund-Raising Counsel Trust for Philanthropy, 25 West 43rd Street, New York, NY 10036; phone: 212-481-6705. Web site: *www.aafrc.org.* Annual survey: "State Laws Regulating Charitable Solicitations."

- Association for Healthcare Philanthropy (AHP), 313 Park Avenue, Suite 400, Falls Church, VA 22046; phone: 703-532-6243. Web site: *www.go-ahp.org*

- The Chronicle of Philanthropy, 1255 23rd Street NW, Suite 775, Washington, D.C. 20037; phone: 202-466-1032. Web site: *www. philanthropy.com*

Domestic and international mail manuals may be obtained by writing to: Superintendent of Documents, Government Printing Office, Washington, D.C. 20402-9371.

- Foundation Center, 79 Fifth Avenue, New York, NY 10003-3076; phone: 800-424-9836; and 1001 Connecticut Avenue NW, Washington, D.C. 20036; phone: 202-331-1401. Web site: *www.fdncenter.org*

- The Grantsmanship Center, P.O. Box 17220, Los Angeles, CA 90017; phone: 213-482-9860. Web site: *www.tgci.com*

- Independent Sector, 1200 18th Street NW, Suite 200, Washington, D.C. 20036; phone: 202-467-6100. Web site: *www.indepsec.org*

- National Catholic Development Conference (NCDC), 86 Front Street, Hempstead, NY 11550-3667; phone: 516-481-6000. Web site: *www.amm.org/ncdc.htm*

- National Center for Nonprofit Boards, 1828 L Street NW, Suite 900, Washington, D.C. 20036-5104; phone: 202-452-6262. Web site: *www.ncnb.org*

- National Society of Fund Raising Executives, 1101 King Street, Suite 700, Alexandria, VA 22314; phone: 703-684-0410. Web site: *www.nsfre.org*

- Society for Nonprofit Organizations, 6314 Odana Road, Suite 1, Madison, WI 53719-1141; phone: 608-274-9777. Web site: *www.danenet.wicip.org/snpo*

# CHAPTER SIX

# Providing Needed Educational Programs

**Preparing a successful educational program requires solid research, planning, and promotion. This chapter will give you an edge in creating high-quality programs that satisfy your audiences and promote the goals of your organization.**

In the nonprofit world, educational programs are often the backbone of an organization's services to its constituencies. Large membership societies comprised of individuals with common interests, charitable organizations that serve the needs of society as a whole, and trade associations that represent whole industries routinely provide educational programs for their members, affiliated groups, and even the general public. Smaller nonprofits, like local civic clubs, churches, and community groups, tend to offer educational programs that are shorter in duration, more narrowly focused, and more likely to produce results that are immediately visible. Although these programs vary in sophistication, approach, and budget, they all have a common denominator: they meet an identifiable need of a target audience.

Not every nonprofit organization is in the education business, or even should be. But if yours is, you have to pay special attention to some basic rules of good marketing, planning, and evaluation. How do you determine the need for education? How do you plan a successful program? What is the most appropriate medium to use? How do you build credibility into your program? Why are promotion and easy access so important? What do you need to understand about your budget? Why is evaluation so important?

This chapter offers answers to these and other important questions that you may ask yourself as you begin to plan your next educational program.

123

## IS YOUR ORGANIZATION IN THE EDUCATION BUSINESS?

Education is a lofty goal, but not all nonprofit organizations are in business to educate. Education is more than just providing information in the form of publications and group meetings. It is the thoughtful effort of assessing the knowledge and skill needs of a specific target audience and designing and executing an effective means of increasing the depth and breadth of that audience's knowledge and skills.

If you are in the education business, your organization's mission and strategic plan should say so. Your allocation of available resources and your program priorities should reflect a clear commitment to providing quality education based on identifiable needs. The lack of such a commitment will cloud your organization's vision of its purpose and direction. It will make it more difficult to allocate the necessary resources to quality education in the face of other interests and priorities.

The importance of having a clear mission statement and strategic plan, and using them to establish program priorities and to allocate available resources, is demonstrated in the following example.

*A statewide charitable community service organization that provided financial help and counseling to needy families decided to develop a series of estate planning seminars for its constituents and the general public. The organization hoped that the seminars would encourage attendees to name the organization in their wills as beneficiaries. Much time, effort, and expense were devoted to developing the content, recruiting presenters, choosing strategically located sites in major population areas, and marketing the program. The result was disappointing. The attendance at most of the seminars was small, and some even had to be cancelled for lack of registrants.*

*From the evaluation data provided by those who did attend, the program content and its presentation were judged to be excellent. In addition, promotion of the program was widespread and repeated through multiple direct mailings and advertisements in the organization's publications. So why did the program fail?*

*The answer is simply that the organization forgot that its mission did not include educating its constituents about a subject (estate planning) that was not directly related to its program mission (providing counseling and financial help to needy families). A random survey of the organization's primary donors revealed that people were suspicious of the organization's motive for offering the seminars and felt that the expenditure of valuable resources in mounting such a program was inappropriate.*

Among nonprofit organizations, there are probably more examples of poorly thought out educational programs than instances of good ones. The adage, "If you're going to do it, do it right the first time," is especially pertinent in the area of education. If your organization is unable or unwilling to allocate the resources necessary to conduct a first-rate educational program, it would be better served if you were to pass up the opportunity.

## HOW DO YOU DETERMINE THE NEED FOR EDUCATION?

*Needs assessment* is the most important prerequisite of a good educational program. It can be as sophisticated or simple, as costly or inexpensive, as the program demands and as your organization's pocketbook allows. An adequate needs assessment does not require an outlay of thousands of dollars and the services of a statistician. It *does* require that you have communicated sufficiently with members of your target audience in the course of day-to-day business to be aware of their perceptions of their own deficiencies in certain knowledge and skill areas. Or, as the staff or volunteer leader in your organization, you might be aware of an emerging issue that will affect your target audience. This issue may form the basis of an educational program. The more you focus your needs assessment efforts, the lower the cost.

### Survey Your Internal Market

The members, donors, clients, and friends of your organization constitute your "internal" market and are closest to the issues that are most important to your organization. What do they perceive as their needs for knowledge and skills? To find out, you can distribute open-ended surveys at group meetings, mail a simple questionnaire with one of your regular periodicals, have informal focus group discussions, poll your board of directors, or conduct a random telephone survey. These are among the most expedient and inexpensive ways of assessing educational needs within your organization.

### Survey Your External Market

Your organization's "external" market can consist of many audiences. The members of other organizations with which you have common interests may be one such audience. A list of prospective donors who may be interested in (but ignorant about) supporting your organization through planned giving may be another. You might even target the general public for your assessment.

Surveying target audiences that are external to your organization requires the use of sophisticated survey instruments and sampling techniques to ensure that the results are statistically valid. Engagement of a professional to advise you is recommended. The cost of designing a valid survey instrument, surveying a large enough population to produce statistically valid results, and the interpretation of those results by a professional can be costly. Remember, however, that the success of your educational program depends heavily on a valid assessment of the needs of your target audience. If your organization is committed to providing quality education, needs assessment is not the place to save money!

## Assess the Competition

A common pitfall in conducting an educational program is to ignore the possibility that some other organization in the community is meeting the same educational need of your target audience. This may be another nonprofit organization, a commercial company, or the local university or community college. An assessment of this competition is vitally important to the success of your own program.

Is your target audience large enough to support more than one educational program? Is the content of your program of higher quality than that of the competition? Is it offered at a time that is more convenient to the target audience? Is your fee lower? Is your faculty more well-known and respected? Have you marketed your program more widely and more aggressively than the competition? These are questions you should ask yourself when comparing your program to the competitions. The bottom line is: If you cannot conduct your program better and with more success than the competition, don't do it at all!

## Analyze the Environment

More often than not, our societal and cultural environments present us with educational opportunities. The political arena, in particular, produces legislation and regulations that lend themselves to interpretation and analysis in the form of educational programs. This is one of the most important sources of exciting and innovative program material. It tends to be on the "cutting edge," causing the target audience to perceive your organization as forward thinking, insightful, and responsive. As you conduct your needs assessment, look around for emerging issues that may affect your target audience.

## HOW DO YOU PLAN A SUCCESSFUL PROGRAM?

Planning and success go hand in hand. Although planning will not guarantee success, the lack of good planning can lead to mediocre results or even outright failure.

Good planning begins with the development of clear program objectives. You can borrow the classic "5 Ws" from journalism to construct an excellent framework for a good program plan.

*WHO?* To whom is your program targeted? How do you reach them efficiently and cost-effectively with information about your program?

*WHAT?* What is the content of your program? Who should be recruited for the faculty, and how? How should the program be structured? Workshop? Seminar? Self-study? Should it be a single presentation or a series?

*WHERE?* What geographical location would be most convenient for attendees? Is there an adequate facility in the area? Is it available at a reasonable price? Is it accessible after normal business hours (for evening sessions)? Is there adequate parking and security?

*WHEN?* When is the best time to schedule your program? Are there competing events and activities? (Avoid scheduling near holidays or summer vacation time.) What is the appropriate length?

*WHY?* This is perhaps the most important question to ask. The answer provides the justification for the program. It identifies the reason that people will be motivated to attend. It ties the program to your organization's mission and strategic plan, and to the results of your needs assessment.

The program plan is your road map. It lists what needs to be accomplished (tasks), when (deadlines), and who will do the work (assignment of responsibility). Make program objectives and associated tasks measurable. This enables you to see to what extent they have been completed. Establish deadlines so you can determine whether your program planning is on schedule and whether interdependent tasks are completed in the necessary sequence. Identify the resources (staff, materials, speakers, etc.) that have to be acquired and assigned to each objective and its associated tasks. Are they readily available? Is the cost reasonable?

It is only through good program planning that you can be assured that all aspects of your program have been thoroughly examined, that everything is in place at the right moment, and that you are prepared for both the expected and the unexpected.

## WHAT IS THE MOST APPROPRIATE MEDIUM TO USE?

In selecting the appropriate medium for your message, remember that true education should increase the depth and breadth of the knowledge and skills of your target audience not merely inform. This requires that you have some means of verifying the acquisition of knowledge and skills once the message has been conveyed. Some media make this relatively simple. Others are designed more for pre-senting information only, rather than for learning.

## Workshops and Seminars

Classroom situations enable the instructor to verify learning through periodic testing and direct interaction with the target audience. They also provide an opportunity for demonstrations, hands-on practice, and other participatory learning techniques. Classroom-style teaching has yet another advantage over most other media: You can convey the latest, most up-to-date informa-tion available during these instructional sessions. One of the pri-mary disadvantages is that to be truly effective, the size of the audience should be relatively small.

Classroom instruction is the most effective way of educating your target audience, but it can be costly. An excellent instructor is critical to the success of the program. Support materials such as textbooks, workbooks, case studies, reading lists, and examinations must be carefully selected or developed to adequately supplement the oral instruction. The preparation time required is extensive, for both the instructor and for you, the sponsoring organization.

The difficulties of this type of educational program are illustrated in the following example. An Oakland, California, affiliate of a major national nonprofit health association sought to develop a heart health education program in elementary schools in the area. With the help of medical professionals, health educators, and teachers, the organization drafted a comprehensive curriculum that included extensive hands-on learning experiences, participatory exercises, and pre- and posttesting to verify learning. Health education stu-dents from a nearby state university were recruited and trained to conduct the program in the classroom in a compact, fast-paced, four-hour module.

*A pilot test of the instructional unit indicated that substantive learning took place on the part of secondary school students who participated in the program. On this basis, plans were made to expand the program in the local school district.*

*Although the program proved to be exemplary from an educational stand-point, and the initial development was relatively inexpensive because of the extensive use of volunteers, the depth and breadth of resources needed to expand the program proved to be beyond the capability of both the organi-zation that developed the program and the local school district. It was sim-ply too expensive to implement.*

If your organization is committed to providing quality education and it has the resources available to do so, classroom instruction should be your first choice. But because programs of this type are usually labor-intensive, it is particularly important to be realistic about the costs and needs of staff.

## Meetings and Conferences

Annual meetings, conferences, seminars, and workshops provide an excellent opportunity to educate a "captive" audience about issues that your organization and its constituents deem important. Typically, annual meetings and conferences offer a combination of general presentations for all participants and smaller breakout sessions for subgroups of the overall audience. This combination provides an opportunity to set the tone of the conference with general presentations on major themes, while using a series of concurrent breakout sessions to address specific issues that relate to these themes.

General presentations and breakout sessions that are part of a conference are more informational than educational. Typically, the number of people in attendance is so large, and the time allotment for each presentation or session so small, that effective learning (and its verification) cannot take place. The advantages are that you already have an interested audience available, and the costs of meeting space and other necessities are more reasonable because the educational program benefits from the economies of scale offered by the entire conference.

If you want to present information about a variety of issues but are not concerned with verification of learning, meetings and conferences should be high on your list of media to consider. (See Chapter 7 for ideas on planning and managing meetings and conferences.)

## Electronic Media

The younger generations have been raised on video games, MTV, *Star Wars* special effects, Walkmans, CDs, personal computers, and other products of the electronic age. The array of technology is dazzling. The production is slick. And the advertising professionals will tell you that use of these media to educate young people is measurable in terms of results. One reason we mention this is that the electronic media are your competition.

If your organization is thinking about producing a videotaped series, a television program, or some other form of educational vehicle using the latest electronic technology, be aware that it will have to compete for attention with the products of the advertising world.

Today, education via electronic media must be as good or better than commercial applications to reach and have any impact on the target audience, especially if your audience is composed of young people. Measuring the results is tricky, at best, and doing it right is expensive.

*The Seattle affiliate of a major national health association decided to educate the general public to the habits of good cardiovascular (heart) health by using a series of television public service announcements (PSAs). The PSAs, developed as part of a research project at Stanford University, had been tested successfully in a small Central California television market. The results showed that, indeed, repeated exposure to the television messages had caused a positive and measurable change in the daily living habits of viewers.*

*The PSAs were reproduced by a Seattle commercial television station (as a public service to the association), with the appropriate "intro" and "extro" using the theme "Enjoy Life with a Healthy Heart." The station then distributed the PSAs to all other television stations in the state of Washington with a request that they be aired in prime time on a regular schedule, over a period of one year.*

*From program logs supplied by the television stations, it appeared that the PSAs were, in fact, receiving significant air time on a regular basis. However, in contrast to the controlled research project done by Stanford University in which the audience was clearly identified and could be reached for evaluation, the extension of the program in Washington state did not lend itself to easy evaluation. To survey the general viewing audiences of each of the state's commercial television stations would have required a significantly large expenditure of the association's funds, and this was not practical. In the end, the association made the assumption that the public service campaign probably had a positive effect on the lifestyles of an unknown number of people, but there were no hard data to substantiate the assumption.*

Given that the use of electronic mass media for educational purposes is an expensive proposition, if you want to reach the masses with a fairly simple message, if your organization has substantial resources to do so, and if you accept that you will not be able to measure the results with precision, electronic mass media can be a powerful and highly visible (to your constituents) means of getting your message across.

Another form of electronic media, the videocassette, lends itself well to use as an educational tool. Although it is still relatively expensive to produce a high-quality program, videocassettes can be used successfully, and often profitably, by organizations to educate their constituents, other special audiences, and the general public.

*A local community services agency that provided job training for people with disabilities decided to take advantage of the business community's growing interest in the Americans with Disabilities Act (ADA).*

*With the help of its clients and the human resources departments of a few local companies, the agency developed a 15-minute videotape that illustrated, through actual case studies and testimonials, why hiring and accommodating people with disabilities is a sound business investment for employers.*

*A large corporation provided funding to duplicate and distribute the videotape to local businesses and other community service agencies serving people with disabilities.*

*In the end, the agency had served an important need of its clients (people with disabilities), had encouraged a commitment by the local business community to the spirit of the ADA, and had done it all at little cost.*

## Internet

What began as an evolution of the application of electronic technology to education and learning has turned into a revolution, thanks to the World Wide Web on the Internet. The Web, as it is commonly called, has not only changed the way information is conveyed to the public, it has dramatically increased the depth and breadth of the information that is available. The power of the Web has captured the attention of educators worldwide and has spawned a whole new way of thinking about how people learn.

One of the primary advantages of the Web as an educational tool is that the younger generations are comfortable with it. They have grown up in the electronic age, and computer technology is a natural part of their daily life. The Web also appeals to their tendency to be visually oriented and interactive in their learning. They see the Web as just another step in the evolution (or revolution) of the information age in which they have been brought up.

Thanks to the Web, learning is no longer confined to the classroom or tied to the calendar or clock, nor is it necessarily the province of a recognized "educational" institution. Learning can now occur at any place and at any time, at the convenience of both the student and the teacher. A typical scenario might be as follows:

*Using the Web, a member of your organization (or of the public) scans a list of courses offered by your nonprofit. He or she registers for a course on-line and pays the required fee using a credit card, again on-line. Registration is confirmed for the student in an e-mail message via the Web. The organization's Web site also provides an e-mail message window for the student to use in asking the instructor about the content of the course. Reference*

*materials for the course are made available on the Web, including "hot"
links to other Web sites that contain information pertinent to the course content. The instructor posts lecture material on the Web, giving students the
flexibility of accessing the text and graphics at their leisure. An ongoing,
interactive discussion among the students and their instructor takes place in
a Web-based chat room. When a student feels that he or she has mastered
the content of the course, an examination can be taken on-line and scores
received returned to the student instantaneously.*

Thanks to the rapid evolution of the Web, the benefits of using
these new technologies to provide a learning environment for an
organization's members are highly tangible. An entire body of
knowledge on nearly any topic is available and accessible 24 hours a
day, instantly. Interaction with other people who have an interest in
the same subject can also occur at any time. The Web has evolved
from a curiosity to a necessity. As our society becomes more global,
our members will need new skills and knowledge to function effectively. The Web empowers them to have greater control over their
learning so they can become more active participants in the larger
world.

## Publications and Printed Materials

Printed materials are at the core of educational programs provided
by most nonprofit organizations. From the local church bulletin to
the annual conference proceedings of a national medical professional society, the printed page has carried the burden of informing
audiences large and small within the area of education.

With publications, you have the ability to treat a topic compre-
hensively. Unlike electronic media, printed publications are not con-
strained by time. You can also use as many pages as you want to
convey your message, provided that the total number of pages fits
within the overall design and construct of your publication. Print
materials are also lasting. Your publication may become a reference
piece on a library shelf.

Publications can be the least expensive medium to use in informing your target audience about certain issues or subjects. However,
they can also be the most *unreliable* in terms of assessing results.
When a brochure, booklet, journal, newsletter, or other publication
leaves your organization's office, you often have no way to be certain
that it is delivered to the recipient, that it is read, or, most important,
whether the information has any impact on the reader.

Publications serve a useful purpose as informational vehicles. But
to be effective tools for education, they must be incorporated into a

more structured educational environment, such as a workshop or seminar, as support or reference materials. They may also take the form of self-study materials, incorporating a testing mechanism that ensures verification of learning.

If you are interested in providing information inexpensively to a large number of people, consider using publications or other printed materials.

## HOW DO YOU BUILD CREDIBILITY INTO YOUR PROGRAM?

Like value, credibility is not an absolute condition. It is more perception than substance. Is your seminar speaker a well-known and respected peer or colleague of audience members? If so, you have probably increased the credibility of your program. Is the author of your organization's new instructional manual unknown in the industry? If so, doubt about the validity of the information presented may linger in the minds of readers.

This is not to say that people outside your organization's sphere of influence cannot do a top-notch job. Thousands of people make their living on the professional speaking circuit, and they come with a long list of credentials and references that you can easily check to increase your comfort. Even so, they are unknown quantities to you and your program's audience, and they pose a risk in terms of the credibility of your program.

The important thing to remember is to check out speakers thoroughly. Talk to people who were responsible for scheduling them for their own organizations. Ask for a videotape of their presentation. (Any professional speaker worth considering has a videotape to lend.) Do everything you can to find out beforehand whether a speaker can do the job you expect and give your program credibility.

### What Else Affects the Credibility of Your Program?

Organization is among the key factors affecting the credibility of your program. Have potential attendees received notice of your program well enough in advance to enable them to schedule it along with other personal and business commitments? Have you offered your program at a date, time, and location that are convenient for your potential audience? Are the program sessions of the right length? People with small children and elderly attendees will want an early start and a program length in the range of one to two hours. Does the price make sense, given what the attendees will receive in return? People are very adept at determining the value they get for the price they pay.

Finally, one of the most effective ways to build credibility into your program is to provide recognition within your organization by awarding *continuing education units* (CEUs). Recognition through obtaining CEUs is becoming more and more important, especially in fields where attendees need CEUs to track their professional or skills development or to maintain professional certification or licensure.

If your program is based on a needs assessment of your potential audience, identifies learning outcomes for participants, includes content and instructional objectives appropriate for the learning outcomes, is presented by qualified instructors, and is evaluated by those participating in the program, your organization may qualify for awarding CEUs. To assess your organization's qualifications for awarding CEUs, contact a local college or university, an association that represents the professional interests of your audience, or the founder and caretaker of the CEU, the International Association for Continuing Education and Training (IACET) in Washington, D.C.

Consider the following example:

*"Arthritis Days" is a seminar held each year by a local medical foundation. Rheumatologists, internists, general practitioners, physical therapists, occupational therapists, and other medical professionals from across the state attend this highly popular conference. Although the program is local in nature, the foundation arranges for persons attending the education program to receive CEUs from their own professional organizations, such as the state medical society and the physical therapy and occupational therapy associations.*

If your educational program is more informational in content and appeals to a broader, nontechnical or nonprofessional audience, CEUs are not nearly as important as giving recognition to those who participate. A signed certificate of completion, notice in the organization's newsletter or bulletin, or an article in the local newspaper goes a long way toward building credibility for your program.

Credibility can make or break an educational program. It can also affect your organization's ability to mount an effective educational effort in the future. Ensure the short- and long-term success of your educational programs by doing everything you can to enhance their credibility in the eyes of your potential audiences.

## WHY ARE PROMOTION AND EASY ACCESS SO IMPORTANT?

The best-planned education program can fail miserably if people do not know about it. Although this sounds like common sense, educational programs are often inadequately promoted by nonprofit organizations that assume if a program is good, the audience will find out about it.

Earlier in this chapter we discussed the importance of identifying the "target audience" of your program. There are two important reasons for being able to identify this group. First, you must know who they are and what is important to them (needs). Second, you must be able to reach them with information about how their needs can be fulfilled (promotion).

## Promotion

Promotion comes in three forms. First, there is paid (or free, public service) *advertising* in the media. This includes display advertising in your own publications, in those of other nonprofits, companies, and community agencies, and in your local newspaper.

Advertising can also take the form of radio and television ads or public service announcements, outdoor display (billboard) advertising, electronic reader boards, or bus cards. But purchasing broadcast air time can be expensive unless you find a creative way to get your message across at someone else's expense.

*A local children's museum in Denver mounted an effective broadcast promotion campaign at no cost. To advertise its annual "Parenting Fair," an event that included an exhibition of products, services, and educational lectures for new and expectant parents, the museum persuaded a popular family restaurant to put a tag line about the fair at the end of one of its radio commercials. The restaurant benefited from its association with the museum, and the museum received some excellent promotion for its education program.*

A second form of promotion is the category of *special events*. These are promotional activities that "piggyback" or make use of an existing vehicle that targets large numbers of people. Perhaps a local radio station is willing to provide free transportation to your educational workshop for the first three people who call in to its popular talk show each day. Or maybe you can strike a deal with the publisher of a national trade or industry journal so that everyone who registers for your educational program will receive a free six-month subscription to the publication.

The third form is *direct mail.* This is the most flexible form because it can be as simple or as sophisticated as you desire, and as inexpensive or expensive as your budget allows. In any case, direct mail can

be one of the most effective ways of promoting your education program. If your organization is a local community group, sending a
one-page, folded self-mailer to your prospective donors may suffice
nicely. If you are targeting the membership of large national organizations, the general public, or others who will be making a significant
commitment of time or resources to attend, you may want to develop
a more professional and eye-catching brochure to interest recipients
and cause them to read and respond positively to your message.

When designing your promotional message, regardless of its form,
there are a few basic concepts to keep in mind:

*Be hard hitting, brief, and clear* in your message. Use action words
that have "punch." Think visual. Use graphics. Remember, you are
competing with the razzle-dazzle of commercial television, Madison
Avenue advertising, and a host of other strong stimuli in today's
society.

*Repeat, repeat, and repeat again!* This is one of the basic tenets of successful advertising. Your message will compete with thousands of
other messages for the attention of your target audience. You will
have to drive your message home again and again if it is to stand out
among those of your competitors.

*Promote early and often.* People in today's society are very busy.
Many families consist of two working parents who have community
and business activities outside normal working hours, young children who must be transported to and from day-care, and teenagers
whose extracurricular activities at school demand parental attention.
Members of professional societies have a wide array of educational
programs offered to them by universities or by other nonprofit
organizations. Calendars are locked in with commitments months in
advance.

Get the message about your education program to your target
audience as early as possible, before their family calendars are full.
And, as discussed earlier, send your message more than once.
Remember that you are competing with an extraordinary array of
messages that your audience has to receive, process, and act on daily.

## Easy Access

Giving your potential audience easy access to your program means
that the price is right and that you make the registration process simple and easy to use.

*Pricing* your educational program at the proper level is not an art
or a science. It is plain common sense. First, you probably want the
program to be, at the very least, self-supporting (to pay for itself).
If so, your starting point for pricing is the program's total cost, less

any sponsorship or other outside underwriting, divided by a realistic estimate of the number of customers. Now compare the resulting price with those of similar educational programs, especially those in your geographical area. Is your price substantially higher? If so, ask yourself whether the perceived value of your program justifies the higher price. If not, you should consider reducing your overall cost so you can lower the price, or plan to incur a loss. If, on the other hand, your price is substantially lower than the prices of comparable programs, you should consider adding a margin that will result in a net profit to your organization. In this event, your educational program becomes, fortunately, part of your fund-raising activity. Taxes on the net profit will be due only if the program is deemed to be "unrelated" business activity by the Internal Revenue Service.

Some organizations have a tendency to offer their educational programs at a price well below that of the competition. They do this as a community service and as a means of making the program available to a larger number of people who might otherwise not be able to afford it. But too often the organization is surprised when few people turn out for this low-priced program.

What we sometimes fail to remember is the concept of perceived value. How you price your product often reflects the value people place on that product. Thus, if your educational program is priced too low, people may question whether it is worth their while to pay for it or to attend.

Recover your costs, compare your pricing in the marketplace, and look at price from the standpoint of perceived value in the eyes of your potential audience. But most of all, use plain common sense.

The right price goes a long way in making your educational program accessible to its potential audience. But pricing is only half the challenge. You must also make it *simple and easy* for a person to sign up for the program, pay the fee, and receive additional information. Although this may sound elementary, the lack of attention to details like these can produce significant barriers to the success of your educational program.

Your promotion materials should include the necessary information to enable a potential attendee to respond:

- Title and description of the program, and to whom it is targeted
- Date, time, and location
- Price
- How to register and get additional information (address, telephone number, etc.)

The registration vehicle that is easiest and simplest to use is a 24-hour, toll-free telephone number that people can use to give their names and addresses and to charge the registration fee to a credit card such as MasterCard or Visa. Typically, this form of registration is used when the potential market for the educational program is relatively large and scattered geographically, or when the program is targeted to people unaffiliated with your organization. Although telephone registration is, by far, the easiest method for the target audience, from the standpoint of the sponsoring organization it may also be the most expensive. A careful study of the cost versus benefit of using telephone registration should be done before a decision is made to proceed.

Membership organizations now frequently offer registration through their Internet Web site. If your membership or target audience is "on-line" and comfortable with using the Internet, this can be the most efficient way to handle registrations. Secure handling of credit card registrations is essential.

A printed registration form is commonly used for educational programs that do not rely on telephone or Internet registration. The form asks for name, address, phone, choice of program dates or elements (if the program is a series or if it has multiple parts that registrants can sign up for separately), the dollar amount enclosed, and method of payment. A more comprehensive form, like that for a multiday educational conference, may have numerous options from which to choose and also ask for additional information about the registrant, such as the following:

- Member of your organization?
- Name preferred on name badge?
- Any special needs (dietary, access for persons with disabilities, etc.)?
- First-time attendee?
- Demographics such as age, educational level, vocation, cultural and recreational interests, etc.
- Certified through your (or another organization's) professional certification program?

The important things to remember when designing a registration form are:

- Ask only for information you plan to use.
- Arrange information on the form in a logical order.
- Leave adequate room for the registrant to enter information.

- Indicate clearly where the completed form should be mailed, and by what deadline date.

- Provide a telephone number (and hours when it is staffed) for questions and additional information.

- Keep it simple.

## WHAT DO YOU NEED TO UNDERSTAND ABOUT YOUR BUDGET?

Earlier in this chapter we discussed the need to price your program in the marketplace by looking at the competition and by determining what the perceived value of your program is in the eyes of your audience. We also encouraged you to budget to at least break even financially or, ideally, to use educational programs to raise funds. This is where a detailed and accurate budget for your program can be an important tool.

Program revenues should not be considered in a vacuum but, rather, as part of an overall budget that includes a breakdown of all direct and indirect expenses that can be attributed to your educational program. *Direct expenses* are those costs of goods and services that are purchased specifically for use in planning and implementing the program. These expenses include such things as printing services, postage, telephone calls (especially long distance), supplies, speaker fees, travel and lodging, time of staff dedicated to the educational program, and meeting site charges for room rental, food and beverages, audiovisual equipment, and any special logistical needs.

*Indirect expenses* are generally referred to as overhead or management and general costs. These expenses are simply the basic costs of doing business, of keeping your organization's doors open. Examples of indirect or overhead costs are accounting, salaries and benefits of administrative staff and the executive director, occupancy (office rent, utilities, and maintenance), insurance, legal fees, and equipment. These costs are allocated, on a prorated basis, to all of your nonadministrative activities. Indirect costs should be allocated in a logical and consistent manner, such as via a formula based on the ratio of nonadministrative staff time spent on the educational program to all nonadministrative staff time. If uncertain about a meaningful allocation, you may wish to consult with the outside accounting firm that performs your annual audit to seek its advice about your methodology. Chapter 12 of this book, which details how to set up a meaningful chart of accounts, should also help.

Sometimes there is a tendency to budget only direct costs for an educational program. Certainly, this places less pressure on your budget. But it also gives you an inaccurate picture, one that understates the real costs of planning and implementing the program. Having an accurate budget is especially important when you decide to evaluate the program on the basis of cost versus benefit.

Once you have developed a realistic and accurate budget, the next step is to undertake a *break-even analysis,* which is simply a determination of how many paid attendees you need for your program in order to cover its fixed costs.

*Fixed costs* are expenses incurred that do not vary with the number of attendees. Generally, these are the costs of planning and promoting your educational program, such as travel and meeting expenses for your program planning committee, the costs of printing and mailing of promotional and registration materials, advertising, telephone calls, and preparing and mailing correspondence. They may also include nonrefundable deposits for meeting room rental, food and beverage guarantees, audiovisual equipment rental, and certain speaker fees and travel expenses. These are "up-front" or committed expenses that will not vary with the number of attendees.

*Variable, or nonfixed, costs* are those expenses that are incurred only if someone attends your program. These typically include the costs of registration, confirmation of the registration, name badge, meals, and handout materials. If a person does not attend the program, you will not incur these costs for that person.

To calculate the *break-even point* for your educational program, first subtract the per-person variable cost from the registration fee. Then take the resulting figure and divide it into the total fixed cost. This will give you the number of paid attendees you will need in order to cover your fixed costs.

Break-even analysis can be very useful in determining "go" or "no go" in a marginal program. If you know the minimum number of attendees you need to break even, and you do not have this number of registrants by a certain date, you have the opportunity of doing some last-minute promotion (perhaps via telephone) to increase the number of registrants. You also have the option of cancelling the program and minimizing your out-of-pocket costs by not having to pay speaker travel expenses and full fees, audiovisual charges, and, possibly, some other fixed costs.

Exhibit 6–1 is a simple example of the break-even analysis for a small workshop conducted by a nonprofit's volunteers.

The registration fee is $45.00 per person. By subtracting the variable cost of $20.00, you end up with a $25.00 contribution per person toward the fixed costs of your workshop. Dividing the total fixed costs of $1,025.00 by $25.00 gives you 41 paid attendees needed to cover your fixed costs.

**Exhibit 6–1**   Sample Break-Even Analysis

| | |
|---|---:|
| Fixed Costs: | |
| Print promotional fliers and envelopes | $  250.00 |
| Bulk rate postage | 150.00 |
| Telephone calls | 25.00 |
| Meeting room rental | 100.00 |
| Staff time | 500.00 |
| Total Fixed Costs | $1,025.00 |
| Variable Costs: | |
| Handout materials (per person) | $      4.00 |
| Box lunch (per person) | 10.00 |
| Morning and afternoon coffee breaks (per person) | 6.00 |
| Total Variable Costs | $    20.00 |

Larger organizations should calculate break-even points for educational programs, seminars, and even conventions in much the same way.

## WHY IS PROGRAM EVALUATION IMPORTANT?

The process of evaluation lets you determine whether, or to what extent, you met the objectives set forth in your program plan. This, in turn, gives valuable information that you can use in planning future educational programs. In order to be a viable tool, evaluation must meet the following conditions:

- It must be done immediately, while the experience is fresh in the minds of the audience.
- The questionnaire (or other evaluation vehicle) should be simple and easy to use, and ask only what you need to know.
- The questionnaire should be designed so that tabulation of the responses can take place quickly and inexpensively.

There are many different vehicles for evaluating an educational program. The questionnaire is probably the most common but suffers from the inherent drawback of incorporating the biases of the respondent. Formal testing is apt to produce less biased data, but it also is more expensive. Postprogram telephone surveys, focus groups, and other more personal kinds of data gathering also can be used.

Regardless of the type of evaluation vehicle you choose, design it around your program objectives and the needs of your audience, as indicated in your preprogram needs assessment. By doing so, you can accurately measure the success of the educational program against your original assumptions. As you design the questions, also think in terms of the information you want as a program planner, such as the following:

- Did the program's promotional materials accurately reflect the content of the program?
- Was the presenter's style appropriate for the program content?
- Was the room setup comfortable and conducive to learning?
- How far did you have to travel to attend the program?
- What topics would you like covered in future programs?

The program evaluation also provides an opportunity to "test the waters" for new ideas about program content, format, and geographical location. In addition, you can collect specific demographic information about your attendees that may be useful in developing future educational programs.

Your evaluation tool also should be designed with the total expected attendance in mind. If the education program draws a relatively small number of individuals, the evaluation questionnaire can be somewhat longer and can include more open-ended (subjective) questions. If, however, you have hundreds of attendees at your program, you should try to make the evaluation questionnaire as brief as possible (but still solicit the data you consider to be important) and limit the use of open-ended questions. Large numbers of subjective responses are very difficult to tabulate into a meaningful summary. They also drastically slow the tabulation process and drive up its cost.

In forming objective questions, stay away from those with "yes" and "no" answers and instead use those with multiple-choice answers and answers that are variable (on a scale of 1 to 5, best to worst, strongly agree to strongly disagree, etc.). These types of questions give you answers that are easier to tabulate and analyze and are more statistically valid.

Overall, a good evaluation mechanism will tell you to what extent the attendees felt their needs were addressed by your educational program, and whether your own program objectives were met. Along with an accurate comparison of the program's actual revenues and expenses to the budgeted amounts, you should have adequate data to judge the success of your educational program and to plan for future programs.

One last thing to remember is that putting the needs of your customers (target audience) first is expected in today's society. They are paying for something of value, and it is your organization's responsibility to deliver that value, requiring only minimum effort on the part of the customer. This is just good, basic customer service and is often the key to "hooking" a person to support your organization or, at the very least, to bring participants back for a future educational program.

Good customer service also means that you subscribe to the notion that the customer is always right. Consider standing behind your educational product with a no-questions-asked, money-back guarantee. Remember, a good experience for your target audience sets the scene for positive referrals and continued support. In contrast, bad news travels fast and can undermine the success of your organization's future programs—educational and otherwise—in pursuit of your mission.

## CHECKLIST FOR EFFECTIVE EDUCATION PROGRAMS

Determine the need for education:

- ☐ Survey your internal market.
- ☐ Survey your external market.
- ☐ Assess the competition.
- ☐ Analyze the environment.

Develop a plan:

- ☐ Identify your target audience.
- ☐ Determine the content of your program.
- ☐ Select a facility or site.
- ☐ Determine the best time to schedule your program.
- ☐ Develop a list of reasons that people should attend.
- ☐ List what needs to be accomplished (tasks).
- ☐ Establish when the tasks need to be completed (deadlines).
- ☐ Draft specific objectives and make them measurable.
- ☐ Identify resources (staff, materials, etc.) needed to achieve the program's objectives and complete the tasks.

Choose the most appropriate medium to use:

- ☐ Workshops and seminars?
- ☐ Meetings and conferences?
- ☐ Electronic media (including the Internet)?
- ☐ Publications and printed materials?

**Build credibility into your program:**

- ☐ Select qualified speakers and presenters.
- ☐ Organize the program's elements well and plan for the unexpected.
- ☐ Ensure that date, time, site location, length of program, and registration process are convenient for the target audience.
- ☐ Price the program so it is competitive with similar programs.
- ☐ Arrange to grant continuing education units, if appropriate.

**Promote the program and provide easy access:**

- ☐ Choose the right promotional medium (advertising, special events, direct mail, etc.).
- ☐ Design your message to be hard-hitting, brief, and clear.
- ☐ Repeat your message again, again, and again.
- ☐ Schedule your promotion early and often.
- ☐ In addition to pricing the program competitively, encourage early payment by giving an "early bird" discount and by accepting major credit cards.
- ☐ Make registration simple and easy by using a printed registration form and offering telephone and Internet registration.
- ☐ Stand behind your product by offering a money-back guarantee.

**Develop a budget:**

- ☐ Calculate direct and indirect expenses.
- ☐ Calculate fixed and variable costs.
- ☐ Perform a break-even analysis.

**Plan your program evaluation mechanism:**

- ☐ Provide for immediate feedback at the program site.
- ☐ Make the evaluation form simple and easy to use.
- ☐ Design the evaluation form so that tabulation is quick and inexpensive.

# CHAPTER SEVEN

# Making Your Meetings Work—For You and Your Members

**With the right plan and careful execution, you can conduct a meeting that meets your objectives, enhances your organization's reputation, and even raises money. This chapter provides step-by-step guidance on developing the overall plan and tracking the details of a successful meeting.**

Skilled executives of nonprofits put as much effort into meeting management as into any other operational function. Whether the meeting is small—say, a critical gathering of the executive committee—or as large as an annual membership meeting, attention to detail and planning are essential.

Americans attend meetings. They want to participate, to contribute, to know what's going on, to network, to learn, or perhaps simply to not be left out. Planners must know the needs and expectations of their audience.

Meetings are a tool for sharing information, generating ideas, hearing a presentation, planning for the future, and getting together with colleagues. The substance of a meeting must reflect your organization's goals and objectives, as well as address current concerns and challenges.

Participation is a key to the attendees' feeling good about a meeting. Think of times when you have felt best about a meeting you have attended. It's undoubtedly been when you have spoken up, asked questions, and had your opinions count. Receiving a report on operations may be important, but debating a future course of action is much more satisfying. In meetings large and small, structuring the program or agenda to increase discussion is an art form practiced by the most successful.

Still, every meeting planner knows that it's the details that can kill you. Room size, seating arrangements, lighting, food, efficiencies, and comforts do make a difference.

A successful meeting is a product of good planning. Regardless of the type of meeting, its location, or its size, you will need to organize the function piece by piece as you would an elaborate puzzle, all the time paying close attention to what may seem to be an endless chain of details. Your task is to create a meeting or event that runs without a hitch and meets its goals. It is probably no exaggeration to say that everyone has sat through a meeting that had little coherence, little educational value, and no uplifting results. With the right plan, you can create a meeting that achieves your objectives, enhances your organization's reputation, and produces a surplus of income over expenses.

Meetings have two basic components: the content of the meeting and the administration of the meeting. The content is the substance of the meeting, which includes speakers, panels, the venue, and the basic flow and structure of the event.

Responsibility for content rests with the executive director, usually working in close coordination with the elected president or a meeting committee from the membership or the board of directors.

The administration of the meeting is the oversight component. Ideally, this responsibility should be assigned to an experienced meetings manager. The task will be both anticipatory and reactive, to meet the expectations and needs of the meeting attendees. Regardless of how much planning effort has been expended, there are virtually no meetings that will proceed from the opening event through adjournment without requiring some tactical response to events.

In this chapter we look at the steps to be taken in planning a typical meeting of 300 to 500 people. The same basic process applies to smaller meetings (scaled back perhaps) and can be extended to organizing even the largest of meetings.

## DESIGNING YOUR MEETING

There are three steps to consider in designing a meeting.

1. Consider your purpose and your audience: who they are, why are they meeting at this time, what type of information they are seeking, what location is preferable, why this conference will be valuable to them personally, and what kind of social events are appropriate. Is continuing education in

demand? Is raising awareness of a specific issue or issues the goal? Is the principal purpose to promote the organization and its activities to present members or to future supporters? If you carefully determine these details and spell out exactly what it is that your audience will be able to take away from the meeting (both tangible and intangible), you will be well on your way to a marketable and successful event.

2. Set the specific framework for your meeting. What is the desired outcome of the meeting for the organization? What are the expectations of those who will attend? How will the meeting be structured to ensure that those expectations are met? Participants must leave the meeting feeling it was worth their while. Know the demographics, education, career level, and so on, of the expected audience.

   Have the logistics taken into account the needs of potential attendees? Ease of transportation and timing, so that there are no conflicting events, holidays, or competing meetings, is a priority.

   It is important to understand clearly all of this information and how it interrelates. This understanding will allow you to select the appropriate site, build a functional schedule of events, present relevant speakers, attract the desired audience, and add to their understanding of the subjects discussed.

3. Designate and empower the meeting's coordinator. The role of this person is analogous to that of a symphony conductor, the planning committee's to that of the composer; the coordinator must be the leader of the actual performance, with all the details firmly in mind and on paper.

Conventions, trade shows, banquets, or any larger meeting will benefit from the services of a professional meeting planner. Often, the savings a professional can achieve will more than make up the professional's cost.

Although the following discussion pertains mainly to conference and convention planning, many elements are essential for other kinds of meetings as well.

## MEETING SCHEDULE

If planning a new meeting, look at those run by other organizations and those you have attended in the past. If, as is often the case, you are building from the model of a previous meeting, analyze what worked well and what did not. The form may be dictated by content, number of days, or how the sessions fit together. Develop a working grid or chart representing the time and length of sessions; such a chart can quickly demonstrate how events fit together and minimize conflicts, particularly if the meeting breaks into concurrent sessions. Do not overlook adequate time for breaks, lunch, and the time it takes to move from session to session. Even smaller, less complicated meetings require a schedule. Blocks of free time should also be built into most schedules.

Regardless of length, a meeting theme or key issue should run consistently throughout the event (although a concurrent session or workshop may address other issues or include a separate value-added topic). In planning a conference, consider a general session of as much as one hour to open the event, during which the keynote speaker will set the tone for the entire conference. The general session is also a chance for your organization's officials to make announcements about the organization, to indicate changes in the schedule, and to give a brief overview of what the time spent at the event will deliver to the audience.

In a similar vein, the closing session should end the conference on a positive note. If placed at the end of the conference—after all seminars and breakout sessions—and featuring a speaker of some import, the closing session may prompt people to stay through the final day. If final sessions are sparsely attended, that lesson should be remembered for next year's conference planning.

## SPECIAL EVENTS

Special events can offer opportunities to share an experience or add a social event to a meeting. In some cases, special events can draw attendance to the conference. They must, however, be thought of in relationship to the overall meeting. Consider how the special event will meet the overall event objectives, sponsor(s) goals, audience expectations, budget parameters, and fit the locale. Special events can run the gamut from a special opening ceremony to a luncheon banquet with a celebrity speaker, a breakfast session, a night of entertainment, a night on the town, or a 10K run. Other possibilities are recognition, by the mayor or other official, of significant accomplishments of your members or the announcement of the formation of a special task force.

When beginning to plan the special event, consider all possibilities. Be creative. The best special events are those that engage, celebrate, create connections, and provide for dialogue among attendees. Search for ways to break the ice, to involve participants, and to create a memorable environment. Detail each component of the event as carefully as you detailed the overall meeting schedule. Tap into all available resources of both the facility you are booking and the community.

## Choosing Speakers

After the design of the conference is set, potential speakers can be chosen and contacted. Speakers and panelists are often recommended by members of your organization or by other community members. It is important for the coordinator to make sure that people recommending speakers are well informed about the theme and the goals of the meeting and how the session fits the objectives. A poor speaker can put a damper on any meeting. Many organizations do not permit a speaker to be engaged unless one of the key board or planning team members has actually heard a presentation by that speaker. You can also increase your comfort level by checking references, listening to tapes of previous engagements, or conducting interviews with potential speakers.

The keynote speaker sets the tone for the meeting and poses specific questions for which participants should seek answers during the rest of the meeting. The opening ceremony should crystallize in the attendees' minds their reasons for attending the conference and help them to shape their personal plans of action to reap the greatest benefits.

Speakers need to know:

- The audience profile and the audience expectations, as well as the potential size of the audience.

- The key points you expect to be covered in the presentation. What is really essential for your audience to get? You may even suggest some points for your speaker to incorporate.

- The total time on stage and how much time is reserved for questions and discussion. This question time is often the most valuable and highly rated by audiences. Canned presentations are one thing, but the opportunity to ask questions of an expert on a particular issue is almost always well received. Always "seed" a couple of questions to get this period started smoothly.

- What kind of audiovisual support will the speaker need? Will he or she stand at the podium or walk around a lot? (Encourage movement; obtain wireless microphones.)

- What are the fee/honorarium, travel, accommodation requirements, and what stipulations are there with regard to taping sessions? Be sure to clarify all expenses to avoid awkward situations later.

Similar attention should be given to panelists and moderators. For small meetings, a designated facilitator can guide the participants to accomplish their task in the time allowed.

All of the information specified in the preceding list should be captured and confirmed in writing to all parties involved, especially the speakers. Be sure to confirm with the speaker the date, day, length, and location of the presentation, as well as any fees that were discussed, even if all the other questions have not been answered. A speaker should want to spend time in this discussion time with you to ensure all objectives are met. It also helps to confirm to the speaker your planning objectives/theme for the event.

Early confirmation of speakers allows your organization to use the identities of the speakers in your marketing campaign; "name" speakers can draw extra attendees. Sometimes early confirmation is not possible, particularly with politicians who are unable to predict whether they will be free. Be aware that political speakers sometimes cancel their appearances. You will have to consider backups, just in case.

If a controversial figure is chosen to speak, the heads of the organization should be notified before the contract is signed. This could preclude any embarrassment to the sponsor; however, some organizations may value a lively discussion. Keynote speakers are generally paid an honorarium of $1,000 to $10,000, depending on the size and type of the meeting (superstars, such as network newscasters or other celebrities, are much more expensive). The honorarium for speakers for smaller sessions should be the same across the board, and lower than for a keynote speaker. Sometimes reimbursement of travel, hotel expenses, and free admission to the conference is the fee. Contracts or letters confirming arrangements should be precise on both fees and expenses.

Speaker contracts may include the following:

- Permission to release biography and photograph of the speaker to potential attendees and the press.
- Permission for the organization to tape the session.
- Request for copies of presentation, if in written form.
- Needs for special equipment.
- Arrangements for room and transportation (if rooms are billed directly to your organization, the hotel should understand that incidentals, such as long distance telephone, are not included).
- Date of final confirmation.
- Any special security arrangements.
- Contracts with an entertainer or talent agent should put in writing the agreement as to dates, fees, travel, accommodations, commis-

sions, substitutions, staff costs, equipment costs, and stipulations concerning cancellation.

## Site Selection

At first glance, the selection of a site may seem easy. It may appear as simple as asking: What is the site at which members of the organization feel comfortable? Is there an unusual site that may be available? Which city would people in the organization like to visit? But finding the right site is not a simple task. It must take into consideration the facilities available in a given place, the kind of atmosphere desired, the housing situation, the cultural and/or sports activities possible, and the tours possible from the site before, during, and/or after the conference. And, of course, the projected number of attendees will determine the size of facilities needed. Check, too, the availability dates of the facilities and consider weather conditions at the site for the time of year you will be there.

The choice of housing—for a convention, conference, or any meeting drawing attendees from out of town—can depend on its cost, its location, its accessibility to physically handicapped guests, and its availability at the time you need it. Also consider the physical layout of the facility for your desired traffic flow and the types of rooms (both sleeping and meeting) to be sure you can meet your objectives.

The first contact at a hotel is usually its sales or convention services department. The variety of meeting rooms available is very important. For example, a meeting of 30 people is best facilitated in a small meeting room and with a hollow square or a U-shape configuration (in which long tables are set in either a U or a box shape). The opening session of a conference for 2,000 persons requires a large, auditorium-style room. Workshops may need tables set up in classroom style, so each participant has a hard surface on which to write. If you are unsure as to the expected numbers, the utilization of space through use of airwalls (walls that can be pulled open or closed to create rooms of different sizes) is a critical discussion between you and the facility manager. Consider how many concurrent sessions you will have and whether there are enough rooms available. Find out how soundproof (*or not*) the walls are and what might be happening in the foyer outside the session space (light, sound, etc.). Traffic flow during the conference should be taken into consideration; concurrent sessions may cause problems. Know the number of rooms and the floor plan of the location. (See the suggested checklist for site selection at the end of this chapter.)

Keep in mind that flexibility in timing can add greatly to your negotiating strength with hotels and other facilities. Published rates should be only a starting point for your discussion.

In addition to hotels, there are many other places to consider as potential sites: restaurants, banquet halls, universities, convention centers, country clubs, theaters, museums, and resorts.

When a particular site or event has been successful, do not repeat that event or presentation at a similar meeting of the same attendees too soon after that success. Although it may be tempting to repeat a successful event, it may not work the second time and may diminish the luster of the original event.

*A nonprofit organization in Washington dedicated to helping local courts deal with rising caseloads held its 10th annual meeting and reception in a reserved room at the U.S. Supreme Court. The site ensured a good turnout of judges from the local superior and district courts and of practicing attorneys, who were rewarded when a Supreme Court justice welcomed attendees and spoke briefly on the role of juries. But, wisely not repeating itself, the next year the organization held its meeting at a downtown site closer to the local courts, featuring a presentation by a local city leader.*

## BUDGETING A MEETING

Which comes first, the chicken or the egg? Projected income or expenses? The objective of your meeting will dictate this philosophy, but whatever it is beware of the temptation to overestimate income and underestimate expenses. Be realistic, cautious, and conservative. It is easy to overlook hidden costs (liability insurance, music licensing fees, taxes and gratuities, the cost of room rental penalty fees, if negotiated food and beverage or sleeping room usage is not realized).

There are, of course, differences between developing a budget for a one-day meeting or educational seminar and developing one for a large convention with exhibits. Exhibits at smaller meetings are most likely to be educational in orientation and usually do not generate significant revenues. Consider inexpensive tabletop displays as a starting point if your group represents a potential market. When well planned and established, an exhibition can bring in a substantial amount of money for an organization's year-long operating expenses. But establishing an exhibit can be a long process, during which profit is not always come by so easily. Creating a successful trade exhibition takes several years and is quite labor-intensive.

Corporations may be willing to sponsor luncheons or other events if they are given credit in the program or on display posters at the meeting. Without an income-producing exhibit or sponsorships, most of the income will come from fees paid by the participants. Estimates of registration fees should take into account early-bird as well as later registration fees.

Nonprofit organizations can also obtain grants from other groups or support from an organization joining the meeting as a cosponsor. Paid ads can be placed in the meeting's program. Food and beverage functions not included in the conference fee can be sold on an à la carte basis to bring in additional income; through ticket sales, you will be able to make accurate food and beverage guarantees. Local corporations or suppliers to a trade association's members often sponsor luncheons or other events. Other potential sources of income are sales of audiotapes, publications, novelties and mementos, and tours (see Chapter 4 for more ideas on income-generating programs).

The first budget estimates are based on general calculations, determined by site, numbers expected, days of the conference, and so forth. A budget can be finalized only late in the planning process, and it still will not be penny-exact. Although the coordinator should be the keeper of the budget, the final responsibility lies with the executive director. The most efficiency can be gained by setting up a computer program for the budget that will recalculate expenses and income and total budget when changes are made.

Computer-generated spreadsheets offer an opportunity to conduct "what if" analyses: What will the effect be on my bottom line if I increase the program fee by $25 per person while holding my projected registration constant? What will happen if 25 percent fewer people attend than I originally projected? What will be the effect on my bottom line if I do an additional mailing that results in a 10 percent increase in registration? These are all considerations you can, and should, look at when planning the budget.

Every possible expense should be budgeted, with a contingency (5 percent) set aside for unexpected charges. It is prudent never to surprise or be surprised when dealing with financial projections. In your overall plan, set dates (90, 45, and 30 days out) where you can reevaluate and make changes. Preregistration numbers should be reviewed, and the entire planning team should review the budget and possible cutbacks. It is possible that no cutbacks will be desirable, but the team should give this their consideration and make a decision.

A working format for developing a meeting budget is shown in Exhibit 7–1.

**Exhibit 7–1**   Budgeting Meetings

| Income | Expenses |
|---|---|
| Abstract fees | Audiovisual equipment/supplies |
| Advertising revenue | Awards/gifts |
| Audio taping royalties | Computer programming |
| Continuing education fees | Contract services |
| Corporate sponsorships | Deposits |
| Exhibit fees | Entertainment |
| Miscellaneous | Equipment rental |
| Program sales | Exhibit costs |
| Registration fees | Food and beverage |
| Sponsorships | Gratuities |
| Sports day fees | Insurance |
| Spouse program fees | Interpreters |
| Suite assessments | Labor |
| Ticket sales | Marketing expenses |
| Tour fees | Photographs |
| Transportation rebate | Press room |
| | Printing |
| | Security |
| | Shipping/freight |
| | Signage |
| | Speakers |
| | Staff time charges |
| | Supplies |
| | Telephone costs |
| | Transportation |
| | Travel |
| | Xerox |

## Critical Dates List

The early creation of a timetable for your event is essential. The dates when actions should be completed will vary with the complexity and size of the meeting you are planning. Exhibit 7–2 is a critical dates list that can be used as a working tool in completing a list of your own. The time frames vary, of course, depending on the size and complexity of the event: Major trade shows execute site contracts five or more years in advance, whereas smaller meetings can be pulled together in a few months' time. Give yourself as much time as possible and be sure to add completion dates and name of the person responsible for each action.

**Exhibit 7–2**   Critical Dates Checklist

(Revise to accommodate special requirements; size of meeting is the major variable)

Two years in advance (can be compressed if necessary):
   Select dates.
   Commit to location.

Twelve months in advance:
   Discuss program and contact potential speakers.
   Begin designing promotional materials.
   Establish budget.

Ten months in advance:
   Finalize program and begin speaker selection.
   Finish promotional materials and send to printer.

Eight months in advance:
   Obtain registration mailing lists.
   Identify services required, such as entertainers, special amusements, A/V, and begin selection process.
   Begin placements of magazine ads if used.

Six months in advance:
   Contact catering department for initial menus and confirm prices.
   Develop floor plans for meeting.

Four months in advance:
   Mail first group of registration forms.
   Request audiovisual requirements, biographies, etc., from speakers.
   Ads begin to appear.

Two months in advance:
   Begin rooming list/assignment of VIP suites.
   Reconfirm all suppliers and communicate final requirements.

One week to one day in advance:
   Give hotel, food and beverage guarantee counts (usually 48–72 hours).
   Assemble and ship registration materials.
   Check in and observe meeting room set-ups.

Supervise meeting.

Post procedures:
   Thank-you letters to hotel, speakers, and memo to staff.
   Pay invoices.
   Make master list of expenses for future reference.
   Review evaluations and start planning for next year.

## Contracts

Solid contracts are the result of clear and documented understandings by both parties. Their importance can not be overemphasized, even for a small meeting. Contracts, or written letters of agreement, should be prepared and co-signed by a qualified representative of the sponsoring organization and the providers of ground and air transportation, hotel and/or other facilities, entertainment, decorators, security, temporary personnel, and any professional speakers. As a general rule, all contracts with facilities and suppliers should clearly state:

- Day, date, to/from time of commitment or performance, to/from time for setup and teardown, location.
- Compliance with hotel/motel fire safety code and applicable federal, state, and local laws, including the Americans with Disabilities Act (ADA).
- Liability and insurance coverage.
- Terms of usage or commitment (day-by-day sleeping room block, meeting space usage, special considerations).
- Financial considerations, deposit, balance due, and past due dates and penalties.
- Name(s) of responsible parties who will be contacts or provide services.
- Quantities, types, and sizes of food and beverage requirements.
- Complimentary commitments to include accommodations (one "comp" sleeping room night per 50 is standard), complimentary suite for key volunteer or reduced-rate staff/speaker rooms, and complimentary meeting space because of food and beverage service.
- Cancellation and/or attrition clauses stipulating the respective responsibilities of both parties and the penalties that will be suffered if terms are not met. Actual dates, quantities, and dollars should be clearly reflected.

All items that require a contract or written agreement are negotiable. Never hesitate to seek final arrangements that meet your overall objectives, and then be certain to confirm in writing.

## MARKETING AND PUBLIC RELATIONS

Have you ever received a brochure that piqued your interest in a meeting? If so, it was probably because the sponsoring organization had a good marketing plan. It understood that you had a need that could be met by the activities that would take place at its meeting, and it communicated that information to you in a clear and interesting way.

Marketing is essential for the planning of a successful meeting, and effective promotion is necessary to stimulate need, build attendance, and reinforce the sponsoring organization's image.

The meeting coordinator should be involved in the marketing plan for the meeting, but because the meeting will probably be only one of an array of products and services offered by the organization, promotion should be a part of the organization's overall marketing plan. (See Chapters 3 and 6 for more information on marketing and meeting promotion.)

Public relations serves a different purpose: to publicize the organization and the special features of its conference. Public relations, however, is more than just an effort to provide one-time publicity; it transmits the image of the sponsor and of everyone involved with producing and running the conference. Like your marketing effort, public relations should be undertaken by a specialist in that area, because generating coverage by the media can be perplexing and even intimidating. It is crucial, however, that the meeting coordinator at least be familiar with the goals of public relations. In large organizations, a public relations staff will conduct the services at a conference, but that staff must remain in touch with the meeting coordinator. (See Chapter 8 on public relations for ideas.)

## CONFERENCE ACTIVITIES

### Registration

Registration is usually the first point of contact for your audience and remains a focal point throughout the event. When registration is efficient and friendly, it bodes well for the meeting. As a rule, a preregistered guest should not have to spend more than a minute on-site to pick up credentials and be on his or her way.

Registration procedures have become much more efficient and orderly with the use of computer programming and Internet registration. A well-thought-out system should be planned before the registration forms are mailed. You can then collect data that are meaningful (be sure to plan for data that can track demographics for later use). Weekly reports will allow you to measure your ongoing registration pickup and the potential financial impact. Advanced information technology enables you to develop customized schedules for individual attendees through a software program often called an "event wizard."

This is useful for complex meetings where registrants choose among a number of concurrent sessions. (Chapter 11 discusses how to choose information technology appropriate to your organization.)

A registration system may include:

- Reminder notices to all delegates, giving them the date and time of the sessions they plan to attend
- Accurate record keeping and financial data
- Accurate counts, meeting room requirements, and food and beverage guarantees
- Valuable information for speakers and discussion leaders, such as an advance list of the people who will attend specific sessions
- A complete, alphabetical advance registration list that is updated weekly (also an exhibitor list, if appropriate)
- A final attendee list ready for distribution at the conference
- A prospective member mailing list that can be used for future conference announcements as well as membership promotion campaigns

In the overall registration process, the first step is to develop a system and procedures that will work for your overall objectives. Then, develop a registration form that will capture all needed information:

- Name
- Business address (first name and title as it should appear on name badge)
- Telephone and fax numbers
- Choice of events if additional fees are charged for optional events such as workshops, tours, banquets
- Reservations for special events
- Method of payment
- Hotel registration form or guidance on hotel registration

Forms should state the sponsor's cancellation policy. VIP registration forms should be designed to accommodate speakers, key organization members, and other special guests.

Hotel accommodations will be very important to participants in an out-of-town event. A housing form can be prepared (although all hotels listed on it must sign off on the form before it is used) and mailed along with your registration form. Another option is to have the hotel provide reservation cards (not easily done if more than one hotel is offered as a choice) that are mailed with the initial marketing piece or along with registration confirmations. A third option is to provide a hotel reservation phone number and have participants call the hotel(s) directly. Your objective should be to ensure that you meet contractual obligations to the hotel and that your participants are handled properly and expeditiously. You must also be sure to communicate the room rate, check-in and -out times, no-show penalties, deposit requirements, the cutoff date, and the credit cards that will be accepted. Discuss the form and the procedure with the hotel convention services or reservations manager. It will also be important to understand exactly how each room reservation will be confirmed to each guest (either by you or by the hotel).

The cutoff date is the date, per your contract with the hotel, when the hotel is (1) no longer required to hold your block of rooms and can release any unbooked rooms to the general public and (2) when the discounted and negotiated group rate may no longer apply and the hotel can sell the rooms at a higher rate. Be certain to take care of all speaker and VIP reservations before this date. After discussion with the hotel on its potential for sellout and your need for additional rooms, you may want to guarantee more rooms. Remember, sleeping rooms are similar to perishable food items. If they are not consumed on a given night, they have no value. The hotel's objective is to sell every available room every night. If you receive "comp" rooms, be sure they are determined cumulatively, not daily.

On-site, the registration desk should be centrally located, with plenty of light and ventilation. The desk should be staffed with adequate personnel, either in-house or outside paid staff or volunteers. Separate preregistration lines can speed traffic flow. Prepared registration packets contain the conference schedule and other information. Badges should be given out on-site rather than premailed, as some preregistrants may forget to bring them.

The registration packet includes a program book or on-site agenda. For a small meeting this may be merely a page or two listing the agenda, speakers, and any other relevant information. For large meetings, and particularly for those with exhibitions, the program book will be much more detailed to orient participants to both the meeting sessions and the exhibition floor. Work on the program booklet should begin as soon as speakers and exhibitors are contracted, but it should be printed as late as possible to allow for changes. Production costs for this book must be included in the overall budget.

Be certain that you have established a solid financial control system that will pass an audit and that money handlers are bonded. Numbered forms and tickets that are assigned and accounted for are a good beginning.

## Specification Sheets

Specification sheets (specs) are written step-by-step directions that are given to the hotel at least 30 days in advance of the actual event. Specification sheets should include the following:

- Event name
- Event day, date, and time
- Assigned room name
- The times setup begins and doors open
- Food and beverage requirements (to include guarantees)
- Setup instructions (table layout as classroom or auditorium or U-shape, for example), 6 ft or 8 ft tables and number of chairs per table, water on tables or in back of room, aisles, staging, etc.)
- AV requirements (35 mm, overhead, video, specifying exact type, screen size; draping, microphones, specifying exact type)
- Billing instructions
- Contact person at your organization
- Any special instructions

## Script

A complete script adds a higher level of professionalism to banquets, award ceremonies, or other critical parts of your event. It should include a minute-by-minute dialogue, including all speeches, awards, light and sound cues, who goes to the stage when, speaker introductions, and so on. As a real-time guide to a successful event, a script can provide immeasurable comfort to all podium participants, the audiovisual support staff, the hotel, and you. A script can make the difference between a flawless performance and one with obvious glitches.

## On-Site Logistics and Staff

Meeting coordinators should arrive at the conference site early, the exact time determined by the complexity of the meeting setup. A pre-conference meeting can resolve potential logistical problems, which can start a meeting off on the wrong foot. This early time should be spent in making sure that all needed supplies are on hand (carefully check off a list of shipping forms to be certain everything has arrived) and reconfirming specifications with the hotel. Are the room sizes still appropriate for your audience (especially important if your numbers have increased or decreased)? You may want to change your room setups on paper before hotel staff moves staging, chairs, and tables into the positions you outlined in your specs. Will there be other groups meeting in rooms adjacent to yours or moving through public spaces at the same time? At this point it isn't too late to discuss crowd and noise control with your hotel convention services manager.

A "precon" meeting with the hotel staff usually takes place on the day prior to the day your event actually convenes and includes all the facility department heads and other key suppliers. Use this opportunity to review and update your specifications. This is your last chance to be sure that the instructions you have detailed were communicated to every responsible hotel department and were understood.

As the meeting planner, you need to be sure that you have enough staff on-site and have preassigned responsibilities and times when certain things must be completed. Staff must understand that if they cannot complete an assigned responsibility, they must find someone else to complete it for them. (Volunteer leaders often make special requests that can pull assigned staff in other directions.)

## Transportation

For a large meeting, the meeting planner negotiates with local transportation companies to provide travel to and from the airport, buses for tours, field trips, and sightseeing, and round-trip shuttle service from hotels to the meeting location (particularly used to transfer attendees from hotels to convention centers and back, which can be a significant distance.) The service records of local transportation companies may help in deciding which group to contract with. Be certain that appropriate insurance is carried by the provider and liability waivers are in order.

A staff person should be appointed as transportation liaison. If outings such as tours and field trips are planned, each bus should have a staff monitor so as to avoid leaving anyone behind at stops along the way.

*Members of a historical society attending a committee meeting went to Monticello, Thomas Jefferson's home in Charlottesville, Virginia, on a special tour after normal visitor hours. The tour was very exciting, as the sun was setting in the west and the group explored Jefferson's masterpiece by flashlight and other portable lights. Five people from the group strayed off and missed the buses when they departed for the hotel. It looked like a long—and probably wonderful—night in Mr. Jefferson's home until the group found the only curator left at the house, which is on a hill miles from town.*

## Special Guests/VIPs

Volunteer leaders of an organization donate a great deal of time and energy because of their personal commitments or beliefs. There are few rewards beyond public recognition for their efforts. However, there are some things you can do for these dedicated and special people at events. Be certain that there are established guidelines or precedents and that if you begin a new form of recognition, you are prepared for it to set a precedent. Special transportation from the airport, a hotel suite or an upgrade to a corner room, or a particular amenity are possibilities that can be negotiated in advance with the hotel. You may also arrange for an advance check in, a late checkout, or a simple welcome note.

## Dealing with Problems

If the planning has been thorough, major problems are unlikely to occur. But something can go wrong at almost any meeting. Keep your calm. Most disruptions or problems can be addressed. If the meeting organizer is visibly upset, everyone else soon will be too. If you project an image of calm competence, attendees will likely take the unexpected in stride.

Careful and complete communication with all parties involved can prevent nightmares, similar to the following, from happening at your special event:

- The band you hired to play light jazz for the next three hours just showed up, 15 minutes late, in boots and jeans and knows only country music.

- The celebratory "sparklers" turn out not to be of the indoor variety and set off alarms and sprinklers.

- You learn that the microphone does not work just as the most senior official begins to make welcoming announcements.

- The after-dinner comedian's raunchy or political jokes insult someone in your audience.

- With preassigned seating, you have mistakenly assigned to a table for 10, 15 people who are not happy while they stand at the table and try to figure where the extra 5 will sit.

- There are no vegetable or kosher plates available for special requests.

- The special awards are not to be found, and everyone is on stage expecting awards, handshakes, and photo opportunities.

- The event went very well, but the final bill is 25 percent over budget.

If you have planned carefully and attempted to anticipate the fore-seeable problems, you will be available to deal with unexpected events (like power outages, more people than you guaranteed show-ing up, the speaker's plane being delayed, or an internal political issue). With poor planning, routine issues will turn into problems and anything unexpected is likely to turn into disaster.

## POSTCONFERENCE ACTIVITIES

### Conference Evaluation

The conference is over and the participants have left for home. You wonder: How well did the meeting go? What did the participants get out of the conference? Did this meeting accomplish its objectives? What worked? What didn't? What kind of changes could be made? What did people learn? How important was this learning? The eval-uation process is one that must be carefully thought out as the meet-ing is planned.

An evaluation of a meeting by the participants can be very valuable in improving subsequent meetings. Your evaluation should measure performance against your event objectives. Speakers should be meas-ured on presentation and content (Was the material presented relative to your own organizational needs? Did you gain practical/applicable information from the presentation?). Make sure that there is a reason for the data you will be gathering; if the information provided by ask-ing a particular question is not relevant, don't ask that question. More information is gathered from brief evaluations, because they are more likely to be returned than long evaluations. There are many different kinds of evaluations. Consider cost, design, collection methods, and the expertise required to format and collect the data. Ask some open-ended questions, particularly, "What would you like us to do differ-ently next year?" and "What was the most valuable event at this meeting?" Be sure to provide an address on the evaluation so that individuals who complete it on the plane or after they get home can send it to your organization. Most important, be sure to read and assess the evaluations, and make changes based on the feedback you receive. Evaluations can be extensive; just be sure they are accurate and reflect membership/attendees requirements.

A summary of meeting highlights is often posted on the organization's Web site. This reminds attendees of the best of the event and tells nonparticipants how much they missed.

## WRAP-UP

A complete financial history of the conference should be completed within 30 days. It should include income and expenses compared with budget, food and beverage actual consumption compared with your guarantees, types of food and alcohol consumed that may be different from what you initially ordered, and final registrant counts. This kind of history will be invaluable in planning your next event.

Thank-you letters to speakers, vendors, staff, and volunteers are in order. They should be prepared within 10 days, recognize specific efforts, and be signed by appropriate organizational representatives. Gratuities may also be given to hotel staff or suppliers for outstanding performance; if you are unsure of the appropriate amounts, a frank discussion with your convention services manager can be helpful in deciding for whom and how much.

### Looking Forward

In the end, a question arises: Shall we do it again? Yes—particularly if your event met its objectives. The coming together of people for a common cause can be extremely rewarding, for both the long and the short term, and it can foster the beginning of positive change. Meetings, whether committee sessions, award banquets, educational seminars, conventions, or giant trade exhibits, can define an organization and enhance its full range of activities. The key is planning, planning, planning.

## CHECKLIST FOR SITE SELECTION

Location:
- Is the site easily accessible by ground and air to your participants?
- Is the site well positioned in relation to planned pre- and postconference events?
- Is the climate at the site at the time of the conference acceptable?
- Is the ambience of the site appropriate for your event?

Past History:
- Check references with others who have used the site for similar events.
- Has the sponsor used this site before?
- Who owns and who manages the property?
- Are there labor negotiations that will take place anytime close to your event?

Service Facilities:
- Is a car rental service provided on-site?
- What recreational facilities are provided on-site?
- Does the site have any arrangements with nearby facilities?
- Does the site charge any fees for using the facilities?
- Are shops located on-site?
- Are there quick-copy or other office services on-site?

Accommodations:
- How many rooms will the property commit for your event?
- What are the different types of sleeping rooms, how many of each, and what is the pricing structure?
- Will early arrival accommodations for officers/VIPs be available?
- Do all sleeping rooms have TV, radio, clock, coffeemaker, remote control, air-conditioning, state-of-the-art fire detection and alarms?
- Are newspapers, turndown, or other amenities available or standard?
- Is the level of housekeeping acceptable?
- Are sufficient sleeping rooms designated no-smoking rooms?
- Do enough rooms meet the guidelines of the Americans with Disabilities Act, and are they available for your event?
- Is room service available, and during what hours?
- What are the check in/checkout times, and will early arrival be available for staff or VIPs?
- Does the site have express checkout?

Site Personnel:
- Do the site personnel need special orientation?
- Are bell people appropriately dressed and responsive?
- Are front desk personnel polite and efficient?

- Is a concierge available to assist guests?
- Are the site personnel unionized, and, if so, what is the current status of the union contract(s)?

Public Areas and Facilities:
- Are there enough elevators to handle the movement of participants?
- Does the site have signs to welcome participants?
- Does the site have facilities for handicapped persons?
- Are hallways and public areas neat and clean?
- Are public washrooms plentiful, clean, and well equipped?
- Are checkrooms available and staffed?

Financial Factors:
- What type of financial arrangement will the site require?
- Does the site provide complimentary meeting rooms based on your food and beverage and sleeping room consumption?
- Does the site offer an off-season or shoulder rate?
- Are rates different on weekdays and weekends?
- Is a deposit required by either the organization or individual guests?
- What is the site's policy on late arrivals? No-shows?
- What type of currency is accepted?
- Which credit cards can be used?
- Are purchase orders acceptable?
- What is the cancellation policy?
- Are there insurance requirements?
- Who has responsibility for property damage?
- Does the site have any special charge for utilities (electricity, light, labor, air-conditioning)?
- When will the site guarantee room rates?
- What add-ons can be expected (for both additional amenities the site may have that your event can utilize and for extra charges you may incur)?

Safety:
- Are site personnel safety conscious?
- Does each room have a smoke alarm and/or sprinkler system?

- Does the site have a working fire alarm system?
- Does the hotel post evacuation procedures?
- Are exits on each floor clearly marked?
- What is the system for room key assignment and replacement?
- Are safe deposit boxes available?
- Does the site maintain a 24-hour security force?
- Does the site have a house physician?
- How close is the nearest medical facility?
- Are site personnel trained in CPR?

General:
- Does the site provide transportation for site review?
- Is the site planning any construction or remodeling? When and of what kind?
- Are internal communication devices available?
- What other activities are booked into the site at the same time?
- Is the site in full compliance with the Americans with Disabilities Act?

# CHAPTER EIGHT

# Using Public Relations Tools To Reach a Broader Audience

**Enhance your image, increase participation, energize supporters around a critical issue, and support fund-raising through effective communications. Every nonprofit needs effective public relations. This chapter outlines the public relations tools and techniques professionals use to get the word out about their organizations.**

Public relations is the practice of communicating with individuals and groups to influence the success of an organization and the cause, constituency, profession, or industry it represents. Nonprofit groups bring inherent strengths to public relations. Cause-oriented groups and charities are often identified with worthy social goals and can draw upon the enthusiasm of their followers, volunteers, and donors. Associations can speak for entire industries or professions, spotlighting the services and products they provide consumers and the people they employ. Such assets can give nonprofits an extra measure of credibility. As a result, the news media, lawmakers, and others often seek them out for background information and for articulate positions on public issues. Nonprofit groups can also act as lightning rods for controversy by speaking for their constituencies and deflecting criticism from individual members.

Public relations can support many activities in nonprofit groups:

- *Fund-raising*—Present the cause or service as worthy enough to merit support by documenting accomplishments and responsible use of the funds raised.

- *Community Awareness*—Build support by highlighting the services provided to the community, such as education, health care, youth programs, food for the hungry, housing for the poor, and environmental preservation.

- *Member Recruitment and Retention*—Communicate the benefits of membership to prospective and existing members.

- *Lobbying and Issue Advocacy*—Shape legislation and public policies by encouraging the news media to report the group's position and publish supporting editorials.

- *Crisis Management*—Coordinate communications during crises to help those who have been hurt and to present the organization as responsible and responsive in trying circumstances.

- *Special Events*—Stimulate interest in a cause or organization by hosting a focused "happening."

## WHAT IS PUBLIC RELATIONS?

According to a frequently quoted definition, public relations is:

The management function that evaluates the attitudes of important publics, identifies the policies and procedures of an individual or an organization with the public interest, and executes a program of action to earn understanding and acceptance by these publics.*

Public relations is not merely an image-building exercise, although one of the goals is often to improve status and prestige. The most effective nonprofits view public relations as two-way communications. They begin by listening to the groups or individuals to be influenced and learning their attitudes about the relevant cause, industry, or profession. The public relations program then develops messages and initiatives that address their concerns. A truism among communications professionals holds that advertising is bought, whereas public relations is earned. An organization can spend millions on an ad campaign that highlights its greatness, but the impact will always be diminished by the fact that the praise is self-generated. Through public relations, groups set out to earn praise through good deeds, well-reasoned policies, careful work with the news media, and outreach to valuable constituencies. Trying to

---

*Public Relations News*, 27 October, 1947.

solicit praise or support in a self-serving manner often tends to tarnish an image. Organizations that objectively support worthwhile causes and make their case in a factual manner are well positioned for future public relations successes.

## Seek a Shared Vision

Result-producing public relations programs start with a shared vision. Begin with a brainstorming exercise by the leadership or a committee charged with formulating a public relations plan. Initially, this group should analyze the circumstances and consider public relations options, disregarding any constraints imposed by limited resources. The agenda for this exercise should be as broad as possible:

- What are the strengths of the organization: size, history, committed supporters, political experience, valued products or services, importance of cause?

- What are the weaknesses: poor public perception, lack of awareness, weak economic condition, declining support, outspoken critics?

- How do perceptions square with realities? To what extent are perceptions of weakness accurate? Do not rush to conclude that all criticisms are unfounded. It is quite likely that some are on target; groups can build credibility by acknowledging faults and taking steps to correct them.

- How do important constituents feel about the organization? Does it elicit respect, fear, frustration, identification, excitement?

- How would you like them to feel?

- How would the organization operate in an ideal world? How would it be perceived? How would it work with its most important publics, such as supporters, donors, volunteers, members, the news media, lawmakers, community leaders?

The best programs find creative ways to touch a responsive public chord. For example, the campaigns in which guns are exchanged for toys or shoes trade violence for nonviolence. The Doe Fund of New York developed a program to shelter homeless people with a feature that gave it special public appeal: The beneficiaries were given jobs and required to work for their room and board. Employment helps homeless people to build self-esteem and gives them the means to support themselves; their paying for food and shelter covers 70 percent of the program's cost. Critics cannot easily dismiss this effort as a stopgap waste of scarce government funds.

Inner-city schools and community organizations can improve the quality of life through programs with local business and nonprofit trade associations. Businesses can provide mentors, job opportunities, and scholarships to teach students valuable job skills and describe career opportunities. The most ambitious programs can revitalize blighted neighborhoods, often with government help. Food retailers can build state-of-the art supermarkets in inner cities through partnerships with local nonprofit community groups and city governments. City officials provide the zoning clearances and tax incentives, and the community groups help recruit local people to work in the stores. In some cases, community organizations can obtain an ownership stake in the property or stores. A supermarket often serves as an anchor for extensive business development, bringing more jobs, products, and services to the community and fueling the local economy. Local nonprofits should search out such alliances, recognizing both the community benefits and the constructive public awareness that can result.

## Set Strategic Goals

The next step is to set goals, both short- and long-term, that align the public relations program with your organization's overall strategic plan. Two years from now, how much would you like public perception to change? If 40 percent of the public is now aware of a service or cause, the short-term goal may be to raise awareness to 60 percent, whereas the long-term goal may be 80 percent. Goals can be fundraising targets or legislative accomplishments. Is there a message or belief you want to impress upon certain individuals and groups? In the short term, you may want to send the message through various media, such as articles, speeches, and direct mail; for the long term, you would search for evidence that the message was believed.

It is often best to state objectives in specific, measurable terms that lend themselves to cost-benefit analyses, such as the number of potential donors reached, amount of funds raised, or bills passed or defeated. This makes it easier to gauge progress and help supporters to appreciate the value of the public relations program.

## Take a Resource Inventory

In the planning process, organizations must take an inventory of their resources. Staff may be needed to create news releases and advisories, respond to reporters' e-mail queries, prepare background pieces, and issue briefs, consumer pamphlets, speeches, and other materials. Administrative support is needed to copy, collate, stuff, and mail such materials. Other tasks include developing and maintaining mailing lists (including e-mail lists), contacting the news media, organizing news conferences, and maintaining speakers bureaus.

For extensive campaigns, you will have to decide whether some or all of the work should be performed by an outside public relations firm. This is not an inexpensive option, but it enables the organization to continue performing its regular duties with minimal disruption.

Often, the duties can be shared, delegating to the public relations firm those tasks for which the organization lacks the skills or resources to perform well. It is quite possible that the optimum division of labor will change over time with changes in the staff, funding, and mission of the nonprofit group. A less expensive option is to hire freelancers to do the editorial and design work. Chapter 15, on using consultants, provides ideas on pursuing this option.

The inventory of resources should include more than a count of heads, funds, computers, and other physical assets. A nonprofit group can often receive help from its supporters; in fact, volunteers in leadership positions are often the best spokespersons for the organization. Investigate opportunities to join forces with allied organizations sharing common interests. Advocates for consumer and environmental causes often form coalitions, in some cases bringing in labor unions as well. Food banks often receive public relations support from supermarkets and food processors. Environmental groups find willing partners in the business community, whether the cause is planting trees or recycling. Doctors support nonprofit health care agencies. If the program can be designed to offer clear benefits to partners, they may be willing to underwrite much of the costs. Nonprofit groups can also ask supporters to contribute services or equipment instead of funds.

Businesses may be willing to donate computers, software, mailing lists, reference books, and office supplies. They can design and print annual reports, consumer pamphlets, and other materials. Tax deductions may provide a financial incentive. Among your supporters may be professional publicists, reporters, writers, and editors willing to contribute their expertise to a cause they feel strongly about.

The question of resources will ultimately come down to funding. After factoring in the help available from members, volunteers, allies, suppliers, and other sources, what can the organization afford to spend? When public relations programs are considered urgent, organizations have been able to undertake a special fund-raising effort or justify a surcharge on dues. In these instances, nonprofit groups must make a special effort to articulate the benefits of the program in concrete terms—and to keep doing so as long as the program is in place. In effect, a public relations program is needed for the public relations program. All programs need such mechanisms to maintain support, participation, and funding. Groups that rely heavily on new funding sources must make a special effort.

*In a successful seasonal campaign, supporters provide Christmas gifts that are requested by needy persons. A church or other nonprofit group simply provides a Christmas Spirit tree and asks low-income families to list the items they need, such as shoes, warm clothes, blankets, and toys. The requests are detailed on cards and hung on the tree; then supporters select the cards and fulfill the requests. Contributions are summarized in a media release to local reporters and to the nonprofit's members at the conclusion of the campaign.*

## Research Audience and Channels

With goals and resources identified, the next step is to research the audiences that will be the target of the public relations program and the best means to communicate with them. Public relations programs can take a shotgun approach, but it is often more effective to identify the individuals, leaders, and groups that are most important to achieving the objectives. What are their views and attitudes? Their demographic makeup may be useful to know, especially in fund-raising efforts.

The research may begin with readily available materials, such as books, articles, government reports, opinion surveys and polls, Census Bureau data, and other published materials. Organizations often supplement this information with their own research, which can be done through informal meetings with representatives of the target audiences. Use these sessions only to listen and gather information, not to argue with such representatives nor to try to win them over. You may even want to create a standing advisory council of such people to serve as a sounding board for program ideas and policies.

For a more objective reading of audience views, you can hire an outside firm to perform focus group research. The firm invites a small group of people for a meeting of several hours to discuss a list of topics set with the sponsoring organization. A moderator leads the discussion in a neutral manner, while members of the sponsoring group observe through a one-way mirror. This is the best way to learn about the range of views, the depth of conviction, and any misconceptions. In other words, it is useful qualitative research.

For quantitative research, groups often turn to polls or surveys. A common approach is to mail a list of questions on a postpaid return card. The questions should be carefully worded to limit bias. Most should be multiple-choice or true-false, and the list should be short to make it easy for people to complete. The main shortcoming of this method is that it tends to eliminate the respondents who have such a negative view of the group that they throw the card away. For this reason, the survey results are often skewed to the positive side, obscuring problems or misperceptions.

For a truly objective picture, organizations turn to opinion polls in which members of the audience are surveyed by phone. If the audience is the entire public, the calls are made by random dialing. It is best to hire an outside firm to perform such polls.

Nonprofit groups with limited budgets can have polling firms ask several questions as a rider on other surveys.

The research you perform at the outset serves as a benchmark by which to gauge progress over the life of the public relations program. Prepare a report summarizing the initial research, then revisit the key topics every three to six months and return to the sources to track changes. Over time, the critical issues and concerns are likely to change, especially if the group effectively engages its constituents in solving problems, allaying fears, and building enthusiasm about progress.

## INTERNET USE IN MEDIA RELATIONS

The Internet is having a profound impact on the practice of public relations. Internet use is widespread by public relations practitioners and has become an essential communications channel to reach desired audiences. Here is a partial list of the principal uses of the Internet:

- Research issues
- Monitor news about the organization
- Monitor news about other organizations, legislative issues, and so forth
- Research media targets
- Contact media representatives
- Distribute news releases
- Transmit graphics/artwork
- Provide an electronic clipping service
- Handle crisis communications

As part of the Internet strategy for your organization (see Chapter 11), and based on the level of your media relations program, consider adding a "Media Only" section to your Web site. Editor sections specifically address the needs of the working media and provide a quick reference and resource to your organization's news. The content can include news releases, background material, images, profiles of board members, a speakers bureau database organized by areas of specialization, and statistics and research reports. Should a crisis arise, your Web site can become an immediate source for editors to receive the latest information on the situation.

## Identify the Best Channels

The growth of the communications industry has produced myriad channels for sending messages—ranging from the special interest magazine and local-access cable channel to *USA Today* and *60 Minutes*. The rise of the Internet has produced an entirely new spectrum of Web-based publishers that are increasingly key contacts for public relations messages. The proliferation of outlets is especially helpful for programs targeting special audiences. If you operate in a specific area, develop a list of all the local magazines and newspapers—community, neighborhood, daily, weekly—and radio and television stations that have news programs. Many available directories, including the following, list outlets by type, city, and subject.

- *Editor and Publisher International Yearbook: Parts 1, 2, and 3,* $179 (prepayment required). Write to Editor & Publisher Co., 11 West 19th Street, New York, NY 10011-4234; or call 212-675-4380. Covers daily newspapers.

- *Broadcasting Annual,* $75 (prepayment required). Write to *Broadcasting & Cable Magazine,* 1705 DeSales Street NW, 6th Floor, Washington, DC 20036; or call 202-659-2340. Covers most TV and radio news agencies.

- *Bacon's Newspaper Directory* and *Bacon's Magazine Directory,* $285 per volume. Write to Bacon's Information, Inc., 332 S. Michigan Avenue, Chicago, IL 60604; or call 312-922-2400. Good coverage of the trade and specialty media; also lists business/financial editors of 700 daily newspapers.

- *National Directory of Weekly Newspapers,* about $100 (prepayment required). Write to American Newspaper Representative, 4108 Park Avenue, Minneapolis, MN 55407; or call 800-550-7557.

- *Working Press of the Nation.* Five volumes: I, Newspapers; II, Magazines and Internal Publications; III, Radio and TV. Each volume costs $249, and all three cost $439.95 (plus $10 for handling and shipping if not prepaid). Write to R.R. Bowker, 121 Chanlon Road, New Providence, NJ 07974; or call 888-269-5372. Owing to the level of detail and cost, this series is best suited for a high-volume, national public relations effort.

- *Writer's Market*, $27.99 (prepayment required if only one copy is ordered). Write to Writer's Digest Books, 1507 Dana Avenue, Cincinnati, OH 45207; or call 513-531-2222; Web site: http://www. writersdigest.com. Valuable for its comprehensive list of magazines, which includes statements of editorial needs and interests by the magazine editors.

If the target audience has a common demographic feature, specialty magazines may be an ideal vehicle. A gynecologic research foundation whose mission is to detect, prevent, and conquer cancer in women might contact the editors of *Cosmopolitan, Good Housekeeping,* or *Working Woman* magazine. A soup kitchen seeking more support from local supermarkets might approach the state grocers association. Charity leaders in charge of the kitchen might appeal for help in association publications, solicit support in mailings to the members, and speak at the organization's meetings.

The list of news media outlets should include the names of executives who make the editorial decisions and reporters who cover the issues important to the nonprofit organization. The decision makers in the print media appear on the masthead as editors-in-chief. Large dailies also have news executives in charge of major sections, such as the city editor, society page editor, editorial page editor, food editor. At broadcast outlets the people who decide the coverage are usually known as news directors. To identify the reporters, scan the publications, watch or listen to the broadcast outlet, or consult the directories in the preceding list.

In any case, before sending material, it's a good idea to phone the outlet to verify that the key individuals still work there. Because news media outlets have high turnover rates, keeping this contact information current is essential. News media outlets are deluged with mail and e-mail, and the letters addressed to no one in particular or to someone who has departed often remain in a massive pile whose size is best measured in feet or yards. Most journalists lack the time to winnow through the pile for the few nuggets of news it may yield.

## COMMUNICATIONS TOOLS

The public relations field offers many methods for sending messages—ranging from the basic news release to a news conference. These tools must be used with care, always keeping in mind the target audience and the need to have all positions and policies built on a foundation of facts and logic.

## When to Send a News Release

The most widely used communications tool, the news release, is also the most abused. It should be written in a news style and carry a newsworthy message or story. Nonprofit groups have many occasions for sending out news releases:

- Report that your group has expanded, is introducing new services, has moved, or has opened a new office.
- Announce accomplishments in fund-raising over a certain time period, emphasizing the number of donors or the amount raised.
- Announce an especially large contribution from a generous donor or a large grant from a foundation or government agency.
- Report the number of people served, healed, fed, or educated over a certain period.
- Announce new medical breakthroughs that have the potential to save lives.
- Provide a timely public service message, such as how to provide clothing needed by the poor before winter or how to recycle cardboard after Christmas.
- Present the group's position on critical issues. This may accompany a recent speech or testimony that details the position.
- Describe the history of the group or its constituency when it reaches a milestone, such as 10, 25, or 50 years. This is a good time to summarize accomplishments. Contrasting your current state with conditions 25, 50, or 100 years ago often serves to accentuate the progress and value of the group. Juxtaposing photos of the old and new can provide a vivid illustration.
- Describe a moving story that illustrates in human terms the work of the group, such as how a life was saved, a family brought back together, urban youths given career direction, any problem solved through innovation by an individual, group, or company.
- Announce the election of new directors, trustees, or officers.
- Report that the group has adopted a new mission, changing or broadening its services or focus.
- Announce that the nonprofit group has received an award, recognition, commendation, or accreditation from the government, another organization, or a community agency.
- Highlight a member of the group who has been honored for outstanding performance or named to a leadership position in a community, government, or charity group.

- Report the presentation of an award recognizing someone who has made exemplary contributions to the ideals represented by the group. For example, you can honor a generous donor or a government official who has supported the group. You might establish an annual award in the name of a distinguished member or founder of the group.

- Describe a major community event, sponsored by the group, that is open to the public, such as a festival, fair, or demonstration of valuable skills.

- Report the findings of a new survey of consumers, constituents, or community residents, conducted by the group. This can be the same survey used to track the success of the public relations program.

- In December, comment on the progress made in the year just ending and the goals for the year ahead.

By sending a news release, you alert the news media to your existence and advise them of a recent accomplishment or event connected to the group. Most editors do not appreciate nor respond to follow-up calls by phone after a release is sent, unless the story is extremely important and timely. Many reporters feel harassed by follow-up calls and are likely to resent people who call with marginal leads on a regular basis. Do not despair if a release does not immediately generate a story; it may lead to a story at a later date. A steady stream of well written and conceived releases can help establish a group as a reliable source of news, and reporters may start calling the organization on a regular basis. As the coverage increases, so will the volume of calls.

Many nonprofits render services that make conspicuous contributions to the quality of life. News releases need only to document the contributions in a descriptive and factual manner.

## Newswriting Style

Just as important as the content of the news release is the style in which it is written. The prevailing approach is based on the idea that people are pressed for time and want to learn the point of a story quickly. Newspapers are designed to be read or scanned during a 15-minute breakfast or train ride. Most broadcast stories are shorter than two minutes. Web surfers look for key words that catch their attention and give them a reason to stay on the site.

All paragraphs in news stories are short; the first is usually one sentence, and the rest generally consist of no more than two sentences. They deliver the information first and the source second: Instead of "ABC Charity president Joe Smith announced today that contributions tripled in 1999," write, "Contributions to ABC Charity tripled in 1999, announced President Joe Smith today." And the most important part of any news story is the beginning: the lead paragraph and the two to three paragraphs that follow. The first few paragraphs should provide a synopsis of the story or so intrigue readers that they feel compelled to read on.

The story that provides a synopsis is called *hard news*. The reader should be able to learn the essential facts by reading only the first few paragraphs. A second style is *soft* or *feature news;* this approach often tries to hook the reader with a human interest angle. A hard news story may begin in this manner:

CHICAGO, ILL., JAN. 5—The Air Ambulance Service saved 632 lives in 20X2, more than double the number in the previous year, with most of the increase occurring with the blimp explosion over Soldiers Field.

"The record number of saves makes us very proud," said Air Chairman Jack McFly. "We're thankful that the special training in dirigible accidents helped us respond to the Soldiers Field tragedy."

In 20X2 the service saved 312 lives in the blimp accident, another 270 people from drowning, 23 in fires and 27 in other incidents.

The service was founded in 1958 and currently employs 12 full-time workers and operates four helicopters. A nonprofit group, it is supported by public donations, along with contributions from area hospitals. . . .

A feature story on the same topic might read like this:

When Bruce Leonard first heard about the plan to receive special training in blimp rescues, he scoffed, "We haven't had one of those since the Hindenburg. You've got to be crazy."

Leonard's opinion changed dramatically less than two months later, when he was holding his chopper 50 feet above a blazing blimp rescuing 18 terrified passengers—an act of valor that earned him a commendation from the city of Chicago.

The service rescued 312 people in all from the blimp accident over Soldiers Field. This one incident accounted for nearly half of the 721 rescues in 20X2—a record and more than twice the number in the previous year. . . .

News releases written in either style should make liberal use of quotes by leaders of the organization. Quotes add color, emphasis, and human interest. If news outlets do not publish the release, they may pick up some of the quotes.

All releases should observe the conventions of capitalization, abbreviation, hyphenation, and usage that prevail in the news media. The most widely used convention is AP style, as set forth in *The Associated Press Stylebook* (available in many major bookstores or from the Associated Press, 50 Rockefeller Plaza, New York, NY 10020; 212-621-1824). The publication also offers useful grammar guidance.

## News Release Format

All news releases must include certain elements. The first page should appear on the group's letterhead or special letterhead designed for news releases. Special letterhead should include the word NEWS prominently across the top or side, and the name of the group or its field of expertise, such as NEWS FROM THE AMERICAN ACADEMY OF COSMETIC SURGERY or NEWS ABOUT COSMETIC SURGERY. The other necessary elements are described as follows.

*Release Date and Time*—Above the headline, advise the news media when they may publish or air the information. In most cases, the instruction will be FOR IMMEDIATE RELEASE. If you are sending out a release before an event takes place, the instruction should be FOR RELEASE ON (the date and time the event is to occur).

*Contact Person*—Underneath or across from the release date, provide the name of a person the news media can contact for more information, and type a telephone number under the name. You can also add an e-mail address. Provide the contact's home telephone number as well, if calls are anticipated at night or over the weekend.

*Headline*—Summarize the highlights of the story, drawing from the points made in the first few paragraphs. This can consist of a main head and a kicker above or below. View the headline as an opportunity to sell the story, to encourage the editor or reporter to read on.

*Dateline*—Most stories should begin with the city and state from which the release is coming (either where the group is headquartered or the site of the event being described) and the date. For example: PEORIA, ILL., AUG. 3, 2000—. . . . Note that AP style requires that the names of states and months be abbreviated, except for those with four letters or fewer. A dateline is not needed on feature stories that are not time-sensitive.

*Body*—Leave several inches of white space above the headline to give news editors room to edit the copy, revise the headline, and insert type specifications. Do not break sentences or paragraphs from one page to the next. Number pages at the top, using either standard numbers or the traditional news format (ADD ONE for page 2, ADD TWO for page 3—along with a one- or two-word slug line for the story; for example, ADD ONE—RESCUE). Type MORE at the bottom of each page except the last; at the end of the story, type ### or - 30 -.

*Standard Description of the Group*—It is good practice to end releases with a three- to four-sentence description of the organization, its purpose, scope of activities, number of supporters or members, and any other information that can help an outsider to quickly grasp its reason for being. This statement can appear on all materials published by the organization: consumer brochures, research reports, testimony, newsletters, journals, and even the back of business cards. This helps to ensure that the essential facts about the group are disseminated in a consistent manner.

Exhibit 8–1 is a sample of a news release.

**Exhibit 8–1**   Sample News Release

---

*NEWS ABOUT COSMETIC SURGERY*

CONTACT:    Joan Hughes              FOR IMMEDIATE RELEASE
            999-111-0000

**PROTRUDING EYES CAUSED BY GRAVES' DISEASE
CAN BE TREATED THROUGH COSMETIC SURGERY**

PEORIA, Ill., Jan. 29, 1999—One of the many side effects for individuals afflicted with Graves' disease is bulging of the eyes. Many who suffer from the disease are unaware that this condition can be successfully treated through cosmetic surgery, according to a presentation today at the 15th Annual Scientific Meeting of the American Academy of Cosmetic Surgery (AACS).

Cosmetic surgeon Peter Levin, M.D., presented the results today of his experience with orbital decompression in Graves' disease patients with prominent eyes who desired cosmetic improvement.

Graves' disease is the leading cause of hyperthyroidism and reflects a basic defect in the immune system. It causes production of antibodies that stimulate and attack the thyroid gland, causing growth of the gland and overproduction of the thyroid hormone. Similar antibodies may also attack the tissues in the eyes.

In the study, 22 orbits of 12 consecutive patients underwent orbital decompression for cosmetic improvement. All patients had Graves' disease that had been stable for at least 12 months. Excluded from this series were patients with active inflammatory orbital disease, visual loss, diplopia, globe subluxation, or retinal folds.

"The goal of surgery was to reduce, but not necessarily eliminate, exophthalmos (protrusion of the eyeball from the orbit) and to obtain or maintain symmetry between the eye orbits," said Dr. Levin.

Surgical technique was individual for each patient. The surgery involved opening the orbit and the areas around it, and expanding into the sinus region. Once the area was opened or expanded, the fat bathing the eye inside the eye socket was removed. This expansion and fat removal allowed the eye to decompress into a more natural position. "The sinuses are air-filled, so if you remove the wall between the sinus and the eye socket, the eye can sink back naturally," said Dr. Levin.

–more–

The results showed that all patients had decompression ranging from 2 mm to 7 mm, which is considered a normal variance. Virtual symmetry was obtained in all patients. Temporary side effects included only numbness or tingling in some patients.

"Orbital decompression is an option for patients with prominent eyes who desire cosmetic improvement," said Dr. Levin. Graves' disease occurs in less than one fourth of 1 percent of the population and is more prevalent among middle-aged females.

The American Academy of Cosmetic Surgery (AACS) is an accredited council of professionals devoted to postgraduate medical education in the field of cosmetic surgery. Members of AACS are dedicated to patient safety and satisfaction through physician education. AACS is the nation's largest multidisciplinary medical organization that devotes its educational efforts exclusively to cosmetic surgery. AACS operates a toll-free Cosmetic Surgery Information Service for brochures and lists of specialists in a given area: 1-800-A NEW YOU.

# # #

## Media Alerts

An alternative to the press release, and sometimes much more effective in generating feature stories, is the media alert. There is no hard and fixed format, but the media alert would contain the basic who/what/where of the press release, but with more background and without quotes. It is not intended to be published as it is—rather, to get the attention of an editor or reporter who will then interview spokespersons for the organization and write his/her own story. Media alerts are usually hand delivered to editors or reporters—ideally, those who have covered similar events or written about similar organizations in the past—or sent by fax after you have made an initial contact by telephone. Exhibit 8–2 is an example used by the VNA & Hospice of Northern California to gain press coverage of its "Hospice Mask Project" (see also discussion of this fund-raising project in Chapter 5).

## Broadcast News Releases

News releases may also be sent to radio and television outlets in forms suited for those mediums. For radio, the releases are narrated onto cassettes and sent to news directors. The most costly variation is the video news releases designed for television outlets. These are sent either in cassette form or by satellite. The length should fit the short television news format. A video release should be packaged whole and in parts so that producers can easily extract quotes and visuals for

**Exhibit 8–2    THE HOSPICE MASK PROJECT:** Benefiting VNA & Hospice of Northern California

---

WHO

Visiting Nurse Association & Hospice of Northern California (VNA & Hospice), a not-for-profit home health care organization, is hosting the international fund-raising event *The Hospice Mask Project* in San Francisco, CA October 16, 1999. *The Hospice Mask Project* is a collaborative effort between VNA & Hospice, civic and community leaders, elected officials, corporations, and local artists to give visibility and much needed funds to the home hospice care services and programs.

WHAT

Mask creations are by nationally and locally known celebrities from an array of backgrounds including the arts, politics, finance, music, theater, media, sports, and technology. The mask creators are furnished with a plain clay mask, acrylic paints and paintbrushes. Using the tools provided, or materials of their own choice, creators are encouraged to put their best face forward in designing their one-of-a-kind mask, and then sign it.

CELEBRITY—ARTISTS

Over 300 local artists, celebrities, and dignitaries have embraced the Hospice Mask Project. Some of the masks already received include creations by Kirk Douglas, Bob Hope, Robin Williams, Bobby McFerrin, SF Giants Barry Bonds & Rich Aurilia, 49er Ronnie Lott, Katie Couric, Al Roker & Ann Curry of NBC-Today, Steve Miller, Bonnie Raitt, Danielle Steel, Richard North Patterson, Peter Mintun, Charlotte Mailliard Shultz, George Shultz, Dr. Dean Edell, Assemblyman Ted Lempert, Mayor Claire Mack, Mayor Diane Howard, and artists Daniel Merriam, William T. Wiley, Tom Holland, Nathan Oliveira.

GALA DETAILS

**Charlotte Mailliard Shultz & George P. Shultz—Honorary Chairs**

A mega, end-of-the-century Celebrity Mask Gala was held on Saturday, October 16 at the San Francisco GiftCenter Pavilion that featured a live auction at which a portion of the masks was available to the highest bidder. Butterfield & Butterfield conducted the live auction. In conjunction with National Hospice Month in November, the remainder of the masks will be available for online auction via eBay.com. View an exquisite collection of masks on our online gallery at www.MaskProject.com.

INTERNATIONAL APPEAL

The original Mask event took place in 1994 in Israel where it raised one million dollars for a school for handicapped children in Tel Aviv. In 1995, a charity organization associated with Prince Charles used the Mask Project and raised over $250,000 in England. The Mask Project came to the United States and was held in Denver, CO to benefit Hospice of Metro Denver. This fundraiser culminated in a Gala on May 9, 1998 that raised over $450,000. Rezvan Moghaddam of VNA Hospice of Northern California has committed to making the Bay Area host for the Hospice Mask Project in 1999.

**Exhibit 8–2** (*Continued*)

---

PRESS CONTACT

Caroline Rustigian, K-Line Publicity at (415) 477-9391

TITLE SPONSORS

**Visa U.S.A., Absolut, Roxane Laboratories, Sutter Health Systems, Bay Meadows Racecourse and KPIX** are official Sponsors of the Hospice Mask Project.

ABOUT VNA & HOSPICE OF NORTHERN CALIFORNIA

Through its Home Care and Home Hospice Care services, VNA & Hospice makes over 305,000 visits a year, serving more than 17,000 patients in Northern California. VNA & Hospice, the leader in technically proficient and compassionate care at home, continues to reach all segments of the community with its innovative practices. VNA & Hospice is a 501(c)(3) not-for-profit agency and a Sutter Health affiliate. For more information about VNA & Hospice of Northern California, visit *www.vnahnc.org.*

---

use in stories they develop. It is common to send broadcasters a "B" roll of images that can serve as background visuals for the stories. It is best to retain a public relations firm to produce these and tend to the technical details. Beware of costs: Smaller organizations should avoid video production unless they can obtain donated services.

## Background Materials

In many communications activities, you will need to distribute background information that provides a broader context, essential facts, historical perspective, or the status of the issue at hand. At a minimum, you will want to present the basic information about the organization, as described earlier, although it is common to develop a more detailed description running one or two pages.

Background materials help establish a nonprofit group as an objective, credible source of information. This is not the place for emotional appeals. It is best to present the facts in a neutral manner, acknowledge opposing views, and refute them dispassionately. Save the purple prose for speeches, testimony, colorful quotes for the news media, and opinion pieces in newspapers and magazines. Several formats are commonly used:

*Question-and-Answer*—Think of questions that members of your target audience are most likely to ask, and provide brief, straightforward answers. Often, a piece is structured to begin with the most basic questions and progress to the most complex and controversial. Some subjects lend themselves to a chronological approach. Your Web site should have a feature known as FAQs, or frequently asked questions. These can address your group or cause or specific issues and policies.

*Issue Brief*—This format is best for legislative issues. In one section, present the background: the circumstances that gave rise to the issue, problem, or difference of opinion. In another section, describe the status of the issue, such as where a bill stands in the lawmaking process and the steps that remain before it becomes law. Finally, the brief should state your position on the issue. Issue briefs should run no longer than two or three pages. These serve primarily to give public officials, journalists, and other interested parties a quick read on the issue and a sense of where the group stands.

*Fact Sheet*—Use this format to present basic information about your organization, cause, profession, or industry. Charts and tables are often helpful. Summarize the services and programs and whom they benefit; the dimensions of the problem that the group is trying to solve; or the economic performance of the industry or profession. Fact sheets can be copied onto standard-sized sheets or printed in pamphlet form.

*Fact Card*—You can also condense the essential information on a wallet-sized card as a convenient handout, or print it on the back of a business card.

## The News Conference

The news conference is an overused tool, overrated perhaps because we see prominent public figures meeting the press so often on television. Few events or issues are important enough to warrant a news conference. Save this tool for dramatic announcements on matters of great public concern, such as an announcement to launch a relief effort to benefit victims of hunger, homelessness, and natural disasters. A plan to start a national foundation for kidney research is significant enough. Research revealing public health hazards may also qualify, although the group making the announcement should make sure the research is strong enough to withstand scientific scrutiny.

News conferences are useful for responding to emergencies. They provide a timely and efficient way of disseminating vital public information. During disasters, emergency response agencies can use news conferences to request blood, blankets, food, water, four-wheel-drive vehicles, and other items.

Whether a news conference is successful also depends on the size of the city and the intensity of competition for news coverage. What plays in Peoria may not be of interest in New York City. Another consideration is that there are many more journalists in major cities, such as New York, Chicago, and Los Angeles. With a good story, you might be able to draw a dozen reporters, at most, to a conference in St. Louis or Atlanta or San Diego. This can be worthwhile if wire service or television journalists are among these reporters, for they can deliver regional and, possibly, national coverage.

In major news media centers, you may generate a greater turnout, but only if the issue is compelling. Numerous press conferences are held each day in these cities. Here, you have a larger pool of reporters to draw from, but more interests are competing for coverage.

As an alternative to a live news conference, consider hosting a Web news conference. Web news conferences using interactive technology have the advantage of allowing editors in many locations to log onto the conference without leaving their offices. The contents of a typical press kit can be made available in digital format to participating editors. It is also possible to conduct a Q & A session and provide live video of presentation materials.

Yet another alternative is to hold a telephone conference call with the media. Telephone news conferences can draw a broad turnout, as reporters can "attend" simply by making a telephone call. In this format, you forgo television coverage, but it is the least costly means for you and most convenient for reporters.

The logistics to be considered in planning and conducting a news conference include a number of elements:

*Whom to Invite*—Letters or news advisories should be sent to all reporters who regularly cover the group or the issues to be covered at the news conference, along with the news directors and newspaper editors. Ask the local Associated Press bureau to include the conference in the Day Book, the list of events circulated each day to all news organizations. When reporters come to the news conference, have them sign a log to provide a record of who attended.

*Where to Hold It*—Carefully select the site, considering the image that will appear behind the speakers. For example, to emphasize the importance of citizen response to jury summonses, the Council for Court Excellence in Washington, D.C., held a press conference in Washington just outside the entrance to the D.C. Superior Court. Television clips showed the site. Beyond visual considerations, the site should be centrally located, such as at a downtown hotel or press club, and have a large room equipped with chairs, a podium, sound system, and enough electrical capacity for the broadcast media.

*When to Hold It*—The best time is often about 9:00 or 10:00 A.M., to give the news media ample time to meet their deadlines, especially for evening broadcasts and newspapers.

*How Long*—Generally, limit the duration to one hour or less because reporters lack the time to stay longer. A large portion of the time should be reserved for reporters' questions.

*Who Should Represent the Group*—In nearly all cases, the nonprofit's chairperson or top executive should serve as the principal spokesperson. Minimally, this individual should welcome the news media and make an opening statement about the issue at hand before turning the forum over to people with more detailed knowledge of the subject. All senior executives in the group should be on hand to answer questions that the top executive cannot.

*Handouts*—Provide the news media with news releases, background materials, and copies of the statements. These are often placed in a press kit bearing the group's logo, with pockets inside for the materials. Releasing the statements in print form does not eliminate the need to present them live at the news conference, because television reporters must capture them on film.

*Rehearsal*—Speakers should rehearse not only their remarks, but also the answers to questions reporters are likely to ask. Focus especially on the most difficult questions.

## Consumer Information

One of the best ways for nonprofit groups to build goodwill is to educate consumers about matters that affect their health and well-being. Many subjects are suitable:

- How to recycle and otherwise help the environment
- Methods for storing food and preparing it safely
- Tips for healthy living
- First aid information
- Preparing for emergencies
- Vacation ideas
- Recovering from natural disasters
- Programs to mentor or educate at-risk youth
- Aid to local schools, hospitals, police and fire departments, and other community institutions

The information can be provided in numerous forms. Burglar and fire alarm and ambulance services can provide their phone numbers on a pressure-sensitive sticker to be placed on the telephone. Brochures are probably the most popular format; announce their availability to news organizations, saying you will send one free to any consumer who sends the group a self-addressed and stamped envelope. Other formats include the following:

*Public Service Announcements (PSAs)*—These are like the broadcast news releases described earlier, except that the message is public service-oriented. However, the competition for time is intense in most cities, and most outlets reserve the times that command the greatest audiences for commercial advertisements, airing PSAs during the late night and early morning hours. Although the sponsoring organizations do not have to pay for the air time, only the most interesting and professionally produced announcements are likely to be broadcast to large audiences.

*Programs for Schools*—An excellent way of looking after the long-term interests of a group is to educate those who will be your supporters, donors, and consumers in the future. Offer the organization as a resource for teaching classes; veterans in the group may enjoy such an opportunity. Groups can also produce films and videos and other instructional materials. Some organizations prepare instructional kits, including a guide suggesting how teachers can present the subject and booklets for the students. A creative alternative is to design games that children can play in school or at home and learn valuable information in the process.

## Annual Reports

It is customary for organizations of all kinds to publish a year-end report summarizing activities and accomplishments. Such reports are a tailor-made answer to the question, What have you done for me lately? Fortune 1,000 corporations invest large sums designing works of graphic art intended to impress investors. Glitzy reports, however, can be counterproductive for nonprofit groups, for they give the impression that funds are being squandered on style at the expense of substance. Thus, nonprofit groups can save money and produce a better-received report at the same time.

Groups that rely heavily on donations will need to publish some kind of accounting of funds raised and spent. Other small nonprofit groups can dispense with an annual report, perhaps devoting the December issue of their newsletters to a review of the year's achievements. Larger groups should view the report as a means to recruit and retain supporters and as a background piece for journalists, public officials, and community leaders.

Use the annual report to document accomplishments and new programs. Shine the spotlight on those who support the organization and benefit from its services. This is not the place for gratuitous praise or for ego-massaging the group's leadership—features that tend to undermine the credibility of organizations that rely heavily on public trust. As with all background pieces, stick with the facts.

The structure of such reports is open-ended. Think of a half dozen accomplishments or programs over the last year, and devote a section to each. With photos, charts, and several pages of financial information, you should have enough material for a 16-page report—the most economical length for printing. Groups may also conserve funds by publishing reports every other year.

## Speeches

The speech is one of the most effective public relations tools because it is a news event unto itself. To make a statement in a public forum carries more weight than including the same statement in a news release. The news media are inclined to give it more coverage, and the audience may be deeply moved if the speech is well conceived and delivered. Speeches are an especially powerful means for group leaders to strengthen their standing.

Speeches differ from other types of writing. They are written for the ear, not the eye, meaning the style should be conversational, the structure explicit, and the scope narrowed to a few key points. The ideal length is 20 to 30 minutes. Narrow the topic by asking what action you would like the audience to take in response to the speech or what beliefs you would like them to adopt.

In some cases, videos, slides, and other visuals can enhance the presentation. Such props also introduce the opportunity for technical problems. You must rehearse any presentation relying on visual props and have a contingency plan in case the technology fails. Group leaders should also bear in mind that visuals distract the audience's attention from the speaker. If one purpose of the speech is to strengthen the leader's stature, visuals should be minimized or eliminated altogether.

Leaders of nonprofit groups are likely to receive many invitations to speak. Local civic clubs—Lions, Rotary, and the like—offer valuable forums for nonprofit charitable organizations. Seek out forums where you can address the key audiences identified in your public relations plan. As an act of reciprocity, invite the leaders of key constituencies to speak at one of your meetings. After you deliver a speech, broaden the impact by sending copies to the news media and important constituents.

## COMMUNICATIONS TACTICS

Nonprofit groups bring formidable resources to the practice of public relations, but these must be carefully used. Important audiences may be skeptical, and the news media and public officials may assume adversarial postures in some instances. The rewards for adept actions are as great as the penalties for ill-conceived ones.

### Media Relations

No institution is more independent than the media. This quality gives news an air of authenticity—like a third party ruling on the facts. Nonprofit groups should cultivate relations with the reporters that cover their issues. The best approach is to act as a valuable source, providing accurate and timely background materials, articulate positions, and colorful quotes. Do not attempt to wine and dine reporters. Most news organizations prohibit this, and reporters resent the implication that their favor can be bought.

This does not suggest that you should act as a passive participant in the news-gathering process. View the news media as a vehicle for disseminating messages to important audiences while supplying the information requested. Groups should set up a system with the following elements for fielding media calls:

*Identify a Spokesperson*—To avoid confusion and contradiction, groups should clearly identify a spokesperson and discourage others in their group from talking to the news media. The top executive will usually be the primary spokesperson. Larger groups may designate another executive, usually the highest-ranking communications official, to share the role.

*Build in Time to Reflect*—Whenever possible, find out the reporter's topic ahead of time so you can respond in a calm, intelligent manner. The easiest way to buy time is to have someone else answer the phone and inquire about the subject before relaying the call to you. If the subject is especially complex or controversial, you may elect to do additional research before calling the reporter back.

*Respect Deadlines*—Reporters from daily newspapers and broadcast outlets often have only several hours to complete a story. An excellent way to cultivate good media relations is to respect their deadlines by responding promptly to all press calls. If you, as spokesperson, do not know the answer to the question, offer to find out and call the reporter back. Be sure to follow through on that promise; call-backs help to build a source's credibility with reporters.

*Stick with Your Field of Expertise*—Resist the temptation to comment on subjects outside the purview of your group. You may be treading on the territory of other groups that could serve as important allies.

*Don't Comment on the Business of Supporters or Members*—Nonprofit groups exist at the pleasure of their supporters or members. Spokespersons should play up the positive features of their constituency but never offer opinions on the troubles of individual supporters or members.

## Broadcast Interviews

Broadcast media, especially television, pose special challenges. The impact can be powerful, but the format limits the time allotted to sources to sound bites measured in a few seconds. It is common for half-hour on-camera interviews with a source to be reduced to two 15-second clips in a two-minute story. Thus, you have to make every word count. In television the visual dimension adds another challenge. You may say the right words, but your fidgeting hands, tense facial muscles, forced smiles, and gaudy clothes can undermine the message. Exhibit 8–3 is a broadcast interview checklist:

**Exhibit 8–3**    Preparing for the Broadcast Interview

- Find out the program slant (consumer, business, hard news, interview, etc.) and how the interviewer's position compares with yours.
- Within the theme or format of the show, determine two or three important points you want to make during the interview. Rehearse responses to questions likely to be asked.
- Make certain that facts supporting your position come to mind easily and are up-to-date.
- Before the interview, check morning newspaper and broadcast reports for late-breaking stories that affect the issues to be discussed.

*Physical Setting and Body Movements*

- Keep your hands off table microphones, don't drum your fingers on tabletops or tap your feet on the floor or on the side of the chair.
- Don't look down or breathe heavily into a microphone hung around your neck or a lavaliere clipped to clothing.

**Exhibit 8–3** (*Continued*)

- Avoid sudden body movements (standing up, learning back in a chair, etc.) that can take you out of camera range.

*Personal Appearance*

- Dress conservatively. Men should wear dark suits, solid-color shirts, and long socks. Women should wear business dresses or suits, preferably of a solid color.
- Remove loose jewelry and prominent rings (except wedding bands). Women should not wear heavy necklaces or bracelets, diamond or rhinestone jewelry, large earrings, or pins.
- Don't wear sunglasses or Polar-Gray glasses. Remove name tags, lapel pins, and all extraneous items attached to jackets.
- When seated, don't slouch or lean to one side. When standing, don't rock back and forth or put your hands in your pockets.
- Keep your head up, so as not to look guilty, when listening or talking. Avoid casting your eyes toward the ceiling.
- Try to match your facial expressions with the seriousness of the matters under discussion. Do not smile at the wrong time because of discomfort.
- Ask for makeup on your face to control perspiration and reduce light reflection.

*Oral Presentation*

- Answer questions in 10- to 20-second sound bites. Give the headline first, then document the answers if time permits. Avoid time-wasting phrases, such as "That's a good question ... " or "I'm glad you asked me that ..."
- Take a second or two to frame your answer if you need it, rather than thinking out loud. Do not repeat the question, especially if it is hostile. Do not repeat negative words.
- Answer only one question at a time.
- Work in your two or three key points, using conversational techniques. You might acknowledge a related question as a bridge or answer a question in such a way that the interviewer must ask a question related to one of your key points.
- Avoid using large dollar figures or other complicated statistics; percentages are better. Where possible, round off numbers or use small ones.
- Don't be defensive. Enjoy taking the offensive. Above all else, be positive.

## Community Relations

The benefits of community relations are self-evident. Purely charitable organizations promote community relations to raise funds, and others reinforce their value as institutions worthy of support.

Community relations activities are virtually immune from criticism. The possibilities are endless:

- Health fairs offering free cholesterol and blood-pressure tests
- Fun runs, in which either the entry fees are donated to charity or sponsors for each runner donate a certain amount for each mile run
- Tailgate cookouts before football games in which local grocers and restaurants donate the food and the proceeds go to charity
- Litter cleanup days coordinated with local youth organizations
- Building homes for low-income families
- Sponsoring sports leagues for youths
- Mentoring youths to help them stay in school and off drugs and alcohol
- Support for local food banks and soup kitchens
- Demonstrations of your group's services in public forums
- Raffles and lotteries to raise money for worthy causes

Community relations programs require the same attention to detail needed in all public relations programs. Especially when programs involve more than one group, begin coordinating activities months before the joint activity is to begin and clarify the division of responsibilities. This practice builds trust and avoids awkward encounters in which leaders of the sponsoring groups present conflicting messages.

*At the start of every flu season, the Visiting Nurse Association of America sends an army of nonprofit nurses into supermarkets, drug stores, and health clubs to vaccinate people. The group buys the serum in bulk, and nurses donate their time to reduce the cost to about $10 per shot. The program started at the local level, and success has turned it into a national program.*

## Political Action

One often overlooked application of public relations is its role in lawmaking. To the extent that elected officials are moved by public opinion, public relations can influence the legislative process. A newspaper editorial, a column by the leader of a nonprofit, a creative demonstration, or televised testimony can sometimes win more votes than conventional lobbying techniques. For this approach to work, however, groups must show how their legislative goal serves the public interest: how it will help consumers, save money for taxpayers, create jobs, promote health, or serve the needy—in other words, the broad causes that public officials champion when they run for office. If a legislative goal cannot be expressed in broad terms, public relations will not be an effective tactic.

*An editorial campaign helped defeat a measure known as the Beer Baron Bill, which would have exempted beer wholesalers from certain antitrust laws. The supermarket industry was the lead opponent, represented by the Food Marketing Institute (FMI). The beer wholesalers had advanced the measure well over a four-year period, convincing several hundred members of Congress to sponsor it. FMI had managed to block the beer bill in the past, but this time the proponents had attached it as an amendment to budget legislation that had to pass.*

*FMI took an inventory of the groups supporting its position: the Consumer Federation of America, Association of State Attorneys General, U.S. Department of Justice, Federal Trade Commission, the association representing tavern owners, and many others. FMI sent a packet of information to the editorial page editors of the nation's 300 largest daily newspapers. The packet portrayed the Beer Baron Bill as an irresponsible measure that would increase the price of beer and, ultimately, other consumer products. The packet contained the following elements:*

- *A one-page cover letter describing the issue, noting the urgency of the situation and asking the newspaper to provide editorial support*

- *An issue brief providing the technical details of the bill, its legislative history and current status, FMI's position, and a summary of scholarly research documenting the inflationary impact of exclusive territories*

- *A list of groups for and against the beer bill, showing only two proponents, beer wholesalers and brewers*

- *Copies of letters and statements from other groups opposing the measure*

*More than 40 newspapers published editorials opposing the beer bill, including the* Los Angeles Times, Chicago Sun-Times, New York Times, Washington Post, Detroit Free Press, Cleveland Plain Dealer, Baltimore Sun, *and* Des Moines Register. *FMI created posters displaying the editorials and distributed copies to every member of Congress.*

Effective campaigns often target the political districts and states represented by the lawmakers you want most to influence. These legislators can also be members of the government committees who will first consider a proposed law. When their hometown newspapers publish editorials or columns supporting your position, you can influence the course of legislation at the earliest stages.

For maximum impact, have members of your group who are also constituents send copies of the published pieces to their legislators. Have them clip a copy of the newspaper and send it with a short hand-written cover note.

When effectively applied, public relations can affect legislation in a strong and enduring manner. It is best to reserve such campaigns for issues on which nonprofit groups can clearly align their goals with the public interest.

In some cases, government officials can help groups to address serious public relations challenges.

*A national supplier of microwave popcorn called the Popcorn Institute to report that a newspaper in a New England state had just published a statement from the state's deputy director of public health, saying that a family had been hospitalized with severe stomach distress after eating the firm's popcorn. The manufacturer was running extra tests on other samples from the same lot and was confident that there was no contamination or other problem with its product.*

*Potentially, this was a problem not just for this one company but for the entire popcorn industry, which had built its reputation and its marketing program on popcorn as a healthful snack food.*

*Confident that the company involved was conscientious and responsible, the association's director of public affairs called the Food and Drug Administration (FDA) in Washington, talking first to experts in its division of food safety and next with the director of public affairs. Although FDA did not at that time have any independent information, officials stated off the record that they thought it was unlikely that the food product was responsible for the exact symptoms reported.*

*Other newspapers in the first state began to pick up the story. Larger newspapers, some from other states, called the company and the Popcorn Institute to ask for a statement. A few other consumers in the same state began to report distress after eating the popcorn. Supermarkets in the state reported a noticeable avoidance of all popcorn products on its shelves. A potential media disaster was brewing.*

*While the company continued intensive testing, the Popcorn Institute referred reporters to FDA officials. While the Institute knew that the FDA would not make any definitive statements, it was confident that its officials would state that they believed further information was needed before any conclusion could be reached. Reporters from major media decided that the story was too speculative to run, containing the story while further research continued.*

*Within days, the company was able to call a press conference in the New England city to present findings from analyses done by an independent laboratory, meanwhile popping its product on the spot and inviting journalists to sample it. Most took the offer. The paper that had originated the story issued a partial, qualified retraction; other members of the press ate the popcorn, went home, and killed the stories they had been holding.*

*The Institute then persuaded the public health officer of the state in which the story had originated to invite the Centers for Disease Control and Prevention (CDC) to send an investigator. CDC did this, and two weeks later reported that there was no product problem and that the original family had probably incurred the intestinal distress by drinking unpurified water on a camping trip.*

*The Popcorn Institute initially had credibility with reporters beyond that of the company whose product had been questioned. The decision to ask FDA to comment on the issue, prior to further investigation, was a calculated gamble that paid off. The hysteria, although initially damaging, was confined to one state, and even in that state sales returned to normal within six weeks.*

## CRISIS COMMUNICATIONS

Occasionally, events may threaten the integrity of the group or its constituency. Industry trade associations may have to respond to consumer or regulatory issues; a charitable organization may be called on to explain the cost of a fund-raising campaign. In these situations, effective communication is paramount. A group under fire that speaks with many voices or runs for cover may find its reputation irreparably damaged. Those that communicate well that the group is meeting the challenges will find their stature enhanced.

The first step in effectively handling a crisis is to have a crisis communication plan. Crisis communication planning gives you the process you need to deal effectively with those emergencies or other unusual events that may cause unfavorable publicity for your organization. The Public Relations Society of America offers these general guidelines:

- *Have a written plan.* Emergencies are by their very nature unpredictable, but it is possible to list and prepare for such possible negative situations. Set up a communications system that can be activated in almost any emergency. Identify your crisis communication team and make sure that the roles of all participants are known.

- *Know the priorities.* In any emergency, it is important to place the public interest ahead of the interests of your organization. Your first responsibility is to the safety and well-being of the people involved. After the emergency has passed, be prepared to talk to the public factually. Never minimize a serious problem or try to "smooth it over." Conversely, don't sensationalize or blow minor incidents out of proportion.

- *Communicate quickly and accurately.* Your goal is to move the entire process forward to resolution by using positive, assertive communications on the most important aspects of the problem. Media representatives have a responsibility to get the facts, and they will get their information whether or not you cooperate. If you don't comment on a situation, you can be sure that they will find another source. Maintain control by making sure you are at least one of the major sources of media information in a crisis. Stick with the facts. Don't speculate.

Crises often present certain logical points at which to communicate:

- Immediately upon hearing of the incident or controversy, announce your availability to respond to inquiries and plans to gather additional information, where appropriate.
- After a preliminary investigation, provide an initial assessment of what happened.
- When new, significant facts are uncovered, issue progress reports.
- After completing the investigation, give a full account of the incident, what you learned, and how you will avoid future crises of this nature.

Be sure to inform supporters, members, and other constituents in a timely manner. Share with them any statements you are making and your positions on issues raised by the crisis. This will help them frame responses that are consistent with the group's.

*After the Crisis.* Once the emergency has subsided, the crisis communications team should review the experience and consider the need for follow-up actions. You may want to thank publicly any individuals who were especially helpful, and send a word of thanks to members of the news media as well.

## Handling Adverse Publicity

Every group with a high public profile is likely to receive criticism from time to time. National charitable organizations, for example, have had to answer charges in recent years that they were overcompensating executives or using funds unwisely. Resist the temptation to accuse the news media of conspiring to destroy the organization.

Reporters do hunt for controversy, but most are bound by ethical codes that require balance and objectivity.

Make good use of the opportunity to provide your side of a story. If you learn of an investigation that could be damaging, it may be wise to preempt it with a news conference or interview with a competing news organization before the adverse material is published or aired. If some of the charges are on target, you may want to announce corrective measures at that time.

When considering whether or how to answer an adverse report, you have to weigh several factors. First, your response may keep in the news an issue that you would rather have disappear. Dignified silence is often the best course for matters of secondary importance. Second, you can limit the response to correcting factual errors, in the spirit of setting the record straight. This approach is wise if the issue is likely to arise again. An aggressive response should be reserved for matters that threaten the integrity of the organization or its constituency. In all cases, the response should be built on facts and reason; emotion tends to be counterproductive.

If a group's constituency is being investigated, the group can play a valuable role by speaking for its supporters and serving as a lightning rod for any criticism that may have been directed at them. The group can also develop broad-based programs to resolve problems.

Occasionally, groups may want to work with critics to correct problems that they have cited. The critics can be invited to debate issues in public forums with articulate spokespersons from your group. This can provide a full airing of all sides, giving the news media a more sophisticated understanding of the issues, which can improve coverage in the future.

## COMMUNICATING WITH CONSTITUENTS

Almost every nonprofit organization has a core constituency. This group will vary by the type of organization: for a university, it may include all graduates; for a church, its parishioners; for a charity, recent contributors; for a membership organization, its members. Communication to this group must be frequent and in tune with the basic mission and principles of the organization.

Internal communication differs from public relations according to the breadth or extent of the audience you are attempting to reach. Media relations is concerned with a wide audience: the men and women who read newspapers that carry stories about an organization's activities, listeners of radio programs that broadcast listings of public performances or activities, or those outside your usual group of supporters who receive direct mail pieces. Although communications designed for your core constituency may have wider uses as well, the distinguishing feature is that they are written and designed primarily with your constituent audience in mind. That audience must feel, when reading your newsletter or other communication, that it was created specially for them.

Communications vehicles vary from the most direct of memoranda to material provided on "members only" sections of your Web site. Often, the choice of how to communicate itself tells much about the organization. Marshall McLuhan wrote, "The medium is the message." An organization that communicates through a two-page front and back newsletter creates a different image than one that uses an electronic bulletin board. Material that uses academic language, with complex sentences or a specialized vocabulary, creates a different image than one written in journalistic style.

The possibilities—some of them obvious, some more specialized—include:

- Periodic written reports from the president or other executive staff
- Special reports on recent organization activities or analyses of issues affecting the organization or its members
- Regular newsletters, whether short (two to four pages) or more elaborate
- Magazines or other more "glossy" publications, usually including advertising
- Scholarly journals, brochures, or even books sponsored by the organization
- Audiotapes or videotapes designed to communicate information about the organization
- A Web site containing password-protected material for "members only" access or e-mail designed to give members or your constituency immediate news on key actions or initiatives

Internal communications activities evolve as the organization grows or changes. At the earliest stage it may be sufficient for the executive simply to telephone key board members frequently to tell them how the organization is progressing. Soon there comes a time when the number of individuals who should receive information makes this approach impractical. For some organizations, printed communications fill this need and can speak to the organization's role in its community or profession. Other organizations are using totally Web-based communications to handle board correspondence, membership services, publications, subscriptions, registration for meetings, chat sessions on key issues, and more.

The first step, often, is a two-page newsletter photocopied on the organization's letterhead. This should be printed on a different, perhaps two-color, masthead, to distinguish the newsletter from the stock used for letters or memoranda. A graphic artist can give this communication a touch of professionalism. A complex creative design is unnecessary, but the organization's name or acronym can be laid out in a modern, professional manner; the apparent savings realized by doing this yourself risks the price of an amateurish presentation. If yours is a true charitable 501(c)(3) organization with limited funds, a local graphics designer may reduce or even waive the fee.

Although the substance of articles must come from staff administering the projects or following the issues of concern to the nonprofit, it may not be cost-effective for the executive director to write and rewrite stories, or for the director of membership services to learn to use the layout features of a desktop publishing program. Professionals can do these jobs faster and usually do them better. Issues to consider in deciding whether to hire new staff or use outside consultants for these or other projects are covered in Chapter 15.

The costs of production vary from one part of the country to another. Staff time for a newsletter is usually covered in staff salaries. Out-of-pocket costs can be projected carefully. A format like that shown in Exhibit 8–4 can make estimating easier.

**Exhibit 8–4**   Newsletter Cost Estimate Form

Newsletters

Preprints—based on two color (Blk & PMS), preprinting on page 1 of a 4-page newsletter.

| Number of Copies | Preprint Cost |
|---|---|
| 2,500 | |
| 5,000 | |
| 10,000 | |
| 20,000 | |

Imprint with black ink only, folds to #10.

| | 500 | 1,000 | 2,500 | 5,000 |
|---|---|---|---|---|
| 4 pages | | | | |
| 6 pages | | | | |
| 8 pages | | | | |

**Exhibit 8–4**   (*Continued*)

---

Additionals

- Any applicable sales taxes
- Type from disk (desktop publishing)
- Design and layout
- Photos
- Mailing and postage

---

Magazine publishing is best left to organizations with very large memberships. Moving from a newsletter to a magazine is tempting. With a magazine, an organization may be able to sell ads. This may permit greater use of color, sometimes even four-color covers. The magazine can be circulated to prospective contributors or to a wider audience that the organization wants to reach, thus becoming a public relations tool. But the costs go up geometrically. Unless there is the potential for circulation in the tens of thousands (and where that large a market exists, there is usually a competing for-profit publication), writing, editing, production, and distribution costs are likely to be far greater than can be offset by advertising revenues.

Membership organizations sometimes strive to increase the proportion of non-dues income without realizing that a magazine or other publication actually costs more than it brings in. The figure you need to focus on is the bottom line, not the top-line income from advertising or sales. If staff costs are covered in other line items—and it can be difficult to allocate executive time to a publication—the nonprofit organization may not realize how much of its resources a magazine is really taking. If a magazine is not "carrying itself" in the fullest sense—as determined by a realistic analysis, including how much time and attention it is taking away from other activities—it is time to step back and ask, Is this really helping us achieve our mission? Is communication in this form necessary? A publication decision should be *shaped by,* rather than *shape* the strategic plan.

## FORWARD-LOOKING PUBLIC RELATIONS

The ultimate goal of public relations is to anticipate change so that the group can have programs in place in anticipation of future trends and opportunities. Groups that listen carefully to their constituents can identify emerging issues and needs. If you take action to resolve a problem at the neighborhood level, you'll be prepared to address it at the city or state level—or perhaps your action will prevent its spread. At its best, public relations is a means for engaging constituents in constructive dialogue, a catalyst for change that keeps groups a step ahead of their critics. The discipline endows groups with a vision of their broader purpose, providing inspiration for all who are touched by their actions.

## SUMMARY

- Public relations can support many activities in nonprofit groups: fund-raising, community awareness, member recruitment and retention, lobbying and issue advocacy, financial relations, and crisis management.

- The most effective programs view public relations as two-way communications with groups and individuals important to the organization.

- The group should set strategic goals for the program based on a vision shared by the leadership and supporters.

- When searching for public relations resources, the group should see whether supporters can contribute professional skills, equipment, and other items.

- Audience research will help nonprofit groups develop appropriate messages and track the success of a program.

- Nonprofit groups have many occasions for sending news releases, ranging from announcing the introduction of new services to commenting on the accomplishments of the year just ended.

- Releases should be written in a news style, in which the first four paragraphs provide a synopsis of the story or so intrigue readers that they feel compelled to read on.

- News releases should include a release date and time, contact person, descriptive headline, and a description of the group, among other features.

- Mailings to the news media must often include background materials, such as question-and-answer pieces, issue briefs, and fact sheets.

- News conferences should be reserved for dramatic announcements of great public concern or responses to emergencies.

- News conferences must be carefully planned and orchestrated as to the invitation list and site, the time, duration, and the people who speak on behalf of the group.

- Nonprofit groups can build goodwill by educating consumers about matters that affect their health and well-being, such as how to recycle, prepare for emergencies, shop for products and services, and recover from natural disasters.

- Formats for consumer information range from brochures, to public service announcements on radio and television, to educational programs for schools.

- Nonprofit groups should publish annual reports to provide an accounting of funds raised and spent and to document accomplishments and new programs. The most economical length for printing is 16 pages.

- Speeches are especially effective at sending messages because they are news events themselves. The speaker should develop a strong, simple message and deliver it in 20 to 30 minutes.

- Because the news media is an excellent vehicle for disseminating information to key audiences, groups should set up a systematic method for handling media inquiries.

- Broadcast interviews pose special challenges, requiring spokespersons to consider their appearance along with the message they want to communicate.

- A nonprofit group can reinforce its value as an institution worthy of support by improving community relations. There are many ways to do this, such as by sponsoring health fairs and supporting youth groups.

- A nonprofit group can use public relations to pursue legislative goals when its position is clearly aligned with a broad public interest. Methods include urging newspapers to publish supporting editorials and providing dramatic displays in testimony.

- Crisis communications can often make or break a group's reputation, because its every move in such a situation will be scrutinized.

- Even a nonprofit group may experience adverse publicity. In some instances, no response is needed. In cases in which the integrity of the group or its constituency is threatened, the group should respond aggressively, always limiting the response to facts and logic.

- The best public relations programs serve as an early warning system for emerging trends and concerns and endow groups with a broader vision of their purposes.

# CHAPTER NINE

# Getting Political Support for Your Cause

**Whether it is a campaign before the U.S. Congress or the local school board, your nonprofit organization can be a powerful advocate for your donors and constituents. This chapter explains what it takes—organization, research, persistence, and enthusiasm—to have an impact on government.**

Each day in this country at all levels of government, elected and appointed officials are making decisions that will profoundly affect the members and supporters of your organization. Through an effective government relations program, your organization can educate public policymakers, ensuring better decisions regarding matters that concern you.

In addressing an issue—whether it is before the local county board of supervisors or the U.S. Congress, your organization can be a powerful advocate for its members and supporters. This chapter explains the elements of a successful government relations program:

- A defined public policy agenda
- Research
- Specific policy arguments
- A public policy action plan
- Infrastructure
- Grassroots advocacy
- Effective coalitions
- Patience

- Persistence
- Enthusiasm

Your government relations program is measured through the degree of political support you obtain for the public policy goals of your organization. Political support is obtained by communicating your views in a timely, persistent, and effective manner to members of an elected body—city council, county commission, school board, planning commission, state legislature, or the United States Congress—in regard to any of the following:

- The enactment of legislation
- Taking action favorable to a cause, such as the defeat or repeal of a measure
- The creation of a new program
- Modification of an existing program
- The guarantee or entitlement of certain rights
- Provision of funding
- Maintaining the status quo

America is a nation of constituents. Former House Speaker Thomas P. (Tip) O'Neill (D-MA) once said, "All politics are local." By that he meant that elected and appointed officials must be concerned about the views and interests of all their constituents, including the members and supporters of your organization. If these officials ignore their voters or supporters, they won't hold office very long. Government officials are always concerned about "how it plays in my hometown" because they know that in the end, it's the constituents who elect them. Individually and collectively, we seek to educate our government to set its priorities in accordance with our own concerns and values. A government relations program is an organized effort to educate.

## BUILDING YOUR ORGANIZATION'S PUBLIC POLICY AGENDA

Defining those public policy issues that affect the members and supporters of your organization is the foundation of a successful government relations program. Although this may seem easy, the process of prioritizing and selecting issues that affect the majority of your members and supporters, versus those that affect the sometimes vocal minority, can be a painful one.

A successful approach to this situation is to survey your membership, asking them to rank a listing of issues that have been identified by the leadership of the organization. Inform the membership that the organization will select as its public policy agenda for that legislative cycle (usually a two-year time frame) the public policy issues that rank highest. The number of issues that an organization includes in its public policy agenda is determined by the resources the organization has available for a government relations program—staff time and direct expenses—and the urgency of the issues.

Another method for identifying those issues to be placed on a public policy agenda is to ask a committee of your organization, such as a public policy or government relations steering committee, to identify areas where they believe governmental action is needed to assist their organization or its members, or where current programs and policies are troublesome. This identifies an action agenda.

Finally, your agenda may be defined by your organization's having to respond to the legislative agenda of another organization. This may be a friendly situation in which an ally organization may ask for your help and support in achieving a public policy goal. Or it may be a reactionary or adversarial situation in which another organization is trying to infringe on the members and supporters of your organization.

Beware: One of the major pitfalls in a government relations program is trying to be all things to all people. A smattering of work across numerous issues can make it less likely that you will achieve any of your organization's public policy goals, thus causing members to lose their enthusiasm and motivation. Avoid this risk by having a defined and agreed-upon public policy agenda that can be implemented successfully with the resources available.

## The Importance of Data

For your organization to be credible and effective in its education of public officials, you will want data that is understandable by a lay person and that can be cited as to its origin. This data must be of relevance to the constituents of the public official you seek to educate.

So how do you gather and present data that will be educational and persuasive? First, define numerically how your public policy issue affects the constituents whom the official is elected or appointed to represent.

*For example, in 1998 the Association of Local Housing Finance Agencies (ALHFA) had as a public policy goal to increase the availability of "private activity bonds" used to assist first-time home buyers, to build and rehabilitate affordable housing, to create jobs, and to finance other economic development in communities. The organizations proceeded by sharing the number of first-time home buyers and the number of jobs created by these programs in the congressional district with the member of Congress they had approached. This allowed the member of Congress to see concretely the number of constituents positively affected by this program. In addition, these organizations were able to demonstrate the number of constituents that could benefit if more of these bonds were available.*

Second, if possible, produce data demonstrating that your public policy agenda item has a positive economic impact on the nation or the state, as a whole. How much money will it save? or How much money will it cost? is usually the first question asked by an appointed or elected official.

Exhibit 9–1 gives a good example of how to present data on the cost savings of expanding the Medicare program to increase access to a specific type of health care service. Charts and graphs such as this can be very powerful in presenting your position on a specific public policy issue to many audiences.

Many government relations programs underestimate the need for and power of data. Many struggles over public policy issues are won or lost based on available data. Investing in the collection of data, where none exists, can ensure a good return to your organization.

## Public Policy Arguments That Work

A public policy argument will be well received if you take the time to "know your audience" prior to creating the argument. It is quite possible that you will create different arguments for different audiences. What motivates elected and appointed officials who have been small

**Exhibit 9–1**   Example: Presenting Data

---

Estimated Cost of Hip Fractures in the Year 2000 and Potential Savings as a Result of Vision Rehabilitation Services

- Eighteen percent of hip fractures in the elderly are a result of vision impairment (Framingham Eye Study, 1989).
- It is estimated that 63,000 hip fractures will occur in the year 2000 as a result of vision impairment.
- The cost of medical treatment for a hip fracture is approximately $35,000.
- The estimated cost of medical treatment for these fractures is $2.2 billion.
- If vision rehabilitation services prevented only 20 percent of these fractures, $441 million could potentially be saved.

---

business owners may not motivate officials who have been teachers. In addition, it is important to review the voting records or administrative decisions of any officials that have served for at least a year to ensure that your arguments are likely to be well received, given their prior statements. Finally, if possible, determine whether there is a personal connection between the official and the issue. Making this connection has been particularly effective at the federal level with funding for biomedical research directed toward the causes of and cures for specific diseases. The following is a list of resources to help you obtain background information on elected or appointed officials:

| | |
|---|---|
| *http://www.house.gov* | (U.S. House of Representatives) |
| *http://www.senate.gov* | (U.S. Senate) |
| *http://thomas.loc.gov* | (legislation in Congress) |
| *http://congress.org* | (on-line Congressional directory) |
| *http://www.rollcall.com* | (*Roll Call* magazine) |
| *http://www.cq.com* | (*Congressional Quarterly*) |

There will be some public policy issues for which no data are readily available. Although your organization may choose to collect data using either in-house staff or a contractor, there are alternatives. Personal stories and professional endorsements can be used in place of numerical data. The adage "A picture is worth a thousand words" can apply in regard to the emotional connection a story can make. This type of approach—"making something memorable"—helps officials to keep your concerns/arguments in mind relative to all other competing interests.

## HOW DO WE GET FROM HERE TO THERE?
## A PUBLIC POLICY ACTION PLAN

Putting public policy arguments to work for the purpose of achieving a legislative agenda is the goal of a *public policy action plan*. This document must be routinely reviewed and modified. The plan may have to be modified because of a change in the legislative schedule, a change in the resources available for the government relations program, the emergence of a new issue of greater consequence to the members of your organization, or a request from a public policy official for his or her political agenda. The public policy action plan should be a "road map" for your organization's government relations program, but open to tactical revisions.

Here is a list of elements that should be included in your organization's plan. You may find it helpful, from an organizational prospective, to put the plan in a spreadsheet (computer) format.

ELEMENTS OF A PUBLIC POLICY ACTION PLAN

- *Specific, measurable goals.* These goals should match the items listed in the public policy agenda for your organization. The goals should be stated in such a way as to allow for an evaluation that is concrete and not subjective. Here are three examples of well-defined public policy goals.

  1. Increase federal funding for the Home Investment Partnerships Program and the Community Development Block Grants by $50 million and $100 million, respectively.

  2. Increase federal funding for kidney disease research by 15 percent.

  3. Obtain direct funding from a municipal government for two new group homes for young women who have successfully completed drug addiction programs.

- *Strategies to achieve the goals.* Defining goals is a must for a successful government relations program. However, goals without a plan for implementation really do not get you very far. The plan for implementation is a list of activities your organization will conduct to achieve the goals. It states the audiences or targets for the activities—legislative committees, administration officials, staff of elected officials, community leaders, consumer advocates, and others.

Exhibit 9–2 shows an example of a goal and the strategies to achieve this goal. This is from a public policy action plan for a medical society that is concentrating on federal health care policy. However, the strategies could be similar for a state-based legislative concern, as well. The item to be changed would be the audience.

**Exhibit 9–2**   Sample Goal with Strategies

*Goal:* Increase FY 2000 funding for kidney-specific research.

*Strategies:*

- American Society of Nephrology (ASN) staff to submit testimony requests to the Subcommittee on Labor, Health and Human Services, Education and Related Agencies in both the House and the Senate.

- ASN staff to prepare remarks, in concert with the ASN Council, to be given in person or submitted for the record to the subcommittees mentioned above.

- ASN staff to work with members of Congress on the Appropriations Subcommittees regarding questions on kidney disease research. These questions are to be directed to the appropriate National Institutes of Health (NIH) program directors, either in person or in writing, during their annual testimony appearances.

- ASN staff to work with members of the ASN Key Contact Network to host congressional tours. The goal is to have three tours with members of the

**Exhibit 9–2** (*Continued*)

---

House Appropriation Subcommittee and three tours with members of the Senate Appropriations Subcommittee.

- ASN staff to work with ASN Councilors and ASN Key Contact Network members in select states to have a small delegation come to spend a day in Washington visiting their congressional delegation.

- Staff to prepare one-page education papers for congressional staff on a National Kidney Disease Education Program, Advances in Kidney Disease Research, and Workforce issues.

- ASN staff to secure language in congressional reports supporting increased emphasis on kidney disease research at specific NIH institutes.

- ASN staff to organize a site visit for staff of members of Congress to the National Institute of Diabetes, Digestive, and Kidney Diseases, for them to learn more about the types of kidney disease research that are being funded. The visit will include a meeting with senior staff and a tour of the intramural labs, including selected experiment stations.

- ASN staff to draft and secure two members of Congress to give one-minute statements for the *Congressional Record* on new advances in kidney disease research and the need for a National Kidney Disease Education Program.

- ASN staff to secure a member of the House to initiate a "Dear Colleague" letter to increase funding for kidney disease research and emphasize the need for a National Kidney Disease Education Program.

- ASN staff to secure a Republican member of the House and a Democratic member of the House to sponsor a congressional briefing, using the publication of the proceedings from the Renal Research Retreat as the basis for the program.

- ASN staff to create a series of "Action Alerts" for members of the ASN Key Contact Network, their patients, and the general membership of the ASN. These Action Alerts are to be timed to affect positively the funding for kidney disease research. The Alerts are to be placed on the ASN Web site, e-mailed, faxed, and mailed.

---

- *Holding the Plan Accountable.* The plan must be held accountable; that is, those charged with implementing the plan must be held accountable. Every public policy action plan should include three additional columns or fields following each strategy. The first column or field will contain the person(s) who has been assigned to complete the strategy. You may want to pair a staff member or contractor with a volunteer leader from the membership of your organization. The second column or field will contain a deadline for the accomplishment of the strategy. In setting these deadlines, you will want to gather information regarding the schedule of the legislative or administrative body that will be addressing your public policy concern. This will enable your organization to be proactive, versus reactive, in its government relations program. The third column or field will contain the name of the person responsible for checking on the progress of the individuals listed in column 1. This function is usually best handled by the staff of the organization.

## INFRASTRUCTURE NEEDS OF A SUCCESSFUL GOVERNMENT RELATIONS PROGRAM

A good foundation of systems—technology based and otherwise—is imperative for your government relations program to move swiftly toward implementing the public policy agenda. The infrastructure elements that your organization should consider are discussed in the following paragraphs.

### A Government Relations Steering Committee

It is important to create a government relations steering committee to work with staff in designing the strategy for your public policy agenda. If possible, appoint people to this committee who are politically active, particularly in support of the elected officials who are making the key decisions on the issues important to your organization, or who are willing to put in the time and effort to build these contacts. Bipartisanship is important and can be accomplished by having on your steering committee people who are active in support of both Democrats and Republicans.

Include individuals who are intimately familiar with those government programs or policies that are affected by or identified in your organization's public policy agenda.

Some organizations elect to have their governing board or executive committee serve as a de facto government relations steering committee. Although this does work, it is not always the most effective structure, owing to other demands put upon the board.

### Lists, Lists, and More Lists

It is very important to have computerized files configured for a mail merge or labels of the elected and appointed officials that have some jurisdiction or say over the areas addressed in the public policy agenda. You will want to gather the names, mailing addresses, phone numbers, fax numbers, and e-mail addresses.

For any extensive program, you may set up fax broadcast lists whereby you can fax directly from your own office computer system, or through a fax broadcast service with which you contract. For local government programs or others on a smaller scale, you can personalize these communications.

As more and more people become active e-mail users, you will have to develop e-mail lists for the timely dissemination and gathering of information. These lists should include names of public officials, as well as the members and supporters of your organization.

The incidents of frustration that can be prevented by investing the time needed to create these and other lists specific to your individual government relations program are many.

## Technology

With the advent of the Internet, e-mail access to the members and supporters of your organization has become essential, as is a government relations section on your organization's Web site. This allows members to receive information regarding the activities of public officials relevant to the specific interests of your organization. It will also enable your grassroots advocacy to be conducted through the Web site, thus making it easier for members of your organization to educate public officials with letters. The following is a list of Web sites that provide tools or models for design of content or of e-mail communication for government relations.

- *http://www.netcapitol.com*
- *http://capitoladvantage.com*
- *http://www.vote-smart.org* (more comprehensive grassroots tracking, public statements of candidates, etc.)
- *http://www.piperinfo.com/state/states.html* (state and local governments on the Net)
- *http://www.capweb.net*

## GRASSROOTS ADVOCACY: EVERY MEMBER COUNTS

What do we mean by the term *grassroots advocacy*? We mean members and supporters of your organization who contact elected and appointed officials to share their views and expertise. This sharing of information builds the relationship between your members or supporters and your public officials that allows your organization to have an impact on issues of concern, both present and future. Once a relationship has been established, public officials and their staff may begin to look upon your organization, and you as its representative, as an important source of reliable information about policies directed at your profession or personal interests. There are four methods for communicating or sharing your views and expertise with elected and appointed officials—meeting with them, calling them directly, writing them a personal letter, or sending them a personal e-mail message. The fine points of each method are discussed in the following paragraphs.

## Meeting with Your Public Officials

A face-to-face meeting with an elected or appointed official, or with the official's aide who handles the issues of importance to your organization, is often the best way to voice your concerns. Meetings with your member of Congress can take place in the member's state or district office or in Washington, D.C. Meetings with state legislators can take place at the state capitol or in their districts. Meetings with local officials can be more informal, taking place at a neighborhood function or county courthouse.

Here are some tips for meeting with your public officials:

- *Always make an appointment.* Contact your public official's office well in advance of your desired meeting date and request an appointment. If he or she is not available to meet with you, request an appointment with the aide who handles your specific issues. Identify yourself and briefly state the purpose of the meeting. Confirm the meeting one day prior to the scheduled appointment.

- *Arrive on time.* Remember that public officials and their staffs have hectic schedules and many appointments during the day. Five minutes can make the difference between speaking with your member of Congress and losing that opportunity because of a vote on the House floor or a committee hearing.

- *Come prepared.* Do your homework and know the facts about the issue that you wish to discuss. This includes knowing the official's position on the issue, the background of the issue, the specific legislation relating to the issue, and any opposing arguments, so that you are prepared to respond to an alternate viewpoint.

- *Introduce yourself.* Identify yourself and, if appropriate, the organization you are representing. Explain why you are interested in the topic you wish to discuss.

- *State your purpose.* Briefly explain the specific purpose of the meeting. Describe the impact of the issue on you and on the constituents represented by the public official.

- *Convey your message.* Meetings with public officials are usually quite short, so be prepared to convey your message concisely. Remember to share relevant personal experiences to illustrate your points and emphasize the possible impact of a piece of legislation on constituents, if enacted. Avoid taking a self-serving position on an issue.

- *Answer questions.* Be prepared to answer any questions the public official may have regarding the topic at hand. Remember that offering useful and reasonable information in support of your viewpoint can be very helpful to lawmakers who are trying to find solutions to problems involving many competing interests.

- *Provide supporting materials.* Bring a written summary of your position or other brief supporting materials to leave with your elected or appointed representative.

- *Get a response.* Before leaving, get a response regarding your public official's position on the issue.

- *Follow up.* Write and send a short note to the public official and/or his or her staff person, thanking that person for meeting with you. You might include a short summary of your position in the thank-you letter. If, during your meeting, your legislator or staff person requests any additional information, be sure to provide it with the thank-you letter.

## Calling Your Public Officials Directly

You can contact your representative or senator by phone in his or her district or state office or in Washington, D.C. Numbers for the district or state offices can be found in your local telephone directory. You can reach an official's Washington, D.C. office by calling the capitol switchboard at (202) 224-3121. Phone numbers of state or local elected or appointed officials, can be found in a special government section of your local telephone book.

Here are some tips on making phone calls to public officials:

- A staff assistant will probably answer the phone. Ask for the legislative assistant (LA) who handles the issues of concern to you and the organization for the public official. If the LA is not available, leave your message with the staff assistant. Make sure you get the name of the person with whom you are speaking.

- Identify yourself as a constituent and give your name. You can also let the staff person know that you are a member of the specific organization or professional society that you are representing.

- Identify the issue or bill you wish to address.
- State your position and ask what your public official's position is on the issue.
- Leave your name and address so that your public official can send a response to you on the matter.
- Follow up with a note to the staff member with whom you spoke, emphasizing your position and your appreciation of his or her attention to the issue. This can help to build your relationship with the staff person.

## Writing a Letter to a Public Official

The following guidelines can be helpful in writing a letter to a public official. See also Exhibit 9–3.

- *Be brief.* Try to keep your letter to a single page, and cover only one issue.
- *Include a sentence or two identifying yourself and your organization.* Indicate that you are representing a group of individuals in the official's district or state, and that you are a member of an organization or association.
- *State the purpose of your letter.* At the outset, explain why you are writing and why the issue is important to you and other constituents.
- *Be specific.* If you are writing in support of or opposition to a specific bill, be sure to identify it by its number (e.g., H.R. 123 or S. 123) and by its name. Give reasons for your support or opposition to the legislation.
- *Write clearly and concisely.* Know the facts about the issue you are writing about and state them succinctly.
- *Know your members of Congress.* If possible, ascertain the position your elected or appointed official has taken on the issue you are addressing in your letter. You can contact the government relations staff of your organization to discover your public official's position. If he or she supports your position, offer thanks; if he or she opposes your position, provide specific reasons to explain why he or she should change positions.
- *Follow up.* If you do not receive a response from your public official, or if your concerns are not addressed in the response you receive, write again. If the response indicates that your position is supported, send a letter of appreciation.

**Exhibit 9–3**  Addressing Correspondence to Members of Congress

---

To a Senator:

The Honorable (full name)

*__(Rm. #)__(name of) Senate Office Building

United States Senate

Washington, DC 20510

Dear Senator:

To a Representative:

The Honorable (full name)

*__(Rm. #)__(name of) House Office Building

United States House of Representatives

Washington, DC 20515

Dear Representative:

*Note:* When writing to the chair of a committee or the Speaker of the House, it is proper to address him or her as:

Dear Mr. Chairman (or Madam Chairwoman):

or

Dear Mr. Speaker (or Madam Speaker):

---

*The precise office number is helpful but not necessary; letters addressed to your member at "United States Senate" or "United States House of Representatives" will be delivered.

## Sending E-Mail to a Public Official

Members of Congress and their staff now often read and respond to e-mail if the message comes from a constituent and is succinct. These guidelines should help:

- Identify yourself as a constituent at the beginning of your message. To maximize effectiveness, put this information in the subject line of your message so that the legislative staff member reading the message knows not to delete it from the in-box. *Example Subject:* Constituent from Cincinnati, Ohio. Re: Increased funding for kidney disease research.

- Include your standard U.S. mail address at the end of the letter. Most members of Congress will use standard mail to respond to your e-mail.

- Keep your message short. Long, rambling messages tend to be ineffective. State your point near the beginning. Use boldface heads to begin each paragraph. If possible, keep the message to one screen (and never more than two).

- Send your e-mail on Wednesday or Thursday. Most congressional mail arrives on Monday, Tuesday, or Friday. E-mail that arrives on those high-volume days may get lost in the shuffle.

- Avoid the words "Congressman" and "Congresswoman." The preferred titles are "Representative," "Senator," and "Member (of Congress)" because each is gender neutral.

- If you are writing about a specific bill, use the bill number, state its current status, name the bill's sponsoring member(s) of Congress or member(s) of the state legislature, and whether the bill is supported/opposed by the president or the governor. This will show that you are educated on the legislative history of the issue.

- Be both specific and practical. Relate the points of your message to your professional expertise and/or the elected official's committee assignments and/or constituents' interests.

- Ask for a response that clearly states the public official's position on the issue.

- Follow up. If the public official does what you want, say thanks. If he or she does not, e-mail your message of disappointment (but be polite!).

## COALITIONS

Coalitions are formal and informal alliances of organizations created to accomplish a common public policy goal(s). Some coalitions are permanently established to work toward a long-term solution for a particular policy concern. Informal or ad hoc coalitions are usually formed to defeat a single law or encourage the adoption of one specific policy; once the goal is accomplished, the informal coalition usually disbands.

Coalitions are effective because they can marshal the energy of a large number of people through the organization they belong to. For example, in many larger communities there are federations of civic associations and federations of Parent-Teacher Associations (PTAs). When these federations take a position, it often carries more weight in the minds of decision makers than would the position of one civic association or PTA.

All it takes to start a coalition is to recognize a common interest. A coalition of PTAs might be formed in support of increased state funding for local schools or of having elected instead of appointed school

**Exhibit 9–4**   What Makes a Good Coalition?

- Defined Message—All coalition members can articulate
- Strategic Action Plan—Defined goals
- Diversity
- Well-Run Meetings—Don't waste people's time
- Results—Tie coalition actions to end product

board members. A coalition of civic associations might be formed to stop the construction of a major highway through their communities.

Coalitions are effective because they demonstrate that an organization is not speaking from a narrow position of self-interest. Coalitions demonstrate unity and numbers of people committed to a cause. These facts impress key decision makers, particularly those who are, or who work for, elected officials. Organizing your members or constituents for your own government relations program should be your first priority. But once that step is taken, think about organizing or creating a coalition (see Exhibit 9–4).

A coalition usually establishes a steering committee to coordinate and agree on the overall strategy and tactics of a campaign.

*The Patient Access to Specialty Care Coalition (PASCC) was formed by a number of physician and patient organizations in 1994 in response to the frustration of many patients in obtaining specialized medical care in the managed health care environment. The coalition established several fundamental patient protections that it believes should be mandated in federal law:*

- *Assured access to specialty care when needed*
- *A fair and expedited independent appeals process*
- *A consumer information checklist to be provided to all patients so they will be able to measure the performance of their health plan and its ability to provide the full range of care*
- *A ban on financial incentives that result in the withholding of care or denial of a referral*
- *A ban on "gag clauses," which prohibit a provider from giving patients certain information, including treatment options*

*Much of the success of the PASCC can be attributed to the breadth of its member organizations, which represent a wide range of constituencies. The organization is composed of 130 health care provider organizations, such as the American College of Cardiology and the American Urogynocologic Society, and voluntary health or patient advocacy organizations, such as the American Diabetes Association and the Cystic Fibrosis Foundation. The coalition's credibility has been enhanced as a result of provider and patient representatives agreeing on what is best for the patient and working together toward that common objective.*

*To harness the tide of growing public dissatisfaction toward managed care, the coalition hired a public relations firm to conduct a national public opinion survey that revealed widespread support for the PASCC's six principles, the results of which were conveyed to members of Congress through mailers and during lobbying visits. The PASCC also developed brochures to educate consumers on the need for establishing national policy to remedy the problems associated with managed care. These brochures, entitled* Your Guide to Managed Care, Specialty Care Works, *and* How Much Do You Really Know About Your Health Plan? *sought not only to educate patients, but to prompt them to contact Congress in support of federal patient protection legislation.*

*After rallying the national organizations, their grassroots membership, and the public to blanket Congress with its message, the coalition achieved its first major victory in 1997, when the provisions it advocated were included in the Medicare Patient Choice and Access Act, guaranteeing these rights to Medicare patients enrolling in managed care plans.*

*After this initial success, the coalition turned its sights to extending these basic protections to all beneficiaries enrolled in managed care plans. To give a human face to its cause, the PASCC assembled "testimonials" from patients who suffered within the current managed care environment and whose problems would have been largely alleviated by the enactment of the managed care reforms supported by the coalition. Several provider and patient representatives identified by the coalition were called to testify before a congressional committee on the need for federal patient protections. An 800 number, established earlier during the Medicare managed care debate, was reactivated for coalition organizations to use in assisting their own members to call their senators and representatives. Similarly, a Web site was established that provided information on these issues and allowed patients and other Internet users to send an e-mail message to their members of Congress.*

*The recommendations of the PASCC were included in the Bipartisan Consensus Managed Care Improvement Act passed by the House of Representatives in the fall of 1999. Some were also included in a bill passed by the Senate, which differs in other aspects. Recognizing that final passage may not occur in 2000, the coalition is determined to continue its work after the year 2000 federal election.*

## ESTABLISHING A GOVERNMENT RELATIONS PROGRAM AT THE LOCAL LEVEL

State and local nonprofit organizations should not overlook the importance of their state legislatures or city governments. America is a nation of advocates. A PTA is formed to ensure that the voices of the parents and students are heard by the school administration. A civic association is formed to protect a neighborhood from unwanted development and to improve a neighborhood by upgrading government services and programs for its community. A charitable organization serving elderly people may need support from the local city council. This process is a part of our American tradition of free speech and the right of citizens to seek redress from their government.

Nonprofit organizations often serve this cause at the community level. Some may owe their very existence to the appeal of their mission. Government relations actions are most effective if they are organized, rather than sporadic or individual. A government relations program of a nonprofit organization at the state or local level, just like a program at the federal level, must be organized and planned based on the time table of the decision-making process and targeted at key people that must be reached. Government action reflects what the people want only if enough citizens take the trouble to let the decision makers know what they think. If you do not take the initiative to educate local officials, you risk the adoption of views that are diametrically opposed to yours. If elected or appointed officials know that you can marshal a letter-writing campaign or a public testimony campaign to support your interests, they are more likely to be cautious or mindful of your views. Individual citizens can have an impact on public policy, but groups of like-minded people and coalitions of groups can be an even stronger force.

Prior to launching a letter-writing campaign, meeting with local officials, or writing a public witness statement, you need to learn as much as possible about the decision makers you are planning to contact.

- What are their interests?
- What are their backgrounds?
- What is their record of support on the issue you are advocating?
- On which committees do they serve, and what positions do they hold?
- Who chairs the committee that will be considering the proposal you support or oppose?
- Who is leading the opposition?

You should also know as much as possible about the groups and individuals who are arguing against your position, as the decision maker will also hear their arguments. If you know the position and arguments of your opposition, you can address those points or concerns in your presentation to the decision maker. It is better to address these issues and offer counterarguments than to let them go unanswered. The decision maker will appreciate your honesty and efforts to help him or her make a balanced decision.

If you want to know an elected official's position on a specific legislation, pick up the telephone and ask that official's staff member. Most elected officials have offices that can be contacted easily. Let the elected official's staff know that you want a copy of a pending bill, study, report, or hearing record, which can be obtained without cost for constituents.

A successful government relations effort must have clear, easily articulated goals. The campaign should express values of importance to the public—justice, fairness, equality, and truth—as well as the importance of the issue being advocated. Try to frame the issue to appeal to prevailing public opinions and beliefs. For instance, job training for unemployed persons enhances productivity, improving schools helps strengthen the economy of the state, controlling commuter traffic through our neighborhoods improves safety for our children.

Remember that advocacy is a long-distance race. Battles are rarely won or lost with a single effort. Successful advocacy requires persistence, organization, research, patience, and enthusiasm.

*A local school organization mounted a campaign in Arlington County, Virginia, to persuade the school board to keep an alternative middle school open. The campaign was initiated and developed following the school board's unanimous vote to consider whether or not to close the school. It was clear from their discussion that the school board members were all leaning toward closing the school.*

*The PTA notified all parents of the middle school students and its companion high school of the school board vote and then held several large meetings. So as not to distract itself from other activities, the PTA decided to establish a special committee to lobby for the continuation of the school. The PTA elected a committee chair who was well known in the county, particularly by key decision makers. Members of the committee were selected on the basis of their knowledge of the schools, school bodies, curricular issues, school board members, and county board members.*

*A quality document was written and developed that answered the opposition's arguments and advocated the continuation of the school. At a key time before the vote, the document was provided to each of the school board members, the superintendent, and key staff in the superintendent's office.*

*Members of the steering committee made appointments with, and visited, each of the school board members and key staff.*

*Recognizing that the school board had asked staff to study the issue, the steering committee met with the research team and presented information to its members throughout the year.*

*Successful efforts were made to form coalitions with other alternative schools, the Association of PTAs, and the Federation of Civic Associations.*

*Members of the steering committee took several of the more outspoken school board members to lunch for a more social, less formal exchange of views.*

*Three individuals (always including one student) testified throughout the year at each board meeting, outlining arguments in support of continuing the school.*

*Because the school board members were appointed by the county board, the steering committee met with the chairman and several members of the county board, which had expressed support for alternative schools. Because the county board was in the process of selecting a new school board member, the candidates were surveyed on their attitudes toward alternative schools. The results of the survey were distributed to the county board.*

*Throughout the year, the steering committee reported to the PTA, held several large, full-membership meetings, and sent out frequent mailings to the parents to keep them informed and to urge them to write to the school board.*

*Finally, in June, at the school board meeting at which the decision was made, 25 parents, school staff, and students testified. The testimony was polite, well researched, and effective.*

*The school board voted unanimously to keep the middle school open. All five members had started in February to lean toward the view that the school should be closed. By June, because of a well-organized, fully committed, and enthusiastic effort, the school board was turned around. Its members were impressed with the presentation of the faculty and the steady flow of information, letters, and meetings throughout the year; they appreciated not being overwhelmed at the final meeting by 50 or more witnesses and a large crowd of supporting parents, students, and faculty. It was a successful campaign, tailor-made to the situation, the history of the issue, and the position and personalities of the key decision makers.*

## The Two P's: Patience and Persistence

Very rarely does government refine policy or create policy in a quick, expedient manner. Many federal- and state-operated government programs have a specific cycle or time frame for programmatic review. It may be once every two years, once every three years, or once every four years that a review can occur. Moreover, if you are trying to create a new program, you will have to wait for the right opportunity that will allow for favorable consideration, which requires the first of two P's, patience. That does not mean that you sit idly by, waiting for your turn. It is during this time that you need to remember the second P, persistence. Do your research. Create your policy arguments. Set up your organizational infrastructure. Continually meet with public officials to build their support for your public policy goal. By being proactive and persistent, you will achieve your public policy goals.

## Let the Celebration Begin

One way to maintain the enthusiasm of the members and supporters of your organization is to celebrate each small victory. Do not wait to have a one-time celebration when the entire public policy goal is achieved. Break it down into smaller steps or accomplishments. When you sign on a key public official as a supporter, send out the good news and publicly thank those volunteer members who worked to solidify that support. When you have a successful grassroots campaign whereby specific numbers of letters and phone calls were achieved, include a news bulletin in the communication vehicles for your organization, thanking all who participated. Give special awards at your annual meeting for the best advocate or the best government relations supporter. This will maintain the momentum and enthusiasm in your organization. Who ever said that doing well can't be fun too?

## OUTSOURCING TO A GOVERNMENT RELATIONS SPECIALIST

Organizations contract for consulting services when they do not have the time or the skills to do the job properly themselves. Professional consultants are hired based on their tactical government relations skills, their track record for achieving the public policy goals of specific clients, their special contacts or relationships with the decision makers and their in-depth knowledge of an issue that is necessary for a successful campaign. Professional consultants are skilled at keeping track of the progress of an issue; they can tell you when a meeting with your decision maker would be most effective; and they may suggest the best time and way to organize your grassroots advocacy campaign.

Consultants cannot win every time, nor can they work magic. Consultants cannot invent good reasons for your cause if you do not supply adequate facts or generate enough enthusiasm. A good government relations specialist will be able to help *you* make the most effective case to the right people at the right time.

One major advantage of hiring a government relations specialist is gaining access to important information before it becomes general knowledge. Government relations specialists can do this because they maintain close day-to-day contact with the programs and decision makers you are trying to educate. The services of a person who monitors government agencies and legislative bodies can help an organization's volunteers maximize their effectiveness by knowing when, how, and to whom the case should be made.

## Legal Limitations on "Lobbying"

The right to petition our government is basic to democracy. The First Amendment to the Constitution of the United States specifically states that "Congress shall make no law ... abridging ... the right of the people peaceably to assemble, and to petition the government for a redress of grievances."

Congress has, however, limited the use of tax-deductible dollars for lobbying. It is important to note that in this context, "lobbying" is not synonymous with "government relations." For the purposes of tax law, lobbying is the attempt to influence state or federal legislation or the decisions of the president, the vice president, or the top two officials of U.S. cabinet agencies—such as the Department of Commerce or the Department of Health and Human Services. Other government relations activities, such as advocacy programs directed at the regulatory or administrative arms of government, fall outside the legal definitions of lobbying.

Because all contributions to 501(c)(3) organizations are tax-deductible charitable contributions, these groups face the strictest limitations. Federal law provides that these organizations should not engage in any "substantial" use of tax-deductible contributions for lobbying.

Because "substantial" was never defined, most 501(c)(3) tax-exempt organizations stayed clear of lobbying until the law was clarified in 1976. Congress at that time removed all doubt as to the legality of lobbying by nonprofit tax-exempt organizations and permitted 501(c)(3) organizations to replace the subjective limitation with a sliding-scale monetary limitation (described in IRC § 501(h)). Now, according to section 501(c)(3) of the Internal Revenue Code, these organizations have the same right as other organizations (within the limits of sliding-scale monetary limitations) to voice their political concerns.

But 501(c)(3) organizations should not hire a lobbyist or a lobbying firm (including a law firm to work on legislation) or expect any paid staff members to devote the majority of their time to legislative affairs without consultation with legal counsel. Some large 501(c)(3) organizations have established 501(c)(6) organizations—contributions to which are not deductible as charitable gifts on the contributor's own tax form—to carry out their legislative advocacy and other government relations work. This step requires sophisticated legal counsel.

Keep in mind that none of these limitations applies to personal advocacy before any body of government by volunteers or non-salaried members of the organization. The most effective advocates for your cause are usually your board members and other supporters. Unless government relations becomes a major focus of your organization, providing information to your members to use in their personal advocacy work will not put your 501(c)(3) tax status at risk.

However, 501(c)(6) organizations do not face any similar limitations on lobbying activities. Government relations, including lobbying, is the principal reason for some organizations' existence. Although lobbying, no matter how extensive, will not threaten the basic tax-exempt status of a 501(c)(6) organization, the tax deductibility of the portion of dues used for lobbying was limited by a law passed in 1993.

Members of 501(c)(6) organizations can no longer deduct the portion of their dues used to influence the federal or state legislatures or top federal executives. This restriction does not apply if no attempt is made to influence legislation and the contact is made only for the purpose of research or monitoring of legislative activities. Contact with the executive branch is lobbying only if it is directed to the president, vice president, or top officials of cabinet offices or if the purpose is to influence legislation. But local activities are exempt: Any portion of dues used for local government relations activities remains tax-exempt to the extent that dues to the organization are otherwise deductible as a business expense. Expenditures for work with regulatory agencies, as opposed to legislative bodies, also remain fully deductible.

Under the revised law, any 501(c)(6) organization engaging in state or federal legislative advocacy should notify its members that the portion of dues used in these activities is not deductible on the member's tax return. (Alternatively, the nonprofit organization may itself pay a "proxy" tax on its lobbying activities at the marginal tax rate for corporations—currently 35 percent.) Although the revised tax law increases the cost of some lobbying activity, it should not affect a government relations program that is efficiently administered and important to the mission established by your members.

## CHECKLIST FOR CREATING A GOVERNMENT RELATIONS PROGRAM

- Clearly identify the outcome you wish to accomplish through your government relations program or campaign.

- Identify staff responsible for the program and establish a steering committee of officers and other key members of your organization to manage the program or campaign.

- Members of the steering committee should include those with program expertise, as well as those having knowledge of and good relations with the key decision makers you need to reach.

- Collect and analyze the relevant information and develop a document/position statement that best presents the case for your issue. This should include information that counters any arguments being used by those who oppose your position.

- Develop a public policy action plan. The following elements should be considered:

  All key decision makers that you need to visit to present with your arguments and position paper. Do not forget the staff associated with key members.

  A grassroots advocacy campaign.

- Keep the broader membership informed and included in the process.

- Form coalitions with organizations that have similar views.

- Seek out opportunities to testify before public bodies.

- Explore the possibilities for public education campaigns to support your campaign goals.

- Monitor the success of the public policy action plan and modify as appropriate.

- Include people who share your full conviction and enthusiasm. Although enthusiasm is critical, it is important to remain calm and professional in your presentation.

- Say thank you, and do not burn your bridges. Remember that not every key decision maker can agree with you on every issue, but some may well be with you on the next issue.

- You may need to outsource your government relations program in its entirety or for selected parts.

CHAPTER TEN

# Looking Beyond National Borders

**More nonprofit organizations than ever before are exploring common interests with potential members or related organizations overseas. What are the opportunities and what are the problems encountered in extending your activities beyond national boundaries? This chapter provides suggestions as to how professional societies, trade associations, and charitable or advocacy organizations can explore these new opportunities.**

The new millennium marks an age of expanding globalization. Corporations have long considered international ventures integral to their planning, relying on modern technology to operate effectively and efficiently. This international arena is increasingly accessible to nonprofit organizations. Many charitable organizations that haven't looked overseas before will do so in the future. Many already solicit international memberships. Others sponsor trade shows, conferences, or educational programs overseas. Advocacy groups are joining with like-minded organizations overseas to promote common policies. Other groups may promote research toward common goals or distribute an international publication. The opportunities and rewards are boundless.

A nonprofit association may be satisfied with intermittent international efforts, or in the long run may seek many such endeavors or even become an international organization. Whatever the goal, going international takes a great deal of effort, time, and resources, and involves maneuvering around major obstacles not encountered in day-to-day domestic operations. On an international level, simple pursuits can turn complicated and bring unexpected failure. Therefore, these undertakings should proceed slowly and with great caution.

## GOING INTERNATIONAL—GETTING STARTED

The first step to going international is to develop a realistic goal. Perhaps visitors from overseas register for your domestic conferences or express an interest in your association. Others follow, and you recognize the potential for broadening international membership or support for your cause. Or your trade organization members suggest the benefits of exhibiting at a trade show in Latin America—perhaps even cosponsoring one with a government or association in that region. Or your environmental organization sees the benefit of making common cause with organizations in Europe. If your plan can be so precisely identified, you can proceed with market research, focusing on specifics.

Start by studying foreign markets. Who would be interested in the programs or services you have to offer? Which products or services might be needed abroad, such as conferences, publications, or research? If you meet foreign attendees at your domestic meetings, ask them what information might be shared in the future. Determine whether people outside the United States are logging on to your Web page.

Start by thinking small rather than trying to present your association to the entire globe. Consider the trends, opportunities, and costs associated with activities in the major regions of the world. Europe offers more cultural connections, long-standing government relations, established legal systems, and a high level of industrialization. If your goal is to help members find new consumer markets, Asia may be the best choice. Trade across the Pacific surpassed that across the Atlantic long ago, as businesses sought to penetrate first the well-developed market of Japan and then the world's largest consumer base in mainland China. But Latin America also shows increasing trade with the United States, and Mexico provides a convenient starting point for Latin American trade and cultural exchange.

Exploring the possibilities, you may find more opportunities than expected. The United States has an extremely well developed non-profit sector—a distinguishing characteristic that goes at least as far back as the observation of Alexis de Tocquiville in the early 1800s. Nonprofits in other countries, for example, are just beginning to see the value of trying to influence government policy. Only in 1999 did Japan pass a law to facilitate and encourage nonprofit organizations. U.S. groups with well-developed public affairs or social welfare programs can offer useful guidance. Trade shows present another opportunity. Expos in other countries are often limited to product exhibitions; in this case, U.S. associations can sometimes establish their presence by adding complementary educational programs.

Analyze relationships between potential member markets and the services and products you offer. For the long term, successful organizations build an international customer database with a running file on each country, including contacts, customs, counterpart organizations, and economic and political factors that affect their trade, profession, or nonprofit concern. Political and social issues often transcend international boundaries.

Of course, establishing counterpart programs or offering educational seminars overseas must be approached with tact. The "Ugly American" is not dead. However, many foreign organizations are delighted to partner with or cooperate with U.S. nonprofits. In fact, U.S. nonprofits are often met overseas with an enthusiasm that a for-profit would not receive. Volunteers in other countries, to take one notable example, have enthusiastically replicated the home-building programs of Habitat for Humanity.

## Partnering

In the international arena, success and failure can hinge on building strategic relationships with non-U.S. partners. Look to organizations in the local markets you wish to enter. An obvious place to start is an international counterpart or an organization whose members may need your product or service. Also helpful are public relations and advertising agencies, logistics and transportation companies, local business contacts, U.S. consultants, U.S. embassies, and association management firms. This partnering can be extremely important, and even crucial, to the success of your efforts, particularly in the day-to-day business aspects. If you have a question—for example, about local telephone service or printing services—the local contact can recommend resources you may not have thought of.

Partners can mean the difference between a project's success and failure. In the mid-1990s a large and well-established industry group introduced a trade show in Hong Kong. The event was patterned after a successful convention in America that was famous worldwide and yearly attracted some 6,000 international delegates from more than 100 countries, including many from Asia. The group expected that it would succeed on the basis of its name recognition and reputation for offering high-quality educational events. The show, however, did not attract enough attendees.

Promotional efforts proved to be quite difficult, because the group failed to appreciate the vast cultural differences in the Asia-Pacific region. Americans tend to view the Pacific Rim as a homogeneous area, but it could not be more diverse. It is virtually impossible to create an event, for example, that will appeal to both Australian and

Japanese interests. Often the government of China must be involved if you hope to gain support from people and businesses in that nation.

Moreover, the logistics involved in holding a trade show some 2,000 miles from headquarters were quite daunting and costly. After two years, the group decided to cut its losses and discontinue the show. Today it remains active in the region, holding small-scale educational seminars. For these ventures it always has a local partner, either a related nonprofit business association in the region or the government of the host country.

A different trade association, which also had a successful trade show attracting a large number of foreign visitors, decided to move overseas more cautiously. Rather than trying to duplicate its U.S. event overseas, this trade association decided to sponsor pavilions of its members at events already established by local national associations in both Europe and Asia. Grouping its members in U.S. pavilions gave focus to their exhibits and gained visibility for them jointly that they would not have achieved individually. The organization has coordinated more than 10 of these pavilions at international meetings in the last five years, with more than 40 companies exhibiting their products.

Another example: The Delta Society, which promotes animal-assisted therapy and the training of service dogs to aid disabled persons, used a similar strategy in developing an international perspective. This organization, headquartered in Renton, Washington, has evolved in less than 15 years from being an obscure research organization to reaching preeminence in its field. But rather than trying to organize its own meetings overseas, it has worked with similar groups in Europe to organize international conferences, rotating between U.S. and overseas locations, and has provided research materials and guest lecturers for similar organizations now evolving in Japan and elsewhere.

A local organization will know the local business and cultural protocols. Remember, you are marketing a product or service to a foreign buyer who has a different cultural orientation. You must accommodate that buyer. If you are holding a conference in Germany, will the sessions be solely in English, or in English and German? What about French?

The costs of interpretation, whether simultaneous (the most difficult and therefore the most expensive) or even consecutive, can be substantial. If you are offering a publication, in what language will it be printed? Is it socially acceptable to e-mail your announcements to your members or potential attendees in certain European countries without their permission, or is it considered an invasion of privacy? In what currency will your attendees pay for the trade show in Japan?

As an American, how do you introduce yourself at the trade show in Japan? Is the choice of language you use in the marketing brochure offensive to your European audience?

## COMMON INTERNATIONAL MANAGEMENT ISSUES

Every international effort, even the simplest task, is more complicated than it would be in a domestic market. For, immediately, in marketing a service or product to a foreign audience, you will encounter language, cultural, and currency differences that can throw the effort off track. These variables differ from country to country but are intrinsic to all international efforts.

### Cultural Differences

When an association ventures into the international arena, it cannot afford to offend those to whom it is reaching out. In some cases, offense can be inadvertent. As Ronald Reagan got off a plane following a long trip to Brazil, he heartily gestured to the crowd of reporters that everything was "OK." Unfortunately, the U.S. symbol for "OK" is one of the most offensive gestures in Brazil.

Obviously, association executives are not likely to attract the publicity a president of the United States can—the president's picture appeared in all the local newspapers—but a lack of understanding of basic business and cultural protocol can make one's entry into a foreign country awkward and, ultimately, damaging. Therefore, advance research that is country-specific is a necessity. Know what pleases and offends the people you are courting. Even if you don't know how to speak their language, let them know that you come in earnest.

In Mexico, for example, it is customary to inquire about a colleague's wife and family, whereas in many Middle Eastern countries that subject is taboo. Giving a pat on the back is a sign of congratulation in the United States, but in Japan it would be discourteous.

### Language

Next, think generally about language. If you are a Latin American, are you likely to attend a conference or to be satisfied at a conference in Mexico that is conducted in English with Spanish translation? The promotional materials and at least some sessions should be conducted in Spanish with simultaneous translation into English. If you want Brazilian attendees, all sessions must be translated into Portuguese as well. Americans can become somewhat ethnocentric, believing that the English language is universal. It is not—even among English-speaking

**Exhibit 10–1**   Language Tips

---

- Meanings for the same word or words may vary from culture to culture.
- Don't use jargon, slang, or colloquialisms.
- Watch for abbreviations.
- Add country codes to telephone numbers.
- Stipulate the monetary currency.
- Avoid seasonal references, as you may be directing your correspondence to a different hemisphere.
- Avoid indirect references to your own country.
- Be aware of metric and nonmetric systems.
- If you use Fahrenheit, give the equivalent temperature in Celsius.
- If you use miles, give the equivalent in kilometers.
- Don't always portray your country as the center around which all other countries revolve.
- In dates, spell out the names of months.
- Jokes may not be exportable. Literal interpretations may be outright offensive.
- When translating for countries with several dialects, choose the most common.
- Interpretation can be done simultaneously, consecutively, or through an escort.
- Accommodate the extra time required to translate English into Asian languages (a 15-minute speech in English, for example, requires 30 minutes in Japanese).

---

people. Try putting an American, a Canadian, a Brit, and an Aussie in a room together, and within 10 minutes you'll find language differences. Add an English-speaking Frenchman and Spaniard, and the differences will be apparent more quickly. It is therefore crucial to be sensitive to language nuances, be consistent in translations, and offer interpretation services at meetings.

When communicating with the outside world, shed national colloquialisms. For examples, in the United States. we commonly write dates as 3/13/99 or March 13, 1999. Others do differently. We use nonmetric systems; others use metric. The list goes on (see Exhibit 10–1).

## Communications/Delivery of Product

Efficient, user-friendly communications and delivery of services are a given in the nonprofit world in the United States. We rely on 800 numbers, faxes, the Internet, and express delivery services, such as the U.S. Postal Service Express Mail, UPS, and Fed Ex, when necessary. When you cross international borders, the usual guarantee is unavailable, and communications and product delivery can become a logistic nightmare. Sending a fax from Chicago to Melbourne, Australia, in the middle of the night is not a major issue, but a phone call will get you nowhere. More time-consuming and costly are the delivery of programs for a major conference in Brussels or the distribution, to several locations, of the brochures for a Latin American trade show or educational conference. Sometimes a destination may be so remote that the first question may be "Is it more efficient and less costly to produce it there than to produce it here and ship it there?"

*Distribution.* There is no magic formula, just admonitions. If not done effectively, distribution can take months and can be extremely expensive. Finding a local distribution partner is often most efficient. For example, every major European city has remailers. You can drop a shipment to the Netherlands Post Office, cut a deal for bulk rates, and get quick service. But if you are sending materials to Australia, even through an express service, the drop shipment alone takes four days. That's the fastest you can get a piece of paper to Australia without getting on the airplane yourself.

*Customs.* Once your materials arrive at the foreign destination, are they marked properly to transfer through customs? The same applies if the materials are sent directly from your suppliers or printers. If the forms aren't properly marked, the materials may sit at customs awaiting payment, even if payment is not required because they are educational materials. Take CDs, for instance, which are often shipped with conference proceedings. Educational CDs are often mistaken as for-sale music CDs and won't be released without proof of documentation. That can take weeks. Again, it's invaluable to work with a local partner. Consider a local customs broker; unless you have a reliable foreign partner, a broker may be essential.

*Electronic Correspondence.* Organizations successfully distribute information electronically on a global basis. But, again, you need to be aware of the local culture and even the local laws of the areas you are sending to. The Netherlands, for example, is receptive to electronic distribution. Other countries have very strict privacy laws that may not approve of broadcast e-mails. Elsewhere you will find that your target market may not be as sophisticated as your home market and may have trouble translating your electronic messages.

*Printed Materials.* Attention to language nuances is essential for cultural reasons, but also for logistics and cost. If you decide to print your materials outside the United States, keep in mind that most of the world uses paper of different sizes. This will affect any prepublication preparation. If you are printing in a foreign language in the United States, check for any unique characters, such as those used even in German or Spanish—to say nothing of those used in Greek, Egyptian, or Chinese. If your printer or typesetter lacks these characters, the typesetting will be expensive.

## Finance

Unless you trade in pure gold and silver, which is highly unlikely, currency exchange will be a major challenge as you go international. The value of the U.S. dollar vis-à-vis other world currencies can change daily. Foreign currency is considered a commodity. Its price, therefore, is expressed as a rate of exchange and can vary from one foreign exchange supplier to the next.

Supply and demand dictates the exchange of currencies between major industrialized countries. The balance can be affected by the difference in interest rates between nations, the strengths of the national economies, and surpluses and deficits. Rates can fluctuate widely. A welcome development is the adoption by many European countries of one continent-wide currency, the Euro; but be advised that the United Kingdom and Switzerland are not involved.

Currency rate fluctuations cause major headaches in the budgeting process. Let's look at expenses first. These can range from travel expenses, to costs associated with a meeting, convention, or trade show, or the opening of an office in a foreign city. If you agree to make payments in the currency of your foreign supplier, you will lower overall costs. The reason is that you are not paying a price inflated to compensate for the risks of currency fluctuations. One way to do this is to buy forward. A forward contract is an agreement between your association and a foreign exchange supplier in which you agree to purchase a specified amount of the foreign currency on a given date based on a rate of exchange established at the time of the agreement. Or you can budget a currency exchange increase as a contingency line item in your budget in case you need it.

With revenue, the money train is running the other way and is most troublesome concerning dues payments. You have to decide how your non-U.S. members will pay dues. In U.S. dollars? If not, how do you compensate for the extra expense for currency exchange? It may seem like a small amount—until you start multiplying. Moreover, don't forget extra postage charges, which add up quickly. Currency exchange issues will, obviously, accompany every conference, trade show, and meeting held in a foreign country. (See Exhibit 10–2.)

**Exhibit 10–2** International Currency Definitions

---

- *Foreign currency draft:* A negotiable instrument denominated in a specific foreign currency and usually drawn by the seller on a bank account held in the country of the currency's origin.

- *Forward contract:* An agreement between your association and a foreign exchange supplier whereby you agree to purchase a specified amount of foreign currency on a given date, based on a rate of exchange established at the time of the agreement. Once a forward contract is entered into, the rate is fixed and the purchaser must take delivery of the currency on the maturity date of the contract.

- *Wire transfer:* Also known as a telegraphic transfer, this is an expression used to describe an electronic payment order made through bank channels. The transfer is a direct wire from the bank's foreign account in a given country to the beneficiary's account.

- SWIFT: The Society for Worldwide Interbank Financial Telecommunications, which created a system in 1977 to provide secure high-speed transmission of financial information and instructions between members. The system is based on a standardized instruction language and protocol to facilitate interbank comminations.

- *VAT—Value-Added Tax:* A tax imposed by many European countries on goods and services, which is often refundable. If a meeting held in Europe, for example, surpasses a certain expanse level, you may be able to recoup some of the tax paid. Consult a VAT expert regarding how this tax will apply to your association as well as to individual participants.

---

*Developed by Thomas Cook Foreign Exchange Ltd.*

## Technology

The rapid advances in technology have nurtured the trend toward globalization. To be able to sit at a computer in Chicago and contact someone in Japan by e-mail in seconds opens up a world of communications. Information travels fast. The possibilities for associations are numerous:

- Bulletin boards
- Chat rooms
- Broadcasting
- Organized conferencing
- Forums on special-interest subjects
- Technical, product, and marketing information
- Text-searching capabilities

- New member recruitment
- Conference promotional information and registration forms
- Member surveys
- Elections
- Database maintenance
- Special group communication forums
- Distribution of on-line newsletters or magazines

For a detailed discussion of technological issues, see Chapter 11 of this book. Yet, once again, it's important to consider the cultural and business protocol of your international members. For instance, some countries have privacy laws that prohibit broadcast faxes. For others it is more of a cultural taboo. Generally, it's useful to review the language tips given earlier when contacting international members by e-mail or by any other type of advanced electronic communication method. If you are transferring documents electronically, you may have compatibility problems with your receiver that may be difficult to resolve. Several software products can translate text electronically into different languages, although accuracy is questionable.

Satellite videoconferencing is another technology that can successfully bring together far-flung association members and others. Basically, a live video telecast via satellite is produced at one location and downlinked to remote sites through an audio-video hookup. Participants can interact with presenters or speakers who are geographically located all over the world. Although very expensive, videoconferencing can sometimes prove less costly than travel expenses. Timing issues are important, as you may be signaling a half day away. Make sure that the downlink sites have adequate facilities capable of receiving the transmission signal.

When you travel internationally for a meeting, conference, or trade show, it's important to plan ahead to make sure you can use the technology you bring with you. Exhibit 10–3 gives some technology travel tips.

**Exhibit 10–3**   Taking Technology with You

---

- Ensure that your videos can operate on systems in the host country; convert the format if necessary.
- Make certain that computers can run your software and that there are backup systems.
- Be sure that qualified technicians are available to work the equipment.
- Bring telephone jack adapter kits for your modems, along with plug adapters.

**Exhibit 10–3**    (*Continued*)

---

- Carry proof that you bought your equipment in your home country or that you left home with it.
- There is no universal standard for how fast you can set up an ISDN line (a high-speed telephone cable for Internet connections), what it costs, or even whether local technicians can handle the installation. Investigate the use of T1 and T2 lines for high-speed Internet use.

---

## INTERNATIONALLY ORIENTED PRODUCTS AND SERVICES

Nonprofit associations that venture into the international arena are likely to enter through one of three routes: membership, publications, or meetings (conferences and trade shows included).

### Promoting Foreign Membership and Participation

Nonprofit associations, benefiting from the perspective of new international members, can grow and flourish. Opening its membership internationally can enhance the organization's image and prestige, extend its goals and purpose, bring in additional income, and broaden the horizon of domestic members.

International members can be recruited individually or through relationships with affiliated non-U.S. organizations. The key issues are determining what types of memberships to offer—for example, individual, affiliate, or corporate—and the dues structures and benefits.

*The Society of Thoracic Surgeons was established in 1964 to provide educational material and research-orientated conferences for heart and lung surgeons. In 1997, the Society leadership decided to make a concerted effort to recruit new members from other countries. The Society president accepted invitations to appear, speak, or participate in meetings of related surgical societies in other nations. Money from the budget was invested in these travels. The president's travel, coupled with a promotional program carried out through the headquarters office, led to a significant increase in membership. Nearly one third of all applicants now come from outside North America, an increase from about 10 percent in years past. Attendance at the Society's annual meeting in the United States is now 34 percent from outside North America. Broadening the perspective, nearly all of the abstracts accepted for presentation at the Society's conference have other countries represented through their coauthors. Nearly half of the submissions accepted for publication in its prestigious academic journal following peer review are from other nations.*

## Publications—Newsletters, Magazines, Journals, Reports

Going international with publications initially sounds attractive. Yet consider the decisions a professional association would have to make to go international with its monthly four-color magazine. Hypothesize a long-established professional society representing 90,000 interior designers. It has long been associated with foreign societies in Europe, Asia, and South America. By going international, it could reasonably project to expand its membership by 30,000. The magazine is an important product, because interior designers are visually oriented and anxious to view new designs from around the world. In the past few years the non-U.S. subscribers have asked for more international coverage in the magazine.

Changes in the editorial content bring excitement. Of course, any increase in editorial expenditures will be contingent on increased ad revenues minus increased costs for shipping and publishing. At first the editorial staff is full of ideas. At least one issue will be dedicated to international coverage. Each issue will have expanded international coverage, either sprinkled throughout or perhaps in an international column.

But despite this enthusiasm, harder decisions have to be made. Are there any international correspondents on staff? How difficult is it going to be to get material from overseas? On deadline? Do the editors need to think about translating the entire magazine into different languages—French? Spanish? Japanese? And what does that mean for design and production?

What about advertising? Will overseas agents be needed to solicit additional advertisers? How will the society handle the financial transactions? What will shipping to foreign members cost? Should membership fees for international members be higher to cover the increased shipping costs? And remember, the process is somewhat circular. The more advertising pages, the more editorial content, the more pages, the heavier the magazine, and the higher the shipping costs. Decisions must be made.

If you are considering such a venture, a less risky or costly approach may be to seek joint publishing ventures with associations in other countries: Share the advertising revenue and costs to develop the editorial content and distribution of the publication. If the publication is to be translated, have your international partner assume that responsibility. A separate edition could be published in another language, or all articles could appear in two languages in the same publication. Canadian publications offer good examples of the latter, with facing pages often appearing in English and French.

As their international memberships grow, some organizations develop special publications that cover global news about their cause, profession, or industry. Because of its modest cost, a newsletter may be the best type of communication. Consult with your international members when developing the content. Invite them to submit articles, feature question-and-answer interviews with them, and present case studies showing how they have excelled or overcome major challenges. Initially, publish the newsletter in English. As it becomes established, publish editions in the languages used most widely by your international members.

For research reports or other important publications you might simply sell—or even donate—the rights for the publication to an international partner. Charge a flat fee, and have the partner handle all the costs and details involved in translating and printing the publication in a different language and distributing it to the appropriate markets. In such a joint venture, make sure that your organization is given prominent credit as the original author and publisher.

*The Candlelighters Childhood Cancer Foundation was established in 1960 as a local organization in Northern Virginia to provide counseling and guidance to the families of children diagnosed with childhood cancer. Candlelighters is not a research organization, and its financial resources have always been modest. But the concept—that families facing this traumatic experience could gain support from common bonding—took hold. There are now 270 loosely affiliated support groups in the United States and similar organizations in 20 foreign countries.*

*In 1994 representatives from most of these countries met for their first international convention, establishing the International Confederation of Child Cancer Parent Organizations (ICCCPO). Activities to date are limited to one meeting a year and exchange of publications. But the communication links established are encouraging families around the world to search out better care, knowing that the long-term survival rate for childhood cancer in the United States is now 75 percent. Candlelighters' most recent publication, a guide to establishing community support groups in the United States, has now been made available to the parallel organizations in other countries.*

## Meetings, Conferences, and Trade Shows

Start by inviting international participants to a national event—special guests, speakers, or exhibitors. Contact members from affiliated organizations. As the number of international attendees grows, the amenities for those attendees will also increase. You might start simply by providing special assistance for your international attendees at the conference. As the international attendance grows, you might consider adding an international lounge or business center, offering sessions in multiple languages, or holding special international dinners or receptions.

*The North American Association of Food Equipment Manufacturers (NAFEM) (see also Chapter 4), utilizing this strategy, has increased international attendance at its biennial trade show from fewer than 100 people at its first show in 1973 to more than 1,700 in 1999. The trade show opens with a welcome party for international attendees, at which exporting manufacturers of foodservice equipment and supplies network with international attendees, and welcome them to the trade show and the United States. Once the show is open, international attendees enjoy an international business center and lounge, language translators, and a special registration area, all provided as an amenity to them at no additional charge. As a result of its participation in the International Buyers Program of the U.S. Department of Commerce, NAFEM also has that agency's assistance in promoting its event overseas and in providing these services.*

A more adventurous option is to take your meetings, conferences, and trade shows overseas. As noted earlier, holding meetings, conferences, and trade shows outside the United States can be time-consuming and costly. Tax deductibility for business expenses is forgone, other than in some Caribbean countries. But the members may enjoy the unusual travel and the face-to-face interactions with foreign members. Consider adding postconference travel packages to attractive locations, encouraging attendees to bring their families. Another idea is to feature pre- or postconference tours of innovative facilities owned by members of your group or suppliers to your industry or profession.

International conference planners need to pay closer attention to acquiring appropriate accommodations for their groups and, within the accommodations, appropriate services. Visit the site and sample its amenities and services before contracting with a meeting facility. Check the meeting rooms to make sure they have the capacity you need, along with up-to-date audiovisual capabilities. Conference centers will usually cover your travel expenses. Consult with your members in the region and other groups that have used the facility to verify that it can deliver the level of service it promises. Convention bureaus in other countries can provide valuable assistance.

Promoting and preparing for conferences abroad can present special challenges. Take into account that it is common for people in other countries, such as those in Latin American and Asia, to register

**Exhibit 10–4** Logistics Tips for Meetings

- Planning an international meeting will take longer than you expect.
- Accommodations: Facilities are different overseas. With a large group, check hotels for breakout rooms.
- Pay close attention to exchange rates and your budget.
- On the application form, leave enough room for foreign names, which tend to be longer than American names.
- Make sure names are correctly printed on badges and tent cards. Errors can significantly undermine your efforts to show cultural sensitivity.
- Have people on your registration staff who can speak different languages.
- Use the standard international-size paper, which is known as A4.
- Allow extra time for travel and jet lag.
- Advance planning is needed at trade shows to accommodate different exhibition systems.
- Develop a crisis management plan. Know where to go for help if someone needs medical attention.
- Special security arrangements may be required in countries that are politically unstable.

late for conferences. As many as half the attendees may register on-site. As a result, you needn't panic if preconference registration numbers are low. Just prepare for a high number of on-site registrations.

When you are welcoming foreign guests to your meeting, conference, or trade show, whether in the United States, Europe, Asia, or Latin America, it's important to remember that you are the host. If you are courting some of the participants as potential members, you need to offer services that will make them feel sufficiently comfortable and interested in your association to do business with you again in the future. (See Exhibit 10–4.)

## DEVELOPING AN INTERNATIONAL PRESENCE

Most nonprofit organizations sensibly limit their international activities to those discussed earlier in this chapter: developing international memberships, promoting publications and research abroad, helping their members to reach overseas markets, and holding at least some of their meetings and conferences overseas, often in partnership with foreign organizations. These cautious first steps create value for the nonprofit's members and supporters and often stimulate other activities in the United States that relate to what is being done overseas.

For some groups, however, international activities are integral to their mission. This is true not only of such truly international organizations as the International Red Cross or the French Médecins sans Frontières (Doctors Without Borders) but also of other nonprofits, most notably advocacy groups, whose missions require activities overseas to supplement their work at home.

*Founded in 1972, the Center for Marine Conservation (CMC) is a nonprofit organization dedicated to protecting marine wildlife and habitats and to conserving coastal and ocean resources. The organization focuses much of its efforts on a national campaign of science-based advocacy, research, and public education ranging from grassroots to congressional activities. One of CMC's most visible programs is a coastal "cleanup," which began in 1986 with 2,800 volunteers on the coast of Texas and now enlists tens of thousands of volunteers every September in campaigns to pick up and remove unsightly and dangerous trash from coastal areas above and below the waterline. Recognizing that the need for cleaner waterways is global, the organization expanded its annual cleanup effort to an international scope beginning in 1989. By 1998, volunteers in more than 72 countries participated in CMC's International Coastal Cleanup Day. Citizen participation and analysis of the debris by the organization allows it to gain media coverage and increase awareness that debris discarded in waters or along the shore fouls the environment and endangers marine life.*

*Because of its credibility as a science-based organization, CMC has been able to obtain significant corporate and foundation support for its international coastal cleanup and other activities.*

*Recognizing the close proximity of Cuba to the United States and the shared interest in the biodiversity of the Caribbean basin, CMC has been able to gain the cooperation and support of both the United States and Cuban governments for international exchange on marine conservation and research. CMC was one of the first organizations to work with Cuban conservation organizations, conducting binational research on coastal resources and ongoing exchange with Cuban specialists in environmental and marine law.*

## CHECKLIST FOR ASSESSING AND DEVELOPING INTERNATIONAL ACTIVITIES

- Are citizens from foreign countries coming to your meetings? Logging on to your Web site? Asking for information?
- Are there significant foreign markets for either the products or the information developed by your members or your organization?

- Does your mission include shaping public attitudes or helping citizens overseas build a better society?

- Are scientists, researchers, or professionals in other countries contributing to knowledge in your field that should be shared with your U.S. members? Do you or your members have research data or other information that should be better known elsewhere?

- Do you have information that could readily be shared with foreign partners? Are there potential partner organizations overseas with whom you could work?

- Do you have the resources to invest in additional research, travel, or exploratory meetings that probably will not support themselves in the first several years?

If you can answer one or more of these questions affirmatively, your nonprofit organization has a potential role overseas. Move cautiously, with a careful eye on expenses, but don't let excess caution keep you from exploring the opportunities.

# PART 3

# Managing the Organization

# CHAPTER ELEVEN

# The New Information Technology: Powerful Tools for Nonprofit Management, Marketing, and Communications

**Information technology is transforming nonprofit organizations. Desktop computers and interlinked networks have given even small organizations the ability to handle management and clerical tasks much more quickly and efficiently than ever before. The Internet has introduced powerful new modes of communication, marketing, and commerce. Where these technologies will lead remains uncertain, but there is no doubting that they will become central to business and life in the twenty-first century—especially for institutions like nonprofits that rely heavily on communications. These new technologies can be daunting, even to the most experienced executives. This chapter can help you set realistic goals, decide what you need to thrive in the Information Age, and equip your organization with the resources to keep up with the fast pace of change.**

The core functions of nonprofit groups—whether they serve businesses, professions, charities or causes—are to advocate, communicate, and educate. The fast-emerging and fast-changing technologies of the Information Age provide even the smallest groups with strategic tools that can greatly extend their power and reach. The question is no longer *whether* to apply tools such as word processing, e-mail, and Web sites, but *how*.

Organization CEOs once boasted that they had never laid their hands on a computer keyboard. Today that attitude can be a liability. Nonprofit executives must know how to use computers and understand the full range of information technology (IT) applications. If you are not already integrating IT systems into your activities and services, begin now, with a sense of urgency. Information technology is much more than an administrative tool; it is a strategic force. An organization that does not embrace it risks being swept into obsolescence.

Modern information systems are based on computers linked from site to site within an organization's own headquarters, with its members, and with the world at large through the Internet. These systems enable us to manage and use information more accurately and efficiently than ever before.

Computers can automate virtually every administrative function a nonprofit group performs, including:

- Word processing, with templates that speed the creation of letters, memos, meeting minutes, reports, news releases, speeches, tent cards, name badges—just about any written document—and give them a professional look

- Communications by fax (now computer-to-computer), voice mail and e-mail, videoconferencing, Internet meetings, and Web pages, offering greater convenience, flexibility, and speed

- Mailing list management, with features that can group names in all manner of ways, depending on your needs—for example, by committee, zip code, political district, donation amount, publications purchased, meetings attended, and news media segment

- Discussion forums and Internet meetings (through static or dynamic communications) to foster idea sharing among people who are geographically dispersed

- Financial record keeping and analysis that can show whether you are operating within your budget and project future costs and revenues based on historical records

The power of modern IT systems extends far beyond automating basic clerical tasks. Many organizations make the mistake of limiting their use in this manner. They miss opportunities to apply computer technology as a strategic tool, such as the following:

- Research on consumer trends, prospective donors, industry operations, new professional standards, and political opportunities

- Highly interactive communications facilities that allow groups to gather information on member preferences and opinions more accurately and easily

- Desktop publishing of newsletters, professional journals, magazines, annual reports, brochures, and white papers on critical issues

- Creating detailed member profiles to understand their current and future needs and thereby ensure that your organization remains a highly valuable resource

- Use of the Internet to learn more about the group's area of interest, how the news media are covering it, potential adversaries, and relevant laws and regulations

- Managing a Web site to develop a presence in the increasingly wired world. Through the site, you can provide information, sell publications and services, raise funds, register people for meetings, create opportunities for members to share information on subjects of mutual interest, and create links to other sites of interest to your constituency

This chapter covers the development, use, and management of modern information systems—ranging from basic to strategic applications—along with guidelines on how to tap the power of the Internet. Much of the guidance draws from lessons gleaned from experience with such systems in a nonprofit environment.

## DEVELOP A STRATEGIC PLAN

Selecting the right systems depends on the nature of the organization and its goals. Strategic planning should help define the computer tools needed, and good operational planning should drive decisions on how best to manage them.

You might begin by forming a committee or task force to create a plan and perform ongoing oversight. Its members should include leaders who know your operational needs and member services, along with the staff executives and experts who manage your IT systems. Ideally, you need leaders who can foresee how the Information Age will change the future needs and mission of your organization.

Understanding how technology affects your overall organizational goals is an ongoing process. Realize that continuing change in technology will introduce new capabilities that will affect how the group applies IT resources in the future. Simply implementing a system to meet your current needs will not be sufficient in today's changing environment. Set up a process to review your group's technology plan regularly to determine whether it still meets the needs of the members, the organization, and its goals. The lack of such foresight can put nonprofit associations out of business. Some retailer associations, for example, once derived most of their income by serving as coupon clearinghouses for their members. When computers automated this function, eliminating the need for an intermediary between retailers and suppliers, they lost their primary source of revenue and many failed. The groups that saw this technology coming found new income sources, such as adding new member categories and merging with associations representing allied industries.

Nonprofits that rely heavily on conferences for income must carefully watch the advent of so-called virtual meetings that people can "attend" by logging on to their computers. Through Internet links, members can view seminars, question speakers, and learn about issues, trends, and best practices. Trade association members can view new products with the aid of three-dimensional images. Forward-thinking groups are exploring ways to hold virtual meetings and raise income by charging attendees for password-protected access to the communications mediums over which such events are held.

In addition, you can combine face-to-face with "virtual" communications. This allows your organization to extend the scope of conferences and meetings. The information can be made available on-line to those who were unable to attend the actual meeting, or it can serve as a refresher for those who did attend. Making this information available electronically means that more people can see the impact of your organization on its area of interest, which may bring you more members and supporters.

IT systems are changing the dynamics of fund-raising, political action, media relations, publishing, research, marketing, and other activities that involve communications and information management. You need to identify the core activities of your group and the technologies best able to support them.

- Groups that rely on small donations from thousands of supporters may want to purchase the most sophisticated mailing list management systems. They may also benefit from word processing systems that can work in tandem with mailing list software to send personalized letters to thousands of prospects.

- Nonprofits with political missions can use mailing list software that groups mailing lists by zip codes, within political districts. With this capability, they can target action calls to supporters in the districts represented by the members of Congress they want to influence.

- Organizations that work extensively with the news media now equip themselves to send news releases by fax and e-mail, which allow for instant communications. If you automate communications in this fashion, first survey your media contacts and ask them how they would like to receive your releases. An increasing number are expressing a preference for e-mail, but you should first obtain their consent.

- Web site technologies can support numerous nonprofit activities. The strategic questions here are how far to go and where. All organizations should have some Web site presence, which can be accomplished with a modest investment. The costs mount as you venture into Web site publishing, marketing and e-commerce, electronic forums where people can share information, conference registration and scheduling, and virtual meetings and discussion groups.

It is possible to race too fast into this new world, using resources at the wrong time or in the wrong place. Ongoing strategic planning can help your organization to avoid such mistakes and ensure that IT resources are applied consistently to support your core activities and strategic goals. Decisions on technology and the staffing needed to use it effectively will fall into place as the goals and needs remain clear.

## SELECT A SYSTEM FOR YOUR NEEDS

The selection of appropriate information systems must flow from a clear operational plan. Lacking a rigorous assessment of operations and goals, some nonprofits wind up using large and complex systems to accomplish straightforward and simple tasks. The converse is also true: other organizations may try to do complex tasks with small systems pushed beyond their limits. With a clear operational plan, you can select the best information system for your particular needs.

The ability to translate an operational plan into a technology plan, and then into a working system, requires particular expertise. This can be gained over time with study and on-the-job experience, but it is easier for nonprofit executives, once their organization has moved beyond basic word processing, to purchase the services of experts. The major hazard of using consultants is becoming locked into their view of the future and what your capabilities should be. This is where the operational plan must remain clear and flexible. Information system decisions should spring from practical, operational decisions and not from someone's new toy wish list.

Suppose that one of your goals is to track information on your organization's membership. Information for each member would include the usual, such as name and address, but would also include some statistical information. The capacity exists to provide extremely detailed profiles of your members, donors, or constituents, including every manner in which they have interacted with your organization. Some large nonprofits, such as the American Association of Retired Persons, require powerful computer systems because they have hundreds of thousands of members and keep detailed information on each one. A smaller organization may be able to keep all of the information it needs on a single personal computer. The degree of detail needed will influence both hardware and software decisions.

No one can predict the future, particularly in technology; but neither can you predict the services that your organization will be providing five or ten years from now. Purchase your system for the functions you are performing now and will be performing in the near future. Here again, the operational plan should spell out the services that you are currently performing. The selection of technological tools required to perform them will flow from the plan.

## Automate the Basics

With cost no longer a significant barrier, every nonprofit organization should be equipped with a basic IT system, including:

- Word processing to create all written materials
- A spreadsheet program to prepare budgets and project cash flow
- An accounting program to generate regular financial reports
- A database program to maintain member and other records
- Voice mail, e-mail, and Internet access

Computer books and training programs can help teach you how to best use these applications. Because nonprofits are prodigious generators of information and communications, most pay special attention to word processing and desktop publishing applications.

### Word Processing

The most current word processing software comes with numerous features to improve efficiency, accuracy, and the professional look of all written materials. Many nonprofits, however, fail to take full advantage of the powerful tools built into these programs.

In this area, the elders in an organization can learn from the younger employees who grew up with computers. A measure of humility may be required. A major time saver is to create templates for letters, memos, faxes, speeches, plaques, reports, news releases, and other written documents. Use either the templates that come with all state-of-the-art software or create your own standard formats.

Once you have created templates, you will never have to waste time in formatting a new document. Simply open the template, type in the new text, and use the "save as" feature to give the file a name. To save even more time, the templates can include built-in type styles for the basic text and for heads and subheads. You can automate page numbering in headers and footers, along with bullets, tables, and the use of multiple columns. For recurring elements or phrases, use the "copy" or "global replace" function. Make liberal use of macros for boilerplate text; with a few keystrokes, you can end letters and insert a standard description of your organization.

Numerous shortcuts are available by using keystroke combinations instead of pulling down menus, selecting functions, and making changes. For example, you can italicize text simply by highlighting it and pressing the "control" and "i" keys. To make text bold, highlight and press "control" and "b." Laminated cards listing numerous shortcuts are available for all standard word processing programs.

## Desktop Publishing

Computer programs such as PageMaker and Quark and, to a somewhat lesser extent, Microsoft Word and WordPerfect can be used to design and lay out publications. Professional designers commonly use the first two software programs to create slick annual reports, magazines, and brochures. As much as nonprofits may expect to achieve the same results simply by purchasing such software, they cannot unless they hire professionals with the considerable expertise needed to design professional-looking publications.

Smaller nonprofit groups, in particular, should limit their desktop publishing to simple newsletters and other materials that do not require sophisticated artwork and designs. In today's visually oriented world, the public can readily distinguish the work of an amateur from that of a professional. The former typically uses too many typefaces and sizes; the spacing is uneven, and the graphic elements are often clip art that is obviously unoriginal. Publishing such unprofessional materials diminishes your image.

On a strategic level, you must watch carefully the migration of publishing to the Internet and Web sites in particular. Some people speculate that most publishing will be electronic in five to ten years. This trend is already well under way with newsletters and many other text-heavy publications. Whether or not publishing goes electronic, electronic communications is reshaping the Information Age fundamentally.

*Networking Options*

As your nonprofit staff grows from a handful of people to five or more, you may want to network your computers. Networks of individual computers tied together were created originally to share expensive resources such as hard drives and printers. Because the price of these resources has come down precipitously, networks are now used primarily for sharing software, printers, and scanners and to facilitate communication among computer users and with the outside world as well. Most office organizations, even those with small staffs, can benefit from the use of a network. Some nonprofit organizations with as few as four persons on staff work so closely together that a network adds to their efficiency.

In recent years computer utilization has been greatly expanded by the use of e-mail. Most local area networks (LANs) can now carry messages between users with files, graphics, photos, or other items attached. This is a common way to communicate and has completely replaced executive memos in some offices. With connections outside the local network to the Internet, e-mail can be sent to anyone with an electronic mailbox. Some nonprofit organizations use these facilities for communications between their officers, committees, boards, or members in disparate locations. These on-line services also provide a direct link to the Internet.

## CENTRALIZATION AND DECENTRALIZATION

One of the philosophical questions that must be addressed in the development of an IT system is whether to centralize or decentralize the flow of information. The benefit of centralization is control; all information is stored in one place and is, therefore, more secure. The downside is that information users may have more difficulty gaining access to the data and less control over how to use it.

A decentralized model, such as a local area network (LAN), facilitates information sharing. It offers less security and data integrity, but this type of system allows greater access to information. The decision on whether to centralize data or not should be based on such issues as the sensitivity of the data and the needs for accuracy and accessibility.

Modern systems offer the versatility to both centralize and decentralize. One computer, equipped with extensive memory and high-speed microchips, acts as the hub of the system—called the file server. It stores the basic software used by all—the programs for word processing, accounting, and e-mail—along with the text and data files to which all users need access. Programs and files needed by individual users can then be stored on the hard drives of their computers. These can include specialized software for mailing lists, graphics, and desktop publishing.

The future may bring even more versatility through access to programs that reside on the Internet, beginning with the Java software pioneered by Sun Microsystems. Palmtop computers are yet another innovation likely to introduce new computer management options. Highly powerful laptop computers are already widely used; they are fast becoming the preferred system for audiovisual presentations. Software like PowerPoint is outmoding hard-slide shows.

The question of whether to centralize or decentralize may very well become moot. With computer resources residing in palmtops, laptops, individual PCs and file servers, how can you manage access? All organizations must develop policies that govern how these resources are to be shared and where access should be restricted.

## Software, Then Hardware

Once you determine how IT systems can best serve your operational and strategic needs, the next step is to identify the software required. A common error is to shop first for the hardware, and, indeed, today's marketplace offers many alluring low-cost deals. But it is best to base hardware decisions on software needs. If your needs are limited to basic word processing, spreadsheets, and a text-based Web site, you do not need a highly expensive system. You will need progressively more powerful systems as you venture further into graphics, complex mailing lists, databases and member profiles, high-speed Internet access, advanced Web sites, multicolor publications, and other memory-intensive applications.

In the simplest terms, the three most important components of a personal computer are processor speed, memory, and hard disk storage capacity. Read-only memory (ROM) is computer memory on which data has been prerecorded. Most personal computers contain a small amount of ROM that stores critical programs, such as the program that boots the computer. The random access memory (RAM) in your computer is where programs, data, and files are used and modified. You are using this memory when running software, surfing the Internet, and otherwise using the computer. The more programs you wish to run at the same time, the more RAM you will need. More complex operations, such as video and image processing, require additional RAM.

RAM and microchip processors largely determine how fast your computer operates. The hard disk on your computer is where all the programs, data, files, and other information are stored when they aren't in use.

As a general rule when buying hardware, you want enough memory of both kinds to accommodate your software needs. To plan for the future, it is best to buy more memory than you currently need. The additional cost is usually minimal. For example, if you now need 10 gigabytes of ROM and 64 megabytes of RAM, buy or lease systems with twice as much. In addition, ensure that the RAM can be doubled yet again by adding RAM chips. Most computers come with empty plastic slots into which these chips can be easily inserted. For storage and backup purposes, purchase computers with zip and tape drives; these can be internal or external components.

Microchip processing speeds are now measured in hundreds of megahertz. At this writing, 400 to 500 megahertz systems are available at moderate prices. If current trends continue, systems two to three times as fast will be the typical business IT systems in the next few years. This level of speed, combined with the memory capacity cited earlier, can provide a small nonprofit group with an IT system able to support a wide variety of basic and advanced functions.

You may also face the decision of whether to buy a PC or a Macintosh/Apple system. Although the term "PC" is used loosely to describe all computers, it refers to those that run on the original disk operating system (DOS) software platform. Microsoft's Windows program was later superimposed on that platform, and PCs now dominate the market. One notable exception is in graphic applications such as design and printing. If you are heavily involved in design and printing, a Mac computer may be the best choice. Current models are reasonably compatible with PCs. E-mail can be exchanged readily, and computer files can be converted from one platform to the other. The principal advantage of Mac systems is that printing presses can more easily handle their files. If you perform a large volume of printing, having at least one Mac system can provide a valuable resource.

Advances in computer design are occurring so rapidly that it is becoming more and more difficult to keep up—notably with the increases in RAM and hard disk capacity. Before making any computer purchases, check with a computer professional, either in person or through the Internet, to determine the most appropriate system for your needs.

## The 80 Percent Rule

Nonprofits should be wary about creating custom software. When buying computer programs, observe the 80 percent rule; that is, if a program can meet 80 percent of your software needs, buy it. Resist the temptation to custom design software that can support 90 to 100 percent of your work.

*A nonprofit organization with a complex Unix multiuser system developed a customized membership software program. This system was created and supported by the hardware vendor. When the group changed its activities, however, the software had to be changed and only the vendor had the expertise to do it. The organization faced these choices: invest the money to train one of its employees to the level of expertise necessary to make the changes, hire a programmer to do the job, or keep on paying the consulting firm whenever a change was needed. What the organization ultimately did, after several false starts, was to scrap the customized system and buy off-the-shelf software to do what it needed.*

It is also risky to customize off-the-shelf software. One nonprofit purchased a membership package and proceeded to write programs to make it do exactly what it needed. Within one year the program was so customized that when the software company published an upgrade, the nonprofit could not use it.

When you purchase software, you are buying a partner in your business. Make sure that you will receive the training and support you need. This is why many organizations will purchase only industry standard "commercial off-the-shelf software" (COTS). These programs, which typically do 80 to 90 percent of the information processing that a nonprofit organization requires, should be the first option you consider.

*A nonprofit with a large membership base had a customized system with 15 terminals working off one central processing unit (CPU). This included a custom membership package, which could be used for fund-raising appeals, fast word processing, and an excellent operating program. But the system was extremely complex. The operators had difficulty maintaining the system because all the commands had to be learned by rote. The operators did not fully understand why they were doing what they were doing. As a result, any time there was a problem, the consulting firm was called in to fix it. This is an expensive way to do things.*

If you have a process that off-the-shelf software cannot perform, hire a consultant to perform a thorough market search. With the rapid development of new sophisticated software tools, numerous niche markets are being filled by software companies. Most software tools are gaining such flexibility and power that they can perform almost all organizational processes without the organization's having to resort to large customization projects.

## ELECTRONIC COMMUNICATIONS

For decades communications were limited largely to sending written materials by mail or messenger, making telephone calls, and holding face-to-face meetings. Each method had its own constraints: Letters took time; and phone calls, messengers, and meetings were costly if the communications or people had to travel long distances. Fax and next-day delivery services overcame some limitations, but not all of them. Heavy reliance on overnight delivery cost organizations thousands of dollars a year, an expense that many small nonprofits could ill afford. Even as fax communications became widely available, their use was spotty and recipients could not revise them without retyping their entire contents. Multipage faxes could also run up large telephone bills.

E-mail is now sweeping away all these limitations, thanks to the revolutionary innovation known as the Internet. The U.S. military conceived this network as an early warning system for nuclear attack. President Eisenhower gave it high priority after the successful launch of the first Soviet *Sputnik* satellite in 1957. Creating a system that enabled various computers to communicate with one another, however, proved to be quite difficult.

The academic community soon took up the challenge, envisioning a system that would enable researchers across the country to share their findings. More than a decade passed before the hardware and software were developed to make electronic communications possible. The first e-mail was sent in 1973. Thereafter, the pace of innovation gathered momentum until the 1990s, when it began to increase geometrically. At this writing, some 50 million computers are linked to the Internet, giving access to about 200 million users. Access to the network is increasing so rapidly that by the end of the first decade of the twenty-first century, virtually every home and business in the developed world will have access. (To learn more about its history, read the award-winning book *Where Wizards Stay Up Late—The Origins of the Internet* by Katie Hafner and Matthew Lyon, Simon & Schuster, New York, 1996.)

The pioneers of the Internet endowed the technology with two features that led to its widespread use. First, they designed a standard interface system so versatile that it could translate the language of any computer into a common format. Second, they made the data stream so compact that it could travel over existing telephone lines. As the interface systems proliferated, people just about anywhere could gain access to the Internet at the cost of a local telephone call, which made use of this communications network extremely inexpensive. (This is not the case in all countries outside the United States. If your organization has many international members, you must be sensitive to the possibility that Internet use for some will be costly.)

As a result, any organization can easily gain access to the Internet with software already installed on all new computers, by connecting a standard telephone line to its file server or to any computer—including palmtop and laptop units that a person can carry on the road. At your headquarters, you should use a dedicated line to connect to the Internet so it will not interfere with regular telephone calls. As your Internet use grows beyond basic e-mail to needing frequent access to Web sites on the Internet and to managing your own Web site, you should consider installing a more powerful link, such as a T1 or Integrated Services Digital Network (ISDN) line. Cable and satellite links are other emerging options that you should watch closely.

The easiest way to get started is to set up an account with America Online (AOL), Microsoft Network (MSN), or another Internet service provider (ISP). ISPs can equip you with e-mail capability and Web site access and facilitate the development of your own Web site, all at a modest cost. Web site design and management are detailed later in this chapter.

The advent of e-mail, along with voice mail and teleconferencing, has given all organizations a dizzying array of communications options. They have not, however, outmoded traditional forms, such as the telephone, fax, and the venerable written letter (now called "snail mail" by technophiles). Nonprofits must be equipped to use all forms of communications. The greatest challenge is to use them in the most effective and appropriate manner.

Organizations should be careful in using the newer forms of communications, such as voice mail and e-mail. These tools are quite effective in adding convenience and speed to your communications. Overreliance on them, however, can waste time and, more important for nonprofit organizations, result in a loss of the personal touch you need when interacting with members and key constituents.

In his widely acclaimed book *Megatrends,* author John Naisbitt introduced the principle known as "high tech/high touch." His idea is that the more we introduce technology into our work and lives, the more important it becomes to retain a human element. In accordance with this principle, one of the best examples of what a nonprofit should not do is completely automate its telephone answering service. There is no greater turnoff than, upon calling a nonprofit group, to be greeted by a computer that says, "Press one for this service, press two for that, press three for yet another. And if you don't know your party's extension, please type in the letters of his or her last name." Fully automated phone services may be appropriate for some organizations, such as those with vast bureaucracies that provide numerous and diverse services. A lesser degree of automation may be acceptable at nonprofits whose members communicate routinely by voice and e-mail.

Nevertheless, organizations that interact constantly with people must use voice mail with care. As a general rule, a nonprofit should have a person answer all incoming calls that are not directed to a particular individual, in a pleasant and professional manner. For first-time callers, this makes a positive first impression. For important constituents, it reinforces the relationship. Calls that are routed or go directly to individuals may be answered by voice mail. But you should make an extra effort to return such calls promptly and to make voice mail answers the exception rather than the rule.

The high tech/high touch principle applies to e-mail as well. This tool is effective as a means of sharing bits of information, routing drafts of documents for review, setting up meetings, and performing other administrative tasks. Articles, reports, and contracts can be edited, rewritten, and expanded among groups of people quite efficiently by e-mail. You can send high-resolution photos, articles, and news releases to publications instantly, avoiding the cost and delay of overnight delivery. You can communicate by e-mail with distant parties—including people halfway around the world—at a fraction of the cost of a phone call.

However, if you reach the point of communicating almost entirely by e-mail, your relationships with key people will begin to deteriorate. E-mail is an inappropriate medium for resolving conflicts. The recipient of such sensitive messages cannot see the nonverbal cues or easily gauge the tone. Constructive criticism may be misinterpreted. Sensitive communications of any type are best conducted face-to-face or by telephone, giving the parties involved an opportunity to ask questions and clarify meanings.

With technology so widely used in modern day communications, personal contact often has a more powerful impact than it did in the past. Instead of thanking a donor or praising a member by e-mail, send a hand-written note. In today's increasingly wired world, we must try harder to communicate and interact in person whenever it is possible and appropriate.

## Electronic Communications Policies

Nonprofits, like all organizations, should set formal policies governing the use of all electronic communications. These cover appropriate-use guidelines and, more important, protect the organization from violations of privacy rights, copyright claims, sexual harassment laws, antitrust statues, and other legal constraints.

When people are introduced to voice mail, e-mail, and Internet use or when they begin to use these tools in an office environment, they may be inclined to regard them as informal means of communications. Although informality has its place in an office environment, using it in electronic communications can create serious consequences for organizations and their employees.

As part of the discovery process in lawsuits, electronic communications records are routinely subpoenaed. Organizations can provide themselves some protection by having a backup policy to retain, for as few days as possible, any data that could be subject to litigation. Such measures, however, will not protect you from the records held by outside parties. In addition, if your organization is already a party in a legal proceeding, such practices could be deemed obstruction of justice. The key points are that:

- Organizations should treat all electronic communications records carefully.

- Employees should observe strict policies when using electronic communications.

Such policies should cover the following general areas:

- *The organization retains access to all messages*—All communications may be monitored, and employees may not restrict access with electronic locks or other security features.

- *Use electronic communications only for business purposes*—Any personal use should be prohibited or limited to nonworking hours.

- *Guard the confidentiality of information about the organization and its constituents*—Do not send out messages that may divulge proprietary information about the organization or its members or violate the privacy rights of donors, members, or other constituents on which you keep records.

- *Do not forward communications that may be protected by attorney-client privilege.*

- *Take care in using copyrighted information*—Do not download and distribute copyrighted articles widely or software that is not offered for free.

- *Observe e-mail etiquette*—Ensure that all messages are courteous, professional, and businesslike. Do not transmit obscene, offensive, or harassing messages.

- *Judiciously store and regularly delete e-mail messages*—Preserve the organization's computer memory by regularly deleting outdated messages and by printing out and deleting any that should be saved.

The appropriate policies will depend on the size and nature of your organization, how you use electronic communications, and how that use evolves over time, including how the technology changes.

## Advanced E-Mail Applications

E-mail has many applications beyond serving as a means for two people to communicate. You can create electronic mailing lists, grouping a set of e-mail addresses under one name. This might include a nonprofit's officers, its board of directors, the members serving on various committees, or all staff within various departments.

You can also create e-mail groups for important constituents, such as donors, segments of the news media, government officials, and countless others. When setting up groups of e-mail addresses of people outside your membership, it is good practice to obtain their permission to receive e-mail from your organization on a regular basis. Then be judicious about what you send, and how often. This may be particularly important for donors, members of the news media, and government officials. If you send them e-mail consistently and it lacks useful information or value, they will soon regard it as junk mail, which will undermine your organization's credibility.

You can create a more sophisticated type of e-mail group that serves as a forum for communications among all people who subscribe by e-mail. Nonprofits can set this up with a LISTSERV program or have an outside service bureau create and manage such an e-mail forum. This service allows people with a common interest or concern to share information. You might set one up for a committee or for your board of directors. A common approach is to raise an issue or question for the entire group and invite the subscribers to respond. Their e-mails are then automatically shared with the entire group, creating an ongoing electronic dialogue. In one instance, an association set up a LISTSERV forum for members to share solutions to the Year 2000 computer problem. Hundreds of members quickly subscribed, leading to a dialogue filled with solutions to the problem and contingency plans to address potential system failures.

Such forums must be carefully managed to guard against inappropriate or inflammatory statements or comments that might reveal proprietary information or even violate the law. Before they can join the forum, subscribers must agree to strict parameters on what kind of information can be shared. You may want to incorporate language in the subscription terms stating that your organization is not legally liable for comments that violate the law.

Nonprofits may choose not to monitor such forums, lessening the legal liability for inappropriate use. Make this liability waiver explicit to all users who join the discussion forum. You may require that the users police themselves and assume the consequences for abuse of the forum.

We are just beginning to see the many powerful services that e-mail and the Internet can offer. Other advanced applications include Intranets to facilitate information sharing and communication among people within an organization, along with Extranets for entire industries or communities of people with a common interest. Given the remarkably fast pace of change—people are now using the term "Internet speed"—it is impossible to know what new applications may emerge in the next five to ten years. As recently as the mid-1990s, computer mavens as insightful as Bill Gates did not foresee many of the powerful ways in which the Internet would revolutionize communications.

## BUILD AN OFFICE ON THE WORLD WIDE WEB

The global electronic community known as the World Wide Web now extends beyond communications to research, marketing, commerce, and applications yet to come. Visiting a Web site today is becoming more like visiting an office. You can obtain a wealth of information, purchase or subscribe to publications, register for meetings (or even attend a virtual or electronic meeting), join a government relations campaign, or obtain the names of experts and professionals and then go to their Web sites with a click of the mouse.

These powerful IT capabilities have developed in a very short time. The World Wide Web was invented in 1989 by Tim Berners-Lee, a British researcher, who created a highly flexible body of software, computer protocols, and codes. Using these common tools, programmers developed a vast system of Web sites—in effect, a global library of information accessible to anyone equipped with a computer, a modem, and a browser, such as Internet Explorer or Netscape. The tools include the hypertext transport protocol (http), which gives your browser access to Internet Web sites; the common hypertext markup language (HTML), in which all Web pages are written; and Uniform Resource Locator codes (URLs) to identify individual sites. This is why most Web site addresses begin with the letters http://www and end with the URL. The World Wide Web

Consortium in Cambridge, Massachusetts, oversees this network. For more information about the Web's history and how to use it, visit the consortium's site (*http://www.W3.org*).

## Developing Your Own Web Site

Every nonprofit organization should have its own Web site. It serves as a basic assertion, telling the increasingly wired world, "I exist; believe me." Some may fear the expense involved and shy away from the Web as long as possible, hewing to the maxim "Better no Web site than a bad one." This is no longer a viable option. Any organization in the business of communication, education, or advocacy must have a presence on the Web. Otherwise, the group will be perceived as being behind the times.

Bear in mind that a Web site is your organization's face to the world. Ugly graphics, dull copy, bad grammar, and typos will stand out, just as they would in a brochure. Long pages of material routinely posted and out-of-date—dubbed "cobwebs" by savvy users—will drag a Web site down even if the opening home page is attractive.

Larger trade or nonprofit organizations with a national or global scope may well choose to put significant resources into a Web site. This may include hiring a full-time "webmaster" or assigning an on-staff executive to manage the site. It is often preferable to retain a firm that provides Web or Internet services (some ISPs do this) to post new material, discard the old, and look for ways to keep the site fresh and useful.

A smaller organization should be careful not to expend resources that could be better used elsewhere. The initial design for a basic site should be no more expensive than the design for a brochure or similar publication. A local graphics artist or public relations firm—or even one of your employees—may already have designed a site and can do the same for you. Or you may develop a site with the aid of an on-line service provider such as America Online.

Subsequently, the organization's director of communications or executive director should be able to update the site with materials prepared for the newsletter or other communications. In between the elaborate and simple fall a wide range of options.

## Reserve Your Site Name

A step you must take immediately, even before starting work on your Web site, is to register a domain name—xxx.com or xxx.org. You want a name that is as close as possible to your group's name or to your cause. This step is critical because millions of names have already been taken and you may find that your first choices are not available.

The process was once fairly simple. You could register a site name or names by visiting a Web site designated for this purpose (*www.register.com*). There are now multiple sites for doing this, with the process still under debate. You might begin by registering your name at the aforementioned site, and then use a search engine, such as Yahoo, Excite, or AltaVista, to find the most current information on "domain name registration." If you need help, contact a computer service bureau or Internet service provider.

## Develop a Strategic Plan for Your Web Site

The process of planning your site should begin with a strategic plan. What is your goal for the Web site? Some organizations have held one- or two-day retreats, essentially a strategy-planning exercise, just on this topic. At the very least, the executive director, one or two members of the executive committee, or other key members should meet with senior staff for a half day to map out a strategy. They should focus on the basic questions: Why do we want a Web site? . What do we want it to do, and how can it support the goals and activities of our organization?

In a brainstorming session, the practical issues of costs versus resources should not be allowed to interfere at the outset. Decide first what you would like to do; there will be time later to adjust the plan to budget exigencies.

First, who are your audiences—who you want to visit and use the Web site—and in what order of priority? These may include:

- Members and prospective members
- Volunteers
- Prospective financial contributors
- Financial analysts of your association's industry or profession
- Convention attendees or trade show exhibitors
- The news media
- Government officials
- Researchers
- People seeking jobs with your association or with your member companies
- Consumers, suppliers, and patients seeking help
- The public at large

As with any communications program, defining the audience is essential to creating the right materials for your Web site. With the target audiences firmly in mind, the next step is to set Web site objectives. Here, again, there are numerous options:

*Attract new members*—The site would emphasize the member benefits; access to valuable information; discounts for educational programs, insurance premiums, and special services; your strength as an advocate for particular causes. Having a "members-only" section of the site with specialized information and services would support this objective. Of course, these sites should make it easy for visitors to join the organization, filling out the required forms electronically and paying by credit card.

*Political action*—Emphasize the group's success in promoting good laws or defeating bad ones. Feature issue backgrounders, white papers, testimony, issue action calls, and links to government Web sites. The site may also play up the group's involvement in election campaigns and political action committees.

*Provide information*—Sites with this objective might feature newsletter subscriptions, background information on numerous topics, extensive conference listings, a publications section, and regular bulletins on key issues. The contents of the site could be completely indexed by subject, and you would need to update it frequently. Feature a "question of the day" on the home page.

*Revenue source*—Such a site would serve as a marketplace for e-commerce, selling publications, videos, software, and educational programs; registrations for conferences (both physical and virtual); and exhibit space at trade shows. You can also sell advertising space on your Web site to suppliers and supporters of your association or cause.

*Educational forum*—Highlight your group's sponsorship of LIST-SERVs and share groups on various issues and topics, its publications and conferences, its relationships with educational institutions, and the academic credentials of its members.

Next, think about how frequently you will have new material to add—not just documents to fill up memory space, but timely and valuable information that your members or other audiences will log on to read. Keep your audience in mind when making these projections. Do not make the common mistake of organizing the site around the association's internal structure rather than the nature and interests of your primary audiences (see the discussion under "Advanced Web Sites").

With a strategic plan, knowledge of your target audiences and the information and services you can provide, you can now begin setting up your Web site office.

## Develop an Operational Plan

Building and managing your Web site requires a well-conceived operational plan. This begins with a connection to the Internet—a so-called on-ramp—provided by your organization or an Internet service provider, such as AOL, MSN, or a host of other local, national, and even international groups.

Next, you need a plan for developing the site. This should cover the standard steps for an IT project: the technical requirements, design (text and graphics), implementation, and maintenance. As with any project, the more time and thought you give to identifying what you want to do, the easier it will be to determine how to do it. A well-conceived strategic plan facilitates these decisions.

You also have to plan the hosting of the group's Web site. Once a site is created, it must be housed somewhere on a dedicated computer—a web server—and it must be accessible at all times, 24 hours a day, seven days a week. The server may be located at your own office, at your ISP, or at a company that offers Web site hosting, such as AT&T. Bear in mind that full-time access requires that you have backup capability and a disaster recovery plan to ensure that your site has minimal downtime.

Finally, you need a plan for maintaining the Web site: posting information on a timely basis, deleting dated material, and ensuring that the data is accurate and the services are fully functional. Many organizations make the mistake of overlooking this requirement even though it is critical to establishing a Web site as a credible information source and a valuable service. Sites that are updated daily or weekly with "late-breaking news," "tips of the day," or "what's new" content will attract regular visitors and give your group a cutting-edge image. If visitors to the "what's new" page find material that is months or years old, your group's image will suffer accordingly.

## Basic Web Sites

For smaller organizations, the basic Web site usually begins with material already developed for a membership brochure, including the group's mission and objectives. The site is, in effect, an electronic brochure, putting before anyone who logs on the same information you might send to introduce them to your group.

Subsequently, a smaller organization would post information on upcoming meetings, descriptions of material available to the public or to members, press releases, and statements or position papers on public issues.

A nonprofit organization dedicated to answering questions from the public about a product or a public affairs issue will include a link that routes an inquiry directly to the organization. For example, the Candlelighters Childrens Cancer Foundation (*www.candlelighters.org*), whose mission is to provide information and social support to children with cancer and their families, receives and answers several hundred questions from the public each week through an Internet link on its Web page. This Internet link supplements a similar service the group offers through an 800 number, and answering inquiries on-line has proven more effective and less time-consuming than responding by telephone.

As noted above, developing such a basic Web site should not be expensive. Most groups can contract with a graphic artist to design the home page, which is the first page people see when they visit your site. The designer should use the association's name, logo, and other identifying characteristics. Have the designer create basic graphics to highlight new postings, such as a "what's new" heading and icon to alert visitors to fresh material that may not otherwise be apparent. Basic headings usually identify the association's services, such as "events" or "meetings," "publications," "news releases," "contacts," and "about (the organization name)."

To design and maintain a basic Web site of this nature does not require a high level of expertise. A computer-literate staff person can do it. This function can also be outsourced to a consultant for a minimal cost. Or the association can hire a Web site developer, as discussed later in this chapter.

## Advanced Web Sites

Web site technology is advancing so rapidly that any discussion of advanced applications will soon fall under a more "basic" applications category. The best way to keep up is to work closely with your site developer and set aside time on a regular basis to visit as many Web sites as possible.

As Web sites grow in content and sophistication, you must ensure that they are well organized and allow visitors to find the information and services they need easily. It is important to view the Web site as a user would. For example, a professional association may be inclined to organize the site by function, such as government affairs, communications, meetings, publications, and background information. This scheme, although logical, offers little help to visitors searching for information and resources on specific issues.

You can make a Web site more user-friendly by developing site maps and subject indices. The map serves as a table of contents, in effect, with active links to every section of the site. Indices can show visitors all the resources available on a particular topic, such as conferences, publications, speeches, press releases, and government initiatives. To help visitors move swiftly throughout the site, post an index in the margin of the page. It may simply be a small box with a pull-down menu of topics or sections of your Web site. Visitors can then click on the menu item to go instantly to the material they want to review.

Many Web innovations involve trade shows and educational conferences. Trade associations and other nonprofits that sponsor conventions have site features that enable attendees to preview the workshops and exhibitors that most interest them. In some cases, the exhibitors' products can be displayed as 3-D images that can be rotated. If the site offers a "scheduling wizard," attendees can develop their personal itinerary for the show ahead of time.

To venture into e-commerce, you need to equip the Web site with security features that allow users to pay by credit card with the assurance that their numbers will be protected. Your Web developer or service provider can help you equip your site with the necessary safeguards. With these measures in place, you can turn your Web site into a major center of commerce. For example, visitors can:

- Contribute financially to your cause
- Pay dues to join your organization or to renew their membership
- Register to attend or exhibit at conferences
- Buy publications, videos, CD-ROM training programs, and other educational materials
- Purchase software that can be transmitted to them instantly and installed on-line

Some industry associations are starting to use Web sites to create an electronic trading community. The grocery industry, for example, is creating an extranet for this purpose, to be managed by the nonprofit Uniform Code Council (UCC), which already oversees all the technical standards associated with product scanning. This is UCCnet, envisioned as a secure medium whereby trading partners can buy and sell products, coordinate promotional activities, introduce new products to the entire industry, share information about consumer needs in different markets, manage inventory more efficiently, and offer many other business-support services. UCCnet may ultimately become the primary center of commerce for a half-trillion-dollar industry.

Associations are using Web sites to vote on board members, policies, and technical standards. Educational and professional nonprofits are sponsoring Web site forums where visitors can express their views on critical issues.

New Web site applications appear frequently. This makes it all the more important to continually visit sites throughout the World Wide Web, searching for ways to upgrade your own on-line office. Start by looking at the Web sites of organizations most like your own, then expand your search to nonprofit organizations in other areas.

Examples of professionally designed interactive sites are those of two quite different nonprofit organizations, the Center for Marine Conservation (*www.cmc-ocean.org*) and the North American Association of Food Equipment Manufacturers (*www.nafem.org*).

## Pitfalls in Web Design

Although an organization's written documents are usually the mainstay of a site, a Web site is not just a compilation of documents. Postings should be important, and they should be readable.

When designing your site, bear in mind that Web users tend to have a short attention span—as limited as that of a television viewer able to click instantly to countless other channels. The visible field of attention on a PC is smaller than a written page. Scrolling requires the eye to jump rapidly. Lengthy paragraphs, hard enough to read in a written document, become unreadable on a computer screen.

Keep paragraphs and sentences short. Use subject heads frequently. Copy that may look choppy in an article is probably well written for the Web site. Long documents are presented in what may be considered layers. Begin by providing viewers the document title. Clicking on that, viewers can then review an abstract or executive summary. If they want to learn more, the next layer can provide a table of contents, enabling them to read the entire document or certain chapters. This approach offers viewers the option to print out the entire document and read it in a hard copy format, which is easier on the eyes.

The need to keep Web sites up-to-date cannot be overemphasized. The Internet culture demands that information be as current as possible, if for no other reason than the technology makes updates easy to provide. Many associations assign a staff member to ensure that the site is refreshed with new information each day, week, or month. This responsibility can easily become a full-time job. If you assign it as a part-time task to someone who is already preoccupied with numerous other assignments, your Web site is likely to age from neglect.

Scholarly documents or complex position statements are, of course, exceptions; they can't be rewritten for the Web site. Readers often download these resources rather than reading them on the screen.

As in all effective communications, adhere to the rule, "Form follows function." Do not create graphics for graphics' sake, designing a site that serves as little more than a picture gallery. Extensive graphics slow the time it takes to open a Web site; if the site offers little substance or value after this wait, visitors will quickly depart and seldom return.

## Make Your Web Site Known

Simply creating and managing your Web site is not enough to establish it; people need to know it exists. You need ways to inform your members and, just as important, potential members and other interested parties, including journalists, researchers and public officials.

The most obvious method is to direct people to visit your site whenever they request any information it holds. The Web site address should appear on everything your organization publishes, including business cards, letterhead, brochures, conference promotions, newsletters, magazines, journals, and annual reports. Anyplace you list a telephone or fax number should feature your group's Web site address, including all e-mails, where the address can be listed as an active link that recipients can click on to gain immediate access.

There are many stopping off places on the World Wide Web that should also have information on your Web site. These include portal or gateway sites such as Yahoo or Excite, which list sites by subject categories. They have sections on associations, including those that may cover your specific industry, product, cause, or service. These gateway sites offer processes for adding a reference to your Web site, which will ensure that it is listed in the appropriate sections. You should also make your site accessible to the most popular search engines, such as Yahoo, Excite, Alta Vista, Webcrawler, Magellan, and others, that give Internet surfers the ability to search numerous Web sites for information. Unless you are registered with these search engines, your members or potential members may not find your Web site when searching for information about your association, industry, or cause.

## Selecting and Using Outside Resources

The use of outside resources is growing more popular as Web site applications become more sophisticated, requiring considerable expertise to program and manage. In addition, it is difficult to recruit and retain a Management Information Services (MIS) specialist and ensure that this staff member keeps up with the fast-changing world of Web technology. Many organizations are finding it more cost-effective to retain outside technical support services. These include Internet Service Providers (ISPs) that can provide the basic Internet connection and offer hosting and maintenance services, along with Internet developers that specialize in design and upgrades. Having such outside support frees their staff to focus on how the Web site can best provide the services and information that its most important audiences need.

Finding the right ISP for your needs requires some care. To ensure that all your needs are met, develop a "Request for Proposal for Web Site Services." At a minimum, this document should cover the following areas:

*Description of your organization*—Include your mission statement and all the services you provide members and key constituents.

*Your Web site goals and requirements*—State the goals in your strategic plan and detail all the features and services you want your site to provide, including how you want the site organized.

*Bidding company profile*—Ask for a description of the company, its history, annual reports, number of clients, hourly service rates, computer hardware, type of Internet connection, software, backup and disaster-recovery capability, and staff (technical, graphics, support/consulting, and total).

*RFP response procedures and format*—Set a deadline and identify the person to whom the proposal should be sent. Also include a time line showing when you will review the proposals, make a decision, and want the Web site up and running. For screening potential service providers, develop specific questions for Web site developers and hosts, along with a third set to ask the customers who are listed as references.

Here are the questions to ask a potential Web site developer:

- How long have you been developing Web sites, and how large is your staff?
- How many Web sites have you developed in the past 12 months? Show examples of four different types of Web sites you have developed.
- How many different types of Web sites do you develop, and what is the most common type?
- Have any of your Web sites won awards? If so, how are the award winners selected; what are the criteria for consideration?

- Describe your approach to building Web sites. Do you have a standard set of tasks, or is each project unique?

- What tools do you use to help build Web sites? How many templates have you created for Web site development?

- How do you estimate your Web site development projects? For your last three projects, what were the original estimate and the final cost of each project? What are the five main reasons for price increases, and what steps have you taken to prevent cost increases?

- How do you keep your customers involved in their Web development projects?

- Describe the specific techniques you use to attract general visitors to your Web sites, and what techniques do you use to attract specific visitors?

- On average, how much do your customers spend on Web site support and updates for a year? What is the range of spending and the number of customers in each range?

- How do you use databases to reduce the cost of ongoing Web site support? Which databases have you used?

- How do you use graphics in building Web sites? Describe specific advantages and disadvantages of different graphics.

Smith, Bucklin's questions for potential Web site hosting services:

- How many Web sites are you currently hosting? Provide examples of your three largest and three smallest.

- How long has your company been hosting Web sites? How long has your oldest customer been with you?

- How many new customers do you have each month, and how many customers leave each month?

- How do you monitor performance and reliability on your Internet servers, and what specific options are available to improve performance and reliability?

- What kinds of tools do you use to help your customers update their Web sites?

- Describe your connection to the Internet; how do you monitor the performance of your Internet service provider?

- Describe your disaster recovery plan. How often do you back up your systems, and when did you last test your recovery procedures?

- What are the top five reasons your customers choose your company to host their Web sites?

Once you have found strong candidates, here are some questions to ask the customers they provide as references:

- Name, company, role in the project, relative size of the Web site, length of development project, number of hits per month.
- How many projects have you done with this vendor?
- How many vendors did you evaluate before selecting this one?
- What is your relationship to the vendor?
- Did the Web site built (or hosting of the Web site) meet your expectations? If not, what specifically could the vendor have done to make it meet your expectations?
- How many problems have you reported to the vendor since the Web site was developed (or hosted)?
- What problems did you have during the project? Did the overall project planning of the vendor accommodate changes and allow enough time for review and testing?
- What would you like to see changed in the overall process of building (or hosting) your Web site?
- Have you been able to determine a return on investment for the Web site?
- Are you planning a change to your current Web site? If so, are you going to use the same vendor? Why or why not?
- Overall, how would you rate this vendor? (unacceptable, needs improvement, satisfactory, very good, excellent).

After you have selected outside Web site support services and are satisfied with the vendor's initial work, periodically review its performance and rates. Compare its service with others that support Web sites like yours by contacting their clients. You may find good reasons to change outside resources over time as the technology changes and new and more innovative organizations emerge.

## STAFFING YOUR INFORMATION SYSTEM

In order to take full advantage of IT capabilities, nonprofits need someone on staff to manage these resources. Smaller groups (and even some midsized groups) need not hire an MIS expert. The staff person who takes on this responsibility needs to know the functions that computers can perform and how to use them, and must have the aptitude and drive to keep up with fast-changing trends. But you do not need or necessarily want a specialist on staff who can program or service computer systems. These functions can be cost-effectively outsourced to service bureaus, ISPs, or Web site developers. The staff executive responsible for your MIS function should focus on how best to apply the technology without being distracted by the minutia of programming and time-consuming hardware maintenance and upgrades. This individual can then serve as an intermediary between the nonprofit's members and staff and the outside MIS experts. In this position, the executive can help the group use computers to accomplish its most important goals.

Another critical role for the MIS executive in any large or mid-sized nonprofit is to develop training programs to ensure that employees have the skills to use IT systems effectively. The use of computers takes skills that can be learned, but they are different from other business skills. Training is vital for efficient information flow, and your investment in training should equal or exceed your investment in capital equipment. Presently, high schools and colleges do not teach their students the "industry standard" software programs, nor do students always learn them on their own with any degree of competence. Your organization must take it upon itself to ensure that your workers know how to use the tools you are providing them.

There are numerous ways to provide training, and the instruction does not need to be expensive if it is spread out over time. Large leaps can make training extremely difficult, so well-managed organizations make change gradually and constantly so that it is the norm rather than the exception.

## Cross-Training

There are two major information assets in your business: the information in the computer system and, more important, the information in your staff. If only one individual in your organization knows how to use your information systems, you are in for trouble. Because the information systems skill level of many entry-level employees is minimal, training is very important. Equally important is the cross-training of several individuals in your organization on the same tasks. Ongoing training and cross-training keep morale up and workers interested, as well as making your whole staff stronger.

Once you have trained your staff, be prepared for changes. If you have trained your staff well, they will be coming up with ideas for processes, software, and hardware that will make your organization more efficient. It is impossible for one individual to track the myriad changes occurring with technology, but if your staff are alert to watch for new tools, they can have a great effect on their own work environment. Systems do best when they are growing and changing.

## MAINTENANCE AND SECURITY

Like any system, your information system will require regular and periodic maintenance. Once again, the maintenance strategy must be determined by the operational plan and a good look at your resources. For example, if you have a knowledgeable user community, your own staff may be able to diagnose and solve software problems. If you have a large enough group, you can afford to train a particular staff person to diagnose and solve hardware problems. If everyone is occupied with other work, an outside company can be brought in for hardware maintenance or software support.

Software companies usually have free (800) telephone support lines, and although these are crowded and you may be on hold for a long time, you generally get the right answer. There are also computer-user network forums that can be connected to manufacturers that will give advice and answer questions. Sometimes these manufacturers will go so far as to put software upgrades and fixes onto a user network for customers to download. With adequate training, you can be self-supporting.

### Disaster

You must have a competent support network, as well as a complete disaster recovery plan, to take care of any contingencies. Backups should be made and kept on a planned schedule. Large nonprofits may use a daily backup that is kept for two weeks, a weekly full-system backup that is kept for a month, and a full-system monthly backup that is kept off-site. With such a system, the most data that could be lost even in a complete "meltdown" of the systems would be one month's worth.

A disaster recovery plan permits you to keep operating if your building has a fire or becomes uninhabitable for some reason and you have to recreate your complete system in another location quickly. With a complete backup of data off-site, you can rent or buy new systems, restore the information, and be up and running as fast as the new machines can be set up. Think through what you would need in such a situation and keep the system off-site.

## PREPARING FOR CHANGE

One of the basic aspects of any system, whether it is an economic system, a company, the biosphere, or an information system, is that it grows and changes constantly. Many people worry that their systems will be out of date before they can become expert in using them. With the speed at which technology is currently developing, that is probably true, but that is no reason to purchase a system that is more complex than necessary. With adequate training and support, a simple system will perform the functions it was designed to do until the scope of the functions change. Follow your operational plan!

If you purchase off-the-shelf software for your information system, you will inevitably face the option of upgrading your software to new and improved versions. You do not need to examine your present software every time a new version comes out, but you do need to know when your present version of software has been superseded by another generation that truly performs better. Upgrades are justified not by simple improvement in degrees, but in kind.

A clear operational plan, updated frequently with tactical technology changes, has a sweeping effect on how an organization's activities are conducted. As a new technology emerges—say, video conferencing—each nonprofit organization should periodically look at the possible problems and opportunities it represents.

Emerging information technologies illustrate Buckminster Fuller's principle of "ephemeralization." His premise is that progress means doing more with less. The "ephemeralizing" technologies are enabling workers to become independent of time and space. A simple example is the use of e-mail instead of the telephone. With the telephone, both parties must be present on the same line at the same time to have a conversation. With electronic mail, the information is passed *asynchronistically,* meaning that each party gives and receives information at a time independent of the other. The Internet has added space independence to time independence, as your staff are now able to dial into your organization's network from anywhere.

### How Do I Deal with the Complexities?

If you have a good, well-trained staff and expert advice from a consultant, you can keep the issues very simple. The overall technology plan will come directly from the operational plans and the goals contained in it. The installer, the maintainer, and the users will work out the complexities. The evaluation of how well the system is working is simple: Is it meeting the needs that it was intended to meet?

## SUMMARY

- Begin with carefully conceived strategic and operational plans, consulting with outside experts and your staff. Make them as clear and complete as possible, as well as sufficiently flexible to accommodate changing technology. Move constantly and consistently into the future, without extreme leaps forward, by following careful planning. Have goals and time lines with demonstrable milestones. Be prepared to change and modify as the organizational climate changes and different services become available.

- Start with the simplest system that will meet your needs and build on it. It will inevitably become more complex, but as it grows so will the expertise of your users and support staff. Just remember, the care and feeding of your system is the training and professional development of your staff and the addition of hardware and software when the need arises.

- Make intelligent use of communications technologies, such as voice mail, e-mail, and Web sites. All organizations should have some kind of Web site presence. Consult with outside experts to determine the best system for your needs. It is often a good idea to use an Internet service provider to manage the technical requirements of your Web site.

- Enjoy the new technology. With all of the changes in efficiency and increases in productivity, there should be time to appreciate the labor saved, the quality increase in the output, and the added ability to be creative. Allow your staff the freedom to explore this new way of doing business. With an adequate and appropriate information system, the management of your organization should grow easier all the time.

## GLOSSARY OF TERMS

The following terms are basic to understanding modem information systems technology:

*Hardware* is the wiring, circuit boards, microchips, and other physical components that make up computers. These include the *central processing unit (CPU)* and the video monitor, keyboard, network interface cards (NICs), and the assorted cables that connect all the components to the CPU. Peripherals include printers and optional devices, such as scanners, joysticks, plotters, and speakers, which are attached to the CPU as well.

Within the CPU are the *hard drive,* where software and other files are stored, and slots for inserting portable disks, including 3 1/2-inch diskettes, *compact disks (CDs)* and *zip disks.* The latter two can store large amounts of data.

*Software* is the instructions that tell the hardware what to do. Word processing programs (e.g., Microsoft Word and WordPerfect) are used to create written documents. Spreadsheet software (e.g., Excel and Lotus 1-2-3) performs accounting functions. You can create electronic slide shows with presentation graphics programs (e.g., PowerPoint and Harvard Graphics). Other software is designed to accomplish certain tasks. You can have experts write customized software or use what is known in the trade as commercial off-the-shelf (COTS) programs.

There is also *firmware,* which is hardware that has software instructions imprinted or embedded in it so that the instructions become firmly built into the hardware. An example is the computer chip that contains the instructions that the computer uses to "wake itself up" when you first turn it on. This chip instructs the computer how to access the various drives and cards that are contained in the CPU.

A *LAN* is a local area network; a *WAN* is a wide area network. These are groups of computers that are connected together in order to communicate in different physical locations, such as in two offices side-by-side or in separate installations on opposite sides of the globe, to share information.

The *Internet* is all the computers that are interlinked to form one global communications network. Through a common computer language, all systems connected to the network can communicate with each other. An *intranet* is a comparable communications network within an organization. Industries use *extranets* to create an electronic trading community for communications and e-commerce; these may be administered by nonprofit organizations.

The *World Wide Web* is a vast network of electronic sites that computer users can visit to obtain information, make purchases, register for conferences, attend virtual meetings, play games, view videos, and undertake myriad other activities yet to be determined. A Web site is identified by the prefix in its code address—http://www.

## CHECKLIST FOR REVIEWING YOUR INFORMATION SYSTEMS PROGRAM

- Do you have a strategic plan to guide the development of your information system (IS)?

- How does your IS plan reflect your mission statement? Is it coordinated with all other aspects of your overall strategic plan?

- Do you have a timetable for implementing the different elements of your IS plan? Do you have a budget that is appropriate to the size and resources of your organization?

- Does your budget allow for appropriate upgrading of your IS capabilities, both hardware and software?

- Who is staffing your IS system? Will you need specialized staff in the future? What training does your present staff need in order to serve your needs, both present and future?

- Are you utilizing the capabilities of the Internet for communication with your leadership? With members or constituents at large? What are the potentialities for educational programs or for electronic meetings for your organization?

- Have you developed a Web site? Is it appropriate to the needs and resources of your organization? Are you updating it regularly? Is a specific individual responsible for keeping it fresh? Do you have a way to determine if your members use it, and how?

- Have you addressed security needs? At the least, do you have back-up in case of system failure?

# CHAPTER TWELVE

# Financial Management

**Money isn't everything, but without it (and proper financial management) your nonprofit may suffer. You need timely, accurate, and meaningful financial information to assess today's results and plan for the future. This chapter provides an overview of accounting issues to help you better manage your financial resources.**

Regardless of its size or type of organization, every nonprofit, from a university hospital to a local charity, needs to maintain accurate financial books and records. The purpose of this chapter is to explain what is required to maintain the books and records of a nonprofit organization with basic bookkeeping needs. Large organizations with complex transactions, income from multiple sources, or large payrolls will need more complex accounting systems than those described here. However, basic accounting concepts are pervasive. Executives of nonprofits, even those with their own accounting staffs and outside auditors, should understand what their accountants do and why. It is the responsibility of the nonprofit executive, recognizing that the needs of each group are different, to identify those topics that are relevant to the organization's administrative and operational requirements.

This chapter does not attempt to teach you how to invest your organization's funds. It does cover the basic requirements for establishing an accounting function, from implementing an accounting system to generating financial statements. Along the way, practical guidelines are provided, covering:

- Banking
- Staffing
- Establishing a chart of accounts
- Accrual and cash basis accounting

- Budgeting
- Financial statement preparation
- Internal accounting controls
- Audits
- Tax returns
- Policies and procedures

The accounting system is the foundation for understanding your fiscal responsibilities. It does not have to be complex. In fact, it can be quite simple and straightforward, whether you have substantial or limited resources. In any case, accounting is an important function that measures and reports the effectiveness of your organization's operations.

## WHAT IS THE ACCOUNTING PROCESS?

The accounting process encompasses the recording and reporting of transactions affecting the financial status of an organization. Regardless of the size of your nonprofit group, your leadership expects that processes and procedures will be implemented to generate useful financial statements and to secure the assets of the organization. Meaningful financial data cannot be produced without a mechanism to capture, record, review, summarize, and report information. This entire process is called accounting.

Bookkeeping is simply the recording of transactions. Although the terms *accounting* and *bookkeeping* are often used interchangeably, the differences in meaning are significant. Bookkeeping is just one facet of the accounting and financial management function of your nonprofit group. Accounting refers to the entire process of recording and reporting and requires that systems (automated or manual) be in place to facilitate bookkeeping and to produce accurate, meaningful financial statements and management reports.

The accounting process can be described as an ongoing, monthly cycle consisting of:

- Cash receipts and disbursements
- Accrual entries (unless maintaining the records on a "cash" basis)
- Other journal entries
- Closing procedures
- Financial statement preparation
- Review and analysis

The ultimate goal of an accounting system is to generate accurate and timely financial statements that provide meaningful financial data to the readers. Readers may include the leadership of your organization (the governing board), the executive director, donors, lenders, and the public. Although the bookkeeping function may end when the monthly financial statements are issued, the accounting process is not complete until a thorough review and analysis have been performed. The rest of this chapter describes some of the key steps in the accounting process.

## GETTING STARTED: OPENING A BANK ACCOUNT

If your organization does not already have one, you must open a bank account so funds can be deposited and vendors paid. Most nonprofit organizations have relatively simple banking needs. This does not mean that the decision to use a particular bank should be taken lightly. First, you must identify your organization's basic service needs. They usually encompass deposits, withdrawals (usually issuing checks but sometimes using wire transfers), and obtaining bank balances.

Sometimes more extensive banking services may be required: direct deposit for payroll, investing available funds, debit and credit transactions processed through the Automated Clearing House, lockbox services, merchant account (credit card) transactions, loans, or Internet access to bank account information via your personal computer.

Most banks can provide all of these services, and many large brokerage houses have money market accounts that can be used like checking accounts. Assuming that all banks appear to be the same, how can you find the bank that is right for you? One way to start is to contact other groups of a similar size that may have the same service needs as your organization. Using references from other nonprofits is an excellent way of identifying a bank that offers services that meet your needs. The bank you use personally or one that serves for-profit firms may not be the best for serving nonprofits. Visit the bank and discuss your expected needs with the bank officer. Consult with your attorney or accountant for recommendations too.

Use the following criteria when searching for a bank:

*Financial strength*—Although this is not the pressing topic it once was, knowing that your bank is financially stable is important. Although you may not want to investigate capital ratios and liquidity, you can obtain quarterly and annual reports (assuming that the bank is a publicly traded institution) directly from the bank. You can also read analysts' reports on the financial strength of the bank.

*Quality of service*—Ask the referring organizations whether they would choose the bank again if they were starting over. Does the bank process transactions accurately the first time? Is the bank responsive to their needs?

*Clearance*—All banks are now subject to the Expedited Funds Availability Act, which mandates the maximum length of time that checks can "clear" through the system and be made available to the customer. Many banks have implemented processes and procedures that reduce this time. This can be an important factor for organizations with severe cash flow restrictions that need immediate use of deposits. If the source of your funding is national or international, be sure to check with the bank to find out how long it takes to clear checks.

*Location*—Although not critical, given that so many banking services can be performed remotely, access to a bank branch is an important criterion for those organizations that may need to make daily deposits. Sometimes it is necessary to visit with bank personnel, and a nearby branch can save time. Inquire about the availability of a night depository so that deposits can be made after the close of business.

*Experience with other nonprofit groups*—Even though your needs may be simple, your banker may be better equipped to address your concerns and banking problems if he or she is attuned to the particular issues of nonprofit groups. If your organization grows, this may become an important consideration as your service needs change.

*Banking personnel*—It is usually incumbent upon the customer to establish a working relationship with the branch manager. Meet with the manager and determine whether he or she will be responsive to your needs.

*Lending*—Does the bank make loans to nonprofit organizations? If you anticipate the need for borrowed funds, you may want to identify some of the criteria used by various banks for extending credit. Of course, most banks will want to see a history of solid financial results and strong cash flow and will review your organization's credit history with vendors. However, collateral requirements and the approval process vary from bank to bank. Decide whether or not you can establish a long-term relationship with your banker that will some day facilitate such borrowing.

*FDIC Insurance*—Most institutions have government insurance provided by the Federal Deposit Insurance Corporation (FDIC). Make sure the banks you are considering carry such insurance. Should you need to maintain in the bank more than the maximum amount covered by FDIC insurance, ask your banker for suggestions to help diversify and thereby protect your group's money.

*Fees*—Service fees can vary significantly from bank to bank. Make sure the banks you are considering have a clear understanding of your service needs. Banks are entitled to make a profit, but it is your responsibility to ensure that the fees assessed to your account are reasonable and competitive. Review them every six months in case circumstances have changed. If you expect the bank to process a significant number of transactions, you may be able to convince the bank to extend volume discounts. However, most small nonprofit organizations are not initially in a position to negotiate deeply discounted fees.

Banks usually charge fees for maintaining the account and for transactions. For example, transaction fees may be assessed for each check cleared, each stop payment, each deposit, and each wire transfer. You can pay for such costs by maintaining a predetermined balance in a non-interest-bearing account (paying with "soft" dollars) or by paying monthly fees out of an interest-bearing account (paying with "hard" dollars). Your banker can help you determine which method is most suitable for your organization. Be sure to ask about special accounts that may be available only to nonprofit organizations with a limited number of transactions.

Nonprofit groups can establish the following types of bank accounts:

*Demand Deposit Account (DDA)*—This is a transaction account or a basic checking account that pays no interest. It can be appropriate for organizations that want to pay for bank services with soft dollars.

*Interest-Bearing Checking Account*—Available to nonprofit groups, this account simply pays interest on available funds. The interest rate is usually not as high as that paid on money market accounts and savings accounts. However, keeping operating funds in an interest-bearing checking account can eliminate the need to "manage" these funds by transferring dollars in and out of interest-bearing and non-interest-bearing accounts.

*Money Market Account*—Excess funds can be deposited into a money market account that usually pays a higher interest rate than an interest-bearing checking account or savings account. Money market accounts provide liquidity, but there may be restrictions on the number of monthly checks or disbursements drawn on this account.

*Savings Account*—The same savings accounts available to individuals are available to nonprofit organizations. Once again, there may be monthly restrictions on the number of transactions.

Your bank may also be able to assist you in investing excess funds in Certificates of Deposit (CDs), Treasury bills, commercial paper, or other investments in accordance with your investment policy approved by the board of directors.

In sum, your bank should be financially stable, offer a variety of services, and have strong ties to the community. Although banks are certainly entitled to make a fair profit, you have an obligation to minimize transaction costs and to maximize services.

## STAFFING THE ACCOUNTING FUNCTION

Finding the right level of staffing for your nonprofit organization is a challenging task. Determining whether a separate bookkeeping/ accounting function is necessary is also a difficult chore. The size of your operation should give you some guidance in deciding whether a bookkeeper is necessary.

Small organizations can usually maintain the books by assigning this responsibility to a volunteer, part-time staff person, or full-time administrative assistant who has other responsibilities. Although bookkeeping experience is helpful, it may not be required if sufficient guidance is provided and the accounting system is simple. This arrangement may be appropriate for groups with relatively small budgets and limited check writing volume.

An alternative to staffing this position is to outsource the function to an independent bookkeeper, accounting firm, or management firm. Such outsourcing can be cost-effective and efficient because direct supervision will not be required, there are usually no payroll issues in using independent contractors, and presumably the person or firm performing such services has the resources and the expertise to meet your particular needs.

Organizations with larger budgets may require an accounting staff consisting of (1) a chief accountant with nonprofit experience to oversee the operation and (2) assistance from one or two bookkeepers who may separate the accounts receivable (cash receipts) and accounts payable (cash disbursements) functions.

## ACCOUNTING SYSTEM

Establishing an accounting system, although not directly fulfilling a nonprofit organization's mission, is nevertheless a critical administrative task. A well-designed system, even if it consists solely of manual ledgers, can mean the difference between timely financial information and incomplete, unsupported records. The accounting system is really just the mechanism that facilitates the recording of transactions into (in the case of computers) or onto (in the case of a manual ledger) various files or ledgers that can be used to generate financial statements.

Usually, the number of transactions (deposits, checks, and journal entries) determines whether it is cost-effective to automate the accounting process. A manual system may be the most appropriate choice for a small operation with a limited number of transactions. Small groups with no paid staff and limited assets may simply "keep the books" in a checkbook supplied by the local bank. Some groups may write enough checks to warrant the purchase of a check register accounting system, whereby checks are manually recorded in a ledger at the same time they are prepared. This combination check-book-and-expense-distribution journal provides a simple way of recording receipts and disbursements while maintaining the checkbook balance.

Some organizations may maintain manual ledgers and then send the ledgers to an accounting firm each month. The accounting firm, often certified public accountants, will input the data into its own system and generate financial statements for the organization. This process may work well for groups that have a close working relationship with their accountants. However, it can also give a false sense of security. The fact that the statements are printed from a computer system on a laser printer does not mean that they are accurate or complete.

An automated system does not have to be a complicated one. There are numerous "off-the-shelf" accounting applications available that do not require any previous accounting or bookkeeping experience. Such systems can be installed and maintained by the nonprofit's paid or volunteer staff. Typically, accounting packages include a general ledger, an accounts receivable subsidiary ledger, an accounts payable subsidiary ledger, and sometimes a payroll module.

Using an Application Service Provider (ASP) is an alternative to acquiring your own accounting package. An ASP allows organizations to use software on-line through the Internet for a monthly fee. Benefits include a lower up-front cost for software, automatic software upgrades, and affordable monthly costs. While many ASPs are providing accounting software to large companies which would otherwise have to purchase or lease expensive networks or mainframes to house their applications, there are also many Internet companies catering to small businesses and nonprofit organizations. Some ASPs make available some of the more common "off-the-shelf" accounting packages. Others provide accounting software with more features but at a higher cost. Some of these ASPs price their services by the number of users and others base their fees on the number of transactions. If your organization maintains a relatively high-speed Internet connection, you may want to consider using an ASP to provide your accounting application.

Payroll is a function that many small (and even some large) organizations prefer not to handle because they do not have staff experienced in this area. The task of paying employees, withholding taxes, filing state and federal forms, and paying state and federal taxes is an onerous one. Taxing authorities are usually unforgiving, so penalties and interest accrue quickly if payments or filings are late. The payroll function can easily be contracted out to a firm that specializes in such services. A payroll service can establish direct deposit and arrange for automatic payment and reporting of all taxes at reasonable prices.

Automated accounting systems can run using the most basic personal computers available. They are easily installed and maintained. It is important, however, that particular attention be paid in establishing the chart of accounts (see the following section). When identifying an automated accounting package, be sure to consider the following criteria:

- How easy is it to use?
- How easy is it to install?
- What hardware capacity is necessary to process adequately all anticipated transactions?
- What reports can be printed?
- Can data be uploaded and downloaded to diskettes for use in other applications (such as Lotus 1-2-3 or Excel spreadsheets)?
- Is the vendor reputable?
- Do you know of other, similar organizations using the software?
- Is the cost reasonable?

## CHART OF ACCOUNTS

Once a system is identified, you must establish a chart of accounts, the account numbers your organization will use to record and report financial transactions. The chart of accounts can be very simple and easy to use as long as it is not too detailed. A separate account number is not needed for every type of revenue and expense anticipated. Ask yourself what is important to monitor and if this information should be specifically identified in the financial statements.

There is one complicating factor that must be addressed in establishing the chart of accounts. Nonprofit organizations should report their results using functional classifications as well as natural classifications. Functional reporting reflects revenue and expenses by major programmatic activities or functions, such as research, community services, membership services, and public relations; and supporting activities, such as general, administrative, and fund-raising. Natural accounts are those that can be used across functional categories. Natural account numbers can refer to specific accounts, including both income—such as contributions, membership dues, or other income—and expenses, like those for meetings, salaries and fringes, printing, rent, telephone, and so forth.

In devising the chart of accounts, use a numbering or lettering scheme that refers first to the functional classification. Programmatic activities and supporting activities are functions that are usually two or three digits long. They are usually assigned numbers so that they are printed in numerical order (see Exhibit 12–1).

**Exhibit 12–1**  Sample Functional Category Table

| Function Number | Function Description |
|---|---|
| 001 | Balance Sheet |
| 100 | Research |
| 110 | Community Services |
| 120 | Membership Services |
| 130 | Public Relations |
| 200 | General & Administrative |
| 210 | Fund-Raising |

Natural account numbers are usually three or four digits long and can be used throughout your chart of accounts in the appropriate functional categories. Be sure to use the same natural account numbers throughout the functional categories. You should use a series of numbers that group the natural account numbers by financial statement category, as shown in Exhibit 12–2.

**Exhibit 12–2**  Sample Natural Account Table

| Natural Account Number Range | Financial Statement Category |
|---|---|
| 1000–1999 | Assets |
| 2000–2999 | Liabilities |
| 3000–3999 | Net Assets |
| 4000–4999 | Revenue |
| 5000–9999 | Expense |

The chart of accounts provides a location for posting all transactions within the general ledger. For example, based on Exhibits 12–1 and 12–2, an organization can record postage expense for a membership mailing to 120-7760. Or cash received can be recorded in 001-1010. Fund-raising revenue might be recorded in 210-4200. Both the function and the account number are used in coding transactions.

The chart of accounts is important because it is the basis for generating your monthly financial statements. Most accounting packages print reports that are based on a combination of functions and account numbers, so it is important to develop the chart of accounts with reporting in mind.

## ACCRUAL AND CASH BASIS ACCOUNTING

Although not required, many nonprofit organizations follow generally accepted accounting principles, rules promulgated by the Financial Accounting Standards Board, in preparing their financial statements. One of the basic tenets covering financial statements is that accrual basis accounting must be used.

In accrual basis accounting, revenue is recognized when earned rather than when received, and expense is recognized when incurred rather than when paid. The use of accrual basis accounting can produce prepaid expenses (when goods or services are paid for in advance) and prepaid or deferred income (revenue received for goods or services that have not yet been received or performed). In addition, revenue relating to the current year but not collected until the next year is reflected on the statement of financial position as accounts receivable, and on the statement of activities as revenue. Expense relating to the current year but not paid until the next year is reflected on the statement of financial position as accounts payable, and on the statement of activities as expense.

At year end, your group should perform a thorough review for items that should be accrued as revenue or expense. Generally, revenue that is expected but not received before the end of your fiscal year will be recorded as a receivable. Examples of such accruals are advertising income and publication sales. In addition, an expense that is incurred but not yet paid will be recorded as a payable. Recording such entries before the books are closed for the year will minimize the number of audit entries that must be posted retroactively. The year-end statements will provide a more accurate picture of your organization's net assets if accruals are made. Accrual basis accounting allows for a better matching of revenues and expenses within an accounting period.

Your organization, however, may determine that keeping the books on a cash basis, during the year, is sufficient. If your financial reporting needs are not significant and you have limited staffing for the accounting function, it is easier to record revenue when cash is received and to record expense when disbursements are made. Conversion to the accrual basis of accounting can then be performed at the end of the year. During the year, however, you should be aware of expenses that have been incurred but not yet paid so as to avoid overspending your budget or altering your cash position.

## CASH RECEIPTS

The accounting process starts with cash receipts, a function common to all organizations regardless of size or purpose. In accounting terminology, cash also means funds from checks, travelers checks, credit card payments, and wire transfers. Nonprofit organizations receive cash for dues, conference registrations, contributions, grants, investment income, advertising income, sales of merchandise and special events, or any services to members or the community from whom they obtain fees.

For most nonprofit organizations, checks are mailed directly to the office, where they should be recorded or logged in by one person and deposited by another. This segregation of duties helps mitigate the risk of loss or misappropriation. Recognizing that some groups do not have enough staff to segregate these duties, it is incumbent upon the leadership to develop a mechanism that helps to ensure that all checks received are deposited into the correct account on a timely basis. To address the lack of segregation of duties, rotate certain functions among the staff, assign the responsibility for opening mail to different people throughout the year, review the journals or logs periodically, and compare these subtotals to the deposit slips and entries recorded in the general ledger. All amounts received should be deposited promptly; do not hold back any cash for the petty cash fund. When that fund needs to be replenished, a check should be cashed for the amount needed.

All checks should be restrictively endorsed upon receipt. A rubber stamp can be readily obtained from the bank. Cash and checks should be deposited the same day they are received or secured overnight in a fireproof safe.

If the volume of receipts is significant, you can establish a lockbox system with your bank or with a third-party vendor that specializes in customized processing. Checks can be sent directly to the bank in your organization's name. The bank will deposit those checks and send you batch totals with supporting documentation. The benefits of this system include the timely deposit of funds, enhanced internal accounting controls, and convenience. Of course, these services can be costly, as there are usually fixed and variable bank fees associated with lockbox services. Your banker can tell you if such a service is appropriate for your group.

Documentation should be available for every deposit made. A copy of the deposit slip and copies of checks or other notations should be filed in chronological order. As the deposits are made, code them in accordance with your chart of accounts and organize them so they can be entered into your accounting system.

## CASH DISBURSEMENTS

Cash disbursements include the processing of checks, wire transfers, and petty cash. This function is a critical one because it entails direct access to one of your organization's most valuable assets, cash. Even if your staffing resources are limited, your group must implement internal accounting controls to safeguard your funds and to ensure that disbursements are authorized and appropriate.

Ideally, the cash disbursements function includes the following:

- Approve invoice for payment
- Authorize that a check be issued
- Prepare and record the check
- Sign and mail check to vendor
- Reconcile bank account
- Review bank statement, bank reconciliation, and check register

The critical internal control feature inherent in this function is that the person authorizing and signing checks is not the same person preparing the checks and recording them in the general ledger.

For those groups with limited staffing, there are steps that can be taken to enhance controls even if you cannot segregate the duties as suggested here. First, pay from original invoices only. Do not pay from statements, because this can increase the likelihood of duplicate payments. Next, authorize the invoice by signing and dating it and circling the amount to be paid. Mark or stamp it paid once the check is issued. Insist that approved supporting documentation be attached for every check so that you are assured that the expenditure is authorized and legitimate. In some cases, it may be appropriate to require more than one signature for disbursements in excess of a predetermined amount. An extra precautionary step in a small organization is to have the bank statement sent directly to the executive director or another senior person who is not an authorized signer. The executive director will then have a chance to review the cancelled checks and deposit listing for any unusual transactions. Periodically, the bank reconciliations should be reviewed in detail and tied into the general ledger to ensure that no unauthorized transactions have occurred.

When a disbursement is made, it must be coded and recorded in the general ledger. File a copy of the check with the supporting documentation by vendor.

## ACCRUAL ENTRIES AND OTHER JOURNAL ENTRIES

Posting accruals and adjusting journal entries is a standard process within the accounting cycle. As noted previously, accruals are made to record revenue and expense in the proper period, whether or not funds have been received or disbursed. After month end, review the files to determine whether revenue collected in the subsequent month should be recorded as a receivable the month before. Advertising and royalty income are examples of items that may require accruals.

On the expense side, review the open payables file and record invoices that have been received but not yet paid. In addition, if an expenditure is material (significant), accrue for items or services that have been received but have not yet been billed. Recording these entries in the monthly financial statements can generate a more complete financial picture of your organization's assets and liabilities.

## CLOSING PROCEDURES

Closing procedures entail a review of key asset and liability accounts. Each month, a series of accounts should be reconciled against subsidiary ledgers and other supporting documentation. It is possible that during the month, entries have been miscoded and misposted, and therefore ending balances will not be accurate. Closing procedures include the process of posting balances to the general ledger and performing an internal control, called the analytical review.

Cash is the first account that should be reconciled or "closed" as part of your organization's closing procedures. Cash can be closed by preparing a bank reconciliation and having it reviewed by someone other than the person posting entries to the general ledger. You may have an accounts receivable subsidiary ledger that must be reconciled and posted to the general ledger. Other asset accounts that may require special attention include deposit accounts, clearing accounts, and prepaid expense accounts. Make sure that all account balances have support or some type of corroborating documentation that ties into the numbers on the statement of financial position.

Liability accounts should also be reconciled as part of the closing process. Many accounting systems use an accounts payable subsidiary ledger, which must be closed and then posted to the general ledger. This closing procedure may include the recording of last-minute invoices and the crediting of payments after issuing checks. The accounts payable ledger should tie into the general ledger each month. Other liability accounts that may require some type of reconciliation include clearing accounts and prepaid income.

Although analytical review procedures are especially appropriate for large organizations with more complex financial reporting, executives of smaller organizations should know what they entail and how they may be able to benefit from them. Analytical review is the review of current account balances as measured against some other criteria. Your closing procedures can include a comparison of current results with those from the same period last year. Balances can be compared with your budget, and ratios can be computed and monitored from month to month. Results can even be measured against external standards as a means of identifying potential problems. The numbers should be reviewed to see whether they make sense, given your knowledge of the organization's activities. These steps can be performed as part of the review and analysis procedures described later in this chapter.

## BUDGETING

Budgeting is a process that must be tailored to the individual needs of your organization. No matter how distinctive your organization is, however, there are some practical considerations common to all groups. Keeping in mind that a budget is a benchmark for measuring the results of your operations in fiscal terms, you should develop a budget based on historical information, trends, industry conditions, and the economy.

Normally, the executive director develops the annual budget and submits it to the board for approval in accordance with the nonprofit's bylaws. As this approval process usually takes a few months, many nonprofit executives begin to prepare the budget at least three or four months before the end of the year.

First, examine last year's results and this year's most recent financial information in order to identify trends and variations from your expectations. In projecting revenues, identify the most likely income sources first and the period of time over which this revenue will be recognized. Membership dues, publication sales, and investment income are some revenue categories that are usually more predictable than others. Fund-raising receipts, other donations, grant income, and in-kind contributions are more difficult to project. The budget for these categories is based more on historical information and the executive director's specific knowledge of these areas.

There should be a direct relationship between projected revenues and the expenses that will be incurred to carry out the nonprofit's mission. Preparing the revenue side of the equation first will make clear the extent of programs and services that can be rendered. Ask the appropriate association employees or volunteers to estimate expenses and to indicate when they will be incurred. You may want written explanations for amounts over a certain percentage of last year's budget or actual expenditures.

Budgets should be prepared on a "calendarized" or seasonal basis. If the organization is operating under the accrual method of accounting, reflect revenues and expenses when earned and as incurred. If the cash method is used, show in each month the projected cash receipts and disbursements. Reflecting the budget in this way will make the monthly financial statements more meaningful when results are compared with the budget.

Do not forget to develop a capital budget, one that encompasses the purchase of fixed assets such as computer equipment and furniture. Although they are usually not recorded as expenses within the financial statements, these purchases can entail a significant amount of money and are therefore subject to the same kind of approval and review as other expenditures. Capital expenditures can be more easily predicted because the number of such transactions is small as compared with those of the organization's day-to-day operations.

Although the budget is often considered a working document, its purpose is to make estimates of future revenues and expenses and thus to serve as a management tool. There are usually no right or wrong budgets. Because a budget will never be perfect, those who prepare it should do the best they can with the information available, be prepared to defend it, and then utilize it as one measure of the success of the nonprofit's programmatic activities. Understanding and responding to significant variances from the budget is probably one of your most important fiduciary responsibilities.

## FINANCIAL STATEMENT PREPARATION

The accounting cycle is almost complete as financial statements are generated and then reviewed. Financial statements should include a statement of financial position (balance sheet), a statement of activities (income statement), and a statement of cash flows.

The Financial Accounting Standards Board Statement of Financial Accounting Standards No. 117, *Financial Statements of Not-for-Profit Organizations* governs the presentation of financial statements for nonprofit groups of all sizes. This pronouncement states that the results of operations must be reported by identifying changes in permanently restricted net assets, temporarily restricted net assets, and unrestricted net assets. Both the statement of financial position and the statement of activities will report the balances in these classes of net assets.

A statement of financial position (see Exhibit 12–3) reports the assets and liabilities of an organization at a particular point in time. It usually includes three sections: assets, liabilities, and net assets. The assets section includes checking, savings, and/or money market accounts; investments and/or reserve funds, if any; the organization's fixed assets, including furniture and fixtures; and accounts receivable and other items of value to the organization.

**Exhibit 12–3** Sample Statement of Financial Position

*The Food Distribution Network, Inc.*
*Statement of Financial Position*
*As of November 30, 20XX*

| | |
|---|---:|
| Assets: | |
| Cash | $ 55,600 |
| Accounts receivable | 2,750 |
| Investments | 59,900 |
| Fixed assets, net | 32,375 |
| Total assets | $150,625 |
| | |
| Liabilities and net assets: | |
| Accounts payable | $ 16,250 |
| Accrued liabilities | 2,400 |
| Total liabilities | 18,650 |
| | |
| Net assets: | |
| Unrestricted | 131,975 |
| Temporarily restricted | 0 |
| Permanently restricted | 0 |
| Total net assets | 131,975 |
| Total liabilities and net assets | $150,625 |

The liabilities section includes trade payables (amounts owed to vendors), deferred income (income to be recognized in a future period), and other obligations the group has incurred.

The net assets section reports the cumulative net worth of the organization, consisting of the difference between total assets and total liabilities.

The statement of activities (see Exhibit 12–4) measures, in fiscal terms only, the effectiveness of the organization's ability to carry out its mission. It reports revenues and expenses and shows the change in net assets from one year to the next. Exhibit 12–4 is an example of functional reporting.

You can also combine a functional and a natural report, as shown in Exhibit 12–5.

Exhibits 12–4 and 12–5 reflect column headings that are appropriate for monthly financial reporting. Audited financial statements would differ by showing yearly results only.

A supplementary statement of activities (see Exhibit 12–6) is an additional report that can (must, for certain types of organizations) be included as part of your audited financial statements. It reports revenues

**Exhibit 12–4** Sample Statement of Activities (functional basis)

The Food Distribution Network, Inc.
Statement of Activities (unrestricted class only)
For the 11 Months Ended November 30, 20XX

| | Current Month Actual | Current Month Budget | Current Month Variance | Year-To-Date Actual | Year-To-Date Budget | Year-To-Date Variance | Annual Budget |
|---|---|---|---|---|---|---|---|
| **Revenues** | | | | | | | |
| Contributions | $9,200 | $9,000 | $200 | $111,000 | $99,000 | $12,000 | $108,000 |
| Fees | 900 | 1,000 | (100) | 8,000 | 11,000 | (3,000) | 12,000 |
| Fund-raising | 4,000 | 5,000 | (1,000) | 58,900 | 55,000 | 3,900 | 60,000 |
| Investment income | 225 | 200 | 25 | 3,050 | 2,200 | 850 | 2,400 |
| Other income | 1,100 | 1,000 | 100 | 8,000 | 11,000 | (3,000) | 12,000 |
| Total unrestricted revenues | 15,425 | 16,200 | (775) | 188,950 | 178,200 | 10,750 | 194,400 |
| **Expenses** | | | | | | | |
| Restaurant pick-ups | 4,400 | 4,000 | (400) | 46,500 | 44,000 | (2,500) | 48,000 |
| Hotel pick-ups | 2,000 | 3,500 | 1,500 | 31,600 | 38,500 | 6,900 | 42,000 |
| Distribution facilities | 3,150 | 2,500 | (650) | 24,200 | 27,500 | 3,300 | 30,000 |
| General & administrative | 4,750 | 5,000 | 250 | 56,850 | 55,000 | (1,850) | 60,000 |
| Fund-raising | 400 | 500 | 100 | 4,900 | 5,500 | 600 | 6,000 |
| Total unrestricted expenses | 14,700 | 15,500 | 800 | 164,050 | 170,500 | 6,450 | 186,000 |
| Increase in unrestricted net assets | 725 | 700 | 25 | 24,900 | 7,700 | 17,200 | 8,400 |
| Net unrestricted assets at beginning of year | — | — | — | 107,075 | 107,075 | 0 | 107,075 |
| Net unrestricted assets at end of period | — | — | — | $131,975 | $114,775 | $17,200 | $115,475 |

299

**Exhibit 12-5** Sample Statement of Activities (functional and natural account basis)

The Food Distribution Network, Inc.
Statement of Activities (unrestricted class only)
For the 11 Months Ended November 30, 20XX

| | Current Month Actual | Current Month Budget | Current Month Variance | Year-To-Date Actual | Year-To-Date Budget | Year-To-Date Variance | Annual Budget |
|---|---|---|---|---|---|---|---|
| Revenues | | | | | | | |
| Contributions | $9,200 | $9,000 | $200 | $111,000 | $99,000 | $12,000 | $108,000 |
| Fees | 900 | 1,000 | (100) | 8,000 | 11,000 | (3,000) | 12,000 |
| Fund-raising | 4,000 | 5,000 | (1,000) | 58,900 | 55,000 | 3,900 | 60,000 |
| Investment income | 225 | 200 | 25 | 3,050 | 2,200 | 850 | 2,400 |
| Other income | 1,100 | 1,000 | 100 | 8,000 | 11,000 | (3,000) | 12,000 |
| Total unrestricted evenues | 15,425 | 16,200 | (775) | 188,950 | 178,200 | 10,750 | 194,400 |
| Expenses | | | | | | | |
| Restaurant pick-ups | | | | | | | |
| Meetings | 45 | 100 | 55 | 1,105 | 1,100 | (5) | 1,200 |
| Miscellaneous | 1,800 | 1,750 | (50) | 18,745 | 19,250 | 505 | 21,000 |
| Postage | 75 | 70 | (5) | 895 | 770 | (125) | 840 |
| Salaries and benefits | 1,600 | 1,500 | (100) | 18,750 | 16,500 | (2,250) | 18,000 |
| Telephone | 225 | 200 | (25) | 2,055 | 2,200 | 145 | 2,400 |
| Travel/transportation | 655 | 380 | (275) | 4,950 | 4,180 | (770) | 4,560 |
| Total restaurant pick-ups | 4,400 | 4,000 | (400) | 46,500 | 44,000 | (2,500) | 48,000 |
| Hotel pick-ups | | | | | | | |
| Meetings | 0 | 40 | 40 | 810 | 440 | (370) | 480 |
| Miscellaneous | 945 | 1,735 | 790 | 13,050 | 19,085 | 6,035 | 20,820 |
| Postage | 75 | 80 | 5 | 1,355 | 880 | (475) | 960 |
| Salaries and benefits | 560 | 1,095 | 535 | 7,800 | 12,045 | 4,245 | 13,140 |
| Telephone | 110 | 155 | 45 | 1,935 | 1,705 | (230) | 1,860 |
| Travel/transportation | 310 | 395 | 85 | 6,650 | 4,345 | (2,305) | 4,740 |
| Total hotel pick-ups | 2,000 | 3,500 | 1,500 | 31,600 | 38,500 | 6,900 | 42,000 |

| | | | | | | | |
|---|---|---|---|---|---|---|---|
| **Distribution Facilities** | | | | | | | |
| Meetings | 80 | 65 | (15) | 385 | 715 | 330 | 780 |
| Miscellaneous | 40 | 50 | 10 | 365 | 550 | 185 | 600 |
| Postage | 95 | 70 | (25) | 495 | 770 | 275 | 840 |
| Rent and utilities | 500 | 500 | 0 | 5,500 | 5,500 | 0 | 6,000 |
| Salaries and benefits | 1,550 | 1,400 | (150) | 14,355 | 15,400 | 1,045 | 16,800 |
| Telephone | 110 | 125 | 15 | 835 | 1,375 | 540 | 1,500 |
| Travel/transportation | 775 | 290 | (485) | 2,265 | 3,190 | 925 | 3,480 |
| Total distribution facilities | 3,150 | 2,500 | (650) | 24,200 | 27,500 | 3,300 | 30,000 |
| **General & administrative** | | | | | | | |
| Audit | 0 | 75 | 175 | 2,100 | 1,925 | (175) | 2,100 |
| Bank charges | 65 | 50 | (15) | 650 | 550 | (100) | 600 |
| Depreciation | 45 | 45 | 0 | 495 | 495 | 0 | 540 |
| Insurance | 100 | 100 | 0 | 1,100 | 1,100 | 0 | 1,200 |
| Miscellaneous | 1,200 | 1,300 | 100 | 15,590 | 14,300 | (1,290) | 15,600 |
| Postage | 50 | 70 | 20 | 675 | 770 | 95 | 840 |
| Rent and utilities | 700 | 700 | 0 | 7,700 | 7,700 | 0 | 8,400 |
| Salaries and benefits | 2,400 | 2,400 | 0 | 27,500 | 26,400 | (1,100) | 28,800 |
| Telephone | 65 | 60 | (5) | 545 | 660 | 115 | 720 |
| Travel/transportation | 125 | 100 | (25) | 495 | 1,100 | 605 | 1,200 |
| Total general & administrative | 4,750 | 5,000 | 250 | 56,850 | 55,000 | (1,850) | 60,000 |
| **Fund-raising** | | | | | | | |
| Miscellaneous | 65 | 0 | (15) | 520 | 550 | 30 | 600 |
| Postage | 135 | 160 | 25 | 1,795 | 1,760 | (35) | 1,920 |
| Telephone | 175 | 200 | 25 | 1,905 | 2,200 | 295 | 2,400 |
| Travel/transportation | 25 | 90 | 65 | 680 | 990 | 310 | 1,080 |
| Total fund-raising | 400 | 500 | 100 | 4,900 | 5,500 | 600 | 6,000 |
| Total unrestricted expenses | 14,700 | 15,500 | 800 | 164,050 | 170,500 | 6,450 | 186,000 |
| Increase in unrestricted net assets | 725 | 700 | 25 | 24,900 | 7,700 | 17,200 | 8,400 |
| Net unrestricted assets at beginning of year | — | — | — | 107,075 | 107,075 | 0 | 107,075 |
| Net unrestricted assets at end of period | — | — | — | $131,975 | $114,775 | $17,200 | $115,475 |

**Exhibit 12–6** Sample Supplementary Statement of Activities

The Food Distribution Network, Inc.
Supplementary Statement of Activities (unrestricted class only)
For the 11 Months Ended November 30, 20XX

| | Restaurant Pick-Ups | Hotel Pick-Ups | Distribution Facilities | General & Administrative | Fund-raising | Total |
|---|---|---|---|---|---|---|
| Audit | $0 | $0 | $0 | $2,100 | $0 | $2,100 |
| Bank charges | 0 | 0 | 0 | 650 | 0 | 650 |
| Depreciation | 0 | 0 | 0 | 495 | 0 | 495 |
| Insurance | 0 | 0 | 0 | 1,100 | 0 | 1,100 |
| Meetings | 1,105 | 810 | 385 | 0 | 0 | 2,300 |
| Miscellaneous | 18,745 | 13,050 | 365 | 15,590 | 520 | 48,270 |
| Postage | 895 | 1,355 | 495 | 675 | 1,795 | 5,215 |
| Rent and utilities | 0 | 0 | 5,500 | 7,700 | 0 | 13,200 |
| Salaries and benefits | 18,750 | 7,800 | 14,355 | 27,500 | 0 | 68,405 |
| Telephone | 2,055 | 1,935 | 835 | 545 | 1,905 | 7,275 |
| Travel/transportation | 4,950 | 6,650 | 2,265 | 495 | 680 | 15,040 |
| Total expenses | $46,500 | $31,600 | $24,200 | $56,850 | $4,900 | $164,050 |

**Exhibit 12–7**   Sample Statement of Cash Flows

| *The Food Distribution Network, Inc.*<br>*Statement of Activities (unrestricted class only)*<br>*For the 11 Months Ended November 30, 20XX* | |
|---|---|
| Cash flows from operating activities: | |
|   Change in net assets | $24,900 |
|   Adjustments to reconcile change in net assets to | |
|     net cash provided by operating activities: | |
|     Depreciation | 495 |
|     Increase in accounts receivable | (1,050) |
|     Increase in accounts payable | 5,775 |
|     Decrease in accrued liabilities | (600) |
|       Net cash provided by operating activities | 29,520 |
| Cash flows from investing activities: | |
|   Purchase of equipment | (3,500) |
|   Proceeds from sale of investments | 10,250 |
|   Purchase of investments | (4,050) |
|     Net cash provided by investing activities | 2,700 |
| Cash flows from financing activities: | 0 |
| Net increase in cash | 32,220 |
| Cash at beginning of year | 23,380 |
| Cash at end of period | $55,600 |

and expenses by natural categories. This statement can be useful in comparing common types of expenses across functions or programs.

The statement of cash flows (see Exhibit 12–7) is a required statement that accompanies the audit opinion, other financial statements, and footnotes as part of the annual audit. This statement reconciles cash flows from operating activities, investing activities, and financing activities. Small nonprofit organizations do not usually prepare this statement on an interim (monthly) basis.

## REVIEW AND ANALYSIS

It is incumbent upon your organization's leadership, usually the treasurer, to review the monthly financial statements in order to identify errors, trends, and unusual transactions. Particular items should be considered:

- Examine the cash balance to ensure that balances maintained in checking accounts are adequate but not excessive

- Note the investment balance, if any, and identify any significant changes from month to month
- Examine the balance in prepaid expenses and prepaid income to ensure that increases or decreases in balances are appropriate, given the timing of your group's activities
- Examine the balances in fixed asset accounts and make sure that there are no significant increases or decreases without prior knowledge and approval
- Ensure that the accounts payable balance remains in line with expectations
- Examine the payroll liability accounts for unusual increases
- Examine major sources of income to determine whether actual results are in line with the budget. Obtain explanations for significant variances
- Examine all expenses that exceed the budget. Obtain explanations for significant variances
- Examine expenses for programmatic activities and obtain explanations for significant variances

You should also review the check register each month in order to note readily identifiable unauthorized disbursements. Review the listing for unusual payees and identify those payees that are not familiar. In addition, review the listing for unusual amounts, including even dollar amounts, and obtain explanations for such disbursements.

Periodically, the executive director should review the bank reconciliation to ensure that reconciling items are researched and resolved on a timely basis.

## DOES YOUR ORGANIZATION NEED AN AUDIT?

Although your organization may not be required to have an audit, it is generally recommended that an audit be performed, even if your operating budget is less than $100,000. An unqualified audit opinion from a certified public accountant (CPA) stating that the financial statements present fairly the balances and results of operations is sometimes critical in fund-raising, borrowing, and accepting government grants. Within your organization, an audit will help provide assurances that the financial statements are accurate and complete.

An audit of your organization's financial statements can give the leadership confidence that the fiduciary responsibilities have been fulfilled. Your auditor will perform tests of your accounting system, review the internal accounting controls, examine corroborating documentation, perform analytical review procedures, and confirm cash accounts and other balances in order to render an opinion on the financial statements taken as a whole. The auditor will review the accounting principles being followed and the financial statement format to determine whether they comply with generally accepted accounting principles.

Generally, the board of directors chooses an auditor after receiving a recommendation from the executive director. When choosing an auditor, consider the auditing firm's experience with nonprofit organizations, the firm's resources, the individuals assigned to the audit, their availability, their commitment to advising your organization on a variety of business matters, and the anticipated fees (you may be able to negotiate a lower fee if the work is performed during the "off season"). Check the auditors' references and ask them what differentiates their firm from others that provide the same service.

You should be aware of the various types of audit reports that can be issued by your certified public accountant. The most comprehensive audit includes procedures that test the organization's compliance with generally accepted accounting principles. These procedures are performed in accordance with generally accepted auditing standards, which require that the auditors satisfy themselves that material transactions are properly reflected in the financial statements and are disclosed in the footnotes. The completion of these procedures results in a complete audit.

An audit includes an opinion, a statement of financial position, a statement of activities, a statement of cash flows, footnotes, and, sometimes, a supplementary schedule reporting results by natural accounts as well as by functional areas. The footnotes are an integral part of the audited financial statements. They disclose the nature of the operations, a summary of significant accounting policies, a description of significant events, the nature of any related-party transactions, and detailed information on the organization's commitments and contingencies.

Upon completion of the audit, your auditors will require a management representation letter addressed to them that acknowledges management's responsibility for the fair presentation of the financial statements. Typically, the executive director and selected board members (usually the treasurer and the president) are asked to sign the letter. If you are not familiar with this procedure, ask your auditor for a copy of the letter that must be signed before issuance of the financial statements. In addition to the audited financial statements, the auditors should provide you with a management or internal control letter in which they discuss any suggestions they have for improvements in your policies and procedures.

An auditor's review of financial statements includes procedures that are not as comprehensive as those included in a complete audit. A review report indicates that the testing performed is less than that of a full audit and that only analytical review procedures were applied. Corroborating evidence, including confirmations, is not a part of the review procedures. A review provides only limited assurances that the financial statements are complete. It may be appropriate when an organization cannot afford an audit or when an audit is not necessary, given the limited scope of its operations.

A third type of service that auditors can perform is a compilation. A compilation report states that the account balances presented are those provided by management. The auditor will take absolutely no responsibility for any of the numbers or for the adequacy of the footnotes or other disclosures. Compilations may be appropriate for organizations that retain certified public accounting (CPA) firms to prepare their monthly financial statements or for those groups that want a professional presentation without any assurances that the numbers are correct.

## TAX RETURNS

If your organization's gross receipts are in excess of $25,000 per year, IRS Form 990, Return of Organization Exempt from Income Tax, must be completed and filed by the 15th day of the fifth month after year end. A penalty totaling $20 per day will be assessed by the Internal Revenue Service if the tax return is late or incomplete. However, IRS Form 2758 may be used to obtain an extension if necessary.

Information that must be completed in the tax return includes the following:

- Details of the revenue and expenses in the year to recalculate the final net assets at the end of the year
- Details of expenses by program services, management, and fundraising
- A description of activities related to your organization's exempt purpose
- A statement of financial position at the beginning and end of the tax year
- List of officers, directors, and trustees, including compensation paid to them

If your group is exempt from federal income taxes under section 501(c)(3) of the Internal Revenue Code, you must also complete Schedule A of Form 990. Schedule A requests other information, including a listing of the five highest-paid employees other than officers and directors, the five highest-paid persons for professional services, and further detail of revenues for the four years preceding the audit year.

You may be required to file IRS Form 990-T, Exempt Organization Business Income Tax Return, if your organization has $1,000 or more of gross income from an unrelated business, such as advertising revenue or the sale of lists and labels to for-profit organizations. This income, net of allocable expenses, is subject to federal tax (and possibly state tax). The 990-T and related tax payments are due by the 15th day of the fifth month after year end.

Your nonprofit is required to maintain a copy of your Form 990 tax return on file and available for public inspection.

You may want to ask your auditors to complete the annual tax return and extension request if necessary. They can also advise you with regard to unrelated business income tax and local tax filing requirements.

## POLICIES AND PROCEDURES

To ensure that the accounting cycle is completed as directed by management, your organization should develop and maintain a fiscal policies and procedures manual. Such a manual does not have to be lengthy, but it does have to be formalized and the staff should be instructed to follow it at all times. The manual should include the following topics:

- Financial statement presentation
- Distribution and timing of the financial statements
- Chart of accounts
- Bank account reconciliation procedures
- Investment policies
- Check-signing procedures
- Travel expense policy
- Revenue collection and recording
- Payroll policies

- Insurance
- Controls over fixed assets
- Controls over inventory, if applicable
- Budgeting
- Corporate tax filings
- Conflicts of interest

Not all of these topics are relevant to the day-to-day operations of small organizations. The fiscal policies and procedures manual can be an evolutionary document that expands as your group's operations become more complex. If followed and maintained, such a manual can help to mitigate some of the inherent internal control issues prevalent in many small nonprofit organizations. It should help to define the responsibilities of those involved in the financial affairs of your nonprofit organization. It should also promote operational efficiency, which will, in turn, permit you to concentrate on providing services and carrying out your organization's mission.

# CHAPTER THIRTEEN

# Your People and Their Environment

**Your organization will thrive with proper management of its most important resource: its people. This chapter provides a summary of human resources principles and practices that can improve your organization's working environment.**

Most nonprofit organizations start out small and are preoccupied with identifying their mission and establishing programs and plans to carry it out. The founding member of a children's health clinic situated in a church basement, for example, will probably be more concerned with fund-raising and public relations than with managing staff and office resources. This young nonprofit will most likely have a small staff and scant office needs. This situation, however, can change quickly.

For example, what happens when the willing lender of a computer needs the equipment back? Or if the neighbors who graciously let the group use their copying machine move away? Or when a professional, full-time staff member is needed to do a job that volunteers have so far handled? Soon that church basement doesn't have sufficient space for the organization's staff and office equipment or for meetings that inevitably conflict with church activities. The organization is growing and its needs changing. It is time to adopt a more professional position.

It is in making this jump that promising nonprofit organizations may falter. The stumbling block for many is generating sufficient funds to grow, through either program revenues or community support. However, the basic activities of managing the office and directing the staff often place unnecessary stress on a growing nonprofit.

If managed properly, both the staff and the environment can reinforce the nonprofit's goals. Given an awareness of the principles of human resources and office management, management tasks can evolve along with the organization. Who ultimately supervises these activities is dependent on the size of the office. These duties will likely be spread among a small staff; a large office will have individuals specifically responsible for human resources and office management—and there is a wide range between these two situations.

The important thing is to proceed methodically, maintaining the spirit of the organization without letting the administrative tasks overwhelm you. Managing human resources and overseeing the office environment are, of course, means to achieve the organization's goals; they should not become goals in themselves. The measure of a successful organization is not the size of the staff it supports or how well decorated the offices are, but whether the people, equipment, and surroundings are the right ones to help move the organization forward to achieve its strategic objectives and fulfill its mission.

Certain principles of personnel management (now generally called *human resources*) and office management apply to all organizations regardless of their size. Each is addressed, in a separate section of this chapter, from the perspective of a growing nonprofit organization.

## HUMAN RESOURCES

A nonprofit organization succeeds because of its people—because of their commitment, enthusiasm, intelligence, and drive. Therefore, it is crucial to find and choose the best employees possible. To act otherwise is to invite failure. Human resources is concerned not only with finding good leaders but also with forming a group of people with different skills who work congenially together for a common good.

Once the staff is hired, trust must be built between employer and employee, manager and worker, to heighten chances for success. If such trust is elusive, the nonprofit's goals are impossible to meet. Managing your human resources will also involve promoting creative responses to challenging work, as well as guarding against unethical or unlawful practices.

Human resources activities can be grouped in five broad categories:

1. Hiring and placement
2. Fair and equitable compensation
3. Communication between staff, management, and volunteers
4. Compliance with local, state, and federal employment laws
5. Maintaining and enhancing an organization's image

## START-UP AND GROWTH

As mentioned earlier, the start-up of a nonprofit may be more reflex than planning. But as your organization grows, it will be necessary to identify the tasks and staff needed to reach its goals. This is true even if your organization cannot yet afford the entire projected staff. Begin to construct an organizational chart that can be your guide to growth. How large is the staff now? How large will it be five years into the future? Who is responsible for which tasks? What is expected from each individual? How will the team interact? How might growth affect the organizational chart? Will some work be outsourced to consultants or performed by volunteers?

At the same time, realistically assess how far the funds budgeted for staff will stretch. Some members of the staff initially may have to take on duties that ultimately may be given over to new employees as the organization grows. Sometimes it may be impossible to predict growth patterns, but it is useful to document the realistic and the ideal. Ultimately, as your organization grows, it will be more important to establish clear and precise descriptions of what is expected from each individual in order to avoid confusion. For smaller groups, however, tasks may shift among the work force, depending on the issue. Assume that in the beginning you realize that with your limited resources you can't hire all the full-time staff you need. There are other ways to perform services. Part-time employees may be appropriate for specific tasks, but because benefits are not always part of their compensation, part-time employees may be hard to attract and keep. Volunteers can be an extremely important pool of labor. Nonprofits, such as museums, homeless shelters, soup kitchens, advocacy groups, and others, would not be able to function without their volunteer armies. Maintaining a good volunteer troop, however, takes attentive management, positive interaction, and strong leadership. The larger the number of volunteers, the greater the need for a volunteer coordinator as a full-time, paid staff member.

To find loyal volunteers, an organization needs to effectively promote the altruistic or educational endeavors of its mission. A small museum, for example, can offer volunteers in-depth training and easy access to knowledgeable staff members. A soup kitchen offers a unique opportunity for volunteers to get involved with the community. Once involved, volunteers need recognition and thanks for the contribution they make to your organization. They won't be receiving paychecks, so their worth should be acknowledged in other ways: special awards, certificates of merit, mention to the local press, an annual luncheon. Volunteers should be encouraged to contribute to the larger whole; that is, their suggestions and observations should be solicited and taken seriously by the staff.

Another source of labor and expertise is independent consultants, who can be called on to accomplish tasks that the staff cannot perform because of a lack of expertise or time. For instance, if you decide to mail a bimonthly newsletter to your supporters, a consultant may be called in to design the newsletter and produce it too. Tasks for consultants can range from the production of newsletters and brochures to public relations projects to fund-raising (see Chapter 15 on using consultants). Some consultants, particularly those seeking to make a name in your community or who are committed to a cause, may be willing to volunteer their services. The qualifications of consultants should be carefully checked, and most jobs (if not volunteered) should be bid out to three contractors before a contract is signed. If projects are continuous, it is sometimes less expensive to enter into a long-term contract with a particular consultant. Such an arrangement can also provide continuity for the special projects. For some tasks, especially those such as data processing, equipment maintenance, cleaning, and food service, look to larger service providers.

## FINDING AND HIRING STAFF

### Job Descriptions

Finding and hiring staff starts with a clear, concise job description. If there is no written job description, the hiring process is handicapped from the beginning.

At a minimum, a job description should include the following:

- Basic skills required, both technical and educational
- Duties and responsibilities
- Any other information that defines the scope of the job, particularly any indication of multiple duties

Job descriptions later become a barometer, for both employees and the employer, for performance appraisals, promotions, salary raises, and the like. Job descriptions should be reviewed once a year, as well as in the event of a significant shift in responsibilities.

Cause-related nonprofits may theoretically find two very different kinds of candidates: those with an empathic feeling for the cause but, perhaps, without the managerial or technical skills needed to fill the position; and candidates with the desired skills and experience but less personal commitment. (Actually, there is a third kind of candi-

**Exhibit 13–1**  Job Description Format

JOB TITLE

JOB SUMMARY
The job's responsibilities and duties—its supervisory, technical, or administrative scope.

SKILL AND EDUCATIONAL REQUIREMENTS
Experience, educational background, and training desired.

ACCOUNTABILITY
Title of person to whom this employee reports. Relationships within and outside of the organization.

SPECIAL ATTRIBUTES
Any specific talents that apply to this job.

date, who combines the best of the two preceding types, but skilled *and* committed candidates can be hard to find.)

Each organization establishes its own style in regard to official documents. For job descriptions, Exhibit 13–1 can be used as a guide.

## Getting the Word Out

Ads placed in a local newspaper's classified section may bring a slew of responses. Professional journals are useful for highly specialized positions, although the typical monthly format may not offer timely announcements and responses. For certain positions, posting ads at community centers can be effective. Postings on your organization's Web site can often attract applications from excellent candidates. The least structured, but sometimes useful, method is word of mouth, such as from an employee to a friend; sometimes a job seems crafted for a specific person known to the organization. A professional network can also provide likely candidates. Like the job description itself, any advertisement or announcement of an open position should be accurate and concise.

## Reviewing Resumes

As resumes arrive, develop a fair and systematic process to review them, always keeping in mind the skills that are required to fill the position. With experience, each reviewer will develop his or her own rating system. Obviously, the basics of the resume are all-important—education, experience, skill levels, and any demonstrable communication and interpersonal abilities. The applicant's interest and commitment to an organization's mission should be noted.

Start judging a candidate as soon as you open the envelope. Does the resume look as though it was written with care? Is it free of typographical or spelling errors? Is it orderly and easy to read? Is the cover letter direct and cogent, or rambling and ineffective?

To uncover more intangible qualities in a candidate, look for evidence of:

- Sustained interest in a job or cause
- Loyalty to an organization
- Ability to be a team player
- Ability to communicate
- Ambition
- Detail-oriented skills
- Knowledge about the job being pursued

## Interviews

Conducting a good interview is a learned skill and requires careful preparation, execution, and follow-up. It is perhaps hardest to master the techniques of putting applicants at ease. Proceed with the general understanding that applicants will be nervous. Try to remain objective rather than subjective in reaction to the applicant's appearance, personality, or background. A person who does not fit your image of the ideal candidate may turn out to be an excellent employee. During the interview, address administrative issues, such as compensation and benefits, travel requirements, starting date, and special job requirements.

To make objective and fair comparisons, ask interviewees a common set of questions that can help determine each candidate's job-related skills and experience, general intelligence and aptitude, attitudes and personality. An expert interviewer, Robert Half, suggests the following questions in his book *Finding, Hiring, and Keeping the Best Employees:*[1]

*"What was your single most noteworthy achievement or contribution in your current job?"*
*"What specific strengths do you bring to this job and this organization?"*
*"How do you make important decisions?"*
*"Why have you decided to leave your present position?"*

---

[1]Robert Half, *Finding, Hiring, and Keeping the Best Employees* (New York: John Wiley & Sons, 1993).

*"What risks did you take in your last few jobs, and what was the result of having taken those risks?"*

Obviously, the overall goal is to learn as much about each candidate as possible, as well as to determine whether that candidate's resume is accurate. Generally, an interviewer should try to determine the candidate's ability to do the following:

- Plan tasks
- Prioritize
- Delegate
- Work on a team
- Solve problems
- Apply knowledge
- Know limitations
- Take initiative
- Learn on the job
- Communicate with associates

Versatility is an attribute sought by most nonprofit organizations.

Your interviewing technique is significant. Candidates should not be rushed into answering questions and should not feel threatened when asked to explain some point further. Pay attention to the individual applicant by soliciting small talk and tailoring questions to previous answers. Remember, you are trying to sell yourself as well as hire an employee. Don't lead the candidate to a short "yes" or "no" answer without an explanation, if an explanation is what you are seeking. Be cautious with a candidate who appears overqualified. It is possible that soon after employment, that person may become disenchanted or bored.

Secure a candidate's approval for your soliciting references. The candidate may wish that his or her present boss not be called, but rather someone on the staff of his or her current organization or a former employer. Realize, too, that references often can be subjective.

## Choosing the Candidate and Making the Offer

A particular candidate may stand out as the final choice for a position. It is likely, though, that no one person is the perfect candidate and that some compromises may have to be made. If the hiring process has been carefully considered and executed, however, the odds of making a mistake are minimized.

Once a candidate has accepted a job offer, it should be confirmed by a letter accurately restating the job offer, as the letter can be used in a court of law as an official document.

A personnel checklist should be filed for each new employee and should include the following:

- Employment application
- Formal job offer letter and employee acknowledgment
- Social security number
- Completed I-9 Form (for all employees)
- Federal, state, and local tax withholding forms as applicable
- Insurance forms—health, group life, disability, other
- Record of the job description and performance evaluations
- Retirement plan application
- Receipt for benefit plan options, where applicable
- Compensation—salary and benefits

Setting salary levels is a difficult task for any organization. You must research comparable salaries elsewhere. One avenue of inquiry is to look to salary surveys of nonprofit industries. You can also contact other organizations like your own and inquire about their salary structures. Traditionally, nonprofits have had a reputation of offering low salaries. That, however, may be misleading in the twenty-first century, as many of your best employees now expect salaries that are competitive with the for-profit sector.

The type of benefits offered may provide an extra incentive for a candidate to join the organization, such as medical and dental health care insurance, disability, life insurance, and tax-deferred retirement plans. Where full-time employment is concerned, it is unusual to find an organization that does not offer what are called "absorbed benefits," such as vacation leave, sick leave, and bereavement time off, as well as holidays. Sometimes a lower salary can be offset by an attractive benefits package or a shorter work week.

For budgeting and planning purposes, it is helpful to list the salary range of each position, even though you cannot afford the top ranges. When salary and benefits are set, you can then document the true cost of keeping a staff member by combining salary with health insurance costs, unemployment insurance costs (in some jurisdictions), worker's compensation, and pension plan contributions—any cost that the employer pays for the employee. On the other hand, staff members should be aware that their pay will reflect federal and state tax withholding and Federal Insurance Contributions Act

(FICA) contributions. Every position must be classified as exempt or nonexempt to comply with the Fair Labor Standards of 1934. (Exempt employees are exempt from overtime payment. Nonexempt employees must be paid time and a half for time worked over 40 hours in a calendar week.)

## ON THE JOB

### Manager/Employee Relationship

An organization's executives set the tone for the office environment. Human resources, however, has a role in promoting practices that respect, motivate, and reward employees and retain their interest in the organization. If the revolving door turns too fast, the staff loses a sense of continuity, especially a small staff.

Employees should be respected for their dedication, creativity, innovation, ideas, and individuality, even if it is often easier for managers to negatively critique performance than to acknowledge gains. If harsh criticism is necessary, try it first in private rather than as a public rebuke. Encourage enhanced performance whenever possible and reward an employee who is responsible.

Challenge is an important part of a person's job. Employees increasingly seek opportunities to advance ideas, to be part of the greater good, to contribute to important decisions and projects. This is called "risk-taking" or, more recently, "empowerment," which, if handled correctly, can ultimately be of great value to an organization.

### Performance Appraisal

The performance evaluation is a tool to review past performances, as well as to discuss future activities. Performance appraisals, which vary from the informal to the highly structured, are usually held once or twice a year. As a nonprofit grows, such reviews will be more formal. Regardless of style, an evaluation should be objective and fair.

Basically, the appraisal starts when an employee is hired. The job description becomes the basis on which an employee's performance is evaluated. How well has the employee reached the specified goals? Each time an employee is evaluated, new performance goals are set, in agreement between employee and employer. In six months to a year, these goals are checked, with the process continuing onward. If an employee has performed badly or has not lived up to your expectations, you can emphasize the need to correct this performance in the future. Performance appraisals are most valuable, both for the organization and the employee, when open lines of communication already exist between the executive and the employee.

There will be instances when management finds an employee's inadequacies to be too great. A negative review should be forthright and clear. A dismissal will call for documentation.

Performance appraisals are often used to justify salary increases. However, discussions of salary can dilute the appraisal objectives and should be handled separately.

## Promotions, Raises, and Rewards

A reassignment can be beneficial if an employee grows complacent and needs a new challenge. Promotions can also be used to reward a good employee, overcome salary caps, and honor seniority. Generally, organizations set a salary range for a particular position, but allow some growth within and above that range. Raises are definitely awards, but mean less when a raise simply meets a cost-of-living allowance. Budget realities, however, may temper your desire to monetarily reward even your best employees. In lean years, those committed to your organization's mission may agree to delay personal salary expectations.

Recognition, rather than financial rewards, will have to satisfy your cadre of volunteers. Such recognition can take the form of special awards, certificates of merit, mention in the local press, or an annual luncheon.

## DOWN . . . AND EVENTUALLY OUT

### Stress and Burnout

Unrealistic expectations—and the work that can come with them—may place undue stress on your employees. Sometimes, stress levels rise and fall with a particular project. If problems remain after completion of that project, if there is a loss of caring, lack of interest, and negative attitude on the part an employee, you may need to reshuffle responsibilities or further investigate the nature of the stress. Burnout will turn the revolving door.

### I Quit/You're Fired

The reasons for an employee's resignation can include limited opportunities for advancement, lack of recognition, unhappiness with management, inadequate salary or benefits, boredom with the job, or a need to try something different. Resignations can be countered with new job responsibilities, but may eventually have to be gracefully accepted.

Firing an employee is unquestionably a difficult task and needs substantial backup. Employees can be fired for failure to perform, insubordination, or embezzlement and other crimes.

Budgetary or programmatic changes may result in a need to reduce the work force, even in the most successful organizations. Sometimes, as a consequence of success, for example, advocacy organizations attract less funding and fewer contributions if the government is perceived as more sympathetic to their goals. Laid-off workers may receive some kind of compensation or outplacement services (such as employment counseling) and may be eligible for unemployment benefits. Firings and layoffs should be done in private, supervisor to employee.

## PERSONNEL POLICIES AND PROCEDURES

An organization must have official documents on hand. Personnel policies and procedures should be documented in a manual that is available to current and prospective employees. Small nonprofits may not have a formal presentation of these policies and procedures but must somewhere have policies and procedures written down. The information should be as up-to-date as possible. Exhibit 13–2 is a sample table of contents of a personnel policies and procedures manual.

**Exhibit 13–2**   Sample Table of Contents

Table of Contents
Personnel Policies and Procedures

THE ORGANIZATION
  Introduction
  History
  Mission
WORK SCHEDULE
  Workday
  Workweek
  Lunch Period
  Holidays
  Personal Days
  Vacation
  Sick Leave
  Family and Medical Leave
  Leave of Absence
  Bereavement Leave
  Severe Weather Conditions
  Jury Duty
  Time Off Without Pay

**Exhibit 13–2**    (*Continued*)

COMPENSATION
  Paydays
  Overtime and Compensatory Time
  Change of Employee Status
  Salary and Performance Reviews
EMPLOYEE BENEFITS
  Social Security
  Workers' Compensation Insurance
  Unemployment Insurance
  Retirement Plan
  Benefits for Part-Time Employees
CODE OF CONDUCT
  Bulletin Boards
  Business Attire
  Emergency Procedures
  Harassment
  Housekeeping
  Personal Conduct
  Security
  Smoking Policy
  Visitors, Vendors, Suppliers
RECRUITMENT
  Equal Employment Opportunity
  Employment of Relatives

## Compliance with Local, State, and Federal Employment Laws

In our litigious society, the legal ramifications of personnel policies and practices are significant. Although lawsuits have been thought to be a problem of the for-profit world, nonprofits are covered by the same laws; even a small or mid-sized nonprofit organization can be severely affected by legal action of a present or former employee. Therefore, it is important that an attorney knowledgeable in employment law review the organization's personnel policies and procedures, hiring practices, firing practices, rules of employee conduct, workplace safety and security, performance reviews, salary increases and promotions, and other actions or documents with legal implications.

At the least, the implications of the following should be well known:

- **Federal minimum wage.** The Fair Labor Standards Act sets the minimum wage, pay for interns, and the status of exempt and nonexempt employees.

- Equal employment opportunity. Title VII of the Civil Rights Act of 1964 outlaws discrimination in employment practices toward individuals based on age, race, religion, sex, color, or national origin.

- Job safety and health. The Occupational Safety and Health Act requires each employer to comply with safety and health standards in the workplace by maintaining the workplace free from recognized hazards.

- Accessibility. The Americans with Disabilities Act forbids discrimination against disabled workers in hiring, compensation, and advancement and mandates accessible office space for handicapped persons in offices with more than 15 employees.

## THE OFFICE ENVIRONMENT

Do not be intimidated by the sound of the term "office management." The most important requirements are that the office environment be pleasant and functional, that equipment and supplies meet the employee's needs, that the communication system is reliable, and that the mail is properly handled. Efficiency and cost-effectiveness are the goals of a well-organized office system and can translate into significant savings for nonprofits.

Nonprofit organizations can benefit significantly from two practices: receipt of in-kind services and competitive bidding. "In-kind" refers to any supply, equipment, or professional aid that is donated or offered at a very low cost by for-profit organizations. The donor gets the benefit of a tax deduction and can save the cost of disposal of old furniture or equipment.

Purchases, especially of equipment and furniture, should be considered in terms of the entire office needs. A good rule of thumb in purchasing is to use a bidding system, in which the purchaser, if possible, bases the decision on the bids of three vendors. The vendors should be aware of the bidding process.

Equipment acquisition should be reviewed in terms of buying or leasing. For some products, such as copiers and computer equipment, leasing agreements offer options to update the equipment periodically. Leasing should also involve the bidding process mentioned earlier.

## Office Space

Office rental can be a big part of the monthly bills. Therefore, before signing a lease, it is worthwhile to see whether any free or especially inexpensive space is available. Be creative in considering office space—a room in a local church, school, or community center, for example. Or look for space that can be shared with an affiliated or nonaffiliated organization. This arrangement can be advantageous to both parties and can include the sharing of such features as meeting rooms, rest rooms, receptionist services, copiers, other equipment, and security systems. Or office space can be tucked into a corner of a nonprofit's operational headquarters—for example, at a soup kitchen, shelter for abused women, or educationally oriented program.

Other factors to consider as you look for office space include the following:

*Terms of contract.* Will you lease or purchase space? This factor is dictated by the size and financial status of the organization as well as the office space market in the city in which it is located.

*Location.* A determining factor if the nonprofit has close ties to a specific neighborhood. If a particular location is not necessary, modest rates may dictate your choice.

*Size.* Ideally, an office should provide approximately 200 sq ft of space per person, including common space. At the start, the office space may be tight, so try to anticipate growth. Also take into consideration needed space for volunteers or board members.

*Anticipated growth.* The potential growth of the organization must be anticipated to the extent possible, inasmuch as leases are usually offered on a multiple-year basis. It is often difficult and expensive to break a lease and move to a new location.

*Utilities in lease.* If the cost of utilities—heat, air-conditioning, and electricity—is included in your lease payment, the building owner will handle monthly payments, but be aware that those rates may automatically increase each year. Utility rates are based on the consumer price index. If your hours are irregular, check to make sure that the building will be heated, cooled, and lit when you have to be there.

*Utilities separate from lease.* If you are in a nontraditional building, control of utilities—and the bills—is separate from the lease agreement. Landlords should be able to give estimates of monthly utility payments.

*Cleaning service.* How the office is cleaned can also be tied to the lease. In some larger office buildings, the landlord often adds janitorial services to all leasees. In other instances, the office manager may have to hire a janitorial service in a separate contract.

*Security and life safety.* Some security and life safety measures are the responsibility of the lessee, regardless of the type of office building. If a security system is required, it must be installed by the lessee; in some locations some security may be offered, but only at the main entrance—such as in the form of a key pass or a security guard.

*Space configuration.* It is essential to meet local codes, such as by providing accessible fire extinguishers and fire exits. Offices with more than 15 employees must adhere to the Americans with Disabilities Act, which sets strict rules concerning accessibility in offices for disabled persons.

*Furniture and equipment.* The most obvious way to furnish an office is to buy, lease, or rent new furniture. Look into buying used furniture. Clearinghouses link donators of used furniture with nonprofits looking for used, but decent, office furniture. Buying used equipment is tricky. For example, to update an older computer system may cost more than the purchase of a new one. When purchasing more sophisticated used equipment, it is advisable to get an expert opinion.

Before signing an office lease, consult your lawyer.

## Communications

The phone system is one of the more expensive items acquired and is usually leased. The system selected should be based on the number of staff and lines required. Single-line phones can easily service a start-up organization with one to two people. The next step is a multiple-line "key" system that can support 20 to 30 people. When the staff reaches 100 persons or more, a PBX (private branch exchange) system becomes a requirement.

A basic backup system for your telephones, either with a basic answering machine or answering service, is essential for member relations and efficiency. Better yet is "voice mail," which is now readily accepted as an alternative to a switchboard operator who answers every call personally. Just be sure that all calls are answered quickly, usually the same day, or that the voice mail message clearly tells callers that the person is out of town or will not be able to answer his or her calls that day, if that is the case.

Fax machines and e-mail have become basic to offices large and small. As costs have dropped, these systems are within the resources of even small nonprofits and add greatly to efficiency and the speed of communications. (See additional information on e-mail in Chapter 11.)

## Copying

It is unrealistic to think that even the smallest office can do without a copier for its routine needs. Access to copying equipment is a modern day must. For start-up, estimate daily copying needs for a month-long period. Then actually track a few months' volume. A leasing agreement can provide periodic trade-ins for new equipment and for equipment of different sizes and features.

It may be more economical to send out large projects such as form letters, annual reports, and newsletters to a copy/printing company. Printers most often provide mail service.

## Mail and Delivery Service

An organization's daily postage flow should determine the necessary postage equipment. The most basic mailing system consists of stamps and a scale. When volume increases, special metering equipment will be more cost-effective and can be leased from a mail equipment vendor. Sophisticated, computer-driven equipment is generally not cost-effective until the average number of daily pieces reaches 2,000.

To reduce mailing costs, nonprofits use reduced bulk third-class postage for mail that is not time-sensitive, such as membership solicitations. Contact your local post office for Form 3624, Application to Mail at Special Bulk Third-Class Rates.

Mail houses provide stuffing, labeling, and mailing and are up-to-date on technical specifications pertaining to factors that can affect postage charges, such as weight, size, folding, and placement of labeling. Mail houses are also more capable of using ZIP+4 and pre-sorting mail. Remember, however, that as a nonprofit organization with third-class bulk mail privileges, you must register independently with the appropriate post office.

## Office Supplies

Buying supplies in bulk saves money. How do you determine your needs when you first start up? The answer: Keep track of your needs for six months to a year. Those records can be a guide to the future purchase of supplies, including stationery. When buying in bulk, negotiation is the key; seek out three vendors and inform them that you are seeking competitive bids. Be careful not to overstock supplies that may not be in demand at a later time.

## Insurance

Three types of insurance are needed for an office environment: liability, theft and fire, and vehicle (if vehicles are used by the organization). Insurance companies' provisions will vary widely, and it is wisest to consult an insurance agent. Recommendations on the selection of an agent in a particular area can be obtained from other nonprofit organizations, lawyers, or accountants.

## SUMMARY

In a broad sense, the people and the place make an organization. An organization that hires and employs wisely and equips well enhances its own image in the world at large. That doesn't necessarily mean that money equals image equals success. The most successful nonprofits, even those that are well-funded, run lean organizations and cannot offer the stock options or other enticements of for-profit organizations, but they also can offer more fulfilling work. For nonprofits, great things will come through choosing the best and the brightest, allowing them to grow in their jobs, and rewarding them for their efforts.

# CHAPTER FOURTEEN

# Knowing Important Legal Requirements

**Like the foundations of a building, legal underpinnings are an essential part of your nonprofit's structure. As a manager, it is your duty to ensure that the essential legal documents—such as tax-exempt forms, bylaws, and articles of incorporation—are handled properly. This chapter outlines the rights, privileges, and obligations that your nonprofit has under the law.**

Managing the affairs of a nonprofit organization within the laws of the United States and the various state and local jurisdictions is not tricky or difficult. The law actually provides some help to the executive in the everyday conduct of the organization's activities. A competent executive should, however, make him- or herself familiar with a few basic principles and provisions of the law to take advantage of the help they can provide and to avoid making any missteps that may result in trouble.

## FORMING A NONPROFIT ORGANIZATION

"In the beginning was the Word," and in the beginning of any nonprofit organization there should also be *the words*. There are three fundamental or "organic" documents that serve as the basis for establishing and operating a nonprofit organization:

- Articles of incorporation
- Bylaws
- IRS tax exemption letter

These documents should be kept securely on file at the headquarters of the organization. They prescribe the scope and limits within which the organization operates, and they can also be the instruments that keep a nonprofit executive out of trouble.

## Articles of Incorporation*

Strictly speaking, a nonprofit organization does not *have* to be incorporated. But failure to incorporate exposes the organization and the individuals involved to a variety of unhappy consequences, not the least of which can be personal liability for the organization's debts.

Corporations are created under the statutory authority of a state, and all states have specific statutory provisions relating to the formation of nonprofit corporations. Typical of the items required to be included in articles of incorporation for a nonprofit organization are the following:

- Name of the corporation
- Duration of the corporation (usually perpetual)
- Purposes for which the corporation is formed
- Provisions for conducting the internal affairs of the organization
- Names and addresses of the incorporators
- Names and addresses of the initial board of directors
- Address of the initial registered office and name of the initial registered agent of the corporation
- Provisions for distribution of the assets of the corporation on dissolution

The statutes of each state are different, however, and legal counsel familiar with the requirements of the state chosen as the state of incorporation should be consulted to ensure conformance with the particular requirements of that jurisdiction.

It is important that the articles qualify the organization as a nonprofit corporation by stating the nonprofit purpose of the organization. The stated purposes in the incorporating document should be broad enough to enable the organization to evolve as necessary to serve its constituency. Satisfying state law requirements for amending the articles of incorporation of the organization can be a nuisance

---

*"Certificate of incorporation" and "charter" are alternative terms used in some jurisdictions.

if later circumstances warrant a significant departure from purposes that were too narrowly drawn originally.

## Bylaws

"Constitution" is a term sometimes used in place of "bylaws" or "articles of incorporation." However, because of the potential for confusion between the terms "constitution" and "charter," which sometimes refers to the incorporating document, use of the term "constitution" is not recommended.

Articles of incorporation provide only a broad outline of the organization's form, and the initial board of directors should quickly approve a set of bylaws that supplement the articles by prescribing more detailed rules for governing the organization. Bylaws provide the discipline required for orderly operation of the organization, and they should be written with an emphasis on fair treatment.

Bylaws often begin with a restatement of the name and purposes of the organization consistent with the articles of incorporation, but they add basic rules for operating the organization:

- The frequency, notice, and quorum requirements for organizational meetings
- Voting qualifications, proxies, and procedures
- The number and term of the board of directors, scope of authority, method of nomination and election to the board, and provisions for filling vacancies
- List of officers, method of nomination and election, terms of office, powers, duties, and succession
- Title and scope of authority of the chief staff executive
- Record keeping and financial reporting responsibilities
- Bylaw amendment procedures and provisions for dissolution of the organization

Other provisions may also be included. For example, membership organizations may include a dues or participation fee structure (but never the rate), a definition of categories of membership, and qualifications for membership.

It is wise, however, to stop short of having too much detail contained in the bylaws so that the organization can retain some flexibility to change its operations without bylaw amendments. Bylaw amendments, although simpler than amendments to the articles of incorporation inasmuch as the laws of the state are not involved, nevertheless often require a vote of the full membership of the organization, which can hamstring an executive and the officers and board in creating new operating structures to meet changing needs.

An illustration of the type of operating flexibility that should be preserved for board action is committee structure. In most instances, the bylaws should prescribe the membership and authority of only two standing committees: an executive committee, which is made up of officers who must make policy decisions between board meetings, and the nominating committee (unless nominations for officers come directly from the membership at large). Beyond that, the bylaws should provide only that the board has authority to establish any other committees with whatever jurisdiction it prescribes. By preserving such organizational flexibility, the board is able to form new committees or, perhaps more important, eliminate obsolete committees without amending the bylaws.

Healthy organizations change over time. Suppose, for example, that a nonprofit organization is formed for the protection of local wildlife. The organizers decide that a banquet to raise funds for wildlife food would be a good activity, and they establish a committee responsible for the event. Initially, the event is successful, but after a few years attendance at the dinner declines, and the organizers decide to abandon the banquet and raise funds by commissioning and selling wildlife replicas. If the bylaws specifically mandate the existence of the banquet committee, the organization will have to labor through an amendment to make the operational change needed for the evolution to the new activity. It is better for the board to have authority to abolish the old committee and establish a new one so that it may proceed with the new project.

With the articles and bylaws in place, most for-profit organizations have what they need for their basic organizational documents. Not so with a nonprofit organization. By their very nature, nonprofit organizations must take one more step in establishing their operations.

## IRS Tax Exemption Letter

Nonprofit organizations must establish their tax-exempt status with the Internal Revenue Service (IRS). Section 1.501(a) of the Internal Revenue Regulations provides that there shall be an exemption from income taxation for qualified organizations. Section 1.501(c) of the regulations defines the organizations that qualify for the exemption and classifies them according to type. The 25 categories listed in section 1.501(c) include religious, charitable, scientific or educational organizations, (c)(3); social welfare organizations, (c)(4); labor organizations, (c)(5); business leagues, (c)(6); fraternal societies, (c)(8); and credit unions, (c)(14).

Application for exempt status should be filed with the IRS using either Form 1023 (for 501(c)(3) organizations) or Form 1024 (for most other section 501(c) category organizations). Copies of the organization's articles of incorporation and bylaws must be included with the application, and a full description of the purposes and activities of the organization must be provided. IRS Publication 557 provides detailed information on the filing of applications for exempt status.

Nonprofit organizations formed for purely charitable or public interest purposes qualify for tax exemption under the provisions of 501(c)(3) of the IRS code. Contributions to 501 (c)(3) organizations are deductible on personal and business tax returns as charitable contributions, to the extent otherwise provided by law. Such organizations must meet particular organizational and operational tests to be eligible for that designation. In general, an organization will qualify for status as a 501(c)(3) organization if it is organized and operated for one or more of the following purposes:

- Religious
- Charitable
- Scientific
- Testing for public safety
- Literary
- Educational
- Prevention of cruelty to children or animals

These general purposes have been defined in much greater detail through IRS rulings and regulations. For example, "educational" purposes may be evidenced by the granting of scholarships, the offering of lectures, or other typical educational activities. "Charitable" organizations must provide that upon dissolution, all of the donated funds will be used for charitable purposes and will not revert to the founding organization. "Scientific" organizations qualify only if the results of their activities are available to the public.

The business league category of tax-exempt organization, 501(c) (6), includes trade organizations, chambers of commerce, and boards of trade. The purpose of such an organization is to promote the common business interests of its members, and not to engage in a regular business of a kind that is ordinarily carried on for profit. Its activities are typically directed to the improvement of business conditions in one or more lines of businesses, and not the performance of services for individuals. Dues or other payments are ordinarily deductible as business expenses, but not as charitable contributions.

In some cases, a nonprofit organization that is qualified as tax-exempt under section 501(c)(6) of the tax code may decide to form a second nonprofit organization under the 501(c)(3) provisions of the code. There are many reasons for deciding to undertake such action, including eligibility for receiving tax-deductible gifts, objectivity and independence from the sponsoring organization's interests, and availability of favorable postal rates.

A sponsored foundation is formed in the same manner in which the sponsoring group was formed: through the creation and filing of articles of incorporation and bylaws. A separate application for tax-exempt status must be filed with the IRS for the sponsored organization. Because of these details, nonprofit executives would be wise to contact competent counsel to assist in the formation of any sponsored foundation.

If the IRS determines that an organization has met the test for exemption, it will issue a "determination letter," which should be kept safely on file with the other fundamental organizational documents. Issuance by the IRS of tax-exempt status does not eliminate the need for the organization to file annual information returns with the IRS. Tax-exempt organizations, other than private foundations, must file Form 990, or Form 990EZ, which is a shortened form designed for use by small organizations.

The nonprofit executive also should watch out for the potential need to obtain tax-exempt status from the state in which the organization is operating or is incorporated. Many states simply replicate the federal tax exemption regulations, whereby qualification under the federal regulations automatically qualifies the organization in the state. The District of Columbia is an example of a jurisdiction that requires an additional application for tax-exempt status and the filing of annual tax returns; the executive should determine the requirements for the particular state in which the organization is located.

## Membership Structure

As noted above, the bylaws should spell out qualifications for membership. If the organization is a *membership*-type organization, the basis for membership is usually a commonality of interest. Such organizations are often more concerned with persuading members to join than with keeping them out, but qualifications for membership must be sufficiently specific so that they include only those who are truly interested in the purposes of the organization. If membership qualifications are too broad in scope, the group may not be able to establish specific goals or interests. On the other hand, if the qualifications are too narrow, the group risks failure because of insufficient support for its programs and activities. An organization may, of course, have separate *classes* of membership with distinct qualifications and prescribed rights and privileges. The organization may, for example, establish a nonvoting "associate" class of membership consisting of individual or company members who have an interest in the overall purposes of the organization, but whose interest is somewhat different from that of the primary class of voting members. Suppliers of goods or services to the primary members for whom the organization was formed are an example of an associate class of membership.

Other common classes of membership in addition to "regular" or "active" members, include honorary, affiliate, inactive, or student members. It is also not uncommon for an organization to bestow "life" membership on individuals who have made a particular contribution to the organization. The life member designation does not mean that the organization cannot subsequently change the terms or conditions of such membership or even abolish the membership category in which the life member held membership.

A nonprofit organization also may define a specific geographic area that it serves and from which it will accept members. For example, a nonprofit organization may be formed to serve an international, national, state, or local constituency.

Any organization that wishes to limit membership must approach the issue of membership exclusivity carefully. Although membership in an association is not a right explicitly guaranteed by the Constitution, organizations may not violate the civil or property rights of potential members by arbitrarily excluding them from participation. The more important an association is to its potential members, the more careful it must be to ensure that membership is not denied to anyone except upon strictly objective criteria related specifically to the purposes and goals of the organization. If the organization serves business or professional members, the basic principle of membership eligibility is that the organization may not exclude potential members for the purpose of reducing competition.

## Electing Officers and Directors

The minimum number of directors required for the board of a nonprofit organization is commonly prescribed by the statutes of the jurisdiction under which the organization is formed. The Model Non-Profit Corporation Act specifies a minimum of three directors.

Beyond the statutory minimum, nonprofit organizations are at liberty to specify in their bylaws any number of directors, and the bylaws may be amended from time to time to increase or decrease that number.

Membership-type organizations usually provide for election of directors on a rotating basis, and in some cases directors elected to represent specific categories of members may be elected only by the members in that category. In other types of nonprofit organization the incumbent directors may appoint their successors. In such cases, if new directors are not appointed, the incumbent directors may continue to hold office indefinitely unless they are removed "for cause" pursuant to "due process" by a majority of the other members of the board. This method of choosing new directors can create problems if a group of incumbent directors uses it to perpetuate their authority or policies to the detriment of the organization. Consequently, a mechanism for selecting new directors with fresh outlooks and energy is desirable.

In addition to specifying the number of directors on the organization's board, the bylaws of the organization should provide for the mechanics of selection. Nomination of directors is often undertaken by a nominating committee appointed by the board chairman or president, with the approval of the other members of the board. Local law may specify the duration of the terms of office for board members, but the organization's bylaws must specify the terms of office and the terms should be staggered to provide for continuity. The bylaws also should provide a method for filling vacancies in any director position. It is common to provide that the chairman or president should appoint a new director to fill the unexpired term of office of the vacant seat, with the approval of the remaining directors.

Officers of the organization may be elected directly by the members in the case of a membership organization, or they may be elected or appointed by the board members. In either case, it is wise to provide for a nominating process to ensure the selection of qualified individuals who have adequate background and experience with the organization and its activities.

## MINUTES, RECORD KEEPING, AND REPORTING REQUIREMENTS

Proper operation of a nonprofit organization entails sound practices for keeping records of the organization's official acts and filing the required reports with the appropriate authorities.

## Minutes

Who should keep the formal minutes of an organization's meetings? Recording and issuing the minutes of meetings is a burdensome task, and it may be difficult to motivate an elected volunteer secretary to generate them on a timely basis. It is often wise for the nonprofit's executive director to undertake the burden or to see to it that the responsibility for producing the minutes lies within his or her domain. Although the minutes are subject to subsequent amendment and approval, the nonprofit executive will have significant influence over the outcome of the meetings if he or she is willing to accept the responsibility for producing the minutes. In this way, at least, the executive can be sure that the minutes will be kept.

By accepting the responsibility for the minutes, the executive can make certain that all of the relevant discussions and decisions are accurately reported, and that any off-hand, thoughtless, or potentially harmful comments are appropriately expunged. If a remark or observation at a meeting is worth preserving, it should be contained in the formal, typed minutes. A complete record of everything that everyone said at the meeting is burdensome and unnecessary. The minutes should accurately record the decisions made at the meeting, with only as much of the discussion as necessary to provide a record of the basis for the decisions. Handwritten notes from a meeting should be destroyed after the formal minutes of the meeting are typed and distributed. You should think of meeting minutes as a public document, because they can be obtained by the plaintiff in any lawsuit against the organization or its members, and you should have no reason to want to prevent them from being examined.

## Annual Reports

Finally, there is the matter of filing required reports with governmental authorities. The jurisdiction in which the organization is incorporated will typically require the filing of an annual report. Normally, such reports simply require information regarding the identities of the officers and board of directors and confirmation of the name and address of the resident agent who is available to receive any service of legal process. In addition, an organization doing a substantial amount of work in a state that is not the state of its incorporation may be required to "qualify" to do business in that state. Additional reporting requirements may be imposed upon the organization by any jurisdictions in which the organization is "qualified" to conduct business.

## Tax Returns

Any nonprofit organization with gross receipts in excess of $25,000 per year must file IRS Form 990, Return of Organization Exempt from Income Tax, by the 15th day of the fifth month after the close of its fiscal year. There is a penalty of $10 per day if the return is late or incomplete; however, exemptions can be obtained if there is cause for a delay (use IRS Form 2758). The return must, among other information, list officers, directors, and trustees, including compensation paid to them (see Chapter 12, "Financial Management," for further detail on information to be included).

## Public Disclosure

Under regulations that became final in June 1999, nonprofit organizations must make its annual tax return, including all attachments (except for the name and address of any contributor to the organization), its application for tax exemption, and any relevant documents issued by the IRS, available to the public on request. The organization must respond within 30 days to any request in writing, but may require payment in advance for minimal copying and postage costs. Any member of the public is also entitled to examine these documents at the organization's principal and regional (if any) offices. Summaries of tax returns are also now being posted on the Internet at *www.guidestar.org.*

These public disclosure requirements are intended to increase public scrutiny of tax-exempt organizations, thereby increasing their accountability to the public and their members. Organizations that are conducting their affairs responsibly should have nothing to be concerned about. The most important thing is to have procedures in place to make the documents readily available on request.

## SALES TAX EXEMPTION AND POSTAL RATES

Charitable organizations and some other nonprofits are entitled to some special benefits under state laws and the U.S. Postal Service. You will want to explore these possibilities.

## Sales Taxes

Certain nonprofit organizations may also enjoy special privileges with regard to local and state sales taxes. State laws often contain sales tax exemptions for charitable and educational organizations, and state laws typically follow the definitions contained in the federal statutes and regulations. Consult with the state and local tax authorities to determine whether your organization qualifies for the sales tax exemption, which can be a very substantial benefit.

## Postal Rates

Nonprofit organizations are often eligible for favorable postage rates that may not be available to for-profit organizations. And because many nonprofit organizations rely heavily on the distribution of publications, solicitations, and other forms of communication through the mail, special attention should be paid to the opportunities for favorable rates.

Postal service regulations provide that a nonprofit organization may qualify for subsidized postal rates if its purpose is religious, educational, scientific, philanthropic, or agricultural, or if the organization is a labor, fraternal, veterans, or political organization. To qualify for such subsidy, none of the net income of such an organization can benefit any private person. If an organization has received an IRS designation as tax-exempt under section 501(c)(3), 501(c)(5), 501(c)(8), or 501(c)(9) of the IRS code, it is presumed by the postal service to qualify for the subsidized rates. Trade organizations qualified as tax-exempt under section 501(c)(6) of the IRS Code do not qualify for the subsidized rates.

## AVOIDING POTENTIAL LEGAL PITFALLS

Executives in any organization must be careful to comply with local, state, and federal laws relating to the employment of workers and other aspects of conducting a business. These issues are discussed in Chapter 13. Nonprofit organizations, of course, must be watchful to avoid legal problems that relate to their particular status.

## Officer, Director, and Executive Liability

The officers and directors of a nonprofit organization have positions of trust vis-à-vis the organization. The fundamental power and authority of the organization reside in the organization itself and, in the case of a membership organization, in the collective members. The officers and directors are the custodians of that authority and have a responsibility to be faithful stewards of the organization's interests.

The nonprofit executive should be aware that the test of good faith can extend to any of the actions or decisions of the officers and directors. Conflicts of interest are a hazard, which may increase as the organization becomes more successful. The executive should be careful that decisions or actions are not made for the benefit of one or more of the officers or directors. Contracting for services with the firm of one of the officers at a higher price than may be obtained through a competitive bidding process is a good example of the type of activity that can fail the good faith test and render the decision makers liable for restitution to the organization. Excessive compensation to executives, or compensation disguised as benefits, is a trap into which some major nonprofit organizations have recently fallen.

## Sanctions for Self-Dealing or Excess Compensation

Until recently, the only recourse available to the IRS in cases of self-dealing or excessive compensation to executives or board members was to end the organization's tax exemption. That remedy is so extreme that it has rarely been used. In 1996, responding to a number of instances in which the executives of charitable organizations appeared to have abused their trust, Congress passed a law providing "intermediate sanctions"—penalties for abuse short of terminating the organization's tax-exempt status.

These penalties apply to public charities and tax-exempt social welfare organizations, including churches, hospitals, and universities as well as charitable or professional organizations exempt under provisions 501(c)(3) and 501(c)(4) of the tax code. Such organizations should be aware of these penalties, which are severe. Penalties include a 25 percent tax on any "excess benefit," to be paid by the person who received that benefit. Full "correction" of the excess benefit—repayment to the nonprofit institution—is also required within the tax period, and there is an additional penalty tax of 200 percent if this correction is not made within the required period.

What is "excess compensation" for purposes of this law? Unfortunately, the IRS has not yet provided any useful guidance and the law will probably evolve over the next several years in response to the first cases and subsequent legal decisions. Executive compensation that significantly exceeds that paid to executives of comparable tax-exempt organizations, including fringe benefits, tax-free loans, housing allowances, or the like, can be vulnerable. IRS agents are also likely to scrutinize payments to board members for services provided to a tax-exempt charitable organization to determine whether any such payments exceed fair market value for those services. Remember that compensation paid to executives or board members, as reported on the annual tax return, is now available for inspection not only by the IRS but also by any member of the public.

Only because of the lack of specific guidance from the IRS are these new intermediate sanctions potentially troubling. Will the IRS use this law only to correct true abuses, or will overzealous agents use it to attack executive compensation that might have seemed too high for a nonprofit organization in times past, but is fully justified by the executive's present responsibilities? For further discussion, see *Intermediate Sanctions: Curbing Nonprofit Abuse,* by Bruce R. Hopkins and D. Benson Tesdahl.[1]

## The Antitrust Laws

A major area of law that is of particular importance to nonprofit organizations of competitors within an industry or profession are the U.S. antitrust laws. The penalties for violation of these laws can be very severe, and nonprofit executives of business or professional organizations should be thoroughly familiar with the basic tenets of such laws to ensure compliance.

America's antitrust laws were established to preserve free economic competition in response to the development of industrial monopolies. The Sherman Act established that "combinations . . . in restraint of trade" are illegal. Because nonprofit organizations are frequently organized as "combinations" of competing members, the first criterion for establishing illegal activity under the Sherman Act is inherent in the nature of the organization. The Supreme Court has adopted a "rule of reason" to determine whether a combination or agreement violates the law.

Although the Supreme Court has determined that not *every* combination or agreement between competitors is a violation of the law, nevertheless it has held that there are some agreements between competitors that may be illegal regardless of their reasonableness. Such agreements, known as *per se* violations of the antitrust laws, include *price-fixing agreements, group boycotts, joint refusals to deal, market allocations,* and *tying arrangements* (the requirement by a seller who has dominant market power that a buyer must purchase a second distinct product as a condition for being allowed to purchase the first). Nonprofit executives should put an immediate stop to any conversations between competing members of the organization that

---

[1]Bruce R. Hopkins and D. Benson Tesdahl, *Intermediate Sanctions: Curbing Nonprofit Abuse* (New York: John Wiley & Sons, 1997).

relate, even if in jest, to matters that may constitute a *per se* violation of the antitrust laws.

The Clayton and Federal Trade Commission Acts added to the list of activities that may be deemed to be an illegal restraint of trade. The Clayton Act covers tying arrangements, exclusive dealing contracts, price discrimination, mergers and acquisitions, and joint ventures.

To protect themselves and their organizations from becoming entangled in an expensive and time-consuming antitrust litigation, executives of nonprofit organizations representing businesses or professionals should frequently remind their members about prohibited subjects and activities. Formal adoption of a set of "antitrust guidelines" for the organization is a worthwhile exercise, providing evidence of the organization's explicit intention to operate within the law. The minutes of meetings should reflect that members of the group were reminded of their responsibilities under the law, and a formal agenda for every meeting will help to establish that there were no prohibited subjects on the agenda for discussion at the meeting.

## Standards and Codes of Ethics

A common and useful area of activity for a nonprofit organization is the development and promulgation of standards or codes of ethics. Standards can take many forms, including product standards and standards of conduct. Nonprofit organizations are natural vehicles for the development of standards, because within them may reside the greatest concentrations of expertise in the subject areas involved.

Codes and standards can, however, be a source of substantial legal trouble for a nonprofit organization and its executive, and they must be carefully and thoughtfully prepared. The general public may place great reliance on such standards to protect their safety and well-being. The sponsor of a standard on which the public relies has a duty to be reasonably sure that the standard is thorough, appropriate, and trustworthy.

## Statistical Reporting

Another area of activity that is a natural for nonprofit organizations is the gathering and reporting of statistical data. Sound judgments can be made only on the basis of accurate facts, and nonprofit organizations involved in advocating public policies and providing social benefits must provide factual justification for their views and activities. Moreover, any business or profession must have accurate information about conditions in its field in order to compete effectively.

Nonprofit organizations often have access to the individuals or companies that possess needed data, and they are best able to collect and
aggregate the data to develop a basis for decisions.

If the data are gathered by a nonprofit organization representing
competing members or companies, legal difficulties can arise in connection with statistical reporting activities when they cross the line to
become an agreement between the participants regarding future
prices, production, or conditions of sale. The key to propriety in statistical programs is to restrict the data collection to *past* prices and
transactions and to stay strictly away from reporting future intentions. Even if there is no express agreement between competitors
regarding future prices, the mere reporting of future intentions provides the necessary basis for competitors to adjust their behavior in
a subtle and unspoken conspiracy.

These are just some of the areas in which a nonprofit executive
might find him- or herself on the wrong side of the law in connection
with management activities. Other areas that must be handled with
care include responsibility for the activities and liabilities of affiliate
groups, lobbying activities and the deductibility of membership dues
for lobbying expenses (see Chapter 9), and a host of other activities
such as buying organizational headquarters. As always, it is wise for
the nonprofit executive to find good legal counsel upon whom he or
she can rely for regular oversight of the organization's activities. It is
much less expensive to have counsel keep you out of trouble than to
get you out of trouble once you are in it.

## Unrelated Business Income Tax (UBIT)

Having gone to the trouble of establishing tax-exempt status for a
nonprofit organization, the nonprofit executive cannot presume that
all revenues generated by activities that the organization undertakes
are exempt from taxation. Revenues from a trade or business that a
nonprofit organization *regularly carries on* and that is *unrelated to the
exempt purposes* for which the organization exists may be taxed under
section 1.511 of the IRS regulations. The objective of this provision of
the tax code is to prevent unfair competition by nonprofit organizations with for-profit organizations.

With that rationale in mind, the nonprofit executive should
remember the three touchstones that determine when revenues are
subject to taxation: (1) They result from a "trade or business," (2) they
are "regularly" carried on, and (3) they are "unrelated" to the exempt
purposes of the organization.

What kinds of activities have been found by the IRS to generate taxable revenues? Depending on the specific circumstances involved,

such activities may include renting mailing lists, selling goods or services to the general public, operating a broadcast radio or TV station, or performing laboratory test services.

Here is one example provided by the IRS of unrelated business income that is taxable:

*W is an exempt business league with a large membership. Under an arrangement with an advertising agency, W regularly mails brochures, pamphlets, and other advertising materials to its members, charging the agency an agreed amount per enclosure. The distribution of the advertising material does not contribute importantly to the accomplishment of the purpose for which W is granted exemption. Accordingly, the payments made to W by the advertising agency constitute gross income from an unrelated trade or business activity."* (Section 1.512(a)-1(e))

Publication of a periodical or magazine is a common activity among nonprofit organizations, and the nonprofit executive should remember that revenues from advertising in such publications are subject to unrelated business income tax (UBIT). Although such publications typically serve the exempt purposes for which the organization was founded, the revenues from advertising are firmly held to be unrelated business income. The direct costs involved in producing the advertising may be deducted from the gross revenues in determining the taxable income.

There are a number of important exceptions in the UBIT provisions that the nonprofit executive should remember:

- If all the work in carrying on a trade or business is performed for the organization without compensation, it is *not* an unrelated trade or business.

- Selling merchandise, substantially all of which has been received by the organization as gifts or contributions, is *not* an unrelated trade or business.

- Conducting activities over a period of only a few weeks does not constitute the regular carrying on of a trade or business.

- Income from dividends, interest, and annuities, as well as capital gains, are generally excluded in computing unrelated business taxable income. (A 1999 proposal by the Clinton Administration to subject such income to taxation is unlikely to be passed by Congress.)

## Expulsion of Members

Earlier, this chapter reviewed the basic principles for defining allowable restrictions on membership. But what about the awkward and uncomfortable situation in which some members want to toss another member or group of members out of the organization for some real or imagined misconduct? This circumstance is fraught with legal danger for the organization and for the executive.

Denying renewal of membership to a member who fails to pay the required dues is not a problem and may be done summarily as a matter of course. Other members pay their fair share of the burden of operating the organization, and a member who refuses to pay has no right to be carried by the others. The bylaws of a nonprofit organization typically provide for automatic expulsion of members for nonpayment of dues. Any other action to expel a member should be handled with the utmost care, in consultation with experienced legal counsel.

## Directors and Officers Liability Insurance

Because of the litigious nature of the society in which we live, it is wise to obtain some protection for the executive and the volunteer leaders through the purchase of Directors and Officers (D&O) Liability Insurance. Such insurance will offer coverage for the payment of legal fees and expenses in defending against legal actions, but careful attention should be paid by the executive to the terms of the policy to ensure that it covers all types of claims (such as administrative proceedings under the Equal Employment Opportunity Act or an investigation by the Internal Revenue Service or the Federal Trade Commission) and to be sure that the requirements for claiming indemnification are not overlooked in case of trouble.

## SPECIAL CIRCUMSTANCES REQUIRING THE HELP OF COUNSEL

By becoming familiar with the basic principles related earlier, the nonprofit executive will be able to use the law as a tool to help manage the affairs of the organization and will largely be able to keep out of trouble. Sometimes, however, the activities of a nonprofit organization involve direct interaction with government, and in such cases the executive may need the help of counsel with particular expertise in the subjects involved.

## Lobbying, Advocacy, and Regulatory Negotiation

As the government has become increasingly active in the business affairs and everyday lives of our citizens, it has developed mountains of laws, policies, and regulations that touch virtually every aspect of our lives. Americans have the right and the responsibility to "petition" their government in connection with these laws, but the government may prescribe rules and regulations for such activities and can also limit the tax-deductibility of expenses incurred in the activities.

President Grant coined the term "lobbying" to describe the job seekers who would linger in the lobby of a hotel he visited, waiting for an audience. Since then, the term has acquired a very specific definition. The Federal Regulation of Lobbying Act says that lobbying is the solicitation or collection of funds principally to aid or influence federal legislation. In the Omnibus Budget Reconciliation Act of 1993, the term "lobbying" is defined as attempts to influence federal or state legislation or to influence official action by "covered" executive branch officials at the federal level. Under the 1993 Act, taxpayers are not allowed to take deductions for lobbying or political expenses, including any deduction for the portion of membership dues paid to a nonprofit organization that is used for lobbying expenses. A nonprofit executive of an organization with dues-paying membership that attempts to influence state or federal legislation should determine the effect of the law on his or her organization. (This issue is also discussed in Chapter 9.)

## Filing Lawsuits and Amicus Briefs

Occasionally, the members of a nonprofit organization will want the organization to pursue legal redress for a wrong that the members have suffered. The first step that must be taken in deciding on such an action is to determine whether the organization has a sufficient interest in the nature of the injury to give it the necessary "standing" to sue. Early cases held that only the party that has directly suffered the alleged injury has the necessary standing, but more recent cases have greatly liberalized that standard, and many nonprofit organizations have been found to have the necessary standing to file lawsuits on behalf of their members' interests. In addition, nonprofit organizations may undertake to file "amicus" briefs in support of a legal action involving one or more of its members. The filing of such briefs can be a substantial benefit for the parties and interests served by the organization, and can address issues of law that might not otherwise be fully explored.

Clearly, the initiation of such activities by a nonprofit organization requires the participation of legal counsel and should be undertaken only after exhaustive review of the wisdom of the action by the organization's officers and board of directors.

## IN CONCLUSION

There are other areas in which the nonprofit executive will want to seek out the particular expertise of specialized legal counsel who know the "prescribed formula" for achieving some legal end, such as trademark registration, copyright protection, the formation of for-profit subsidiaries, or the operation of political action committees. Such counsel is readily available and need not be expensive. Executives should keep current on legal developments affecting nonprofit organizations and repeat often, "The law is my friend."

**CHAPTER FIFTEEN**

# Selecting and Using Consultants

"Outsourcing" became a buzzword in the 1990s, and many nonprofits continue to turn to outside experts for help. This chapter provides insight and guidance on knowing when to seek outside assistance and then finding and hiring the right consultant.

## HOW TO SELECT AND USE CONSULTANTS

The responsibilities of nonprofit organizations are wide, but their staff resources are usually limited. To carry out its strategic plan, almost every nonprofit organization uses outside services at some time. Even the largest for-profit organizations often use consultants. But a nonprofit organization is even more likely to find that the expertise and resources it needs to get its job done fall outside the experience and available time of its professional staff and of those board members and volunteers willing to commit to getting everything done.

The earlier chapters of this book outline how nonprofit executives and their in-house staff can carry out a range of complex activities. The ideas and case studies presented should make it possible for you to take on activities you may not have thought you could handle. But there is always a limit to time and staff, and it is a mistake to spread your staff too thin. The director of marketing who takes on additional responsibilities for community education programs may do that very well, but may self-destruct if asked to handle fund-raising.

The nonprofit executive frequently faces the question: Do I do it myself or do I need a consultant? An analogy from the private sector is the "make or buy" decision: Do I make my own gear shifts (pistons, axles, headlights, batteries) or am I better off buying them from a supplier? The same question comes up in a different form for a nonprofit.

## When Should I Use a Consultant?

The first necessity, of course, is having a clear idea of your organization's goals and objectives. The long-range and strategic plans, if they are kept up-to-date, should lead the executive to a plan of action. The first consideration of whether to use a consultant begins as you face serious obstacles or opportunities to meet important goals of your organization.

This decision should not be made precipitously. It is usually a mistake to decide it's time to upgrade your information systems or start an ambitious new service program just because you have been influenced by someone you met at a conference or who came to see you on the recommendation of a member of your board. Similarly, it's too easy to "set up a foundation" or agree with the board member who says, "What we need is a public relations campaign" just because the idea sounds good at a meeting. Although it's fine to get ideas this way, you should not base decisions about whether or when to take on a new project on the basis of personal contact. Improvisation—reacting to circumstances as they change—is sometimes needed in carrying out a project, but not at the point of planning. Choosing to use a consultant should be a need-driven decision that fits within the outlines of your strategic plan.

Assume you have a project—perhaps a membership campaign—that has been planned in advance and is carefully integrated with educational programs or other membership services. There are likely to be a number of pieces to this campaign. There will be letters to write, brochures to design. There is probably an outreach activity, involving staff or members calling prospects. There is research to be done on membership prospects, and an analysis on why present members are (or are not) renewing. There may be prospective member receptions to plan and hold. There may even be a kickoff with a leading figure from the community or profession and media possibilities that go along with one or more of these functions.

Who is going to do all this? Your overworked administrative assistant? The publications director? Your bookkeeper, who took an art course in college and has always wanted to try graphic arts? Even if you think that you or others on your staff can accomplish these tasks, do they really have the skills or time or energy to do it, on time, in addition to their regular jobs?

At this point it may be helpful to make a checklist, such as the example in Exhibit 15–1, of the different tasks that are required for

**Exhibit 15–1** Checklist of Staff Responsibilities

| | PRESENT STAFF CAN DO? | | | |
|---|---|---|---|---|
| | *Well* | *Satisfactorily* | *With Luck* | *Never* |
| Plan Meeting? | | | | |
| Solicit Corporate Sponsors? | | | | |
| Obtain Speakers? | | | | |
| Select Hotel and Negotiate Contract? | | | | |
| Prepare Publicity Brochure and Press Releases? | | | | |
| Develop Mailing List? | | | | |
| Handle Registration and Accounting? | | | | |
| Obtain Press Coverage? | | | | |

this project. Put the different tasks involved on the left margin. On top of the page, write "Present Staff Can Do?" (don't leave out the question mark). Under that, set up four columns with these headings: "Well," "Satisfactorily," "With Luck," and "Never."

Go through this list twice, with your present staff in mind. The first time, just think of their abilities and preparation. If they can be included in any of the first three categories, put their initials in the appropriate box.

Put the worksheet aside for a day. (It's best to do this at home so you don't give in to the temptation to discuss it with your staff quite yet.) Then, the next day, review it with a different set of questions in mind: Does this person have the time? Would he or she enjoy doing this? Would I want to give him or her this assignment? And, if you have those initials in the two "maybe" categories ("Satisfactorily" or "With Luck"), is that good enough?

Now you're getting close to your decision points. If you have a staff person in the first category (that is, you're confident that he or she can do the task just fine), you have only to face the question of whether this is the best use of the person's time. Perhaps you will have to take her away from something she's doing now to free up enough time, and you may not want to do that. On the other hand, if it is really an opportunity for job enrichment and learning, that person may be glad to take on the assignment even if it is a stretch.

But if those initials are in one of the "maybe" categories, you don't want to have this task done with present staff if you can help it. Here, of course, budget realities have their impact. Often, in a nonprofit organization (it can happen in a for-profit too) the resources needed to get additional help are just not available, even if you want to. You may have to settle for "Satisfactorily" or gamble on "With Luck." Just bear in mind that this staff person is going to need extra help and coaching along the way, either from you or from a talented board member or volunteer.

## New Staff or Outside Consultants?

If you have concluded that some parts of an assignment are beyond your present staff, you can think about whether it is time to hire someone. If you have the resources and the assignment is likely to be continuing, this may be the right thing to do—but not always.

The decision on whether to use a consulting firm or consultant is highly specific to the individual case. The right decision changes, depending on the nature of the assignment, the nature and resources of your organization, and the relative strengths of both your own organization (which you have assessed earlier) and the services available to you locally that are within your budget.

Look again at your organization's mission statement, the strategic plan, and the one-year plan. You have a job to do and a budget within which to do it. For a complex project, a consulting firm or agency may cost as much or more as bringing a new manager or an experienced professional on board. Why use an outside firm if you can hire your own staff member?

If the budget can accommodate a first-class professional, and if the job is going to keep him or her fully occupied, not just for the first six months but into the future, a new hire may well be called for. But there are a few cautions.

Most managers have an in-built bias toward building up their own organization staff. A nonprofit organization may not have to measure success by increased sales or profits, as a for-profit organization must do. The "bottom line" (size of profit) does not constrain growth as long as revenues cover expenses. As a result, we have heard non-profit managers boast that they have doubled staff since they became CEO, as if the size of the staff is the measure of the organization's success. The best executives approach this inside staff/outside staff decision more analytically.

First, be sure that you have looked at real costs, not just salary and fringes. Estimating overhead accurately can be complicated; we have given some guidelines in Chapter 12, "Financial Management." The fringe benefit costs—Social Security, unemployment compensation, and, most likely, health insurance—add up fast. The new staff person is going to need an office, a desk, and a word processor, probably with an Internet connection. The new hire will entail increased time on the part of your human relations director. Is this new staffer going to require an assistant? At the least, someone to answer the telephone when he or she is not at the desk?

A second question to ask yourself: Can I (or other members of your staff) give this person the guidance that will be needed? Of course, you would look for a "self-starter," someone who knows what he or she is doing and doesn't need much supervision. But chances are that the budget you've established is not going to attract a top-flight professional at the peak of experience. You will probably find that executive guidance is needed, and may find that this guidance is hard to come by. After all, if you really knew how to do this task yourself, you might not be looking to hire.

Third: Will this person really be busy—fully occupied—by the assignment you're giving? For how long? Suppose you put on four educational conferences in the course of a year, two board of directors meetings, and one or two major dinners or other events. That's clearly more than you or your administrative assistant can handle. Why not hire a full-time meeting manager? Because, most likely, that meeting manager is going to be extremely busy about half the year, and overloaded for two or three weeks of those six months. The rest of the time that person is going to sit there bored, or pretend that what he or she is doing will make the next meeting better. Travel costs to scout meeting sites will be a bigger item in next year's budget.

Is there a better way to do this?

## Assignments for Consultants

There are certain assignments for which nonprofit organizations are most likely to call on outside consultants for help:

- Accounting
- Audiovisual production
- Audit
- Computer services
- Curriculum development
- Fund-raising
- Government relations
- Graphic arts
- Legal
- Meetings management
- Public relations

- Publications
- Strategic planning

Obviously, there are different considerations in each category in making that "make or buy" decision. Unless the organization is so small that you don't need (or want) an audited annual financial statement, you will have an outside auditor. And only very large nonprofits will have an attorney on staff; if you have a clear legal issue, you're going to contract out.

On the other end of the scale is accounting; most organizations do this themselves. But the choice may not be so obvious. Even fairly large organizations can find that the checks and balances needed for good financial controls are hard to build internally.

*A membership organization with a $750,000 operating budget employed a full-time bookkeeper to manage its financial affairs. The bookkeeper had several years of experience but could not implement financial controls and could not provide the executive director with meaningful information. In addition, the association's software was inflexible, so it could not meet the particular needs of this organization.*

*The bookkeeper became increasingly frustrated and left. Instead of replacing the bookkeeper and purchasing new accounting software, the organization retained the services of an accounting firm to handle the day-to-day responsibilities including cash receipts, cash disbursements, maintenance of the general ledger, and generation of the monthly financial statements. The net savings to this group totaled $20,000 a year and the financial information was both more detailed and more timely.*

## Finding the Right Consultant

Once you have made the decision to go outside, the question is how to locate candidates and how to make the next decision. We stress again: The make-or-buy decision should precede the decision on whom to buy from. Far too many nonprofits do this the other way around: They decide to undertake a project because a consultant sells them on that project. Even if one outside firm brings you an idea for a project that you then adopt, you should still get competitive bids and proposals. (Of course, you then keep the specific operational ideas of the original firm confidential, asking for proposals on a project outlined in general terms. Often, the original bidder wins out in a case like this; but if they object to your asking for competitive bids, it's probably not the right firm for you.)

The bidding process can vary, depending on the nature of the project. Major consulting or public relations projects usually warrant a full-blown request for proposal (RFP). Selecting an attorney or auditor is usually a matter of interviewing recommended firms or individuals and carefully checking resumes. An important factor in deciding on your approach is whether you expect this to be a long-term or a single-project relationship. Another is the importance or financial size of the project—that is, what are the consequences of a mistake? The answers to these questions will affect the amount of time you spend making your selection. Designing a brochure for your major fund-raising event of the year is important, but you aren't necessarily committing to using the same graphic design firm next year. If the design is less than great or if you get a better bid next year, it's easy to change. Choosing an attorney or auditor, on the other hand, builds a relationship that will be harder to change. That person will develop an understanding of the organization and a base of experience that you lose if you start over. More care is required in the initial selection.

The time-honored way of selecting a number of consultants to interview or from whom to request proposals is to gain recommendations from fellow professionals. The experience of people you trust and respect can be invaluable. Sometimes, however, what you get from them are safe, predictable recommendations favoring the established firms. The firms recommended may be excellent, but they are unlikely (if cost matters) to be the low-cost suppliers.

By all means, get recommendations from your peers or the local grapevine. You may already know the names of the dominant firms in the area in which you're looking for help. Include one or two of those best-known or highly recommended firms on your list, but search out at least one small or less known firm for comparison. At the very least, that will keep the established firms on their toes.

Some nonprofits, at this point, simply put an RFP in the mail. That's usually not best. A better course is to ask some of your likely bidders to come by to discuss the project. Describe it to them orally. You'll find some that don't understand what you're after, some that offer sharp ideas right on the spot. You may even find that your RFP is off the mark, that what you're asking for is unrealistic or too ill defined. If so, the sooner you learn that the better; revise your RFP now (even if this means going back to your executive committee) rather than facing reality later.

There is no one universally applicable model for a good RFP. You must spell out what you want the consultant to accomplish and ask for specific recommendations as to how the consultant or consulting firm will execute the project. Ask for specifics on staff to be assigned and billing rates, as well as for information on the consultant's past projects and clients, including two or three you can call for references. Although you need to include all details that will be important to you in making your decision, beware of making the RFP too long or too prescriptive. An overdetailed RFP may signal to potential bidders that you don't really want their advice and ideas and may even discourage the best from responding. (See Exhibit 15–2 for a model RFP.)

**Exhibit 15–2**   Model RFP

---

Request for Proposals

Public Relations and Membership Campaign: Council for a Better Community

*Background:* The Council for a Better Community was founded in 1984 by Crescent City leaders concerned that the social fabric of our city was deteriorating, undermining public safety, schools, and our local economy. Initial support came from five local corporations. Program emphasis has been, and will continue to be, on citizen involvement in community affairs, especially local schools and those government agencies, such as public health, housing, and public safety, that work directly with our citizens.

Although community support has broadened, with over 100 local businesses and several foundations now funding the Council's activities, the Council has never before solicited membership or support from the general public. The board of directors has decided that a broad-based membership would not only widen the Council's base of financial support but would also improve public awareness and encourage greater citizen participation in the organization's activities. (Annual Reports summarizing the Council's recent activities are attached.)

*Assistance desired:* The Council is soliciting proposals from a public relations agency or other capable provider for a two-year program. Elements should include:

- Materials, including a membership brochure, to be used in direct mail and other membership promotion activities;

- Press releases and an action plan for developing media coverage that increases public awareness of the Council's activities and supports the membership campaign;

- Public relations materials and a plan for promoting the Council's annual award dinner, to be held later this year, and for incorporating this event into the new membership campaign;

- Plan of action for a direct mail membership campaign, including development of target lists and a plan of implementation.

The agency selected will report to the executive director and work closely with the Council's executive committee as well as Council staff responsible for communications and member recruitment.

*Details for submission:* The Council requests written proposals from qualified firms, to be submitted in triplicate to the Council's office by (date).

Submissions should include:

- An outline of how the firm would develop the plans and materials cited above;

- Any other suggestions for broadening the Council's membership base and increasing its public visibility and support;

**Exhibit 15–2**    (*Continued*)

---

- Examples of similar materials and summaries of campaigns that the firm created and carried out previously, for either nonprofit or for-profit organizations;

- Budget for the program, detailing the basis for the firm's charges; in particular, state whether the firm proposes to charge a fixed-fee retainer or on an hourly basis;

- List of references.

*Additional information:* please feel free to call (name), executive director of the Council, with any questions about the assistance desired.

The Council's executive committee intends to invite finalists to make a personal presentation of their proposal (next month, etc.). Finalists will be notified by (date).

---

After reviewing responses to the RFP, you should be able to pick out three finalists. The qualifications you look for will differ, of course, by the type of project. Thoroughness, creativity, and ability to work within budget are basic factors. It may be helpful to use an appraisal form in reviewing the RFPs with these qualifications, plus others specific to your project. If more than one person is reviewing the RFPs (a good idea on any major project), ask them to rate the respondents on a scale of 1 through 5 in each category. If there are significant differences, meet to talk through the different reactions. At the end of this process you should be able to identify your three best candidates. Invite them to make their final presentations before your selection committee. Now that they know they are finalists, they may be able to refine their own ideas. You should expect discussions precisely focused on your organization and your specific project; consultants who talk too much about themselves or who give you the same "canned" presentation they make to all prospective clients probably won't give you individualized service in the future either.

Final interviews are usually conducted, for major projects, by groups of three or four interviewers. We all have different questions to ask, and group dynamics are important. Moreover, for a large project, you want key board members to "buy into" the decision.

The agreement should be summarized in a letter of understanding or, for larger projects, in a contract. Usually, this need not be elaborate. It should summarize what the organization expects from the consultant, when the work will be completed (often in stages), and the agreement on compensation. Where applicable, the agreement should spell out terms concerning how either party can terminate the agreement. Very large or complex projects sometimes require detailed contracts and legal review, but this should be avoided wherever possible. If a consultant's work turns out to be unsatisfactory, the only practical course is to terminate the arrangement as soon as this becomes evident. The purpose of the contract or letter of agreement is just to ensure that each party understands the expectations of the other, not to create a legally binding document. (See Exhibit 15–3 for a sample contract.)

**Exhibit 15–3**   Sample Consultant Contract

---

This letter is to confirm and constitute the understanding between WORTHY AGENCY and SUPERIOR CONSULTANTS, a [name of state] partnership conducting the business of fund-raising consultation for not-for-profit organizations.

SUPERIOR CONSULTANTS will design and implement a fund-raising plan to increase contributions from individual donors.

[Person's Name] will coordinate the delivery of service under this contract, with the support of SUPERIOR CONSULTANTS.

It will be SUPERIOR CONSULTANTS' responsibility to:

1. Direct the development of a contributions data base containing information about past and present giving. Train volunteers in basic research techniques.

2. Identify potential contributors to the "challenge fund." Prepare and assist the president and board members in soliciting selected individuals for this purpose.

3. Develop and implement both short-term and ongoing fund-raising strategies involving board members, parents, and friends of WORTHY AGENCY.

4. Review suggestions for fund-raising for WORTHY AGENCY. Help set priorities and advise on the implementation of the best ideas.

5. Outline the basic functions of a development office for WORTHY AGENCY and prepare a model job description for a Director of Development.

6. Develop a proposal for a feasibility study for an Endowment Campaign and advise on sources of underwriting for such a study.

It will be WORTHY AGENCY'S responsibility to:

1. Provide SUPERIOR CONSULTANTS with information on prior and ongoing fund-raising efforts and outreach.

2. Identify key volunteers, donors, and community leaders for fund-raising leadership, and help with involving them in the annual giving program.

3. Enable the Executive Director to work closely with the consultants to ensure full and timely communication.

4. Furnish whatever secretarial and other office services the contributions program requires.

5. Pay or reimburse any out-of-pocket expenses, such as printed materials, special-event costs, and recognition items. All expenditures will be subject to prior approval.

**Exhibit 15–3** *(Continued)*

6. Receive all monies; log and collect gifts and pledges; and provide periodic reports on income and expenses.

7. Implement public relations aspects of the campaign, if any.

WORTHY AGENCY will not be billed for telephone, postage, photocopying, clerical, and similar expenses incurred by SUPERIOR CONSULTANTS in WORTHY AGENCY's offices, or for travel within Home County.

WORTHY AGENCY has the right to cancel this contract upon 30 days' written notice. WORTHY AGENCY is responsible for all authorized expenditures committed up to the date of notification and for the final 30 days' fee owed to SUPERIOR CONSULTANTS.

The period covered by this contract is

[Date] through

[Date]. The fee for these services is [$X,000], payable monthly at the beginning of each service period. Should WORTHY AGENCY wish to continue to receive these services after [Date], SUPERIOR CONSULTANTS will provide them at no increase in fee.

If this letter correctly expresses our mutual understanding, please signify approval by signing the original and the attached copy and returning the original to me at SUPERIOR CONSULTANTS.

AGREED

| [Signature] | [Signature] |
|---|---|
| PRESIDENT | Partner |
| WORTHY AGENCY | SUPERIOR CONSULTANTS |
| Dated _____ | |

*Source:* Nan D. Doty and Barbara M. Cox, "Annual Giving Programs" in *The Nonprofit Management Handbook,* edited by Tracy D. Connors (New York: John Wiley & Sons, 1993), p. 506. Reprinted by permission of Doty & Cox.

## WORKING WITH YOUR CONSULTANT

Experienced nonprofit executives have different views of how best to work with consultants. Some executives simply sign the contract and turn their backs on the project until it is complete. Others will call the consultants every other day and expect them to be present at frequent staff meetings or consultations.

A middle course is usually best and should not be hard to follow. The nonprofit chief executive officer (CEO) or department head in charge of the project should be sufficiently involved to know how it is progressing and to be able to summarize its status. Is the project on schedule? Do preliminary findings confirm or call into question the premises on which the project is based? What changes have been necessary in the plan of action? Are costs under control? The person on staff who is responsible for the project should be able to answer these basic questions at any time.

Overmanagement of consultants may seem harmless, but it can present problems. For one thing, it takes time—both your own time (to reduce your own or your staff's time is probably one reason you contracted out in the first place) and that of the consultant. If you're paying by the hour—typical of contracts with law firms or public relations agencies—every hour these professionals spend in consultation with you or your staff is added to your bill. They should not be spending their time in unnecessary meetings, and neither should you.

Overmanagement can also call into question the basic reason you hired a consultant in the first place: The consultant knows more than you do in his or her field of expertise. At worst, overmanagement of a consultant may invalidate the results of a worthwhile project.

Research projects require realistic goals and the willingness to accept results, which at times can be different from those anticipated by the organization at the outset. An organization that expects a contractor's report to buttress a case to which it is already committed can be disappointed.

The following examples illustrate the importance of being open to research project results.

*The Federated Council of Internal Medicine, representing four major organizations of internal medicine physicians, was skeptical of established projections showing a surplus of general physicians as a result of increased enrollments in medical school. The Council contracted with a recognized health care research firm to study trends in the practice patterns of internal medicine physicians. The consultants interviewed leaders of the sponsoring organizations and physicians at teaching hospitals and in the field. Although different physicians had various pieces of information, none of them tried to force his or her own view on the consultants.*

*The consulting firm, able to "step out of the frame and look at the picture," found several factors that had been overlooked in deriving the projection of a physician surplus. First, it found that physicians working in managed care organizations typically put in somewhat shorter workweeks than those in private practice. It also found that women physicians, perhaps because of family demands but also because of different styles, not only worked slightly fewer hours but tended to spend more time with each patient. With enrollment of women in medical schools rising rapidly, this one factor changed trends sharply. The consultants also pointed out that any change in disease patterns could quickly create greater needs for medical generalists.*

*The study, when released and presented to a special governmental committee recommending changes in graduate medical education, prompted a shift in federal policy to encourage teaching hospitals to emphasize general medical practice and was one factor in changing policies on payments of physicians to increase payments made to general practitioners.*

*At about the same time, another health care organization, whose members provided services to convalescent patients, faced cuts in payment under federal policies and wanted to demonstrate that the cost cutters had overlooked essential costs of providing these services. A major consulting firm, which had done credible work for the association previously, set out to interview association members in the field about their own expenses and cost structures. First, it derived medians of costs in different companies and came up with a model cost structure. Unfortunately, the preliminary conclusion seemed to reinforce the view the association had set out to disprove: that prices were high in relation to costs.*

*The study was extended, and the consultant returned to the field. But the only solution was to construct a new composite from the higher range of costs reported by the higher-cost firms in the industry. This supported the point desired, but at a heavy price; the study screamed, "Tilt!" Although members of the board of directors seemed satisfied—the study now supported their preconception—the association's government relations staff knew the study would hurt, rather than enhance, the group's reputation and credibility. The study was buried in files.*

Both organizations expected, at the outset, that their consultant's study would validate the opinions they held and that it would sway major decisions on health care policy. The first organization was correct; the second made the mistake of thinking the world could be remade to fit its preconceptions and compounded the error by pressuring the consultant into its own bias.

## Controlling Costs

It is not always possible to price every project to the dollar. Research, for example, can justifiably take longer than predicted. But beware: Any adjustments in estimates permitted in the contract will always be upwards. If a supplier comes in under bid, be sure to use that firm next time.

Many projects, such as printing or convention management, are usually fixed-cost contracts. Accounting, audits, and legal services are usually based on hourly charges. Public relations can be either hourly or based on a monthly retainer, often with add-ons for any part of the project not specifically called for in the contract.

Major corporations, alarmed at rising legal bills, have begun in recent years to require that their law firms live with fixed contracts for all but complex litigation. Nonprofits, working with smaller budgets but without the same cost discipline, have been slow to follow their example.

At the very least, insist on timely billings and keep a running tally. (Law firms are notoriously late in billing; this makes it harder to control costs.) Some projects, for which the consultant is managing outside costs, might include a bonus if the overall project comes in under budget.

## Monitoring Performance

For major projects, the contract should have appropriate reporting times built in. For a research project, reporting should usually be quarterly if the project will take a year or more, and monthly if it is a short-term project. Public relations or government relations projects usually stipulate a short monthly summary and a longer quarterly report. Other projects, such as an audit, are oriented to one task; time frames for completion of preliminary tasks should be agreed upon, but there usually won't be any report until the project is over.

Management of projects such as conventions or public events should be keyed to time lines, either as specified in the contract or worked out in detail between you and your consultant. For example, there should be dates by which hotel contracts will be pinned down, promotional pieces printed and mailed, speakers confirmed, and so on (see Chapter 7). The consultant should keep his or her own checklist of actions completed to make sure nothing is missed; it doesn't add to the consultant's cost to share this with you on a frequent basis.

If the contractor is off schedule or over budget, or if performance is clearly differing from what you have expected, it's best to face the situation early. If you let it worry you or sit too long brooding, delay will sap your own energy and increase the risk that you will end up in a confrontation with your consultant at the most critical time in the project. Work out any problems early, when they are most easily corrected. A good consultant will appreciate your honesty; after all, the consultant cannot respond without knowing where you stand.

Occasionally, you will have to take radical action to redirect or even terminate a project. This is hard to do, because it is a recognition either that the project was misconceived in the first place or that you made a mistake in hiring the consultant. If the consultant is tied in with influential members of your board of directors, you're in a worse bind. In that case, if possible, discuss it with that board member or with your executive committee. Ask for advice whether or not to proceed with the project. A smart consultant will be the first to say so if a project isn't working out as expected.

*Soon after new regulations appeared to implement the Americans with Disabilities Act (ADA), an industry organization contracted with a nonprofit organization representing disabled individuals. The second organization, which had expertise in helping service industries hire and promote workers with physical or emotional disabilities, served as consultant and contractor for the seminars and would share in the profit of the meeting after expenses.*

*The first seminar, in Washington, was oversubscribed, and in their enthusiasm the two organizations scheduled another in Chicago four months later. The director of the industry organization, who had been ecstatic at the success of the first meeting, was looking forward to press coverage of the second.*

*But registrations just did not come in. Contracts with some of the speakers had cancellation clauses that would require partial payment; other speakers were consultants also well known to members of the nonprofit organization. Worse yet, the hotel contract had a cancellation penalty.*

*As the deadline for hotel registrations approached, the executive director of the industry group checked with the hotel and found he could negotiate a revised cancellation clause at a reasonable but not disastrous penalty, but only if the cancellation was done immediately. He called a half dozen expected attendees who had not yet registered and found that it was not just delay; they had all attended other seminars on the subject or realized that compliance with the ADA would not be nearly as difficult as early headlines had proclaimed. They could deal with the new law without having to send staff to Chicago for two days.*

*Reluctantly, the executive directors of the two organizations agreed that the meeting should be cancelled, accepting a small financial loss but avoiding the risk of a meeting that would flop.*

## ASSISTING THE CONSULTANTS

It stands to reason that nonprofit executives will be able to help consultants do their work only if they understand what the consultants are doing. Most projects should be a partnership between the nonprofit's staff and the consultant. Communication must be good; usually, this means frequent, but not, as stressed earlier, time-consuming. Two five-minute telephone calls are usually better than one one-hour meeting.

No consultant will know your own business as well as you do. Even if the consultant is a national expert on the cause to which your organization is devoted, he or she probably doesn't understand your local situation as well as you do.

The issue of how you can best work with the consultant, helping that person or firm to produce a report or hold a workshop or prepare a press conference that will serve your purpose, should be addressed in the selection process. How much help does the consultant want from you? How does he or she want to communicate? Rapport is intangible, but if it's not there from the outset, it may be hard to develop later.

## FINAL REPORTS

For some projects—research projects most obviously—the final report is the purpose of the exercise. For other projects, such as fundraising or organizing a meeting, the results will be in the numbers. But a summary of activities carried out under the contract and of results achieved is always useful. You will usually circulate this summary to at least part of your board of directors, and it will be very useful the next time you take on a similar project.

## CHECKLIST/POINTS FOR REVIEW

Deciding on a Consultant

- Make a cost-benefit analysis of doing the project in-house versus using a consultant. Be sure this includes the real costs, direct and indirect, of doing it yourself.

- Cast a wide net in targeting potential consultants; don't just use the first one suggested (long-established relationships are an exception).

- Discuss the project informally with one or two potential consultants even while developing the RFP. Be available to meet with all bidders at their request.

- Develop an RFP. This makes you think through the project, as well as giving potential consultants a guide to which to respond.

- Interview finalists in a small group of your staff or members.

- Delineate expectations and responsibilities clearly and summarize in a letter of agreement or contract.

- Make sure all costs are clearly spelled out and that fixed costs or caps on hourly charges are included.

Working with the Consultant

- Maintain an open line of communication without wasting time in long meetings.
- Make sure you or someone on your staff knows where things stand at all times; don't just write a contract and then walk away from the project.
- Be honest with yourself and the consultant. If things aren't going well, have a meeting and discuss problems openly.
- If it is necessary to terminate a project—no matter what the cause— it's usually better to do this early than to struggle through to an unsatisfactory conclusion.

# Index

Visioning, 12–13
Visiting Nurse Association/Hospice
of Northern California, 102–103
Visiting Nurse Association of
America, 194
Volunteers, 311–312
executive director and, 51
for gift solicitation, 107–108
special consideration for, 162, 318